The Advanced Grammar Book

SECOND EDITION

The publication of *The Advanced Grammar Book, Second Edition* was directed by the members of the Newbury House ESL/EFL team at Heinle & Heinle:

Erik Gundersen, Editorial Director
Bruno Paul, Market Development Director
Jonathan Boggs, Market Development Director
Maryellen Killeen, Production Services Coordinator
Ken Pratt, Associate Editor
Kristin Thalheimer, Production Service Coordinator

Also participating in the publication of this program were:

Stanley J. Galek, Vice President & Publisher
Thomas Healy, Developmental Editor
Amy Lawler, Managing Developmental Editor
Mary Sutton, Associate Market Development Director
Mary Beth Hennebury, Manufacturing Coordinator
PC&F, Inc., Interior Designer and Page Production
Gina Petti, Cover Designer
Margaret Cleveland, Project Manager
Robin Longshaw, Copy Editor
Katherine Hughes, Photo Researcher

Library of Congress Cataloging-in-Publication Data

Steer, Jocelyn.
    The advanced grammar book/Jocelyn Steer, Karen Carlisi. —2nd ed.
        p. cm.
    Includes index.
    1. English language—Grammar. 2. English language—Textbooks for foreign
speakers. I. Carlisi, Karen. II. Title.
PE1112.S73 1997
428.2'4—dc21

97-24076
CIP

Manufactured in the United States of America.

ISBN: 0-8384-4715-5

Heinle & Heinle is a division of International Thomson Publishing, Inc.
10 9 8 7 6

The Advanced Grammar Book

SECOND EDITION

Jocelyn Steer

Karen Carlisi
Pasadena City College

Heinle & Heinle Publishers
I T P *An International Thomson Publishing Company*
Boston, Massachusetts 02116 U.S.A

Text Credits

Art/Photo Credits

Contents

CHAPTER 9:   HEALTH AND FITNESS II 215

Preface

To the Teacher

The *Advanced Grammar Book* is intended for the high level ESL student who has a solid foundation in the fundamentals of English grammar. This text provides the student with a sophisticated analysis of the grammatical structures of English and ample opportunity to practice using them, with the objective of increasing the student's competence in both conversational and written English. The text is designed for both preuniversity and nonacademic students and as such includes a variety of exercises to develop oral and written competence, allowing the instructor to select those exercises that best suit the needs of a particular class.

The features that contribute to the text's effectiveness are: • theme-based grammatical presentation and practice • inductive exercises • well-organized, thorough charts for presentation of the grammatical structures • special notes which focus on exceptions and related structures • ample opportunity for writing • a special problems section in each chapter to focus on common errors produced when using the target structure • and the use of cartoons and authentic material.

Format and Content of Chapters

The book is divided into fifteen chapters that are self-contained yet ordered with some consideration of grammatical sequence; for example, the verb section precedes the passives. Nevertheless, an instructor could teach the chapters in the order that would best satisfy the students' needs.

THEME   Each chapter of the book is based on a theme to capture the interest of the student and provide a "hook" for the grammatical structure being practiced. The theme is introduced at the outset of the chapter through discussion questions and continues to appear throughout the chapter in the written and spoken exercises in order to motivate the student to practice grammar in a meaningful way.

PREVIEW   Following the introduction to the theme of the chapter is the preview section, which consists of a dialogue, letter, article, or interview to further develop the theme while introducing the student to the target structure. Vocabulary from the reading is isolated with definitions, and often a cultural note addresses an aspect of American culture related to the theme and depicted in the reading. An inductive exercise based on the reading requires the student to discover and make generalizations about the form and function of the grammatical point of the chapter.

GRAMMATICAL PATTERNS   The grammatical patterns sections present the grammatical structures of the chapter. The structures covered in the book are those that the advanced student may have studied previously; however, every effort has been made to focus on uses that the student perhaps has not yet encountered or mastered. For this reason, most chapters are divided into two sections: the first, "Grammatical Patterns Part One," is usually a more basic presentation, and the second, "Grammatical Patterns Part Two," is a more complex treatment. Presentation of the grammatical structure is usually done in chart or list form, which can be assigned for homework and reviewed during class after the students have studied and are prepared to raise questions. A variety of spoken and written exercises that encourage meaningful practice help the advanced student to master and use the grammatical patterns rather than manipulate them artificially. These exercise types include rapid drill, paired oral practice, oral and written paraphrase, interviews, and roleplay.

FEATURES   Each chapter contains several special features that provide focus and variety. The "special notes," which are highlighted in boxes throughout the text, contain exceptions to rules and special reminders about the target structure. These can be brought to students' attention during presentation and practice and used as study aids later. The "special problems" sections list common errors that students can make with the grammatical structure. In some chapters there is an excerpt from "authentic materials" written by well-known and respected writers such as the newspaper columnist Ellen Goodman. Each excerpt expands on the theme of the chapter and provides the student with further real-life context for the grammatical structure. At the end of each chapter, students are given a choice of "composition topics" related to the theme of the chapter. These may be assigned by the teacher as homework or journal writing, activities especially useful for classes that combine writing and grammar. Finally, in response to the increasing concern students have about the TOEFL, this text has targetted those structures and types of exercises that may be of assistance to students preparing to take this test. A symbol—■—identifies those explanations and exercises that are "TOEFL-relevant."

Added Features

Many teachers have used The Advanced Grammar Book and appreciated the theme-based approach, the grammatical charts, and the opportunities to practice the grammatical structures through engaging oral and written exercises. For this reason, the guiding principles, approach, and content of the first edition have been maintained in the second edition. The following features have been added to the second edition to improve upon the effectiveness and appeal for advanced students and their teachers.

- **Improved Charts**

  The charts have been revised to present the grammatical points clearly and concisely. With these revisions, the charts can better serve as a useful tool for out of class study, as well as a teaching tool for instructors.

- **Emphasis on Written Activities**

  The second edition places increased emphasis on written activities since students at this level benefit from continual reinforcement of the grammatical structures through writing. Essay and letter writing as well as paraphrasing and editing exercises provide this practice.

  A new section, "Focus on Writing," has been added to each chapter. The purpose of this section is to emphasize the functions or uses of the target grammatical structure most often applied in writing. By setting apart a section focusing on writing, students can be made aware of the specific distinctions in the written and spoken application of the grammar point.

- **Updated readings and topics**

  Since the text is theme-based, any content was outdated has been replaced with topics of interest which will maintain currency over time. In this way, the text will continue to engage students in the grammar as a vehicle for expression.

- **Expanded appendices**

  A number of longer charts originally included within the chapter have been moved to the appendices. By doing this, the flow of the chapter is not interrupted and the appendices provide additional study and reference tools for students and instructors.

- **Workbook**

  The second edition includes a workbook with exercises to accompany each chapter of the text. The exercises in the workbook correspond to the theme of the chapter so that students can get additional practice in applying the grammatical structures for authentic communicative purposes.

- **Revised Instructor's Manual With Unit Tests**

  The Instructor's Manual has been revised to provide teaching suggestions for each chapter in addition to the answer key. For teachers who may be less experienced with advanced grammar, these guidelines will provide the necessary foundation they need to ensure clear presentation and explanation. The instructor's manual will also include a unit test for each chapter to assist teachers in their assessment of student progress.

- **CD-Rom**

  Grammar 3D is an ideal supplement to *The Advanced Grammar Book, 2nd ed.* It provides comprehensive instruction and practice in 34 of the key grammar structures found in the text.

  Grammar 3D is appropriate for high-beginning to advanced students, and allows students to progress at their own pace. Students can access each grammar category at 3 or 4 levels of difficulty. They can then move to a lower level if they need basic review, or to a higher level for additional challenge.

  An instructional "help page" allows students to access grammar explanations before they begin an exercise, or at any place within an exercise. Instruction is also provided through feedback that helps students understand their errors and guides them toward correct answers.

How to Use This Book

The Preview section is an inductive exercise that can be used by the instructor as a diagnostic tool to determine what the students already know. The students can benefit from the exercises as a pretest. If the instructor is uncomfortable with an inductive approach, the preview section can be used as a review after the chapter is completed.

The charts can be studied at home, and students can come to class with specific questions. If used in class, the charts can become an inductive tool. Have students cover the section in the chart identifying the rule, and ask them to generate the rule by examining the sentences. In many cases, the chapter has been divided into basic and more complex treatment of the grammatical structure. The "Grammatical Patterns One" section can be skimmed if it is a review.

The readings can be assigned as homework or read in class. Especially when the reading is a dialogue or interview, assigning roles and reading aloud in class can be beneficial.

Encourage students to cooperate on written activities as well as speaking activities. Even fill-in-the-blank exercises can be completed in pairs to encourage interaction. Very often the student is required to write a response after a short discussion, an activity that also lends itself to paired work.

Acknowledgments

I'd like to thank the ALI/PD-02 support group for listening patiently to my grammatical monologues—especially on the progressive. Special thanks, too, to Dick Yorkey for getting me started on writing materials. Finally, the greatest thanks go to my husband, Jo, for his unending patience, support, and understanding.

Jocelyn Steer

I'd like to thank my students—they continue to inspire me long after they take the grammar out into the world.

Karen Carlisi

The authors and publisher would like to thank the following individuals who offered many helpful insights and suggestions.

Barbara Bliss	Boston University
Glenda Bro	Mt. San Antonio College, CA
Cathleen Cake	Tulane University, LA
Shawn Connelly	CSU, Hayward
Patrice Connerton	George Washington University
Eric Dwyer	University of Texas
Sally Gearhart	Santa Rosa Junior College, CA
Joyce Hutchings	Georgetown University
Robin Lombard	University of Texas-Arlington
Debbie Ockey	CSU, Fresno
Amy Parker	ELS Language Center, CA
Caroline Schwatzwalder	North Shore Community College, MA
Mary Kay Seles	University of Washington
Colleen Weldele	Palomar College, CA

To the Student

As an advanced student of English, you have undoubtedly been studying English grammar for some time and have the feeling that there is nothing left to learn. However, this textbook has been written specifically to address those areas of English grammar that you have not yet mastered or perhaps have never encountered. Therefore, by continuing your study of English grammar with this book, you will build on what you already know and become more fluent in English by being able to use more sophisticated grammatical structures.

This textbook contains fifteen chapters, each centered around a specific grammatical structure and a theme to make your study of the grammar more interesting. Each chapter contains the following parts:

THE READINGS   Although this is not a reading book, you may be surprised to find an interview, article, letter, or dialogue with vocabulary highlighted in the text. In this way, you can see how the structure functions in a sentence.

CULTURAL NOTES   You will find short explanations of cultural aspects of the United States after most Preview sections in each chapter. These notes are designed to introduce you to the cultural information referred to in the Preview readings.

INDUCTIVE EXERCISES   These exercises encourage you to discover and make generalizations about the grammar yourself. Some questions may be more difficult than others, so you will know which structures you need to work on.

CHARTS   The grammar is usually presented in chart form so that you can study at home and bring questions to your teacher. Each chart can also serve as a study aid when preparing for tests. Toward the end of each chapter, you will find a special problems section that lists the errors that students often make with the particular structure being studied.

SPEAKING AND WRITING ACTIVITIES   Each chapter contains a variety of speaking and writing exercises. Because you are often expected to communicate your ideas about the theme of the chapter rather than simply manipulate the structure, these exercises may seem at times quite challenging to you.

COMPOSITION TOPICS   At the end of the chapter, you are given a choice of topics based on the theme so that you can practice using the grammar in your own writing.

TOEFL GUIDES   This book is not a TOEFL book; however, because many of you may be required to take the TOEFL, you can identify those explanations and exercises that may be helpful in preparing for the TOEFL by looking for this symbol—■.

American Culture

Chapter 1

- Count and Noncount Nouns
- Quantifiers
- Possessives

"You deserve a break today—at McDonald's"

DISCUSSION QUESTIONS

1. A "time capsule" is a container that holds objects that reflect a particular time period. What would you put in a time capsule to represent the essence of American culture as it is today?

2. What has your culture "borrowed" from American culture? What has the United States borrowed from your culture?

OBJECTIVES

In this chapter, you will review:

1. Forming regular and irregular plural nouns

2. Distinguishing between count and noncount nouns

3. Using appropriate quantifiers

4. Using possessives correctly

Preview

DIRECTIONS: The following adapted excerpt about the fast food chain, McDonald's, was written by the economics writer, Robert J. Samuelson. Read the selection to find out what Samuelson thinks about the famous fast food restaurant, and then answer the questions that follow.

My Big Mac is Back; Praise Be to Ray Kroc

So what if McDonald's is a crass, arrogant corporate giant? It does what it does just right.

by Robert J. Samuelson

1 I am **thrilled**. The McDonald's that is located a block from my office has reopened. Ever since it closed two years ago when the building was torn down, I have suffered cruelly. Now I can get my Big Mac and fries again. My writing has definitely improved. . . .

2 McDonald's is no ordinary company. It's the greatest restaurant chain in history. A recent survey of the country's best-known brands put McDonald's in the top five (Coca-Cola was No. 1).

3 There are three types of Americans. First are those who, like me, openly **worship** McDonald's. Next is a much larger group that likes McDonald's but would never admit it. These people use their children as an excuse to go—or only visit a McDonald's where they won't be recognized by family and friends. Finally there's a small group of **weirdos** who can't stand the food and regard McDonald's as a symbol of the poor taste of American mass culture.

4 Before Ray Kroc—the man who made the chain what it is today—there were Richard and Maurice McDonald. The brothers McDonald conceived **the golden arches** and the basic ideas behind fast food. In 1948, they converted a successful conventional restaurant in San Bernardino into **the prototype** of every subsequent fast-food restaurant. They shortened a long menu to five items (hamburgers, cheeseburgers, fries, milkshakes and sodas). They cut prices (a hamburger went from 30 cents to 15 cents). And they adopted assembly-line cooking.

5 Kroc improved and franchised the brothers' system. He was **fanatical** about cleanliness, because he realized that dirty restaurants would kill family business. McDonald's set strict standards on everything from meat quality to frying potatoes. In 1961, it created Hamburger University to train its managers.

6 I admit that the resulting food **colossus** has many uncharming aspects. The work is boring and demanding, although (. . .) these jobs do teach vital employment skills: punctuality, teamwork and customer courtesy. (. . .) There's also **an arrogant edge** to McDonald's that reflects its combativeness and success.

7 McDonald's uniformity was a response to social changes in **postwar society** that created fast food. As Americans became more **mobile** and **harried,** people looked for something that was familiar, quick and dependable. McDonald's uniformity and quality satisfied these needs. The same formula is now working abroad.

8 It's impossible to overstate the quality control. Once in Tokyo, I had a Big Mac. A Japanese Big Mac doesn't merely taste like an American Big Mac. It tastes exactly the same. **Ditto** for the fries. Put another way, if other American companies had McDonald's quality control, Japanese exports to the United States would be half today's level.

VOCABULARY

thrilled: very happy about; excited
worship: to regard someone or something with great respect and reverence
weirdos: strange people
the golden arches: the yellow arches that characterize McDonald's restaurants
the prototype: the original model
fanatical: excessively attentive to
colossus: something of enormous size
an arrogant edge: a sense of superiority
condemning: criticizing harshly
postwar society: American society after World War II
mobile: not fixed in one place
harried: very busy
ditto: (informal) The same is true for . . .

CULTURAL NOTE/DISCUSSION

This article praises McDonald's for running an efficient business and controlling quality to provide a uniform product. Many Americans agree with Samuelson and could not imagine a world without fast food. What do you think about the predominance of fast food in this country? If you have been to a McDonald's in another country, how was it similar to or different from a McDonald's in the United States?

FOCUS ON GRAMMAR

The following questions are based on the preview text and are designed to help you find out what you already know about the grammatical structures in this chapter. Some of the questions may be difficult and some of them may be easy. Answer as many of the questions as you can. Work with a partner if your teacher tells you to do so.

1. Can you explain why the author uses no article before the **bold** nouns in the following sentences?

    a. "He was fanatical about **cleanliness**. . . ." (paragraph 5)

    _____

    b. "McDonald's set strict **standards** on everything" (paragraph 5)

    _____

2. Can you explain why *a* is used before *McDonald's* and *an* is used before *excuse* in the following sentence: "These people use their children as **an excuse** to go—or only visit **a McDonald's** where they won't be recognized by family and friends."

_____

3. "**The work** is boring and demanding, although (. . .) these jobs do teach vital employment skills: **punctuality, teamwork** and **customer courtesy**."

   Could the nouns in bold be made plural? Why or why not?

_____

   Would you use *much* or *many* in the following blanks? Explain your choices.

not _____ teamwork

not _____ employment skills

not _____ customer courtesy

Grammatical Patterns Part One

I. Count Nouns

In general, nouns in English can be classified as either count or noncount. As you will see in greater detail below, count nouns can be counted or easily divided. Count nouns have both singular and plural forms. The term *noncount nouns* refers to nouns which cannot be easily counted, and these nouns do not have a plural form.

	Singular	**Plural**
COUNT NOUNS	a hamburger a french fry	hamburgers french fries
NONCOUNT NOUNS	jazz quality	XXXXX XXXXX

1.1 Written Drill: *Plural Formation*

DIRECTIONS: Provide the **plural form** of these nouns. Refer to the charts in Appendix 417, which outline the rules and exceptions for plural formation. Be ready to cite the rule for forming the plural of similar nouns.

Example   memorandum: *memoranda*
Rule: words that end in *-um* form their plural by changing the *-um* to *-a*.

1. odyssey _____   6. goose _____
2. Filipino _____   7. mouse _____
3. phenomenon _____   8. belief _____
4. potato _____   9. attorney _____
5. fish _____   10. syllabus _____

Provide the **singular** form of these nouns.

11. hypotheses _____   16. fungi _____
12. indices _____   17. stimuli _____
13. criteria _____   18. data _____
14. series _____   19. media _____
15. species _____   20. shelves _____

1.2 Editing Activity: *Plural Formation*

DIRECTIONS: Read the following student essay, which contains errors in plural formation. Underline the nouns that have faulty plural formations and make the necessary corrections. Refer to Appendix D on page 417 for information.

I am a second generation Mexican-American women. Even though I was born in the United States, I feel as if I live between two cultures. I experience this a lot when it comes to believes about the role and function of "la familia," the family. Familys in my parent's country of origin were extended. They included the husbands and wifes and the childrens, and also aunts, uncles, mother-in-laws, father-in-laws, and so on. All the memberes of the familys shared in childcare and provided support for everyone in the family. As you know, familys in the United State are smaller, sometimes called "nuclear familys." I love my extended family, but it can be very difficult for me to find a balance between my own time and the time I feel I should be giving to my relatives. Of course, in crisises, I want to be available for my family, but when I have a lot of homework to do, I feel guilty when I go off to the library to study. The peoples in my family don't always understand how important my school and career are for me

■ II. Noncount Nouns

There are two types of noncount nouns: mass and abstract, as follows.

Mass nouns cannot easily be counted or divided. They are always singular.	• Please pass the **milk.** • Buffalo had two feet of **snow.**
Abstract nouns refer to general concepts and ideas. They are always singular.	• McDonald's **uniformity** and **quality.** • Kroc was fanatical about **cleanliness.**

A. Mass Nouns

There are many types of mass nouns. Here are some common examples.

CATEGORY	NOUNS	EXAMPLE SENTENCE
1. Liquids	wine, beer, milk, water, coffee, tea, etc.	• I bought some **milk** for breakfast.
2. Food These can be solid or granular.	sugar, salt, pepper, rice, flour, etc. cheese, meat, butter, bread, yogurt, etc.	• Pass the **salt,** please. • I'd like to buy some **bread.**
3. Natural Elements These include terms relating to the weather and also to natural resources.	weather, rain, snow, hail, ice, wind, heat, etc. wood, oil, gold, iron, petroleum, copper, uranium, etc.	• We didn't have much **snow** or **rain** this year. • The **fog** is beautiful in San Francisco. • A lot of **wood** for construction comes from Canada. • **Uranium** is a valuable resource.
4. Problem Noncounts These noncounts often cause problems for students. Study them carefully!	advice, clothing, equipment, furniture, hair, homework, information, jewelry, luggage, mail, money, news, slang, travel, vocabulary, work	• Can you give me more **advice** about marriage? • I bought a lot of new **furniture** yesterday. • Have you learned any new **slang?** • I've learned a lot of **vocabulary** this week. • The factory sold its outdated **equipment.** • I just washed my **hair.**

1.3 Rapid Drill: *Noncount Nouns*

DIRECTIONS: Identify the following nouns as *count* (C) or *noncount* (NC).

advice	mouse	news	knowledge
luggage	information	furniture	suitcase
slang	mail	assignment	smog
toy	medicine	hypothesis	bottle
people	sheep	traffic	fog
homework	deer	vocabulary	rice
work	jazz		

1.4 Recognition Drill: *Count or Noncount?*

DIRECTIONS: Read the following paragraph, which is a continuation of the Preview selection by Robert J. Samuelson. Underline the nouns and identify them as *count* or *noncount*.

> In the end, McDonald's exemplifies what I have called "the Big Mac Principle." It holds that a Big Mac tastes better than "two all beef patties, special sauce, lettuce, cheese, pickles, onions on a sesame seed bun." The whole, in short, is greater than the sum of its parts. Or, if you think a Big Mac tastes worse than its ingredients, you have the Big Mac Principle in reverse. Companies, politicians, sports teams, bosses, entire civilizations—in fact, almost anything—can be understood as either the Big Mac Principle or the Big Mac Principle in reverse.

1.5 Paired Activity: *Count and Noncount Noun Equivalents*

DIRECTIONS: Often noncount nouns in English have count noun equivalents. For example, study this sentence from the Preview text:

> "The **work** is boring and demanding, although these jobs do teach vital employment skills . . ."

Work is a noncount noun and the count equivalent is **jobs**.

In the following exercise, work with a partner to find a noncount equivalent for each count noun provided.

Example   CUE: **a suitcase**
       STUDENT A: **suitcase** (count)
       STUDENT B: **luggage** (noncount)

1. a letter _____

2. a chair _____

3. an assignment _____

4. an idiom _____

5. a job _____

6. a dollar _____

7. a dress _____

8. a possible answer to a problem _____

9. a bracelet _____

10. an editorial _____

B. Abstract Nouns

Abstract nouns refer to general concepts and ideas. Here are some examples.

CATEGORY	EXAMPLE NOUNS	EXAMPLE SENTENCE
1. Concepts and Ideas	democracy freedom socialism	• Most Americans believe in **democracy.** • Some Americans take **freedom** for granted.
2. Emotions	anger, fear, sadness, joy, happiness, love, hate	• Great **love** can erase **anger** and **hate.** • Both **sadness** and **joy** can cause a person to cry.
3. Qualities and Traits	wealth, poverty, beauty, luck, intelligence, trust, patience	• **Wealth** is often considered a sign of success. • **Beauty** is in the eye of the beholder.

1.6 Recognition Drill: *Preview Text*

DIRECTIONS: Return to the Preview text on McDonald's on page 2 of this chapter. Underline all the noncount nouns in the passage. Circle the noncount nouns which are also abstract.

1.7 Written Activity: *Stereotypes*

DIRECTIONS: Stereotypes are general statements that people make about people or things based on popular conceptions rather than actual experience or research. Many of the stereotypes we hold are formed by images from films and television. Select among the following categories and write a paragraph describing how popular television and film portray these people, emphasizing the stereotypical characteristics. Underline the abstract nouns that you use in your paragraph.

cowboys
Indians
members of organized crime (e.g., the Mafia)
medical doctors
housewives
members of a certain religion or culture

Special
Note

> The first letters of the names of countries, nationalities, races, and religions are **capitalized,** whether they are used as nouns or adjectives:
> - My best friend is **Mexican.** (adjective)
> - He comes from **Mexico.** (noun)
> - He went to a **Catholic** school. (adjective)
> - His father works in a **French** restaurant in **Mexico** City. (adjective; noun)

III. Nouns That Are Both Count and Noncount

Some nouns can be both count and noncount. Compare the following examples and note how the meaning changes when the noncount noun becomes a count noun.

NONCOUNT MEANING	COUNT MEANING
1. Americans are drinking more **juice** these days Noncount meaning: in general	**1.** Have you been to that new juice bar? They serve **15 different juices.** Count meaning: kinds or types
2. Coffee is the preferred breakfast beverage in the United States. Noncount meaning: in general	**2.** I'd like **two large coffees** to go, please. Count meaning: servings, cups of
3. Many families eat **turkey** at Thanksgiving. Noncount meaning: meat from an animal	**3.** He cooked **two turkeys** for Thanksgiving. Count meaning: the entire animal
4. Education is the most important issue in the local elections. Noncount meaning: The concept in general	**4.** Every American child is entitled to **a free education.** Count meaning: a specific instance of the general concept
5. Glass is used in building many skyscrapers. Noncount meaning: a reference to the general substance or material	**5.** The baby broke **a glass.** Count meaning: an object made from a substance or material

1.8 Written Drill: *Noncount or Count?*

DIRECTIONS: Read the following sentences and indicate whether the bold noun is *count* (C) or *noncount* (NC). Then explain the meaning of the noun by referring to the five cases listed above.

$$\underline{C}$$

Example   I'd like to order **two teas**, please.
              Meaning: *two servings*

1. My aunt bought me an **iron** for Christmas.

    Meaning: _____

2. His two children are the **joys** of his life.

    Meaning: _____

3. The cafe down the street is now offering a new **coffee**.

    Meaning: _____

4. **Poverty** is a fact of life in many cities in the United States.

    Meaning: _____

5. Bill Gates has **a wealth** that most people can't even imagine.

    Meaning: _____

6. Many Americans go into **business** for themselves.

    Meaning: _____

1.9 Written Activity: *Noncount to Count Changes*

DIRECTIONS: Write two sentences for each of the following nouns, clearly demonstrating the change in meaning caused by the noncount to count shift.

Example   democracy: Democracy is based on the will of the majority.

              a democracy: The United States is a democracy.

1. beer: _____

    a beer: _____

2. life: _____

    a life: _____

3. business: _____

    a business: _____

4. noise: _____

    a noise: _____

5. love: _____

    a love: _____

Grammatical Patterns Part Two

Expressions of Quantity

I. Count and Noncount Expressions of Quantity

Note the different expressions of quantity used with count and noncount nouns.

MEANING	COUNT NOUN QUANTIFIERS	NONCOUNT NOUN QUANTIFIERS
1. A sufficient or great amount of something	The following quantifiers can be used with both count and noncount nouns. (Note that **ideas** is a count noun and **information** is a noncount noun.) • **some** ideas/information • **a lot of** ideas/information • **lots of** ideas/information • **plenty of** ideas/information Note which quantifiers are used with count and noncount nouns. • **many** ideas • **several** ideas • **a couple of** ideas • **(quite) a few** ideas	 • **much** information • **a little** information • **quite a bit of** information
2. Expressions for a sufficient or great amount	**FORMAL EXPRESSIONS:** • **a great number of** ideas • **a large number of** ideas • **a great many** ideas **SLANG EXPRESSIONS:** • **millions of** ideas • **tons/loads of** ideas • **a bunch of** ideas	• **a great amount of** information • **a great deal of** information
3. An insufficient amount; emphasis is on the negative.	The following quantifiers may be used with both count and noncount nouns: • **a lack of** ideas/information • **hardly any** ideas/information • **not all (the)** ideas/information • **almost none of the** ideas/information Note which quantifiers are used with count and noncount nouns: • **(very) few** ideas • **not many** ideas	 • **(very) little** information • **not much** information

SPECIAL NOTE

MANY VS. MUCH

Keep the following in mind when you are trying to decide between using *many* and *much*.
- Use *many* with count nouns: **Many Americans** own cellular telephones.
- Use *much* with noncount nouns. Avoid using *much* in affirmative sentences. Use a different expression, such as *a great deal of*, instead.
(awkward): Americans send **much** information by fax.
(better): Americans send **a great deal of** information by fax.
- Use *not much* in negative sentences: Businesses do **not** have **much need** for electric typewriters anymore.
- Use *much* in questions: Do you have **much** software for accounting?
- *Much* can replace the noun phrase in questions and negative statements:
(questions): Do you have **much** to do?
(negative): No, **not much.**

1.10 Written Activity: *Quantifiers*

DIRECTIONS: Technology has changed drastically in the United States during the past twenty years. Read each of the following statements about technology in the United States today and then write a comparative statement using the time frame provided. Use a different quantifier in each of your sentences; avoid using the quantifier provided at the beginning of each sentence.

Example   CUE: Many people in the United States wear "pagers" today so that they can be reached at all times; [ten years ago], fewer people wore them.

ANSWER: _____

1. A great deal of money is spent on computer technology in American colleges; in the past, _____

_____.

2. Most college libraries have computerized indexes; ten years ago, _____

_____.

3. You don't hear many human voices when you call businesses on the phone these days. A lot of businesses have computerized phone systems that connect you from one automated voice to another; in the 1970s; _____

_____.

4. A lot of mail is sent electronically now—many people have an "e-mail" address in addition to a street address; in the past, _____

_____.

5. An increasing number of people are "telecommuting"—a great deal of work is done at home and transmitted electronically via fax, telephone, and modem; twenty years ago, _____

_____.

■ SPECIAL
   NOTE

> **UNITS OF MEASUREMENT**
>
> Many noncount mass items are measured in terms of count units. Study the following examples.
> See if you can think of any other units of measurement.
> - **a quart / gallon / carton / bottle of** liquid
> - **a loaf of** bread
> - **a pound of** cheese / meat, etc.
> - **a stick of** butter
> - **a can of** soup
> - **a tube of** toothpaste
> - **a head of** lettuce

1.11 Paired Activity: *Expressions of Quantity*

DIRECTIONS: Potluck dinners, parties to which each guest brings a dish or beverage, are becoming more popular in the United States as families have less time to prepare an elaborate dinner for a large group. Imagine that your English class is planning a potluck dinner for the end-of-the-term party. How much or many of the following items will be needed for your class?

Work with a partner to prepare a list of possible items to bring to a potluck party. Use the suggested items below, or include your own ideas. Identify an exact amount for each item. (See Special Note: Units of Measurement above.) Note that count nouns must be made plural.

Example   bread <u>two loaves of bread</u>

1. pita bread
2. soda
3. coffee
4. chicken
5. fried rice
6. hummus
7. potato
8. salad
9. napkin
10. flower
11. egg
12. paper plate
13. sushi
14. ?
15. ?

II. (A) Few/(A) Little

DIRECTIONS: Read the following story about Carlos and Maria and then study the chart on quantifiers that follows.

Students who were not born in the U.S. often respond to "culture shock" in different ways. Maria is an example of a student who adjusted well to life in the U.S. She has been in the U.S. for a little over three years. She has had few problems making the transition to speaking English and attending American schools. She has had a few part-time jobs to supplement her family's income. She has made a few friends at work and school, and she spends a little of her leisure time with them.

Carlos, on the other hand, is not very satisfied with his American experience. He doesn't have many friends, and the ones he does have don't live close by. He feels lonely and sad, so he spends his weekends writing letters to his family in South America. He also stays in on the weekends because he's on a tight budget. Since life in the U.S. is much more expensive than he had imagined, he doesn't have enough money to pay for a dinner out or even an evening at the movies.

MEANING	EXAMPLE	NOTES
POSITIVE QUANTIFIERS		
a few not many, but a sufficient amount	Maria has **a few** friends.	Use **a few** with count nouns.
quite a few many	Carlos has **quite a few** problems.	Use **quite a few** with count nouns.
(only/just a) a little some, but not a lot of	Maria works part-time, so she has **a little money.**	Use **a little** with noncount nouns.
NEGATIVE QUANTIFIERS		
few not many, not enough, hardly any	Carlos has **(very) few** friends.	Use **few** with count nouns; use **very few** to add emphasis.
very few, little, very little hardly any; an insufficient amount	Carlos has **(very) little** money for weekend fun.	Use **little** with noncount nouns; use **very little** to add emphasis.

Here is a summary of the uses of *(a) little* and *(a) few*:

Negative –	Positive +
Carlos has **few friends.**	Maria has **a few friends.**
Carlos has **little money** for fun.	Maria has **a little money.**

1.12 Oral Drill: *Few* and *Little*

DIRECTIONS: Choose five of the following phrases and make sentences using *(quite) a few/(very) few* or *a little/(very) little*. Be honest in your answers and be prepared to disagree with your classmates!

Example   CUE: snow in Florida
          ANSWER: There is very little snow in Florida.

1. money in your pocket
2. friends in this city
3. problems with count and noncount nouns
4. free time in the evening
5. great leaders in the world
6. cheap housing in New York City
7. tests in this class
8. teachers like this one
9. intelligent students in this class
10. chance for peace in the world

1.13 Written Activity: *(A) Few/(A) Little*

DIRECTIONS: Imagine that a friend from another country is coming to your city or community to work. Write a letter to him or her describing various aspects of life in your city. Include things you think would be surprising or that might be difficult for him or her to understand. Use a variety of quantifiers in your letter, including *(a) few/(a) little*.

1.14 Written Activity: *All Expressions of Quantity*

DIRECTIONS: Read the following sentences which compare 4-year and 2-year colleges. Paraphrase these sentences using any appropriate expression of quantity from the list on page 14 (for example, **a great deal of, plenty of, few,** etc.).

Example   CUE: An American university professor may give 50 to 100 pages of reading per night.
          ANSWER: An American university professor may give a great deal of reading per night.

1. A four-year university is likely to have all types of recreational activities on campus—movies, concerts, plays, and even bowling.

2. Many students attending community colleges live at home with their families and commute to school.

   _____

   _____

3. In private colleges and universities, however, you will find more students living in dorms on campus.

   _____

   _____

4. A foreign student might be surprised at the amount of "partying" that goes on in the campus dorms of a large university, especially on the weekends.

   _____

   _____

5. It may be difficult for students to complain about the noise, because not many students seem to mind it.

   _____

   _____

6. At the end of the semester, however, most students have a lot of work, and the noise level is substantially reduced in the dorms.

   _____

   _____

7. In community colleges, many students take classes in the evenings, because they work during the day.

   _____

   _____

■ **1.15 Chapter Review:** *Settling the New World*

DIRECTIONS: Choose any appropriate answer to complete the following sentences about settling the New World. **Some may have more than one correct answer.**

1. _____ Pilgrims came to Massachusetts in the seventeenth century.

   a. Many   c. A great number
   b. Much   d. A number of

2. About the same time, _____ noblemen from England were settling in Virginia.

   a. some   c. quite a few
   b. much   d. a great deal of

3. Unfortunately, _____ settlers from the first permanent English

   settlement in Jamestown, Virginia, survived.

   a. hardly any   c. not many
   b. few   d. not much

4. In Virginia, the land was rich. As a result, _____ colonists were

   able to prosper from the land and build luxurious homes.

   a. many of the   c. many of
   b. many   d. a good many

5. Life was hard in Massachusetts for the early settlers. _____ of

   their land was as fertile as that in Virginia.

   a. Very little   c. Not much
   b. Very few   d. Not many

6. Native American Indians inhabited the land in Virginia; when the European settlers moved to

   Virginia and decided to cut down _____ of their pristine land for

   tobacco, the Native Americans were quite unhappy.

   a. very little   c. much
   b. some   d. a good bit

III. Special Problems

Pay special attention to these very common errors.

PROBLEM	EXPLANATION
1. Use of **much** in statements: [(AWKWARD): A doctor makes **much** money.] (BETTER): A doctor makes **a great deal of** money.	1. Use **much** only in questions and negative statements. Use another quantifier instead.
2. No plural after **of** phrases: [INCORRECT: There are a great number **of car**.] CORRECT: There are a great number of **cars**.	2. A plural count noun follows **of** phrases like *a great number of*.
3. Count and noncount problems: [INCORRECT: We bought some **furnitures**.] CORRECT: We bought some **furniture**.	3. Study count and noncount nouns carefully. Remember noncount nouns can never be plural.
4. Plural spelling problems: [INCORRECT: How many **countrys** are there?] CORRECT: How many **countries** are there?	4. Watch out for the spelling of irregular plural nouns.

■ 1.16 Error Analysis: *Count* and *Noncount Nouns*

DIRECTIONS: The following sentences were written by students. Correct any errors in count and noncount noun use, *a/an* use, and quantifiers. **Some sentences may have more than one error.**

1. In small private colleges, you will find a great amount of students living in dorms.

2. At the end of the semester, however, most students have a larger number of work.

3. At the end of the semester, a great deal of student have a lot of work.

4. A foreign student might be surprised at the great deal of partying that goes on.

5. At the end, most students have plenty work.

6. At the end of the semester, you have very few noise in the dorms.

7. In small private colleges, you'll find a great many of students living in dorms on campus.

8. Bettina would like to take a class in American slangs so she can improve her conversational vocabularies.

9. She bought three pianos for her rental studios.

10. You can get much informations from your advisor about applying to an U.S. university.

11. The automobile factorys in the midwest of United States still have some equipments that are not operated by robots.

12. The table's leg got chipped in the move.

13. There were much letter to the editors on the topic of illegal immigration.

14. The mother gave her twin two-years-olds a handsful of cherries.

focus on Writing

Possessive Nouns

Use a possessive form with nouns and pronouns to show ownership. Note from the example below that the possessive for the noun (Ray Kroc's) is formed by adding an apostrophe (') and an "s" to the end of the noun.

• **Ray Kroc's** empire was built on the success of **his** restaurants.
   (noun)   (pronoun)

Below are the basic guidelines for forming and using possessives.

RULE	EXAMPLES	NOTES
1. Add an apostrophe + s to singular nouns and plural nouns which do not end in -s.	• the girl**'s** book (singular noun) • the men**'s** department (plural noun)	
2. Add an apostrophe (but no -s) to a singular noun that ends in -s or -z.	• the boss' orders • Liz' paper • Arkansas' governor • Lopez' house	**Exceptions:** If the noun is **only one** syllable, you may add an apostrophe + -s: (e.g., the boss**'s** orders; Liz**'s** paper).
3. Add an apostrophe (but no -s) to plural nouns that end in -s.	• the teachers' room • the Senators' wing	
4. Add an apostrophe + s to the end of compound nouns.	• my mother-in-law**'s** present • the homeroom teacher**'s** desk	Be careful not to confuse the plural formation with the possessive formation of compound nouns. (e.g. plural: mothers-in-law; possessive: mother-in-law's)
5. Avoid using the possessive apostrophe + s with nonliving things. Use **of** instead.	• the color of the room (not: the room's color) • the taste of the food (not: the food's taste)	This rule is flexible. Many expressions do not follow it. (See Special Note on page 20.)
6. Do not use an apostrophe with pronouns (e.g., *my his, her, your, etc.*)	• The dog is in pain. **Its** leg is broken.	Note that **it's** is a contraction for "it is."

1.17 Editing Activity: *English Only*

DIRECTIONS: José wrote a letter to the editor of his local paper on an old typewriter. The apostrophe key was not working, so all the apostrophes (') are missing from the following "Letter to the Editor." Edit the passage, inserting the apostrophes where necessary.

Dear Editor,

My mothers family came from Mexico and my fathers family came from the United States. All their childrens first language is Spanish because my mother always spoke Spanish at home to her kids. But we all learned English as soon as we went to the local schools, because none or our teachers could speak Spanish. In fact, they reprimanded us when we spoke Spanish among ourselves, so we learned to speak English in public and Spanish at home. I know that those teachers intentions were well-meaning, but I feel that I should have the right to speak the language I choose with my friends and family.

That is why I am opposed to the "English Only" proposition which wants to make English the only language in this country. My familys heritage is important to me, and a big part of that is the language of my culture. Speaking Spanish is part of the Ramirez family tradition, and I would have a very difficult time accepting the governments mandate that I speak only English at school and at work.

Sincerely,

José Ramirez

José Ramirez

SPECIAL NOTE

Possessive nouns are usually used to show ownership of living things. There are a few exceptions to this general rule.
- To refer to relationships in nature (e.g., *the earth's rotation; the ocean's ebb and flow; the sun's rays*)
- To express an amount or quantity (e.g., *a month's salary; one dollar's worth of change*)

1.18 Written Activity: *Possessive Nouns*

DIRECTIONS: Complete the following sentences by providing a possessive form of the cue words in parentheses. Use an apostrophe + -s form whenever possible; use an *of* phrase when necessary.

Example: CUE: (Americans/love affair with big cars)

It is easy to trace _____.

ANSWER: *It is easy to trace Americans' love affair with big cars.*

1. Each generation has its love affair with cars. In the 1950s, people fell in love with (Cadillac/fish-tailed curves) _____ .

2. These cars symbolized success and opulence, which were (that generation/dreams) _____ .

3. In the 1960s, sports cars matched the (Baby Boomers/daring moods) _____ as they purchased their first cars.

4. The Ford Mustang, the Camaro, the Corvette—these cars were designed to catch the eye of (teenage boys/girlfriends) _____ .

5. In the 1970s, larger American cars lost their glamour as the energy crisis hit. The (cars/great consumption of gasoline) _____ led to (big car/demise) _____ .

6. (The 1980s/trend) _____ was to buy smaller, more fuel-efficient foreign cars. Le Car from Renault and the Yugo from the former Yugoslavia were common sights on the road.

7. These cars saved people (hundreds of dollars/worth) _____ of gas annually.

8. They also conserved a great deal of (the earth/natural resources) _____ .

Composition Topics

1. Many children of first generation immigrants find themselves between two cultures—that of their parents and that of the United States. Interview a student whose parents are immigrants. Find out about the difficulties and joys of being part of two cultures. Then summarize what you learned in the interview in an essay.

2. Many states in the U.S. have endorsed "English Only" initiatives which state that English is the official language of the United States. What is your opinion on this issue? Do you think that everyone in this country should master English, or do you believe that it is important to preserve and encourage immigrants to speak and write their own language? Discuss your ideas in a composition.

3. In the Preview text on page 2, the author, Robert J. Samuelson, maintains that McDonald's is a model for quality control in business. Agree or disagree with his point of view and provide reasons for your ideas.

A Quick Review

The next three chapters will present information about and practice in using verb tenses. Some sections may be a review for you, and others may be new and challenging. After studying each verb tense individually, you will have a chance to put everything you have learned together. The sequence is as follows:

Chapter 2: Overview of the Verb Tense System; The Simple Tenses

Chapter 3: The Perfect Tenses

Chapter 4: The Progressive Tenses; Integration of Tenses

Objectives

In this chapter you will:

1. Review forming the simple present, past, and future;

2. Practice using time words with these tenses;

3. Review forming irregular verbs.

Preview

People *have always told* me that I am an adaptable person. However, when I came to the United States to study, I found out that I am not as adaptable as I seem. I had already studied six years of English before I left my country, Indonesia. I had been studying conversational English with an American teacher for about a year before I left. So I really didn't expect to have any problems communicating with Americans. I thought to myself, "I will just go to my classes and learn everything I can. Then by the time the TOEFL test arrives, I will have learned everything I need to get 550 on the TOEFL. I'll enter the local university for my M.B.A."

Well, I really wasn't ready for my first months here. At the first orientation meeting at the English school, the Americans were talking to me so fast that all I did was smile and nod. I still don't know what they said to me! I had more surprises—my accent was hard to understand, I didn't like the American food at the cafeteria, the pace in the city was too fast. But the biggest surprise was my progress in English. I didn't get into that university right away.

I'm still studying English. In fact, I've been studying for two semesters now. If all goes as planned, I'll be entering the M.B.A. program next semester. I'll have been living in the United States for an entire year by then. I am able to understand just about everything, and most people understand me. But guess what? I'm still not used to American food!

There are three basic **times** in English: present, past, and future. Each of these times combines with an **aspect**: simple, perfect, and progressive. The chapters that follow will explain these aspects in detail.

Before you learn about the more precise meanings and uses of the times and aspects, it is important to learn the names of the verb tenses. The names of the tenses are created by combining the time and the aspect expressed in a specific tense. Consider the verb in the sentence, *I was eating*. The time expressed is past (*was*) and the aspect expressed is progressive. (You know this because the verb has an *-ing* ending.) Therefore, the name of this verb tense is **past progressive.**

The chart below summarizes all twelve verb tenses. To read the chart, choose the time (at the top) and combine it with the aspect (on the sides). For example, the past progressive tense is *I was eating.*

ASPECT	TIME		
	Present	**Past**	**Future**
Simple	I eat.	I ate.	I will eat.
Perfect	I have eaten.	I had eaten.	I will have eaten.
Progressive	I am eating.	I was eating.	I will be eating.
Perfect Progressive	I have been eating.	I had been eating.	I will have been eating.

FOCUS ON GRAMMAR

In order to gain the most from the chapters on verb tenses that follow, it is very important that you know the **names** of all the verb forms. Use the above chart to help you to identify all the verb forms in the previous passage written by an Indonesian student living in the United States. Underline the verbs in the passage and label them from the list below:

simple present   simple past   simple future
present perfect   past perfect   future perfect
present progressive   past progressive   future progressive
present perfect progressive   past perfect progressive   future perfect progressive

Grammatical Patterns Part One

I. Overview of the Simple Present and Simple Past Tenses

The information in this section is probably not new for you. Review the following chart and then move on to the sections that follow. They will highlight some of the persistent problems that even advanced learners of English may still have with the simple present and past tenses.

TENSE	USES	EXAMPLES
Simple Present	• To express habitual actions	1. I **have** my economics class every Thursday. 2. She **goes** to the gym regularly.
	• To express opinions and preferences	3. She **prefers** hard rock music to jazz. 4. I **think** B. B. King is the best blues musician alive.
	• To state permanent truths and facts	5. Water **freezes** at 32°F. 6. Birds **watch** over their nests. 7. A dollar **buys** less today than it did in 1950.
Simple Past	• To describe completed actions	8. The neighbors **complained**. 9. The band **played** until dark. 10. The robbery **occurred** at midnight.
	• To express habitual past action . . . (**Used to** and **would** also express habitual past actions. Chapter 12 explains these in detail.)	11. I **spoke** Spanish when I was young. 12. I **used to speak** Spanish when I was young. 13. I **would** always get in trouble when I was young.

II. Special Problem One: *Time Words and the Simple Present*

Adverbs of frequency are time words that answer the question "How often?" Students often have difficulty with the **placement** of time words because they can occur in three positions in a sentence: at the beginning (initial position), in the middle, or at the end (final position). Study the following chart, which summarizes this information.

POSITION OF TIME WORDS	EXAMPLES
Initial Position These time words appear at the **beginning** of the sentence: • every (day; week; month, etc.) . . . . • on (Mondays; Tuesdays, etc.) . . . . • sometimes . . . . • usually . . . . • often	**1. Every week** I get a massage. **2. On Tuesdays,** we eat with our neighbors. **3. Sometimes** we get Chinese takeout. **4. Usually** if I cook, he does the dishes. **5. Often** I pay by credit card in stores.
Middle Position Most time words can be placed **before** the main verb or **after** the verb, be. • regularly (habitually, normally, uniformly, etc.) . . . . • always . . . . • usually . . . . • rarely (never; hardly ever, etc.)	Compare: **6.** He **regularly** goes to the gym. *(before verb)* **7.** He is **regularly** late. *(after be)* **8.** She **always** arrives before him. **9.** She is **always** on time. **10.** He **usually** quits before her. **11.** He is **usually** the first one out the door. **12.** She **rarely** leaves before him. **13.** She is **rarely** the first to leave.
Final Position Most time words (except *always*) can appear at the **end** of the sentence. • regularly . . . . • sometimes . . . . • usually . . . . • every day . . . . • rarely	**14.** He goes to the gym **regularly**. **15.** She accompanies him **sometimes**. **16.** He quits before her **usually**. **17.** She doesn't go **every day**. **18.** He misses school **rarely**.
Note Don't separate the verb from its object with a time word.	CORRECT: He lifts weights **regularly**. [INCORRECT: He lifts **regularly** weights.]

2.1 Paired Activity: *Time Words*

DIRECTIONS: Work with a partner and discuss how you act in different social situations. Describe yourself and your actions using the following time words: *usually, rarely, sometimes, often.*

Example   ANSWER: I am **rarely** quiet at a party. I **always** talk to people.

> ## NEGATIVE ADVERBS IN INITIAL POSITION
>
> Negative adverbs (e.g., *never, rarely, seldom, barely, scarcely*) can occur in initial position in a sentence. Note that this is not a common placement. When these adverbs appear in initial position, use **question word order** after the time word, as is shown in the examples below.
>
> **Rarely** does my sister go out on Saturday night.
>   aux   subject verb
>
> **Never** does my brother stay home on a Friday night.
>   aux   subject verb
>
> **Seldom** is the grocery store closed on Sunday.
>   verb   subject

2.2 Rapid Drill: *Negative Adverbs in Initial Position*

Directions: Restate the following sentences, beginning each with the negative adverb found in the sentence.

Example   SENTENCE: John rarely goes out on Saturday night.
           ANSWER: **Rarely** does John go out on Saturday night.

1. Guillermo rarely goes to the cinema anymore since the tickets are so expensive.
2. I never entertain in my home—I just don't have the time!
3. Loretta seldom goes to a disco since the music is so loud.
4. My parents never go to a rock concert; they prefer the symphony.
5. José's grandparents rarely sit through an entire concert without falling asleep.
6. Gladys never rents videos because she prefers to go to movie theaters.
7. Mr. and Mrs. Dupont hardly ever attend the Hollywood parties which they are invited to.
8. Construct your own sentences using *rarely, seldom, never.*

■ 2.3 Error Analysis: *Time Words*

DIRECTIONS: Find any errors in the use of adverbs in the following sentences. Correct the error clearly above the sentence.

1. Usually do I drink a beer.
2. We often organize at night barbecues around the swimming pool.
3. Never I stay at home to do my homework when I can go out with my friends.
4. My boyfriend is every day at my house.
5. Rarely the recreational facilities at this institution are fully utilized.
6. My roommate goes often to the Hard Rock Café.
7. Always I stay out late on Saturday night, but never do I do that on weeknights.
8. My friend invites often her class to her house for parties.
9. My sister throws lavish parties always on the 4th of July.
10. Seldom I have gone to nightclubs in my city.

III. Special Problem Two: *Irregular Verbs*

Some verbs are not regular in their past and past participle forms. Refer to the list of these verbs in Appendix A on page 411. Make a note of the verbs you still don't know and practice them regularly until you do.

A. Possible Spelling Patterns for Irregular Verbs

There are no exact rules for forming irregular verbs, but many of the verbs follow similar patterns. These are outlined below. Keep these patterns in mind when you are studying the verbs.

POSSIBLE SPELLING PATTERNS FOR IRREGULAR VERBS	EXAMPLES		
	Base	**Past**	**Past Participle**
1. These verbs **remain the same** for all three parts of the verb.	cut burst let	cut burst let	cut burst let, etc.
2. The past and past participle forms are **the same** for these verbs.	bend build mean	bent built meant	bent built meant, etc.
3. Note how the end of the base form (*-eep*) changes to *-ept* in the past and past participle of these verbs.	creep sleep keep	crept slept kept	crept slept kept, etc.
4. Note how the *-in* in the middle of the base form changes to *-an* in the past and *-un* in the past participle of these verbs.	drink sing ring	drank sang rang	drunk sung rung, etc.
5. Note how the middle vowel in the base form changes in the past and past participle for these verbs. Note also how you add *-n* to the base to form the past participle.	grow draw drive forgive forsake give	grew drew drove forgave forsook gave	grown drawn driven forgiven forsaken given, etc.

2.4 Paired Drill: *Irregular Verbs*

Directions: Work in pairs. Have your partner cover up the past and past participle columns of the list of irregular verbs in Appendix A on pages 411–414. Choose any fifteen verbs and test your partner's knowledge of the irregular forms. Then switch roles. Keep a list of the verbs your partner needs to study and then test him or her again in the next class.

2.5 Crossword Puzzle: *All Irregular Verbs*

DIRECTIONS: Complete the crossword puzzle by using the appropriate forms of the irregular verbs from the list in the appendix.

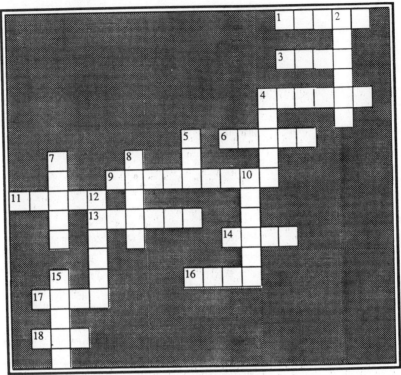

Across Clues

1. After she stopped smoking, Gloria _____ she would never smoke another cigarette in her life.

3. The small wound _____ profusely.

4. Maria was excited because she had been _____ for the "Student of the Year" award.

6. The hurricane _____ through Miami and knocked down all the trees.

9. Will the baseball game be _____ on national television?

11. I was _____ three aces in my poker game yesterday.

13. The criminal was _____ in the public square for all to see.

14. The car went over the bridge and _____ into the river.

16. The telephone rang before John _____ up his coat.

17. The car slid on the ice and _____ around three times.

18. The waiter _____ the woman's cigarette.

Down Clues

2. Have you ever _____ a camel?

4. The soldier _____ carefully through the forest to avoid being seen by the enemy.

5. Have you _____ the dog yet? He must be hungry.

7. Someone had _____ a caricature of the disliked teacher on the board.

8. To make flatbread you need to _____ the wheat berries into a fine powder.

10. David _____ out of his chair when he saw his old girlfriend.

12. The baseball had been _____ so hard, it went into the outfield.

15. Daniel _____ the cake into two pieces and offered one to his mother.

IV. Future Forms

Note the different ways in which the future may be formed and used.

Form	Use/Explanation	Example
Will + Main Verb	Use *will* + **main verb** for: 1. Predictions 2. Scheduled events 3. Promises 4. Offers 5. Requests	1. It **will rain** tomorrow. 2. The music **will start** at 9:00. 3. I **will meet** you there.* 4. I'll **pick** you up if you need a ride. 5. Will you **marry** me?
Be Going To + Main Verb	Use *be going to* + **main verb** for: 6. something planned or thought about ahead of time 7. a sure or certain future event.	6. I'm going to take **my sister to the new jazz club.** 7. **I'm going to have** my baby in March.
Simple Present	Use the **simple present:** 8. for scheduled events 9. with verbs such as *start, begin, finish,* etc. and *leave, depart, arrive,* etc.	8. The music **starts** at 9:00. 9. The plane **leaves** at 4:00.
Present Progressive	Use the **present progressive:** 10. for most future events, except predictions and offers 11. when the future time is clear from the context e.g., in (10) *tonight* indicates the future.	10. **I'm having** dinner at John's tomorrow night. 11. **I'm running** late tonight.

*Shall can replace *will* here, but this is more common in British English. (*I shall meet you there.*) In American English, *shall* is usually used as an invitation or suggestion, as in, "Shall we dance?" or in tag questions, "Let's go, shall we?"

2.6 Oral Activity: *Future Forms*

DIRECTIONS: Choose two or three of the following topics that you would like to respond to by using an appropriate form of the future. Be ready to respond orally when asked by your teacher.

1. Make a prediction about your life in ten years.
2. Tell the class about your weekend plans.
3. Offer to help your teacher with some aspect of the class.
4. Make a prediction about the next music trend.
5. Ask your neighbor about his or her plans for this evening.
6. Answer that question.
7. Try to guess about the activities and content of your next English class.
8. Offer to take your teacher out to a nice restaurant.
9. Make a promise about coming to class on time and doing all the homework.
10. Make a promise to the class about a future party.

2.7 Written Drill: *Be Going To* or *Will?*

DIRECTIONS: Fill in the blanks with *be going to* + verb or *will* + verb, depending on the meaning of the sentence. Indicate when both forms are possible.

1. According to all the forecasts from this year's food critics, restaurants serving low-fat entrees (continue) _____ to do well. They also predict that low-fat Mexican restaurants (grow) _____ in popularity. The expensive, "nouvelle cuisine" food that was so popular among yuppies in the 1980s (lose) _____ many customers since people prefer not to spend so much money on so little food.

2. Coffee bars have proliferated in the United States during the past five years. The famous Seattle chain, Starbucks, has become a trendy meeting place for many people. It's not uncommon for people to say, "I (meet) _____ you at Starbucks in half an hour." In addition, the servers are extremely congenial. They (prepare) _____ your coffee drink just the way you want it—with nonfat milk, with decaffeinated coffee, with a double shot of espresso. Starbucks is expanding; in fact they (open) _____ six new shops in my city this year. I think I (talk) _____ to my financial broker today about buying some stock in that company!

2.8 Written Drill: *All Forms*

DIRECTIONS: Circle **any** correct answer. Each item may have one, two, three, or four correct answers.

1. It _____ tomorrow.
   a. will rain
   b. is going to rain
   c. is raining
   d. rains

2. "Mr. Williams _____ up his wife at 3:00 later this afternoon. He won't be back in the office after that. Shall I have him call you tomorrow?" the secretary told the caller.

   a. will pick

   b. is going to pick

   c. is picking

   d. picks

3. I'm sorry that I can't stay longer at this meeting, but my child's play _____ in one hour. I can't miss that!

   a. will start

   b. is going to start

   c. is starting

   d. starts

4. "I _____ your exams tomorrow," the teacher said. "I promise!"

   a. will return

   b. am going to return

   c. am returning

   d. return

5. "Do you have any toothpaste left?" asked John. "No, but I _____ some for you when I go downtown," Kim said.

   a. will get

   b. am going to get

   c. am getting

   d. get

focus on Writing

Spelling Rules

Students sometimes have difficulty with the spelling of present and past verbs. Some of these trouble spots are outlined below.

TROUBLE SPOT	PRESENT	PAST
1. When the verb ends in **-y:** **a.** Change **-y** to **-i** and add **-es** (to form the present tense for third person singular) or add **-ed** to form the past tense. **b.** When **-y** is preceded by a vowel, just add **-s** or **-ed.**	• carry-carries • bury-buries • play-plays • stay-stays	• carry-carried • bury-buried • play-played • stay-stayed
2. When the verb ends in **-s,** **-z, -ch, -sh,** add **-es** or **-ed.**	• wash-washes • kiss-kisses • watch-watches	• wash-washed • kiss-kissed • watch-watched

Continued on next page.

Continued from previous page.

TROUBLE SPOT	PRESENT	PAST
3. To form the past tense of one-syllable verbs **a.** If the verb ends in one vowel and one consonant, double the consonant. **b.** If the verb ends in two vowels and one consonant or one vowel and two consonants, do not double the consonant.		• hop-hopped • pat-patted • help-helped • beam-beamed • rain-rained
4. To form the past tense of two-syllable verbs **a. Double the consonant** if: • the stress is on the second syllable (when pronouncing the verb), and the verb ends in one final vowel + consonant **b. Don't double the consonant** if: • the stress is on the first syllable and the verb ends in one final vowel and consonant. **c. Don't double the consonant** if: • the verb ends in two final vowels and a consonant. (The stress can be on either syllable in this case.)		• ad**mit**-admitted • pre**fer**-preferred • **mas**ter-mastered • **sof**ten-softened • refrain-refrained • succeed-succeeded

2.9 Editing Activity: *Simple Present*

DIRECTIONS: Edit the following paragraphs for spelling, subject-verb agreement, and time word placement. **Don't forget the -s on third person singular!**

1. Mrs. Nelson Whitney will be hosting her annual Charity Ball on Friday. She organize every year this event to benefit the Children's Hospital. Usually the ball is held in the Ballroom of the Hilton Hotel. Rarely less than 400 people attends the event since it is considered to be **the** social event of the season. Last year, Mrs. Whitney postponed the event due to the untimely death of the mayor. Let's all hope it happen this year.

2. Mindy wanted to know what it would feel like to "free fall" from 8500 feet, so she tryed "tandem jumping." She was tied to a harness, and straped to the instructor's chest. They went up in a small airplane and then got releassed into the air. She said that it was something like being on a roller coaster and her stomach felt compresed into a tiny metal ball during the first 20 seconds. Then when she rememberred to arch her back as she had been told by the teacher, she began to feel as though she were flying. After the teacher pulled the parachute, they floatted through the air, weightless, until they landed on a dirt mound. Tandem jumping is not cheap; it usually cost about $200 per trip.

Composition Topics

1. Describe a place at your school (or in your city) where you go to be by yourself. What does it look like? Why do you like that place? Provide enough details so the person reading your description can visualize that place clearly.

2. In the United States, sports fans eagerly await the biggest football event of the year—the Super Bowl. People have parties or go to restaurants with big-screen televisions to watch the game. Describe a similar sporting event which you have enjoyed. Use details to make the event come alive to your readers.

3. Students eagerly await their "breaks" from school. What are your plans for the next school break? Describe what you will do, where you may go, and so on.

Taking It Easy

- ## The Perfect Tenses

"Don't Worry, Be Happy"

DISCUSSION QUESTIONS

1. How do you like to spend your free time?
2. When you are feeling tense, what do you do to relax?
3. If you won a free trip around the world, where you would go? What would you do?

OBJECTIVES

In this chapter you will learn:

1. To form the present perfect, the past perfect, and the future perfect tenses

2. To recognize differences in uses between simple and perfect verb tenses

3. To use appropriate time words with each perfect verb tense

Preview

DIRECTIONS: Read the following conversation between Cheryl and Patty, who work in the same office. They are talking about where they went on their honeymoons. Find out why Patty can't join Cheryl on her vacation.

PATTY: Where did you and Ted go on your honeymoon?

CHERYL: We went to Las Vegas. Can you believe it?

PATTY: *Las Vegas!* I've never been there before. What was it like?

CHERYL: It sure wasn't what we had expected. Neither one of us had been there before, so we were surprised at how crowded and noisy it was. Some people think it's a romantic place, but we didn't like it. How about you? Where did you go?

PATTY: We went to Hawaii. Now **that** was romantic! Have you ever been there?

CHERYL: Oh, I love Hawaii. I've been there three times so far. In fact, we're going there for Christmas this year. Have you ever gone back?

PATTY: No. John and I haven't taken a vacation since our honeymoon three years ago.

CHERYL: Then why don't you two join us in Hawaii for Christmas? By then, we'll have gotten the bonus the company promised us and we'll have some spending money. Think about it. It could be a lot of fun. You deserve a break.

PATTY: Oh, Cheryl, I wish we could, but we can't. We've just bought a new car. Maybe next year . . .

FOCUS ON GRAMMAR

The following questions are based on the preview text and are designed to help you find out what you already know about the structures in this chapter. Some of the questions may be hard and some of them may be easy. Answer as many of the questions as you can. Work with a partner if your teacher tells you to do so.

1. Cheryl says, "We went to Las Vegas" in line two. Could she also say, "We have gone to Las Vegas"? Why or why not?

   _____

2. What time word indicates that an action was repeated in the past and will probably be repeated in the future?

   _____

3. Consider the following sentence from the dialogue: "It wasn't what we had expected." Can you explain why the first verb (*wasn't*) is simple past and the second verb (*had expected*) is past perfect?

   _____

4. When Cheryl says, "Neither one of us had been there before," what does she mean by "before"? Before what?

_____

5. Find the one sentence with the future perfect tense (**will have** + past participle). Could you use a simple **future** tense here? Why or why not?

_____

Grammatical Patterns Part One

I. Perfect Aspect

A. Forms

To form a perfect tense, use an appropriate form of the auxiliary *have* and the past participle of the main verb.

TENSE	FORM	EXAMPLE
Present Perfect	Use the auxiliary *have* or *has* with the past participle of the main verb.	• I **have been** there three times so far.
Past Perfect	Use the auxiliary *had* with the past participle of the main verb.	• Neither one of us **had been** there before.
Future Perfect	Use the auxiliary *will have* with the past participle of the main verb.	• We **will have** gotten our bonus by then.

3.1 Written Drill: *Forming Perfect Verbs*

DIRECTIONS: Provide the correct form of the verb, as indicated in parentheses.

Example (present perfect/sing)
Michael Jackson *has sung* for the Academy Awards before.

1. (past perfect/perform)

   Michael Jackson _____ on television in "The Jackson Five" with his siblings when he decided to go solo.

2. (present perfect/become)

   Jackson _____ a famous entertainer all over the world.

3. (present perfect/change)

Many Americans _____ their opinion of Jackson, however, due

to his unconventional behavior.

4. (future perfect/forget)

Although he was suspected of sexual misconduct, the next generation of fans

_____ about that incident.

5. (past perfect/live)

Jackson _____ with his wife, Lisa Marie Presley, the daughter of

Elvis Presley, less than two years before they got divorced.

B. Comparison: Simple vs. Perfect Tenses

SIMPLE TENSES	PERFECT TENSES
Use a **simple tense** to talk about one single event in the past, present, or future, without relating that to another event or state in time.	Use a **perfect tense** to relate one event or state that occurs **before** another event or state in the past, present, or future. A point of reference is always stated or implied.
─────X───── event I	─────X─────────────X───── event I event 2
• I **went** to Las Vegas in 1971. • I **will go** there again in ten years.	• I **had** never **been** to Las Vegas before I went there on my honeymoon. *(stated point of reference)* • I **have been** there before. *(implied point of reference)*

■ C. Uses: The Present Perfect

The following chart summarizes the differences in uses between the simple past and present perfect tenses.

SIMPLE PAST TENSE	PRESENT PERFECT TENSE
1. Use the simple past for events which occurred at a **definite** time in the past • We **went** to Las Vegas in 1988. *(1988 is a definite date.)*	1. Use the present perfect for events which occurred at an **indefinite or unspecified time** in the past • We **have been** there before. *("before" is indefinite; the exact time is not specified.)*
──X──────────┼── 1988 now	──???──────────┼── unspecified time in past now

Continued on next page.

Continued from previous page.

SIMPLE PAST TENSE	PRESENT PERFECT TENSE
2. Use the simple past for **continuous, completed** events or states in the past • Cheryl **smoked** from 1980 to 1990.  1980 1990 now (Cheryl doesn't smoke anymore.)	**2.** Use the present perfect for **unfinished events or states** in the past, which continue to the present • Patty **has smoked** since 1980.  1980 now (Patty still smokes)
3. The simple past also expresses **repeated events** in the past; this implies the event is not likely to recur. • We **went** to Hawaii three times in 1985. *(This sentence does not imply that the speaker plans to return to Hawaii in the future.)*  1985 now	**3.** The present perfect can also be used for **repeated events** in the past, which are likely to continue in the future: • I **have been** to Hawaii three times so far. *(This indicates that the speaker is likely to return.)*  unspecified time in past now (I may go again.)
4. Use the simple past for a **recently completed** event • We just **bought** a new car.	**4.** Use the present perfect for a **recently completed** event, which has some effect on the present. • We've just **bought** a new car, so we can't afford to take a vacation. • I've **broken** my watch, so I don't know the time.

3.2 Recognition Activity: *Present Perfect Tense*

DIRECTIONS: Read the following sentences about the Rock and Roll Hall of Fame Museum, which were written just after the hall opened in 1996.

Identify the precise meaning of the present perfect verbs (in italics in the sentences) and label each verb with one of the following:

(1) Indefinite time in the past
(2) Unfinished event in the past, continues to present
(3) Repeated events in the past, likely to continue
(4) Recently completed event.

1. The Rock and Roll Hall of Fame Museum in Cleveland *has* just *opened*, to the delight of many rock 'n roll fans. _____

2. Investors *have spent* $90 million on a 150,000 square foot building for the museum. _____

3. Many people believe that rock and roll *has* only *been* in existence for forty years, but the director of the museum assures people that this musical form has actually been around for an entire century. _____

4. The Director reminds us that Chuck Berry, whom many people think of as the father of rock and roll, *has played* music for a while now—and he's still going strong. _____

5. The collectors *have gathered* an impressive assortment of rock and roll memorabilia—Pete Towshend's (The Who) guitar; John Lennon's (The Beatles) "Sergeant Pepper" vest, and clothes from Carl Perkins. _____

6. Many rock and roll fans *have visited* the museum several times. _____

3.3 Oral Drill: *Effect on the Present*

The present perfect tense, when used to describe a past, completed event, indicates that the event has some effect on the present. Complete the following statements with a sentence which makes that relation clear.

Example   Ben has returned from a swim in the ocean, *so his hair is all wet.*
          Anna has already seen that play, *so she wants to go to a different play this evening.*

1. I have never been to a rock concert, so . . .
2. Our teacher has had a vacation, so . . .
3. The news has just announced a hurricane, so . . .
4. Ken has bought a surfboard, so . . .
5. The concert has sold out, so . . .
6. The World Cup finals are on television tonight, so . . .
7. The new Steven Spielberg film has come out on video, so . . .

8. Public Broadcasting has come out with a twelve-part series on the history of rock and roll, so . . .

9. George has received his black belt in Tae Kwan Do, so . . .

10. I have heard some French rap music, and . . .

3.4 Written Activity: *Past or Present Perfect?*

DIRECTIONS: For answers 1 and 2, read the questions and select answer (a) or (b), as appropriate. Remember to use the present perfect tense when the past activity still affects the present situation. Use the simple past tense when there is no effect on the present situation.

For number 3, write questions for the answers given. Your answers should demonstrate the difference between the present perfect and simple present tenses.

Example   CUE: A. Gary has bought a guitar.
                       B. Gary bought a guitar

1. Why is Gary so happy? _____A_____ (*The past event is making Gary happy now, so use the present perfect tense.*)

2. What did Gary do yesterday? _____B_____ (*This sentence is describing a completed past event; since there is no relation to the present, there is no need for the present perfect.*)

1. A. She has sung in a coffeehouse.

   B. She sang in a coffeehouse.

   a. Why couldn't Georgette make it to the party? _____

   b. Her occupation for the last 30 years: _____

   c. Does she have any experience as a singer? Yes, _____

   d. How did she earn a living in 1967? _____

2. A. He saw Whitney Houston in concert.

   B. He has seen Whitney Houston in concert.

   a. Why does Mark look so happy?_____

   b. Why is Mark talking to the newspaper reporter? _____

   c. What did Mark do in New York last summer? _____

   d. Mark doesn't care if he goes to another concert in his life because

   _____

3. Now, write your own questions to the following answers.

   _____?

   I was at an outdoor concert in Central Park.

   _____?

   I have been at an outdoor concert in Central Park.

_____?

Jack was at Kickers Night Club, a country dance place.

_____?

Jack has been at Kickers Night Club, a country dance place.

_____?

She has learned to box.

_____?

She learned to box.

D. Time Words: Present Perfect

The following chart identifies time words which are often used with the present perfect tense. Make a note of which time words are used with each of the following types of event—indefinite, unfinished, or recently completed.

USE	TIME WORDS	EXAMPLES
Indefinite Time In the Past	1. before 2. in the past 3. ever (for questions) 4. yet 5. already	1. I have been to Paris **before**. 2. I've studied this **in the past**. 3. Have you **ever** seen a UFO? 4. I haven't seen a UFO **yet**. 5. I've **already** taken Spanish 101.
Unfinished Action	6. for (+ period of time) 7. since (+ a specific date or time) 8. until now 9. up to now 10. so far 11. thus far	6. He's been sick **for a month**. 7. He's been sick **since June**. 8. We haven't had snow **until now**. 9. We've had good weather **up to now**. 10. We've had three storms **so far** this year. 11. They've had six children **thus far**.
Recently Completed Activity	12. just 13. recently 14. barely	12. I've **just** finished my test. 13. George has **recently** moved. 14. The show has **barely** begun.

3.5 Written Drill: *Time Expressions*

DIRECTIONS: Provide a time word to justify the use of either the simple past or present perfect tenses in the following dialogue. Refer to the chart on page 42 for present perfect time words.

Example   My sister has seen that movie __before__ .

MIKE: Have you even been skydiving _____?

1

KATHY: Funny you should ask me that. I tried it for the first time _____, and it was great.

2

I can't believe that I've lived _____ without ever trying it before.

3

MIKE: I've done it six times _____, and you know, it still scares me to death! I keep doing

4

it, though, because I love the thrill. Hey, I'm going tomorrow. Why don't you join me?

KATHY: I'm sorry, I can't. I've _____ made plans to have lunch with Nancy. Well . . .

5

maybe I can talk her into trying it!

3.6 Oral Drill: *Since and For*

DIRECTIONS: Choose three of the following cues to respond to, using **since** or **for,** as indicated. Your answer will be made with the negative form of the verb. Remember the following:

- Use a specific date or time after since (e.g., *I haven't been to a county fair **since I was a child.***)
- Use an expression of duration, a period of time after for (e.g., *I haven't been to a county fair **for twenty years.***)

Example   CUE: gone to a movie/since

ANSWER: I haven't gone to a movie since 1988.

1. got a haircut/for
2. read a novel/since
3. spoken my native language/for
4. written to my family/since
5. told a joke/since
6. had an argument with my mother or father/for
7. gone to the beach/for
8. done the dishes/since
9. taken a test/for
10. gone to the dentist/since

3.7 Written Activity: *Past and Present Perfect Tenses*

DIRECTIONS: Read the following situations describing Kumiko's leisure activities. Then construct sentences using the simple past or present perfect verb tenses.

Example   Kumiko was in Paris in 1980 and 1990. She is thinking about going there next year.
Kumiko has been to Paris twice so far.

1. Kumiko recently returned from seeing the movie, *Philadelphia,* and she is feeling very sad.

   _____

2. Kumiko is not exactly sure when she went to Yosemite National Park.

   _____

3. Kumiko went to Magic Mountain Amusement Park in California three times when her children were young, but she never wants to return there again.

   _____

4. Kumiko started skiing in 1975. She loves it and goes every winter.

   _____

5. Kumiko only went to Las Vegas once in 1995. She lost all of her money, so she doesn't plan on returning there.

   _____

6. Kumiko went shopping for five hours. She is exhausted now and is taking a nap on the couch.

   _____

3.8 Written Drill: *Simple Past or Present Perfect?*

DIRECTIONS: Fill in the blanks with the appropriate tense—**simple past** or **present perfect**. If both tenses are possible, write both answers.

1. A. _____ you ever _____ (go) to Yellowstone Park before?

   B. Yes, I _____ (go) there three years ago.

2. Jill _____ (be) to Disneyland five times before. Last year, Jill _____ (take) her parents there when they _____ (come) to visit her.

3. Jennifer is quite excited about going to the Rolling Stones concert since she _____ (never/see) them in concert before.

4. A. Can you give me a ride downtown?

   B. Sorry, I can't. I _____ (just/have) an accident and I'm a nervous wreck.

5. Dear Mom,

   Sorry that I _____ (not/write) you last week, but I _____ (be) so busy lately at the hospital. Three of the doctors _____ (be) sick and so I _____ (have to) fill in for them all last week.

Daniel and I finally _____ (go) to see the Bolshoi Ballet. I _____ (never/see) such a crowd at our local theater! Our seats _____ (be) quite good, and we could see the dancers very well. We _____ (be) all surprised, though, when the prima ballerina _____ (slip) and _____ (fall) during the first act. She _____ (break) her leg and they _____ (take) her to the hospital immediately.

I _____ (not/make) airplane reservations for Thanksgiving yet, but I promise I will very soon. I can't wait to see all of you again. Write soon.

Love,

Jack

Grammatical Patterns Part Two

I. Past Perfect Tense

The following chart compares the simple past with the past perfect tense.

SIMPLE PAST TENSE	PAST PERFECT TENSE
The simple past describes **one** event (or state) which occurred in the past: • Cheryl **went** to Las Vegas in 1992. • Pete **was** in excellent physical condition in 1992.	When **two** events (or states) are stated or implied, the past perfect is used to describe the earlier event (or state): • Cheryl **had graduated** from college before she went to Las Vegas. • Pete **had gotten** into shape before he entered the race.
──────×──────┼────── 1992 now	────×¹────×²────┼──── had graduated went to LV now had gotten entered

3.9 Written Drill: *Past Perfect*

DIRECTIONS: Read the following sentences and underline the past perfect verbs. Be ready to identify the stated or implied second event.

Example   When I got to the beach, dark clouds <u>had moved in</u>.
Everyone <u>had</u> already <u>left</u>.

had moved in—second event: got to the beach, stated.
had left—second event: got to the beach, implied.

Walt Disney, the U.S. pioneer of animated film cartoons, had had huge success in Hollywood before he even considered building his amusement park. He had created such animated film classics as *Snow White and the Seven Dwarfs* (1938) and *Pinocchio* (1940). By the time Disneyland opened in Anaheim, California in 1955, Donald Duck and Mickey Mouse had already become well-known cartoon characters. Disney World followed in Orlando, Florida. Unfortunately, because he had died in 1966, Walt Disney never got to see his success spread worldwide to amusement parks in Japan and France.

SPECIAL NOTE

WHEN THE PAST PERFECT IS OPTIONAL

If the sequence of past events is clear from the adverbs and the context of a sentence, then many native speakers of English will not use a past perfect tense. For example:
- After the Little League game (had) finished, the team went out for ice cream.

After in this sentence makes it clear that first the game finished and then the team went out, but you would not be wrong to use the past perfect in this sentence. However, in cases where the sequence is not clear, the past perfect is required:
- When the player had scored a home run, the coach sat down.

In this case, the past perfect is necessary to understand which action happened first.

II. Time Words: Past Perfect

The following time words are often used with the past perfect tense.

TIME WORDS	EXAMPLES	NOTE
1. before 2. after 3. already	1. I (had) graduated from college **before** I got married. 2. I got married **after** I (had) graduated from college. 3. I had **already** graduated from college when I got married.	In conversation, the simple past is often used with **before** and **after**.
4. by the time	4. I had graduated from college **by the time** I got married.	Use the simple past in the **by the time** clause and the past perfect in the other clause.
5. until	5. He (had) never skied **until** he moved to Colorado.	The use of the past perfect is optional here.

Continued on next page.

Continued from previous page.

TIME WORDS	EXAMPLES	NOTE
Compare: **6a. when** *(meaning before)*	**6a.** The president **had already been assassinated when** the revolution started. *(The president was assassinated first; then the revolution started.)*	**6a.** In this case use the past perfect to describe the event which happened first.
6b. when *(meaning right after)*	**6b.** The military general **was assassinated when** the revolution started. *(Immediately after the start of the revolution the general was assassinated.)*	**6b.** In this case, use the simple past in both clauses to show that both events occurred almost at the same time.
6c. when *(meaning at the same time as)*	**6c.** The crowd was watching **when** the general was shot. *(These two events occurred at about the same time.)*	**6c.** In this case, use a simple past or past progressive tense (See Chapter 4 for an explanation of the progressive.)

3.10 Oral Drill: *Past Perfect*

DIRECTIONS: Be ready to respond to four of the following statements. Note that *before* is followed by the *second* (most recent) event and *after* is followed by the *first event*.

Example   CUE: **Before** I came to class today . . .
ANSWER: Before I came to class today, I had already eaten breakfast.

CUE: I came to class **after** . . .
ANSWER: I came to class **after** I had eaten breakfast.

1. Before I graduated from high school, . . .
2. I learned English after . . .
3. Before I met my current boyfriend / girlfriend / husband or wife, . . .
4. I learned to talk after . . .
5. Before we studied this chapter in the book, . . .
6. I laughed after . . .
7. Before I came to this school, . . .
8. I stopped smoking after . . .
9. I ate dinner yesterday after . . .
10. Before I stopped studying, I . . .

3.11 Written Activity: *Baseball*

DIRECTIONS: Work with a partner, making sure that one of you is familiar with the game of baseball. Complete the following sentences describing the sequence of events at a baseball game.

1. The baseball game began after _____

    _____

2. The pitcher did not throw the first ball until _____

    _____

3. After the pitcher threw the ball, _____

    _____

4. By the time the outfielder caught the ball, _____

    _____

5. The crowd went crazy when _____

    _____

6. After the batter hit three strikes, _____

    _____

7. When both teams were tied at the ninth inning, _____

    _____

Now select another sport which you know and enjoy. Write a brief (100 words) paragraph in which you describe a game that you saw. Use a variety of time words and the simple past and past perfect tenses to indicate sequencing of events.

3.12 Written Activity: *Using When*

DIRECTIONS: Read the following sentences with *when*. Then paraphrase them so that the sequence of events is clear.

Example   The dishes fell off the counter when the earthquake hit.

      Immediately after the earthquake hit, the dishes fell off the counter.

1. In 1995 an American tourist was gored by a bull when he ran with the bulls in Pamplona, Spain.

    _____

2. The tourist, Matthew Tassio, had just graduated from college when he decided to take a summer vacation in Europe.

    _____

3. There hadn't been a death in fifteen years when Tassio was killed.

    _____

4. Tassio was gored by a bull when another bull knocked him down.

_____

5. Officials in Pamplona said that many tourists, and especially Americans, sustain injuries because they run with the bulls when they are intoxicated.

_____

3.13 Paired Activity: *Using Past Perfect Time Words*

DIRECTIONS: Here is a jumbled series of events recounting how Tim and Jean met, fell in love, and got married. In pairs or small groups, reconstruct this story in the correct order. First number the events as you imagine they happened. Then write up the story, combining events into one sentence and using the time words listed in the chart on page 47. Feel free to add any details to make the story more interesting. There may be several correct versions.

1. How Tim and Jean Met

> Jean said she had to think about it.
> Tim talked to Jean.
> Tim watched Jean come into his store every day for several weeks.
> Jean got a good job offer in another city.
> Jean made him her favorite lasagna dinner.
> Tim asked Jean out on a date to a movie.
> Tim came over for dinner every night.
> Tim asked Jean to marry him.
> They fell in love.

2. How Monique and Peter Met

> Peter learned to use the Internet.
> Monique was feeling lonely.
> Monique and Peter started "chatting" on the computer.
> They set a time to meet.
> Peter bought a new computer.
> Monique's friend told her about meeting people on the Internet.
> Monique got divorced.
> Monique decided to try to meet someone on the Internet.
> They grew to like each other.

3.14 Written Drill: *Past, Present Perfect,* or *Past Perfect?*

DIRECTIONS: Fill in the blanks using a **simple past, present perfect,** or **past perfect tense.**

I will never forget the worst summer vacation of my life. My parents (decide) _____

to go to Florida with the six children in our family because they (go/never) _____ there

before. We all (wake up) _____ early the morning we were supposed to leave. My

mother (pack) _____ all the bags and (make) _____ a picnic lunch for all o
4   5

us. We (pile) _____ into the station wagon amid luggage, beach balls, and coolers. I
6

(be) _____ a sweltering day. Unfortunately, the air-conditioning in our car (break
7

_____ the day before and my father (have/not) _____ time to fix it before we
8   9

(leave) _____.
10

I remember that it was hot, hot, hot. The heat never let up as long as we were on the road. By

the time we (arrive) _____ at our destination, we (lose) _____ our patience
11   12

and our enthusiasm for the trip. And our bad luck continued. The city (issue) _____ a
13

beach warning because a shark (attack) _____ a girl two days before we arrived. My
14

mother wouldn't let any of us go in the water. To top it off, we had to leave Florida early because

of a hurricane watch. When I (think) _____ about that trip today, I can finally laugh.
15

Needless to say, I (go/never) _____ back to Florida since that vacation!
16

3.15 Paired Activity: *Simple and Perfect Tenses*

DIRECTIONS: Work with a partner and write a 10–12 line dialogue for one of the following scenarios. Write sentences which have a **simple past, present perfect,** and **past perfect** verb in them. As your classmates listen to you present the dialogue to the class, have them listen for verbs in those tenses.

SCENARIO ONE: You and your spouse are 70 years old. You are reminiscing about your 45 years together as a couple.

SCENARIO TWO: You are a foreign student on a scholarship. If you are not accepted into a university in the United States this year, you will no longer be eligible for your scholarship. Unfortunately, you only have 545 on your TOEFL, and the Admissions department of your preferred university will not admit you. Try to convince them to let you in.

SCENARIO THREE: You and your friend are traveling in a foreign country. Suddenly you realize that you have lost your passport. Have a conversation with your friend to try and remember what might have happened to the passport.

III. Future Perfect Tense

Note how the future perfect is different from the future.

FUTURE	FUTURE PERFECT
The future expresses **one** event (or state) in the future: • We **will get** our bonus on December 15.	The future perfect is used to express one event in the future which is completed before another event in the future. • By the time Christmas arrives, we **will have** gotten our bonus.
(timeline: now ——— ✗ December 15 / bonus)	*(timeline: now ——— ✗¹ December 15 / bonus ——— ✗² December 25 / Christmas)*
The future is used for **states**: • I **will be** 48 years old by Christmas. (The state = being 48 years old)	Do not use the future perfect for states, only for events or points in time: • I **will have celebrated** my 48th birthday by Christmas. (The event is a celebration.)

3.16 Written Drill: *Future* or *Future Perfect?*

DIRECTIONS: Fill in the blanks with a future or future perfect form of the verb in parentheses, as appropriate.

1. Many sociologists predict that people (have) _____ more free time in the next few decades.

2. They believe that advanced technology (perform) _____ the work of people.

3. Many economists worry that this (mean) _____ more unemployment.

4. Other economists believe, however, that by that time social scientists (find) _____ a solution to the unemployment problem.

5. They think that in the next century, the government (discover) _____ ways to reduce the number of working hours and increase wages.

6. Yet a recent book on the productivity of Americans indicates that this (not/be) _____ the case.

7. Americans are working more and more, and they have less and less free time. Many have two or more jobs. Therefore, the author of this book probably believes that by the next century, people (work) _____ longer hours.

8. Workers say that they have heard this story before. When computers first came out, social scientists believed it would mean more free time. Such workers think that by the next century, not much (change) _____. As the French saying goes: "The more things change, the more they stay the same."

Special Note

"By the Time"

The time expression, **by the time,** can be used with the past perfect and future perfect tenses as follows:

Past Perfect: Used to show relations between two past events.

- **By the time** I <u>arrived</u>, the plane <u>had left</u>.
                simple past   past perfect

Future Perfect: Used to show relations between two future events.

- **By the time** I <u>graduate</u>, I <u>will have lived</u> in this city for five years.
           present   future perfect

3.17 Written Activity: *A Three-Year Plan*

DIRECTIONS: The chart below represents the three-year plans of Sarah and Clark, who are neighbors and friends. Read the chart, and in the section entitled YOU, fill in events and accomplishments that might happen to you. Then complete the sentences that follow. Be ready to compare your answers with your classmates'.

	In 1 Year	In 2 Years	In 3 Years
Sarah	—	Gets married	Writes her first novel
Clark	Has his first grandchild	Retires from work	Moves to Florida
You			

1. By the time Sarah gets married, Clark _____.

2. By the time Sarah finishes her novel, Clark _____.

3. By the time Clark moves to Florida, I _____.

4. By the time I _____, Clark _____.

5. By the time I _____, Sarah _____.

Now complete the following sentences with a partner.

6. By the time (my partner) _____, I _____.

7. By the time I _____, my partner _____.

3.18 Written Drill: *Future* or *Future Perfect?*

DIRECTIONS: Fill in the blanks with an appropriate form of the **future** or **future perfect**.

1. Tomorrow is an important day for Colette. She (go) _____ to the high school prom, an annual formal dance for high school seniors.

2. She (wear) _____ a long dress, and her date, Jason, (wear) _____ a tuxedo.

3. Today she is quite busy getting ready for tomorrow's event. Hopefully, by tomorrow at six o'clock, she (go) _____ to the hairdresser and her mother (pick) _____ up her dress from the store. Her father (buy) _____ her the pearl earrings he promised.

4. Jason is busy too. This afternoon, he (rent) _____ his tuxedo and (get) _____ his hair cut. By the time he picks Colette up, he (wash) _____ the car and (buy) _____ her the corsage he ordered.

5. Today Colette looks like an ordinary teenager in jeans and a T-shirt. By tomorrow, she (be) _____ an elegant woman in formal attire.

IV. Special Problems With Simple and Perfect Tenses

Pay special attention to these very common errors.

PROBLEM	EXPLANATION
1. Use of the present perfect with *ago*. [INCORRECT: I have arrived here three months ago.] CORRECT: I arrived here three months ago.	Use the **past** tense with *ago*.
2. Use of the present tense with *since* and *for*. [INCORRECT: I am here for three months.] CORRECT: I have been here for three months.	Use the **present perfect** with *since* and *for*.
3. Incorrect use of *since* and *for*. [INCORRECT: I have been here since three months.] CORRECT: I have been here **since January**. I have been here **for three months**.	Use *since* with a specific time or date. Use *for* with a period or amount of time.

■ 3.19 Error Analysis: *Simple* and *Perfect Tenses*

DIRECTIONS: Correct any errors in the uses of **simple** and **perfect** verb tenses in the following sentences. Do not change anything that is already correct. Some sentences may not have any errors.

1. When I came to the United States for the first time, I have had difficulty understanding the sales clerks in the stores.

2. Ronald Reagan has been president for eight years before he retired.

3. The band plays since three hours. Do you think the players will take a break soon?

4. The movie starts at 9:00. It's 9:10 now, so by the time we get there, we will have missed the first 30 minutes.

5. Have you chosen your china pattern yet? I'd like to buy you a place setting for your wedding present.

6. Pete is getting married next year. By then, he will know his fiancée for five years.

7. I hope I can use verbs correctly in English when I will finish this course!

8. My family and I are in Alaska since five years, and we still aren't used to the long, dark winters.

9. I am here for six months, and I still can't speak English.

Focus on Writing

Shifting Time Frames

It is very common to begin a written passage in one verb tense and then shift to another. For example, note how the author begins the following paragraph in the present perfect to describe an **indefinite time** in the past and then shifts to a simple past as the time frame becomes more **specific**.

I **have had** many memorable experiences traveling in foreign countries. Perhaps the most memorable trip **was** in 1995, when I **went** to a small town in Mexico to learn Spanish. I **found** the people to be extremely friendly. Even though my Spanish **was** quite elementary, everyone **was** patient as I **struggled** to communicate.

It is also common to move from a **present time frame** to a **present perfect** as you relate past events to present states. Note how the following author describes his present state in the first sentence and then details how he brought about that state.

I **am** quite proud of my progress in learning English. During the past six months I **have progressed** from a beginning language learner to an advanced one. I **have worked** diligently in my language classes and I **have spoken** as much English as I can. I **have taken** advantage of every opportunity to improve my English.

3.20 Written Activity: *Shifting Time Frames*

DIRECTIONS: Write two paragraphs using the paragraphs above as models. In paragraph one, move from **indefinite to definite time**. In paragraph two, relate **past events to a present state**. Select your topics from among the following suggestions, or come up with your own.

I. Indefinite to Definite Time Shifts

- a trip you took
- a memorable restaurant experience
- a musical concert you attended
- a funny or embarrassing experience

II. Past Events Related to a Present State
- how you learned English
- how you got in shape
- influences on a current musical style

3.21 Written Activity: *A First Date*

DIRECTIONS: Write a brief skit (conversation) between a man and a woman on their first date. Include verbs in the following tenses: simple present, future, simple past and present perfect. Incorporate time words to demonstrate your understanding of tenses. Include a discussion of likes and dislikes. Make the conversation humorous if you like. Be ready to present the dialogue with a partner in class.

Composition Topics

1. Imagine your life in ten or fifteen years from now. The first decade of the twenty-first century is right around the corner. What do you think will have happened to you or in the world by then? Write a short paragraph in which you predict events in your personal and professional life. Include possible events in the world (political, technological, artistic, etc.) if you like. Begin your paragraph as follows:

   In ten or fifteen years from now, I will have _____

2. Do you think that teenagers (aged 14–18) should be allowed to go out with friends or on dates without adult supervision? Why or why not?

Making It!

• Progressive Verbs

To Make It: To achieve fame or financial success through hard work or talent

DISCUSSION QUESTIONS

1. How is success measured in your community or in your family (for example, through wealth, fame, intelligence, achievement, etc.)? Do you personally agree with this standard of success? Why or why not?

2. Describe a person whom you consider to be successful. What is his or her "secret to success"?

3. Discuss the importance of the following elements in achieving success—hard work, intelligence, luck, personality, connections, ambition, education, and honesty.

OBJECTIVES

In this chapter you will learn:

1. To form the progressive in all tenses

2. To know when to use the progressive form

3. To recognize verbs that cannot be used in a progressive form

4. To use time expressions with progressive verbs

SUCCESS

To laugh often and love much,

to win the respect of intelligent people and the affection of children,

to earn the appreciation of honest critics and endure the betrayal of false friends,

to appreciate beauty,

to find the best in others,

to give of one's self,

to leave the world a little better, whether by a healthy child,

a garden patch,

or a redeemed social condition,

to have played and laughed with enthusiasm and sung with exultation,

to know even one life has breathed easier,

this is to have succeeded.

Ralph Waldo Emerson

Preview

DIRECTIONS: Read the following letters that Mitsy wrote to Randall. Then answer the questions that follow.

This letter was written in 1985, when many of the so-called "Baby Boom" generation were consumed with their work and making money. Randall and Mitsy were living in San Diego, California at the time. Mitsy was in New York City interviewing for an important marketing position with a very large company.

June 14, 1985

Dear Randall,

1 I really miss you! This afternoon while you were probably **basking** in the San Diego sun, I was having my interview with the Vice-President of Marketing of Smith Corporation. Wow, is he ever a **hard nut to crack!** I've met with him three times so far and I'm having a hard time convincing him that I'm the **top-notch** candidate for the job. He's forever reminding me that I'm too young and inexperienced for this high-stress position. I'll be seeing him tomorrow at 7:00 a.m. to **go over** my **portfolio.** (They sure do start their days earlier here on the East Coast.) **Keep your fingers crossed.**

2 That's enough about my situation out here. What about you? Have you been feeding the dog? Have you been getting my mail for me? I hope you haven't been working too hard.

3 Randall, I've been thinking pretty seriously about your marriage proposal. Don't you think that twenty-four is a bit young **to go to the altar?** Besides, neither of us has a decent job yet and we should really be off to a good start professionally and financially before we **tie the knot.** I'm not saying no, but I guess we just need a little more time.

4 See you on Friday. Let's hope that I'm the new International Marketing Director for Smith Corporation by then.

Love and kisses,

Mitsy

Mitsy

VOCABULARY

basking: lying

hard nut to crack: a person who is difficult to convince of something (informal)

top notch: of superior quality

to go over: to review

portfolio: a sampling of a person's artistic or professional work

to keep your fingers crossed: to hope for a good outcome (informal)

to go to the altar: to get married (figurative)

to tie the knot: to get married (informal; slang)

Now read an e-mail message that Mitsy wrote to Randall several years later. Mitsy got the job as International Marketing Director, but she was fired four years later when the recession hit the country and the company decided to streamline and cut positions. As you can see, Mitsy and Randall did get married. You be the judge of whether they will live happily forever after.

To: Rand527@527EOL.COM
FROM: Mitsy114@UNI.COM
DATE: July 2, 1997
RE: Happy Birthday

Randall, I just wanted to send you a special note on your birthday. I know that we've been having some tough times lately and you've been experiencing a lot of anxiety about our future, but remember that above all else, I love you. All the money in the world couldn't buy me the happiness I have when I'm with you. I think we're lucky that at least one of us has a job, even though yours is only temporary. And I don't mind being a one-car family. I can't wait until you get home tonight. I'm working on a special dinner for us. Happy Birthday, Sweetheart. Love, Mitsy.

CULTURAL NOTE/DISCUSSION

The term *yuppie* was a popular one during the 1980s. It came from the abbreviation for Young Urban Professional and referred to the stereotyped young successful professional, living in an urban setting. Yuppies placed a great deal of value on material wealth. The archetypal yuppie earned a high salary, drove an expensive imported car, and preferred the finer (expensive) things in life.

What evidence do you have from the 1985 letter that Mitsy was or wanted to become a yuppie? What happened to that in 1997? Do you notice any changes in Mitsy? What do you predict for Randall and Mitsy?

FOCUS ON GRAMMAR

The following questions are based on the preview text and are designed to help you find out what you already know about the structures in this chapter. Some of the questions may be hard and some of them may be easy. Answer as many of the questions as you can. Work with a partner if your teacher tells you to do so.

1. Find one sentence in the 1985 letter and another one in the 1995 message in which Mitsy uses the **present progressive tense** (*is/are* + **verb-ing**) to describe her present, ongoing activities.

   _____

   _____

2. Find the sentence in the 1985 letter in which Mitsy uses the **present progressive** to express her frustration with the vice-president who is interviewing her.

   _____

   _____

3. Write down the sentence in the 1985 letter in which Mitsy uses the **past progressive** (*was/were* + **verb-ing**) to relate ongoing activities that she and Randall were doing **at the same time** in the past.

   _____

   _____

4. Mitsy uses the **present perfect progressive** (*have/has been* + **verb-ing**) in her 1985 letter to talk about a repetitive activity that Randall (she hopes) did and will continue to do until she returns home. Write that sentence here.

   _____

   _____

5. In her 1985 letter, Mitsy uses the **future progressive** (*will be* + **verb-ing**) to talk about a continuous activity in the future. Write that sentence here.

   _____

   _____

Grammatical Patterns Part One

I. Simple Progressives

A. Forms

To form the simple past, present, or future progressive, use an appropriate form of the auxiliary *be* and a **verb-*ing*** as follows:

TENSE	FORM	EXAMPLE
Present Progressive	Use the auxiliary *is* or *are* with the **verb-*ing*** form of the main verb.	• I **am having** a hard time convincing him I'm the top-notch candidate.
Past Progressive	Use the auxiliary *was* or *were* with the **verb-*ing*** form of the main verb.	• I **was having** my interview with the Vice-President of Smith Corporation when you called.
Future Progressive	Use the auxiliary *will be* with the **verb-*ing*** form of the main verb.	• I'll **be seeing** him tomorrow at 7:00 A.M.

4.1 Written Drill: *Forming Progressive Verbs*

DIRECTIONS: Provide a **present**, **past** or **future progressive** tense as indicated by the context of the sentence.

Example   I _am reading_ my assignment right now, so please don't disturb me.

Randall (take) _____ a shower right now. Mitsy (put on) _____ her makeup
            1   2

at the same time. They (get) _____ ready to go to work. Both are quite tired this
                            3

morning because their neighbors (play) _____ loud music last night and they couldn't
                                        4

sleep. Finally, Mitsy fell asleep, but Randall couldn't. While Mitsy (sleep) _____ ,
                                                                                5

Randall went down and asked the neighbors to turn the music down. Mitsy and Randall aren't

really concerned, because they are going on a two-week vacation next week. By this time next

week, they (relax) ——————— in Hawaii. Randall (surf) ——————— and Mitsy (sunbathe)
$\quad\quad\quad\quad\quad\quad\quad\quad$ 6 $\quad\quad\quad\quad\quad\quad\quad\quad\quad\quad\quad\quad$ 7

——————— .
$\quad$ 8

■ B. Uses of *Simple vs. Simple Progressive:* A Comparison

Note how the simple progressive tenses differ in use from the simple tenses.

SIMPLE PROGRESSIVE TENSES (PAST, PRESENT, AND FUTURE)	SIMPLE TENSES (PAST, PRESENT, AND FUTURE)
I. Use the progressive to emphasize the **continuous** nature of an activity. PAST: I **was swimming** between 6:00 and 7:00. PRESENT: Mitsy **is swimming** in the pool right now. FUTURE: She**'ll be swimming** in tomorrow's meet.	**I.** Use the simple tenses to talk about **regular, habitual** activity. PAST: I **swam** regularly as a child. PRESENT: I **swim** every day. FUTURE: I**'ll swim** a mile a day for a month.
2. The progressive describes an **activity in progress** which is **intersected** by another activity, which is not continuous. • I **was eating** breakfast when the earthquake hit. was eating ~~~✕~~~→ earthquake now hit	**2.** The simple tenses describe an activity which is **not continuous** and which is **not in progress.** • The earthquake **hit** at 10:00 A.M. yesterday. ✕ earthquake now hit
3. The progressive can be used to describe **two continuous events** which occur at about the same time. • While you **were basking** in the sun, I **was having** an interview.	**3.** The simple tenses can describe **two habitual activities.** • He **cooked** and she **served** the food in their first restaurant.
4. The progressive can be used to convey a note of **annoyance, insult** or **frustration,** especially in conversation. (A time word such as **forever** or **always** is usually used in this case.) • Randall **is** always **leaving** the door open, and it drives me crazy!	**4.** The simple tenses, when accompanied by the time words **always, forever, constantly,** and so on, do not express annoyance; they show habit. • Randall always **leaves** the house at 8:00 A.M.

4.2 Written Drill: *Simple Present* or *Progressive?*

DIRECTIONS: Fill in the blanks with either a **simple present** or **present progressive** form, as appropriate. (Be especially careful with the adverb *always*, which, when not used to express annoyance, must be followed by the simple present tense.)

1. Jack _____ out the garbage on Thursday mornings.
   (always/take)

2. In fact, if you look out the window, you will see that he _____ that now.
   (do)

3. After he _____ out the trash, he _____ in his car and _____
   (take)   (hop)   (speed)

   off to work.

4. His family _____ about him on the road because he _____ over the speed
   (always/worry)   (always/go)

   limit.

5. Today, Jack is late and the chairman of the board of his corporation _____ for him
   (wait)

   impatiently.

6. What the chairman of the board doesn't know is that a police officer _____ Jack a
   (give)

   ticket for speeding.

4.3 Oral Drill: *Present* or *Present Progressive?*

DIRECTIONS: Add a response to the following statements to demonstrate the difference between using **always** to express **habitual activity** and **annoyance.** Add your own statements and responses for 9 and 10, and indicate if the response should be a statement of annoyance or habit.

Example   CUE: He always goes to church on Sunday morning. (habitual activity)
              ANSWER: So he can't take you to the airport then.
              CUE: He's always going out with his friends on Sundays. (annoyance)
              ANSWER: And I wish he would spend time with me instead.

1. He always buys me chocolates.
2. He's always buying me chocolates.
3. My mother always calls me.
4. My mother's always calling me.
5. The teacher always reviews the important information.
6. The teacher is always repeating boring information.
7. My boss always talks to me in the morning.
8. My boss is always asking me to get him coffee in the morning.
9. _____
10. _____

4.4 Written Drill: *Simple Past* or *Past Progressive?*

DIRECTIONS: Fill in the blanks with the **simple past** or **past progressive tense** of the verb in parentheses, as appropriate. Then select one of the stories and complete it in your own words. Be ready to tell your story in front of the class.

1. Last night I (have) _____ the strangest dream. I (walk) _____ through the
               1   2

   park near my house when I suddenly (see) _____ a small tiger coming towards me. I
                                              3

   (be) _____ very frightened, but the tiger (begin) _____ to talk to me. It
            4   5

   said, "Don't be frightened. I am not going to hurt you." But I didn't believe him. The wind (howl)

   _____ and the leaves (blow) _____ around us. Suddenly, the leaves
       6   7

   (form) _____ a big circle around the cat and then . . .
             8

2. Last week when I (shop) _____ at the mall I had a funny experience. I (browse)
                      9

   _____ in a bookstore for a present for my father. A young boy (enter)
     10

   _____ the store and started looking at the magazines. I (watch) _____ as
     11   12

   the boy (put) _____ a magazine under his jacket. The store manager (wait)
              13

   _____ on a customer and the other clerk (arrange) _____ books on the
     14   15

   shelves in the back of the store. So as the boy (step) _____ out of the store. I (scream)
                                          16

   _____, "Hey! you! Come back here." The boy turned around and . . .
     17

3. Describe one of your own dreams using the simple past and past progressive tenses. If you can't remember a dream, write about a strange or funny experience that you have had.

II. Perfect Progressives

A. Forms

To form the perfect progressive, use an appropriate tense of the auxiliary **be** and **verb-*ing*** as follows.

TENSE	FORM	EXAMPLE
Present Perfect Progressive	Use the auxiliary **have (or has) been** with the verb-ing form of the main verb.	• I hope you **have been feeding** the dog.
Past Perfect Progressive	Use the auxiliary **had been** with the verb-ing form of the main verb.	• Randall **had been waiting** for the express mail package for two hours when it finally arrived.
Future Perfect Progressive	Use the auxiliary **will have been** with the verb-ing form of the main verb.	• By the time Randall and Mitsy **get married, they will have been dating** for three years.

4.5 Written Activity: *Forming Perfect Progressive Verbs*

DIRECTIONS: Write about your academic achievements. Complete the following sentences using a **present perfect**, **past perfect** or **future perfect progressive** form, as indicated.

Example   (future perfect progressive) By the time I graduate, *I will have been studying for fourteen years.*

1. (future perfect progressive) By the time I get the degree I want _____

   _____

2. (present perfect progressive) For the past year, _____

   _____

3. (past perfect progressive) Before I started this school, _____

   _____

Now compare your answers with those of a classmate and write his or her achievements in the space below.

_____

_____

_____

B. Uses

Use the **perfect progressive (present, past or future)** in the following two cases.

I. To describe a continuous or repetitive activity which occurs before another point in time:

PAST PERFECT PROGRESSIVE*: The continuous event began before and is intersected by another event in the past:

    a. I **had been thinking** about you when your letter arrived.

            thinking   letter arrived   now

    *See the Special Note "When the past perfect is optional," on page 43 of Chapter 3. The same guidelines apply for deciding whether to use a past perfect or past progressive.

PRESENT PERFECT PROGRESSIVE: The continuous event began before and continues up to the present:

    b. I **have been thinking** about your marriage proposal. *(continuous)*

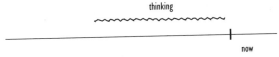

                      thinking

                              now

    The repetitive event occurred before the present and is likely to continue in the future:

    c. I hope you **have been feeding** the dog. *(repetitive)*

             feeding   now

FUTURE PERFECT PROGRESSIVE: The continuous event began before another event in the future:

    d. By the time Mitsy gets home from New York at 2:00 A.M., Randall **will have been sleeping** for two hours.*

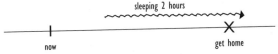

                    sleeping 2 hours

          now   get home

    *The continuous activity is in the progressive.

2. Continuous activity with temporary effects:

PRESENT PERFECT PROGRESSIVE: The temporary effects are still apparent:

    a. He **has been eating** onions and I can smell them on his breath!

PAST PERFECT PROGRESSIVE: The temporary effects occurred in the past:

    b. I could tell that she **had been crying** because her eyes were red.

4.6 Recognition Drill: *Uses of Perfect Progressives*

DIRECTIONS: Read the following sentences and identify the use of the perfect progressive as **PCA** (previous continuous action), **RA** (repetitive action) or **TE** (temporary effects). Then identify the time frame as **past, present** or **future**.

1. Before 1995, the University of California <u>had been admitting</u> 40% of their students on factors other than pure academic merit, including race and ethnicity.

    USE: _____   TIME FRAME: _____

2. In 1995, the University of California decided to change its admissions policy. They decided to eliminate the race and ethnicity factors. Since that decision, many minority students <u>have been protesting</u>.

    USE: _____   TIME FRAME: _____

3. Many white men <u>had been putting</u> pressure on the University of California to eliminate the race and ethnic factors because they believed it was reverse discrimination.

    USE: _____   TIME FRAME: _____

4. Opponents of the new decision believe it is necessary to give underprivileged minorities special preference. This will give them a chance to catch up so that by the time they finish college, they <u>will have been learning</u> and experiencing the same things as the more privileged students.

    USE: _____   TIME FRAME: _____

5. The Governor of California was smiling the day of the decision—you could tell that he <u>had been hoping</u> for this change.

    USE: _____   TIME FRAME: _____

4.7 Oral Drill: *Temporary Effects*

DIRECTIONS: Using the cue provided by your partner or your teacher, form a sentence using a **perfect progressive** form to indicate the recent activities of the person. Pay attention to the verb tense of the cue sentence; this will indicate whether a present perfect or past perfect progressive form of the verb is required in your answer.

Example   STUDENT A: Her eyes are red.
STUDENT B: She's been crying. (*The effects are still present, so use the present perfect progressive.*)
STUDENT A: His eyes were red.
STUDENT B: He had been crying. (*The effects were present in the past, so use the past perfect progressive form of the verb.*)

Jeff and Joan work for a very successful computer software company. Identify these employees' recent activities using the cues provided.

1. Jeff has dark circles under his eyes.
2. Joan has a huge smile on her face.
3. Jeff's desk is full of computer disks.
4. Joan has 25 e-mail messages in her mailbox.
5. Jeff's belt is on the last notch.
6. Joan's appointment book was completely blank last Friday.
7. Jeff's office plants shriveled up and died.
8. Joan's boss gave her a substantial salary increase.

9. Jeff's desk was clean yesterday.

10. Joan was limping yesterday.

C. Uses of *Present Perfect* vs. *Present Perfect Progressive:* A Comparison

The following chart summarizes the differences in use between the present perfect and the present perfect progressive tenses.

PRESENT PERFECT PROGRESSIVE	PRESENT PERFECT
1. To emphasize that something happened recently in the past.	**1. To emphasize that something was completed at an indefinite time in the** *past.*
a. I've been writing a lot of songs lately. *(And I'll probably continue to do so.)* **b.** We've been eating at this restaurant a lot lately. *(This sentence implies repetition and recency.)* **c.** Randall has been feeding Mitsy's dog. *(And he'll continue until Mitsy returns.)*	**d.** I've written a lot of songs in the past. *(And I'm not writing them anymore.)* **e.** We have eaten at that place before. *(Sometime in the indefinite past.)* **f.** Mitsy has taken care of Randall's dog in the past. *(She's not doing it now.)*
2. To emphasize the length or duration of an activity something (still ongoing).	**2. To emphasize the quantity of (recently completed).**
g. Mitsy has been writing **for six hours.** **h.** Jack has been singing in the choir **for many years.**	**h.** Randall has written **six pages.** **i.** June has sung **in six operas.**
3. No difference in meaning. With certain verbs (for example, verbs of living, occupation, and vocation) there is little difference in meaning between a present perfect and present perfect progressive tense. The progressive can imply a temporary state, but doesn't always	
j. I **have been living** here for five years. **k.** The secretary **has been working** at this site for a week.	**l.** I **have lived** here for five years. **m.** The secretary **has worked** at this site for a week.

4.8 Oral Drill: *Present Perfect* or *Present Perfect Progressive?*

DIRECTIONS: Complete these statements to justify the verb tense used. In many cases, an expression of **quantity** or **length of time** can be added.

Example   CUE: I've written . . .
          ANSWER: I've written six letters to my parents.

          CUE: I've been writing . . .
          ANSWER: I've been writing for three hours and my hand is tired.

1. My friend has been talking . . .

2. My friend has talked to me about her problems with her boyfriend . . .

3. Our teacher has taught us . . .

4. Our teacher has been teaching us . . .

5. My government has been working on . . .

6. The news has covered . . .

7. I have talked . . .

8. You have been talking . . .

9. I've never written . . .

10. He's been watching . . .

11. The president has been talking about . . .

12. My father (mother) has been working . . .

13. Elizabeth Taylor has been married . . .

14. In the past year, I've read . . .

15. We've been learning about verb tenses . . .

SPECIAL NOTE

THE PROGRESSIVE FOR A TONE OF COMPLAINT

The present perfect progressive often expresses a tone of complaint more strongly than the present perfect.

- Someone's been eating my chocolate! (And I'm not happy.)
- I've been waiting for you for two hours! (I'm angry.)

4.9 Written Drill: *Present Perfect* vs. *Present Perfect Progressive*

DIRECTIONS: Use a **present perfect** or **present perfect progressive tense**. Be ready to explain your choices. In some cases, both tenses might be correct.

1. I (read) _____ the book you lent me, but I'm not finished yet.

2. I (read) _____ the book you lent me. In fact, I stayed up until 3 A.M. last night to finish it!

3. Who (take) _____ money out of my purse? This is the second time this week that this (happen) _____.

4. The professor (explain) _____ this math problem five times and the class still can't understand it.

5. The professor (explain) _____ this math problem for one hour and the students still can't understand it.

6. I'm really very sorry I'm late. (wait) _____ you _____ long? I got stuck in traffic.

7. Where have you been?!! I (wait) _____ for two hours. I already finished

   lunch.

8. The FBI (investigate) _____ many financial brokers recently for trading

   violations. I wonder if they (arrest) _____ my stockbroker.

9. My sister (live) _____ in Iowa, Ohio, and Wisconsin. Recently her family

   (live) _____ in Dublin, Ireland.

10. Lately, some big companies (test) _____ their employees for drugs. My

    roommate said they (test) _____ her twice so far this year.

4.10 Written Activity: *Present Perfect* and *Present Perfect Progressive*

DIRECTIONS: Read the following biographies and decide which individual has achieved the greatest success in his or her life, according to your own values. Then, write a brief paragraph in which you defend your choice and describe the person's accomplishments. Use the following verb tenses in your paragraphs: **present, past, present perfect** and **present perfect progressives.** Be ready to discuss your choices in class.

Joan Campbell

Age: 33

Education: B.A. Harvard University; Ph.D. Stanford University (Mathematics)

Employment: Currently at University of California, Los Angeles; Associate Professor
 in Math (tenured position)

Publications: 14 articles in major math journal, 2 textbooks for college students

Family situation: Single, no children

José Rodrigues

Age: 54

Education: B.A. State College

Employment: Works with gang members for social service department

Publications: None

Awards: Citizen of the Year Award, 1997; YMCA Recognition of Social Contribution
 Award, 1993

Family Situation: Married, four children

James Caldwell

Age: 58

Education: B.A., Yale University; Law Degree, University of Virginia

Employment: Partner in Law Firm; State Senator, 4 years

Publications: 1992, "How to Improve Health Care"

Future: Plans to run for governor next year

Family Situation: Divorced, two children, who live with their mother

Marsalis Washington

Age: 24

Education: B.A. State College

Employment: Star Basketball Player, NBA team

Awards: Player of the Year, 1990, State College; Best Rookie Player, 1994

Earnings: Over $1 million a year

Family Situation: Married, one child

D. *Future Perfect Progressive* vs. *Future Perfect*: A Comparison

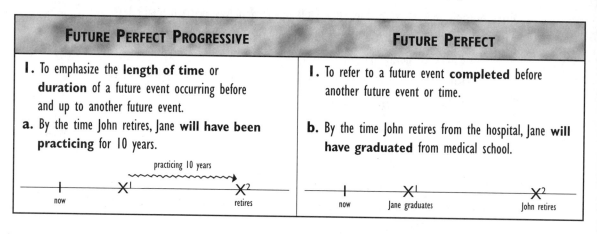

FUTURE PERFECT PROGRESSIVE	FUTURE PERFECT
1. To emphasize the **length of time** or **duration** of a future event occurring before and up to another future event.	1. To refer to a future event **completed** before another future event or time.
a. By the time John retires, Jane **will have been practicing** for 10 years.	b. By the time John retires from the hospital, Jane **will have graduated** from medical school.

4.11 Written Drill: *Future Perfect* vs. *Future Perfect Progressive*

DIRECTIONS: Use a **future, future perfect,** or **future perfect progressive.** Note when more than one tense is possible.

1. A: How much longer (you—be) _____ at this school?

   B: About another year.

   A: By the time you leave, how long (you—study) _____ English altogether?

   B: Eighteen months. I hope I (master) _____ the English language by then!

2. A: Is your sister older or younger?

   B: She's 12 years older. It's hard to believe this, but by the time I graduate next year, she (work) _____ as an X-ray technician for 10 years.

   A: That's like me. By the time I graduate from high school, my brother (work) _____ as a roofer for our uncle for 10 years.

3. A: Have you finished painting your house yet?

   B: Not yet. It's taking me a long time. I'm afraid that by the time I finish the back of the house, I (have to begin) _____ painting the front again!

   A: I know what you mean. It's taking me forever to finish refurbishing our bathroom. Probably by the time I finish, I (remodel) _____ for four years and the wallpaper and colors will be outdated!

4. A: Has your son finished high school yet?

   B: No, he (graduate) _____ next spring. How about your daughter?

   A: Oh, gosh, yes. By the time your son graduates, she (spend) _____ two years at college.

   B: It's hard to believe, isn't it? They grow up so fast. Before we know it we (retire) _____ .

4.12 Oral Activity: *Future Progressive, Future Perfect,* and *Future Perfect Progressive*

DIRECTIONS: Discuss the following in pairs or small groups, using a **future progressive, future perfect,** or **future perfect progressive verb tense.** Remember that a future progressive tense expresses a continuous activity at a specific point of time in the future, (e.g., *I'll be working on the project at 2:00 tomorrow*), but future perfect (progressive) describes a future event which is completed before another event in the future (*I will have been working on the project for two hours by then*).

1. Imagine yourself on this date next year. Describe your activities, your feelings, your friends, and so on.

2. Imagine it is ten years from now. Describe the lives of your classmates and teacher at that time. Describe what they will have accomplished during this time period. Describe what they will have done by then.

3. Imagine it is fifty years from now. Describe life in this country or another; describe the changes in politics, social programs, and so on.

III. Time Expressions

The following chart presents the most common time expressions used with the progressive tenses.

TENSE/TIME EXPRESSION	EXAMPLES
I. Present Progressive this semester today right now at this moment at this time while/when/as in + time word or **expression**	**a. This semester** I am studying English in California. **b. Today** women are having fewer children. **c.** I am reading this chart **right now.** **d.** My brother isn't working **at this moment.** **e.** We aren't accepting any reservations **at this time.** **f. While** you are studying, I'll go grocery shopping. **g.** People are buying more computers **in this decade.**
2. Past Progressive during at that time/moment by then/by that time while/when/as in + time word or **expression**	**h.** The teenager was throwing popcorn **during** the film. **i.** I was selling insurance **at that time** in my life. **j.** Jim got married in 1960. **By then** I was working. **k.** Van's mother arrived **while** he was teaching. **l.** Houses were selling quickly **in the 1960s.**
3. Present Perfect Progressive by now so far up to now this + time word today all + time word since + specific time for + duration	**m.** The soup has been boiling for an hour **by now.** **n.** It has been raining for three hours **so far.** **o. Up to now** I've never been skiing. **p.** I have been getting all A's **this semester.** **q.** I've been cleaning house **today.** **r.** I've been thinking about you **all week.** **s.** I've been writing **since** 9:00. **t.** I've been reading **for** three hours.
4. Past Perfect Progressive by then at that time/at that moment/by that time for/since	**u.** Sue had been running three hours **by then.** **v.** Jack and Jill were divorced in 1966. **At that time** they had already been seeing a marriage counselor **for** three years.
5. Future Perfect Progressive by then for by that time*	**w.** My store will celebrate its anniversary next year. **By then,** I will have been operating the store **for** 10 years. **x. By the time** I leave the United States, I will have been studying English **for** ten months.

*See also Chapter 8 for a detailed discussion of "by that time."

4.13 Written Drill: *Time Expressions*

DIRECTIONS: Do you think how you dress at work can affect your success? How do people "dress for success" in your country? Fill in the blanks in the following sentences using one of the time expressions listed below.

right now	in the 1960s
always	currently
in the next century	at that time / moment
this (+ time word)	today
recently	for (+ time period)

1. In 1975, John T. Molloy wrote his famous book, *Dress for Success*, about the importance of attire and a person's success in the working world. Dark suits and ties have _____ been the uniform of male executives.

2. Although the majority of corporate presidents and vice-presidents are still not female, _____ we are seeing more and more women assuming middle management positions.

3. Women's office fashion has changed since the 1960s. _____ many women were sporting mini-skirts, high heels, and bright jewelry.

4. However, _____ women are wearing conservative suits with discreet accessories.

5. Are women copying men? Or are they simply aware that a more serious approach to fashion results in being taken more seriously? What will the future bring? What will women be wearing _____?

6. On the other hand, many newer companies, and especially those companies with younger employees, are encouraging their employees to "dress down." _____ you sometimes see employees wearing jeans and T-shirts to work on Fridays.

4.14 Written Activity: *Changes*

DIRECTIONS: Write about one aspect of life at the workplace or in school that is changing in your community. Use time **expressions** as appropriate.

4.15 Written Activity: *Milestones*

DIRECTIONS: Write about the milestones, or important events, in your life. Use at least one **time expression** from each of the **progressive tenses** listed on page 72.

QUESTIONS:

1. What did the form letter really want to know?
2. What did she think the letter wanted to know?

Grammatical Patterns Part Two

Preview

DIRECTIONS: Read the following interview between a wealthy American businessman and a newspaper journalist. Then answer the questions that follow.

INTERVIEWER: Mr. McDougall, what do you consider to be your secret to success?

MCDOUGALL: That's not an easy question to answer since each person perceives success in a different way. For me, I believe that my success was a result of hard work.

INTERVIEWER: I see. Didn't luck **enter into the picture?**

MCDOUGALL: Well, yes, I'd have to say that it did. You know, after I made my first million, I thought my luck had **run out.** But it hadn't. My fortune is growing every day, and I'm having a great time watching that happen.

INTERVIEWER: Did you always want to be rich?

MCDOUGALL: I guess I'd have to say that as long as I could remember, I wanted to strike it rich. I have **a strong drive.** I've always had it. I had been wanting to be a millionaire long before I even opened my first fast food restaurant, and I never **lost sight** of my goal. And for me success means money. Who ever heard of a successful businessman who is poor?

INTERVIEWER: One last question, Mr. McDougall. Is money all there is? I mean, don't you ever think about the people around you, the homeless, the environment?

> **MCDOUGALL:** Look here. I'm doing **my share**. I'm providing jobs for people. I'm paying for their health care. If somebody wants a job and is willing to work, send them to me. They don't need to be on the street.
>
> To answer your question more directly—no, money can't buy everything, **as the saying goes**. There's your health, your family, your friends. I've got all three and I can say I'm happy and I'm loving my life.

VOCABULARY

to enter into the picture: to have something to do with it
to run out: to end, to disappear
a strong drive: a strong motivation to pursue and achieve a specific goal
to lose sight of: to forget
my share: my part
as the saying goes: according to the common statement or proverb

DISCUSSION

How do this businessman's values compare with yours? Is he really "doing his share"? How does his viewpoint compare with the idea of success expressed in the poem on page 57.

FOCUS ON GRAMMAR

DIRECTIONS: The following questions are based on the preview text and are designed to help you find out what you already know about the structures in this section. Some of the questions may be hard and some of them may be easy. Answer as many of the questions as you can. Work with a partner if your teacher tells you to do so.

1. Compare the use of *have* in the following sentences. Is there any difference in meaning?

   a. I'm having a great time watching that happen.

   b. I have a strong drive.

   Can you explain why (*a*) uses a progressive form and (*b*) does not? _____

   _____

2. There are several verbs in the interview which describe **mental processes** (for example, *think*).

   Write those verbs here. _____

   _____

   What tense is used with each? _____

   _____

3. *Love* is not usually used in the progressive. For example, we say "I love you." Can you guess why the businessman says "I'm loving my life"? _____

   _____

I. Verbs Not Used in the Progressive

Some verbs cannot be used in a progressive form. The following chart lists these by category.

A. Voluntary and Involuntary Verbs

Verbs of sensory perception can be divided into two groups. Note the differences below.

CATEGORY	NO PROGRESSIVE (THESE ARE NONACTION VERBS.)	EXCEPTIONS (THESE VERBS HAVE A PROGRESSIVE FORM.)
Sensory Perception	**Involuntary verbs** These refer to passive, unconscious activities. **Do not use these in the progressive form.**	**Voluntary verbs** These refer to active, conscious activities. **These verbs can be used in the progressive form.**
Sound	*Hear* • I was unable to sleep because I **heard** the neighbors quarreling.	*Listen to* • I **was listening** to Beethoven's Ninth Symphony when the electricity went off.
Smell	*Smell* • Your hair **smells** great!	*Smell* • Why **was** your dog **smelling** my couch?
Taste	*Taste* • This cake is delicious! It **tastes** just like my mother's!	*Taste* • I burned myself while I **was tasting** the soup.
Sight	*See* • Judy **saw** the photographers as she walked down the runway. (See the special note below for an exception to this verb.)	*Look at/Watch* • Judy **was looking at** the dress in the window. (for stationary objects) • The audience **was watching** Judy as she twirled around in her dress. (for moving objects)
Touch	*Feel* • She **felt** a cold draft in the old house.	*Feel/Touch* • The man **was feeling** his stubbly beard.

4.16 Written Drill: *Voluntary and Involuntary Verbs*

DIRECTIONS: Read the following sentences and fill in the blanks with an appropriate form of the verb in parentheses. In several cases you will need to choose between an **involuntary** or **voluntary** verb, depending on the context of the sentence.

Example   What kind of music (listen to/hear) <u>are you listening to</u> right now? (voluntary verb)

1. Shh! Could you please turn down that music? I (listen to/hear) _____ the

   President's State of the Union address and I can't (listen to/hear) _____ a

   word of what he's saying.

2. Mrs. Jones criticized her daughter because her grandchildren always (watch/see)

   _____ T.V. programs of little educational value.

3. After the seance yesterday evening, Mary and Bob (feel) _____ the

   presence of an unfriendly ghost in their living room.

4. The blind man (feel) _____ the cat's soft fur when she suddenly scratched

   his arm.

5. Quick! Call the fire department! I (smell) _____ something burning.

4.17 Written Activity: *Voluntary and Involuntary Verbs*

DIRECTIONS: Note Dennis' use of both a voluntary **(listen)** and involuntary **(hear)** verb in the above comic. Demonstrate your understanding of the difference between the voluntary and involuntary use of sensory verbs. Write one sentence for each verb listed below.

DENNIS THE MENACE

"HOW DO YOU EXPECT ME TO HEAR YOU WHEN I WASN'T EVEN *LISTENING* ?"

1. **a.** listen to
   b. hear
2. **a.** watch
   b see
3. **a.** touch
   b. feel
4. **a.** smell (voluntary)
   b. smell (involuntary)
5. **a.** taste (voluntary)
   b. taste (involuntary)

SPECIAL
NOTE

> ### SEE = VISIT OR DATE
> Sometimes SEE = VISIT or DATE, as in the following examples. You can use the progressive in these cases:
> 1. **I'm seeing** Gary now; we might get married soon. (He's my boyfriend. We go out on dates.)
> 2. I'll **be seeing** the doctor at 4:00 P.M. (I have a visit with the doctor.)

B. Other Verbs Not Used in the Progressive

Other verbs also do not have a progressive form, and there are exceptions to these as well. The verbs in the left column are nonaction verbs and do not have a progressive form. Some of these nonaction verbs have an action meaning as well; in this case, a progressive form may be used. These exceptions are listed in the column on the right.

NONACTION MEANING (NO PROGRESSIVE)	ACTION MEANING (MAY USE PROGRESSIVE)
Verbs of Possession and Relation 1. She **possesses** many good traits. 2. How many books do you **own?** 3. He **belongs** to a health club. 4. This milk **contains** vitamin D. 5. I **have** three cats now.	 **a. to have = to experience** • **I'm having** a great time watching that happen. • Paula's **having** a difficult time learning chemistry.

Verbs of Emotion and Attitude
6. I **prefer** to live in a city now.
7. She **cares** about her TOEFL score.
8. He **hopes** she will marry him.
9. I **love** to play tennis!
10. He **hates** mayonnaise. . . . .
 	
11. I **want** to be a writer. . . . .
	
	b. love/hate:
	  love and *hate* can be used in the progressive for **very strong emphasis:**
	• How do you like your new job?
	  I'm loving it. (something new)
	• **I'm loving** my life. (emphasis—I **do** love my life.)
	c. Want can be used in the progressive in the **perfect tenses only:**
	• I **had been wanting** to be my own boss for a long time.

Continued on next page.

Continued from previous page.

NONACTION MEANING (NO PROGRESSIVE)	ACTION MEANING (MAY USE PROGRESSIVE)
Verbs of Mental Perceptions and Beliefs 12. She **considers** cheating to be a serious . . . . offense. 13. He **thinks** abortion is immoral. 14. I **don't mean** to insult you . . . . 15. I **didn't recognize** you with your new haircut. 16. I **remember** you from the party! 17. I'm sorry, but I've **forgotten** your name. 18. He **believes** in reincarnation.	**d.** When **think/consider** are used to describe a mental process, you may use the progressive: • I **am considering** taking a trip. • He **has been thinking** about changing careers. **e.** When *mean = have the intention,* use the progressive: • I've **been meaning** to call the doctor, but I've been so busy. **f.** When **remember/forget/recognize** are used to emphasize the uncompleted, step-by-step elements of a mental process, use the progressive: • More and more, I'm **recognizing** the need for regular exercise. • It's so sad. My grandmother is slowly **forgetting** everything.
Verbs of State 19. Laura **is** a teacher . . . . 20. You **look** like a million bucks! 21. It **appears** much easier than it is. 22. You **seem** depressed.	**g.** *be = behave unusually* • Our professor **is being** really unreasonable; she's asked us to write three papers this semester.

4.18 Recognition Drill: *Verbs not in the Progressive*

DIRECTIONS: Reread the preview interview. Circle and identify the verbs in the speech that belong to any of the following categories: Possession and Relation **(P&R)**, Sensory Perception **(SP)**, Emotion and Attitude **(E&A)**, Mental Activity and Perception **(MA&P)**, and Stative verbs **(S)**. If any of these verbs are progressive, be ready to explain why.

4.19 Written Drill: *All Progressive Verbs*

DIRECTIONS: Fill in the blanks below with any appropriate **progressive form** of the verb in parentheses. Be ready to compare your answers with a partner and discuss your choices.

1. Women's presence in the workforce (increase) _____ steadily since the so-called women's movement in the 1970s.

2. More women than ever are now (work) _____ outside the home.

3. Yet while women (contribute) _____ more and more to the workplace, the workplace (not/reward) _____ women with the same kinds of promotions and salaries that men enjoy.

4. Today women (barely/earn) _____ more than what they (earn) _____ twenty years ago when the women's movement started—about 62 cents for every dollar earned by a man.

5. Further, companies today (not/promote) _____ women to senior management positions. Researchers call this the "glass ceiling." It looks as if they can rise above it, but in reality, they are held at the middle level.

6. For example, a man and a woman will start at a company at the same time. Both will move up the ladder in the company, but the woman will stay as a middle manager and the man (get) _____ regular promotions. By the time she realizes that a promotion is unlikely, the woman (put) _____ in long hours and hard work for little return.

7. Recently, more women (open) _____ their own businesses, many of which they operate from their home.

8. In this way, women who (raise) _____ a family can earn a living and be available to their children.

9. Janice, a former employee of an insurance company, (get) _____ tired of commuting two hours a day to work for someone else, so she quit her job and started her own medical insurance billing operation.

10. Before, while she (work) _____ 60 miles away from her family, the babysitter (play) _____ with her kids. Now she can do both at the same time. But she cautions it's not for everyone. "You have to be disciplined, or you won't get any work done!"

4.20 Paired Activity: *A Small Success*

DIRECTIONS: Think about an experience you had that represents a small success for you (for example, performing well on a job interview, performing in a school play, etc.) Describe this experience to your partner, explaining what happened, what you were feeling and thinking at the time. Be ready to describe the experience in written form, if your teacher asks you to do so.

II. Special Problems With the Progressive

PROBLEM	EXPLANATION
1. Use of Simple Present For Current Ongoing Activity [INCORRECT: *I read my economics book now.*] CORRECT: *I am reading my economics book right now.*	Use the present progressive (and not the simple present) for ongoing activity.
2. Use of Progressive To Express Habitual Activity [INCORRECT: *What are you doing for a living?*] CORRECT: *What do you do for a living?*	Use the simple present for habitual activity.
3. Use of Present With *this + time* Words [INCORRECT: *I take 3 courses this semester.*] CORRECT: *I am taking 3 courses this semester.*	Use a progressive tense with *this + time* words.
4. No Progressive To Contrast An Ongoing Activity With A Sudden Action [INCORRECT: *I ironed my shirt when the electricity went off.*] CORRECT: *I was ironing my shirt when the electricity went off.*	When one ongoing activity is intersected by another, more sudden, action, use the progressive to show this contrast.

■ 4.21 **Error Analysis:** *The Progressive*

DIRECTIONS: Some of the following sentences have errors in verb form. Make the necessary changes clearly. **Do not change anything that is already correct. Be ready to explain the mistakes and your corrections.**

1. I wonder what that exotic spice in this sauce is. I am tasting turmeric and coriander, but there is another spice that I can't identify.

2. By the time her husband was awakened by the smoke, she had already been smelling the fire downstairs and called the fire department.

3. I touched the expensive vase when it suddenly fell to the floor and smashed into many pieces. I felt very embarrassed when I told my grandmother about it.

4. Lisa, did you forget everything I taught you about setting a table? You put the fork on the wrong side of the plate!

5. Jim studied in his room when his sister arrived, so he didn't hear the door open.

6. As the elderly man crossed Main Street last night, he was assaulted and robbed by two armed boys.

7. My sister and I take the same classes this semester.

8. During the entire party, I wasn't recognizing the girl in the red dress until she began to laugh.

9. This year, the university works hard to recruit students from Malaysia.

10. Go call the fire department. I am smelling smoke.

11. In spite of many arguments against the idea, John is still believing that men are superior to women.

12. I'm not understanding what you are trying to say right now.

13. My baby sister is being a real brat today, so I am going to the beach.

14. Have you cried? Your face is red and blotchy.

15. These days, American parents are having fewer children than ever before.

16. I'm not agreeing with any of my professor's theories this semester.

17. Lorenzo told Maria that he was thinking that they were seeing too much of each other.

18. I crossed Skyline Drive when I suddenly heard the loud screech of tires. I turned around and there was a huge moving van just a few feet from me. I'm lucky I didn't get run over.

19. Have you drunk whiskey tonight? I am smelling it on your breath.

Focus on Writing

Using the Present Progressive for Contemporary Issues

The present progressive tense is often used when writing about current topics, especially when those contemporary issues are unresolved and in progress. For example, note how the following author emphasizes the ongoing issue of homelessness by using a progressive tense in the following paragraph.

> It is becoming increasingly difficult for the "average middle class" person to ignore the issue of homelessness. Homeless people are now moving into neighborhoods and commercial districts that were immune to this problem ten years ago. Smaller cities are seeing the same kinds of problems that the larger cities began to experience a decade ago. Homeless folks are camping out in vacant lots, city parks, and street corners, a vivid reminder that all is not well in our fair cities.

4.22 Written Activity: *Using the Progressive for Contemporary Issues*

DIRECTIONS: Write a 100-150 word paragraph about one of the following topics. Use the **present progressive tense** whenever possible to emphasize the ongoing impact of the issue.

1. Unemployment in your city (country)
2. Obstacles facing women or minorities in achieving success in a field (e.g., technology, engineering, etc.)
3. The high cost of funding an education
4. The lack of job stability in corporations

Composition Topics

1. Compare your personal idea of success with the philosophy expressed in the poem at the beginning of the chapter.
2. Describe a successful person you know. Explain what he or she is presently doing and how he or she managed to achieve success.
3. "Time is money." "Money talks." "A penny saved is a penny earned." These are some very popular expressions that many Americans use to express their attitude about the value of money. Many Americans believe that money will bring them a certain amount of happiness, and the typical American would like to earn enough money to live comfortably. Buying on credit has become popular in the United States as more consumers wish to have their material possessions now and pay for them later. In a well-written composition, discuss your own attitudes, emotions, and perceptions of money, indicating how they might be similar to or different from those conveyed by the expressions above.

Verb Integration Exercises

DIRECTIONS: The exercises in this section will provide practice using all the verb tenses and forms—simple, progressive, and perfect. They require you to compare and contrast the use of verbs in many different contexts.

1. The following is the passage from the introduction to this unit without the verb tenses. See if you can complete the passage correctly. All twelve verb forms are included. Then compare your answers with the original version on page 23.

People (always/tell) _____ me that I (be) _____ an adaptable person. However, when I (come) _____ to the United States to study, I (find) _____ out that I (be) _____ not as adaptable as I (seem) _____ . I (already/study) _____

six years of English before I (leave) _____ my country of Indonesia. I
(study) _____ conversational English with an American teacher for about
a year before I (leave) _____. So I really (not/expect)
_____ to have any problems communicating with Americans. I (think)
_____ to myself, "I (just/go) _____ to my classes and
learn everything I can. Then by the time the TOEFL test (arrive) _____, I
(learn) _____ everything I need to get 550 on the TOEFL. I (enter)
_____ the local university for my M.B.A."

   Well, I really wasn't ready for my first months there. At the first orientation meeting at
the English school, the Americans (talk) _____ to me so fast that all I
did was smile and nod. I still (not/know) _____ what they (say)
_____ to me! I (have) _____ more surprises—
my accent (be) _____ hard to understand, I (not/like)
_____ the American food at the cafeteria, the pace in the city (be)
_____ too fast. But the biggest surprise (be) _____
my progress in English. I (not/get) _____ into that university right away.

   I'm still studying English. In fact, I've been studying for two semesters now. If all goes as
planned, I (enter) _____ the M.B.A. program next semester. I (live)
_____ in the United States for an entire year by then. I can understand
just about everything, and most people can understand me. But guess what? I'm still not
used to American food!

2. Write your own story about going to a foreign country or new city based on the above text. Try
   to use all twelve verb forms if at all possible. Underline all the verbs.

3. The following chart appeared on page 24. Note that these sentences have little meaning without
   additional information such as time expressions, additional clauses, or explanation. Complete
   these sentences to justify the verb tense used.

I eat	I ate	I will eat
cornflakes for breakfast		
every day.		
I have eaten	I had eaten	I will have eaten

I am eating

_____

_____

I was eating

_____

_____

I will be eating

_____

_____

I have been eating

_____

_____

I had been eating

_____

_____

I will have been eating

_____

_____

4. Storytelling is often difficult in a foreign language because of the many verb tenses required to describe the action in the story. Choose a fairy tale or bedtime story that you learned as a child. Recreate that story in English, in writing. Use as many verb tenses as is naturally possible and underline them. Be ready to share your story with the class orally.

5. Below are three brief biographies of well-known people. Choose one and write a summary of his life in well-composed complete sentences. If you prefer, you can go to the library to research a different individual not represented here. Use the most appropriate verb tenses to express time relationships. Add time expressions.

Thomas Paine

- Born in 1737 in England
- emigrated to American in 1774
- published his pamphlet *Common Sense* in 1776, urging American colonists to declare independence
- writer and radical
- wrote *The Crisis* during the war
- returned to England in 1791
- wrote *The Rights of Man* in 1791–92, defending the French Revolution
- as a result, he left England for France
- returned to United States in 1802 and died there

Pelé

- full name is Edson Arantes do Nascimento
- born in 1940 in Brazil
- considered the best soccer player of all time
- led the Brazilian national soccer team to victory in 1958, 1962, and 1970
- joined the New York Cosmos in 1975
- played with them until 1977
- North American Soccer League gained credibility
- scored 1,281 goals during his career as a soccer player

Malcolm X

- born Malcolm Little in 1925
- U.S. African-American radical
- in prison 1946–52
- converted to Black Muslims during this time
- became their leader in 1963
- founded Organization of Afro-American Unity (OAAU) in 1964
- OAAU supported "brotherhood," not separation
- assassinated in 1965 at an OAAU meeting

6. Compare the following sets of sentences. Decide if the sentences have the same meaning. If not, indicate the difference in the space provided.

Example   A: I read few books.
              B: I am reading a book.

_____ Same meaning

___X___ Different meaning: A. describes regular activity; B. describes what that

person is doing now.

1. **a.** My son eats my leftovers every day.

   b. My son is always eating the leftovers in the fridge.

   _____ Same meaning

   _____ Different meaning: _____

   _____

2. **a.** Just a few people in this class have been doing all the talking.

   b. Just a few people have talked so far. Does anyone want to add anything?

   _____ Same meaning

   _____ Different meaning: _____

   _____

3. **a.** I'll be 60 on Friday.

   b. I will have turned 60 by Friday.

   _____ Same meaning

   _____ Different meaning: _____

   _____

4. **a.** I'm in a pretty good mood.

   b. I've been in a pretty good mood.

   _____ Same meaning

   _____ Different meaning: _____

   _____

5. **a.** I've been living in this old house for six years.

   b. I've lived in this old house for six years.

   _____ Same meaning

   _____ Different meaning: _____

   _____

6. **a.** Elliot has never seen snow.

   b. Elliot never saw snow.

   _____ Same meaning

   _____ Different meaning: _____

   _____

7. **a.** Jack left when Judy arrived.

   b. Jack had left when Judy arrived.

   _____ Same meaning

   _____ Different meaning: _____

   _____

8. **a.** Cynthia cleaned the house before her mother came to visit.

   b. Cynthia had cleaned the house before her mother came to visit.

   _____ Same meaning

   _____ Different meaning: _____

   _____

9. **a.** I've been meaning to do it.

   b. I meant to do it.

   _____ Same meaning

   _____ Different meaning: _____

   _____

10. **a.** He's being a difficult child.

   b. He is a difficult child.

   _____ Same meaning

   _____ Different meaning: _____

   _____

11. Work in pairs. Choose three of the pairs of sentences above. Incorporate each sentence into a three to four line conversation between two people to make the exact meaning of the sentence clear. (You will have six conversations.) Write these down and be ready to present them to the class.

Example   cue: I read few books.

   A: What do you do in your spare time?
   B: I like to ride my bicycle and do stuff outdoors.
   A: Don't you like to read?
   B: No, I'm not that type. I read few books in my spare time.

Health and Fitness

• The Sentence: Introduction (Review Chapter)

Chapter 5

DISCUSSION QUESTIONS

1. Do you consider yourself a healthy individual? What aspects of your lifestyle help you to maintain your health? What bad habits (if any) do you have that are threatening to your health?

2. Are you involved in a sports or exercise program? Is there any sport that you've never tried that you're curious about?

3. What kind of medical system exists in the country where you're living? Is medical care expensive? Do you have medical insurance? How is this system different from other medical systems you've experienced?

OBJECTIVES

In this chapter you will learn:

1. To understand the distinction between phrases and clauses

2. To understand the components of English sentences in a variety of forms

3. To recognize and correct faulty sentences

Grammatical Terms

PHRASE—two or more words that don't contain a subject and verb

>   e.g. *an interesting class*

CLAUSE—contains a subject and verb

>   e.g. **This is** *an interesting class.*
>   (subject) (verb)

SUBJECT—the topic of the sentence; it usually precedes the verb

>   e.g. **Aerobics** *has become very popular.*
>   (subject)

TRANSITIVE VERB—a verb that takes a direct object

>   e.g. *I* **am attending** *a class.*
>   (transitive verb)   (dir. obj.)

INTRANSITIVE VERB—a verb that cannot take a direct object

>   e.g. *Jane* **is running.**
>   (intransitive verb)

LINKING VERB—connects the subject and its complement

>   e.g. *The teacher* **seems** *prepared.*
>   (linking verb)

DIRECT OBJECT—receives the action of the verb

>   e.g. *I like* **aerobics.**
>   (dir. obj.)

INDIRECT OBJECT—the receiver of the direct object

>   e.g. *Jane teaches* **me aerobics.**
>   (ind. obj.)   (dir. obj.)

SUBJECT COMPLEMENT—describes the subject

>   e.g. **Jane** *is an* **aerobics teacher.**
>   (subject)   (complement)

OBJECT COMPLEMENT—describes the object

>   e.g. *Mary finds* **aerobics exhausting.**
>   (dir. obj.)   (obj. complement)

SUBORDINATING CONJUNCTION—connects a dependent clause to an independent clause, e.g. **although, because, if, when,** etc.

COORDINATING CONJUNCTION—connects two independent clauses, e.g. **and, but, so, or, nor, for.**

Preview

DIRECTIONS: Read the following interview between Randy Brown, a leading T.V. journalist, and Joyce Coles, the famous actress who popularized aerobics instruction.

RANDY: Tell me, Joyce. What made you become so seriously involved in **aerobics** instruction?

JOYCE: Well, you know, I've always been kind of a **health nut,** but for years I hadn't been very good about **staying in shape** because of my film career. Then several years ago, I attended an aerobics class here in L.A., and I felt so great afterwards that I signed up for a year of classes. I really **got into** it for a year and then decided to start a class of my own.

RANDY: And now you have your own **fitness center** and a videotape that has sold millions. A real hit!

JOYCE: Yeah, I took some time off from making movies for a while to **get** the fitness center **off the ground.** The video was a fairly simple project because I was already running classes at the center in Hollywood. It was **a cinch.**

RANDY: You know, you've been an inspiration to many people who thought there was **no getting around** the **middle-aged spread.** What is your message to these people?

JOYCE: I want them to realize that we can stay fit and beautiful by **working out** regularly. If our bodies are in shape, our minds work better and we feel better about ourselves.

RANDY: Is working out the only answer? What about diet?

JOYCE: Of course, a balanced diet along with a regular program of exercise is the real key to **getting into shape** and maintaining that condition for an extended period of time. There are too many **fad diets** out there that can be very unhealthy and even dangerous.

RANDY: Well, Joyce, I'm sure you know what you're talking about because you are definitely the **picture of health.** Thanks for talking to us today, and we'll look forward to your upcoming video of aerobics for pregnancy.

JOYCE: Thank you, Randy, it was a pleasure speaking with you.

VOCABULARY

aerobics: an exercise routine set to music and designed to increase the heart rate

health nut: a person who is preoccupied with health

a cinch: very easy

get into shape: improve your physical condition so that you are at your ideal weight and your muscles are toned

staying in shape: maintaining a good physical condition through regular exercise and good diet

get into (something): become interested and involved in something

fad diet: a strict diet that promises rapid weight loss and that becomes very popular

fitness center: a place for physical training usually consisting of a running track, swimming pool, weight room, exercise bicycles, and saunas

get (something) off the ground: get a new project started

no getting around: no avoiding

middle-aged spread: heaviness around the middle of the body that can occur during middle age

picture of health: looking perfectly fit and healthy

a balanced diet: eating the proper amount of food from the major food groups and avoiding unhealthy foods

a cinch: very easy; without effort

CULTURAL NOTE/DISCUSSION

In the last two decades a health craze has swept the United States. Many people are preoccupied with maintaining a healthy diet and a regular program of exercise. Is there much emphasis on health and exercise in your country? What kinds of diets and exercise are popular?

FOCUS ON GRAMMAR

The following questions are based on the preview text and are designed to help you find out what you already know about the structures in this chapter. Some of the questions may be hard and some of them may be easy. Answer as many of the questions as you can. Work with a partner if your teacher tells you to do so.

1. In the following two sentences from the preview, *and* is used to connect two grammatical patterns in one sentence. How is the pattern of the two sentences different based on the function of this connector? How could you change the sentences so that they have the same pattern?

    a. *Then several years ago, I attended an aerobics classes here in L.A., **and** I felt so great afterwards that I signed up for a year of classes.*

    b. *I really got into it **and** then decided to start a class of my own.*

2. What is the difference between the two underlined groups of words in the sentences below?

    a. *The video was a fairly simple project <u>because I was already running classes. . . .</u>*

    b. *I hadn't been very good about staying in shape <u>because of my film career.</u>*

3. Which of the following examples from the interview is an incomplete sentence? How could you make it a complete sentence?

    a. *A real hit.*

    b. *It was a cinch.*

4. In the following sentence identify the subject, verb and object and write them below the sentence.

    Of course, a balanced diet along with a regular program of exercise is the real key to getting into shape.

Grammatical Patterns

I. Phrases and Clauses

The following two examples help to demonstrate the difference between a phrase and a clause. Notice that the clause has a subject and a verb whereas the phrase does not.

CLAUSE: Because <u>I was running</u> . . .
                    (subj.)   (verb)

PHRASE: Because of <u>my film career</u>
                             noun phrase

The chart below provides examples of the different types of phrases and clauses.

EXAMPLES	NOTES

Phrases
1. *Many fad diets* are *unhealthy.*
  (noun phrase)
2. *Diet* **can influence** *moods.*
  (verb phrase)
3. *You should eat breakfast* **in the morning.**
  (prepositional phrase)
4. **Swimming and cycling** *are her favorite*
  (gerund phrase)
ways to exercise.
5. *She really likes* **to swim.**
  (infinitive. phrase)
6. **Knowing the harmful effects of fats,**
  (participial phrase)
Gwen limits her intake.
	Two or more words that serve a particular function in a sentence.
	• A phrase doesn't have a subject and a verb.
	• Phrases can be the subject of a sentence as in (1) or the verb as in (2).
	• Phrases have many other functions, as illustrated in sentences 3–6.

Clauses
1. **Because John has a heart problem,**
  (adv. clause)
he is on a low-cholesterol diet.
2. *You must choose a diet* **which you can live with.**
  (adj. clause)
3. *Sharon thought* **that she would lose 40 pounds on her new diet.**
  (noun clause)
	• A clause contains a subject and a verb.
	• An adverb clause answers the questions *why?, how?, when?,* etc. as in (1).
	• An adjective clause modifies a noun. In (2) it modifies *a diet.*
	• Noun clauses replace nouns in a sentence. In (3) it is the object of the verb.

5.1 Recognition Drill: *Phrase or Clause?*

DIRECTIONS: State whether each underlined group of words is a **phrase** or a **clause**. Identify the type of phrase or clause. Refer to the charts on page 93 for assistance.

Example   <u>Due to the growing interest in better health,</u> many people are joining fitness clubs.
(Phrase) (Type: Prepositional Phrase)

1. <u>Because of the latest trend in health and exercise,</u> health clubs are opening everywhere.

2. My favorite time to exercise is <u>in the morning after getting up and before eating breakfast.</u>

3. A leading expert in the field of nutrition has stated <u>that calories play a more important role in weight gain than anything else.</u>

4. <u>Despite her repeated efforts to lose weight,</u> she has had no success.

5. <u>Getting enough sleep and eating well</u> are essential in order to stay healthy.

6. I go to the health club every day to work out <u>although it is very often an effort to get myself there.</u>

7. Alicia likes any kind of exercise; however, she <u>has never tried windsurfing or kayaking on the ocean.</u>

Notice the difference between an independent clause and a dependent clause.

EXAMPLES	DEFINITION
Independent Clause **1. *She walks to work in the morning.***	• An independent clause can stand alone as a sentence. • An independent clause contains a subject and a verb and usually an object or complement.
Dependent Clause **2. *Although she walks to work in the*** (sub. conj.) ***morning,* *she takes the bus home at night.***	• A dependent clause cannot stand alone as a sentence. It must be joined to an independent clause. • A subordinating conjunction is used to join a dependent clause to an independent clause

5.2 Recognition Exercise: *Dependent or Independent Clause?*

DIRECTIONS: In the passage below, underline the **independent clauses** once and the **dependent clauses** twice.

More and more people are incorporating natural foods and herbs into their diets for better health as well as for medicinal purposes. The use of garlic, for example, has recently become popular for its beneficial effects on the immune system. Although the smell of garlic is not very pleasant, many people eat raw garlic as a nutritional supplement and there are now even garlic pills on the market. Another natural ingredient that has become popular recently is cayenne pepper. Because of a suggested relationship between the use of cayenne pepper and longevity, some people are adding cayenne pepper to their diet. Finally, the use of fresh ginger, which can be combined with lemon and honey to make a tea, can be very effective for coughs and colds.

II. The Parts of a Sentence

A. The Subject

The subject of a sentence can take a variety of forms as demonstrated in the chart below.

Form	Example
Noun	• *Joyce* has her own fitness center.
Pronoun	• *She* teaches aerobics classes at the center.
Noun Phrase	• *The aerobics classes* are very demanding.
Gerund Phrase	• *Staying in shape* requires exercise and a balanced diet.
Infinitive Phrase	• *To avoid the middle-aged spread* is his primary goal.
Noun Clause	• *What form of exercise you choose* affects the kind of results you get.

• See the chapters on noun clauses, gerunds, and infinitives for more explanation.

5.3 Written Exercise: *Identification of Subjects*

DIRECTIONS: Underline the **subject** in each of the following sentences. Work with a partner to identify the grammatical form of the subject.

Example   *The video* was a fairly simple project. (noun phrase)

1. Bill and his friends take kickboxing lessons on Saturdays.
2. Something I really enjoy is hiking in the mountains.
3. Lifting weights and riding the lifecycle are Robin's favorite activities at the gym.
4. The dietary requirements of Weight Watchers can be found in their manual.
5. To become a health nut was never Joe's intention when he became a vegetarian.

5.4 Paired Activity

DIRECTIONS: You are a health expert and you must create a set of guidelines for optimal health. Discuss with a partner your guidelines using each given word or phrase as the subject of a sentence.

Example   Good health . . .

              Good health is a product of balanced nutrition and a regular program of exercise.

1. A regular program of exercise . . .
2. Taking aerobics classes . . .
3. What you eat . . .
4. Junk food, coffee, cigarettes, and alcohol . . .
5. Fad diets . . .
6. Staying healthy and fit . . .
7. The best way to avoid getting sick . . .
8. You . . .
9. What you must always remember is . . .
10. Finding a way to relieve stress . . .

B. The Verb

English verbs can be either transitive or intransitive. If a verb is **transitive**, the action of the verb is received by a **direct object**. If the verb is **intransitive**, the action of the verb remains in the verb and there is **no direct object**. The charts below classify some of these verbs.

TRANSITIVE AND INTRANSITIVE VERBS		

Always Transitive
 Verb + Direct Object
 have, use, do, want, need, say, hold, hit, choose, watch, spend, wear, keep, attend, raise, lay, bring up
	1. Jim **has** a cold.
	        tran. verb dir. obj.
	
	 2. Sue **wants** cake.
	        tran. verb dir. obj
		• These verbs are **always** followed by a direct object.
		 • The direct object receives the action of the verb.

Transitive or Intransitive
 eat, play, begin, finish, practice, leave, ring, sing, teach, see, hear, break, read, write,
	4. I **ate** breakfast.
	        (dir. obj).
	
	 5. I **haven't eaten** yet.
	        (no dir. obj)
		• Some verbs can be **either** transitive or intransitive, depending on the context and meaning.

5.5 Paired Activity: *Transitive and Intransitive Verbs*

DIRECTIONS: Your partner or teacher will ask you a question. Answer the question using the verb provided in parentheses. If the verb can be either **transitive** or **intransitive**, use it in both ways in your answer.

Example What are your eating habits? (eat)
TRANSITIVE: *I try to eat three balanced meals every day.*
INTRANSITIVE: *I always read the newspaper while I'm eating.*

1. Are you a good cook? (cook)
2. What do you do when you don't know the meaning of a word? (use)
3. Are there special clothes for aerobics? (get dressed)
4. Which skills are your strongest in English? (read/write/speak/listen)
5. What happens in your culture if the parents of a child get divorced? (bring up)
6. What is your routine before you go to work or school in the morning? (leave)
7. Where do you sit when you go to the movies? (see)
8. How do you stay healthy? (need)
9. Do you like chocolate? (want)
10. Do you like your fitness class? (teach)

5.6 Written Activity: *A Day in the Life*

DIRECTIONS: You are a journalist for a top-selling fitness magazine. Use the information from the interview in the preview section to write an article about Joyce Coles. Use at least ten of the verbs from the above chart.

TRANSITIVE VERBS FOLLOWED BY AN INDIRECT OBJECT. The transitive verbs below take an indirect object as well as a direct object.		
Verb + Indirect Object + Direct Object **give, buy, tell, take, sell, make, send, bring, get, pay**	1. *He gave **me some advice.*** (ind. obj) (dir. obj)	• Some verbs can be followed by an indirect object before the direct object to indicate the receiver of the direct object as in (1). • The indirect object is usually a person. • When used with an indirect object, **to, for,** and **from** follow the direct object as in (2).
	2. *She sold **a bicycle to me.*** (dir. obj.) (ind. obj.)	
	3. *She sold **me a bicycle.*** (ind. obj.) (dir. obj.)	• If the preposition is omitted, the indirect object precedes the direct object as in (3).
	INCORRECT: She sold to me a bicycle.	

INTRANSITIVE VERBS The chart below shows two types of intransitive verbs.		
Linking Verbs be, seem, appear, become	1. *A regular program of exercise **is beneficial.*** (complement)	• Linking verbs are followed by a *complement,* which completes the verb and describes the subject of the sentence.
Action Verbs walk, run, work, live, sleep, work out, come, go, arrive, listen, speak, rise, lie, talk, get dressed, laugh, grow up	2. *In the afternoons, Bruce **works** out.* 3. *Bruce **works** out every day.*	• Action verbs can stand alone with no object or complement as in (2). • These verbs are often followed by a phrase as in (3).

5.7 Editing Activity: *Transitive* or *Intransitive?*

DIRECTIONS: Correct the error in each of the sentences below based on whether the verb is **transitive** or **intransitive**. Consider the meaning when deciding whether it should be transitive.

Example   [INCORRECT:When parents are growing up their kids, they should teach them about good nutrition.]
            CORRECT: *When parents are bringing up their kids, they should teach them about good nutrition.*

1. In the morning I get dressed my clothes.

2. My aerobics instructor said me about the new music she will use.

3. The dinner was so delicious last night. I never tasted before.

4. I arrive the gym very early in the morning.

5. When my mother was raising, she always emphasized the benefits of fresh fruits.

6. When the moon appears the sky, it's beautiful.

7. We usually listen the music during dinner.

8. My mother brought up with no help from her parents.

9. There's a great new CD by the Bongos. Did you hear?

10. Yesterday I didn't eat the food all day.

SPECIAL
NOTE

TROUBLESOME VERBS

The following verbs are often confusing for speakers of English. Study them carefully.

TRANSITIVE VERBS	**INTRANSITIVE VERBS**
Lay, Laid, Laid: to put or place	Lie, Lay, Lain: to assume a horizontal position
• He *lays* his keys there every day.	• Cats often **lie** on warm cars.
• She *laid* the book on the table.	• He **lay** down on the couch.
Hang, Hung, Hung: to suspend	Hang, Hanged, Hanged:
• The proud owner of the painting	to kill by hanging
hung it on the wall.	• He **hanged** for his crimes.
Raise, Raised, Raised: to lift, to grow, to bring up	Rise, Rose, Risen: to increase
• The student **raised** her hand.	• Prices **rose** 10% last month.

5.8 Oral Drill: *Troublesome Verbs*

DIRECTIONS: Answer the following questions using one of the six verbs listed in the chart above.

1. Your mother was extremely tired yesterday afternoon. What did she do?

_____

2. What does your teacher do with his/her books when he/she comes into the classroom?

_____

3. What happens to the level of water in a river during a flood?

_____

4. Country X is in an inflationary period. What do you suppose happened to food prices?

_____

5. What did the father do with his baby after she fell asleep?

_____

6. Where did you put your coat after you walked into the house?

_____

7. Where do you go when you want to take a nap?

_____

8. What did the soldiers do after they captured the enemy?

_____

5.9 Written Activity: *The Picture of Health*

DIRECTIONS: Describe someone you know who is the "picture of health"—in very good health and physically fit. Use a variety of transitive and intransitive verbs from the chart on page 96.

C. Direct Objects

As you have already seen, a **direct object** receives the action of a transitive verb. The chart below lists the various forms that direct objects can take.

DIRECT OBJECTS	
Form	**Example**
1. Noun	1. Joyce teaches **aerobics** every day. *(noun)*
2. Pronoun	2. She enjoys **it**. *(pronoun)*
3. Noun Phrase	3. Joyce has **her own fitness center and a videotape**. *(noun phrase)*
4. Gerund Phrase	4. Her students like **exercising to music**. *(gerund phrase)*
5. Infinitive Phrase	5. Joyce hopes **to open another fitness center** soon. *(infinitive phrase)*
6. Noun Clause	6. She knows **how to make this business successful**. *(noun clause)*

5.10 Recognition Drill: *Direct Objects*

DIRECTIONS: Underline the **direct object** in each of the following sentences. Be prepared to identify the type of direct object it is.

Many people are taking up Capoeira as one of the latest fads in the fitness craze. Capoeira, which originated in Brazil, integrates the newest aerobic techniques with traditional combat styles. These new workout opportunities offer excellent cardiovascular conditioning, elastic flexibility and superb muscle tone. Capoeira involves working every muscle in your body. The strong kicks help to get the muscles popping. The masters of this sport understand why capoeira is becoming so popular. People appreciate the infectious rhythms, the beautiful sense of balance, and the deeply spiritual element.

D. Complements

There are a few different types of complements as shown in the chart below.

COMPLEMENTS	NOTES
SUBJECT COMPLEMENTS 1. *Joyce seems* **happy.** (adjective) 2. *Joyce is* **an aerobics instructor.** (noun phrase) 3. *Her dream is* **to have two fitness centers.** (infinitive phrase) 4. *Fitness is* **what she really believes in.** (noun clause)	• A subject complement describes the subject. • An intransitive verb links the subject and its complement. • A subject complement can be an adjective (1), a noun phrase (2), an infinitive phrase (3), or a noun clause (4).
OBJECT COMPLEMENTS 1. *Many people consider* **aerobics** (dir. obj.) **the best workout.** (obj. comp.) 2. *Mary finds* **aerobics exhausting.** 3. *Sports Illustrated labeled* **the 80s** (dir. obj.) **the decade of fitness.** (obj. comp.) 4. *Many people regard* **the fitness craze** (dir. obj.) *as* **a wake-up call.** (obj. comp.)	• An object complement describes the direct object. • Verbs such as **consider, find, call, imagine,** and **prove,** which reflect the opinion or perception of the speaker, take noun or adjective object complements as in (1) and (2). • Verbs such as **call, label, name,** which indicate a name or label for the object, take noun object complements as in (3). • A few verbs that are followed by **as** or **for** are followed by object complements as in (4), e.g., *recognize, regard, accept, mistake, take, describe.*

5.11 Oral Drill: *Complements*

DIRECTIONS: Restate the following sentences about soy protein, using the **verb** in parentheses and a **subject** or **object complement**.

1. Many doctors think that soy protein can be useful in preventing heart disease and cancer. *(consider)*

2. They are saying that soy protein is a new wonder food. *(label)*

3. They think that soy may be a replacement for certain drugs that treat high cholesterol. *(regard as)*

4. Genistein, a powerful natural chemical unique to soy, can be effective in slowing down the cancer process. *(seems)*

5. Unfortunately many people think that tofu, the primary food made from soy, is tasteless and unappealing. *(find)*

6. On the other hand, many vegetarians think that tofu is a viable substitute for meat. *(accept as)*

7. Health experts think that soy is a miracle food for its medicinal and nutritional qualities. *(call)*

5.12 Recognition Drill: *Identifying Sentence Parts*

DIRECTIONS: For each sentence below, underline the subject once, circle the verb, and underline the direct object or complement twice. Be prepared to describe each of those sentence parts.

Example   Jim and his wife (eat) three balanced meals every day.

> **Jim** and **wife** are nouns. **Eat** is a transitive verb. **Three balanced meals** is a direct object.

1. What Rachel really enjoys is taking long walks in the evening.

2. Due to the growing number of people at this fitness center, we are expanding.

3. Taking too many vitamins can be harmful to your body.

4. The secret to avoiding stress is managing your time wisely and exercising regularly.

5. Many avid joggers, cyclists, and swimmers have recently begun competing in the triathalon.

6. To be in excellent physical condition is what Grace has always strived for.

7. Michelle and her friends follow a strict vegetarian diet.

5.13 Written Activity: *Verbs at Work*

DIRECTIONS: Identify the parts of the sentence in the following cartoon. Then replace the verb in the cartoon with **exercises**. What other changes do you have to make when you do that?

the neighborhood. Jerry Van Amerongen

© 1988 Cowles Syndicate, Inc.

9-19

Mr. Carlisle probes the very frontier of fitness technique.

III. Sentence Types

A. Sentence Types According to Function

The chart below demonstrates the different types of English sentences according to their function;

TYPE	NOTES
Declarative Headaches can sometimes be attributed to a poor diet.	• Makes a statement • Ends in a period
Interrogative 1. Why is diet important? (wh + verb + subj. + comp.) 2. What time is it? [INCORRECT: What time it is?] 3. Is the new diet working? (aux. + subj. + verb) 4. Aren't you studying? (aux. + not + subj. + verb) 5. You ate onions for breakfast?	• A **wh-** question asks for information, e.g. *who, what, why, when, where, how* • Sometimes a quantifier or noun follows the **wh-** word as in (2). • A **yes/no** question requires **yes** or **no** for an answer as in (3). • A **negative** question asks for confirmation or expresses disbelief as in (4). • A declarative sentence can be used as a question to express surprise as in (5).

5.14 Paired Activity: *Asking Questions*

DIRECTIONS: On the lines below, write five statements of fact about health and fitness. Take turns with your partner relating to each other the facts you have written. After one of you has made a statement, the other should ask a question about the information, using a different type of question each time.

Example   STATEMENT: Some people suffer from environmental illness.
             QUESTION: What exactly is environmental illness?

Statements:

1. _____

2. _____

3. _____

4. _____

5. _____

SPECIAL
NOTE

TAG QUESTIONS

Tag Questions are used to clarify what the speaker assumes to be true. Tag questions are formed in the following way:

Tennis **is** a competitive sport, **isn't** it?
(positive)   (negative)

Jogging **isn't** a competitive sport, **is** it?
(negative)   (positive)

- **If the verb in the main clause is positive, the verb in the tag is negative and vice versa.**

5.15 Paired Activity: *Complex Questions—Tags and Negatives*

DIRECTIONS: Below are some influential statements commonly found on food product labels. Below each statement you will find two explanations for the statements. Discuss with a partner which explanation is correct, making the first explanation a **tag question**, the second one a **negative question.**

Example   "high in Vitamin C"

    a. The food has 20 percent of the vitamin C you need to eat each day.
       The food has 20 percent of the vitamin C you need to eat each day, doesn't it?

    b. The product delivers 10 percent of the daily recommeneded amount.
       Doesn't the product deliver 10 percent of the daily recommended amount?

1. "Cholesterol-free"
   a. The cholesterol has been removed by the manufacturer.
   b. The food was free of cholesterol in the first place.
2. "Light"
   a. The product delivers half the fat.
   b. The product delivers two-thirds the calories of the regular version.
3. "Good source of calcium"
   a. The product has at least 20 percent of the calcium you need to eat each day.
   b. The product supplies 10 percent of the government recommended amount.
4. "Low-fat"
   a. The food gets no more than 30 percent of its calories from fat.
   b. The product has fewer than 10 grams of fat.
5. "Reduced fat"
   a. The fat in this product has been cut by at least 50 percent.
   b. The producer has cut the fat per serving by a quarter compared to its regular product.

5.16 Written Activity: *Follow-Up*

DIRECTIONS: Write a letter to the FDA to clarify the nutrition facts from the previous exercise. In your letter, use a variety of tag and negative questions. Write to the following address: FDA, Office of Pulic Affairs, 5600 Fishers Lane, Rockville, MD 20857.

5.17 Editing Activity: *Question Formation*

DIRECTIONS: Correct the errors in the following questions.

1. How many times you ran around the track?

2. What kind of running shoes they are?

3. Richard came in second in the marathon, did he?

4. What kind of doctor you have?

5. You aren't a vegetarian, aren't you?

6. How often you take these vitamins?

7. How many people you asked about the new equipment?

8. You have a very healthy diet, do you?

9. Who you talked to about your sore arm?

10. When you are going to the clinic?

TYPE	NOTES
Imperative 1. Drink plenty of fluids. 2. Don't forget to take your vitamins. 3. Be careful of drafts.	• Used as a command as in (1), a reminder as in (2), or a warning as in (3).
Exclamatory 1. I lost 5 pounds! 2. What a great teacher she was! (What + noun phrase + subj. + verb) 3. How fascinating! (how + adj.) 4. How interesting that class was! (how + adj. + subj. + verb)	• A declarative sentence in form, used to express strong feelings such as surprise, pleasure, excitement, etc. • An exclamatory sentence ends with an exclamation point. • Errors are often made in word order, e.g., How interesting was that class!

5.18 Rapid Drill: *Exclamatory Sentences*

DIRECTIONS: Use an **exclamatory statement** to respond to each of the following situations.

Example   CUE: You just heard some great news.
                RESPONSE: What great news I just heard!

1. Your workout was exhilarating.
2. Your doctor has a very abrupt manner.
3. Your day at work was very stressful.
4. You feel sick.
5. You have found a great running path in the forest.
6. It's 105° F. today.
7. You just saw a beautiful sunset.
8. You're eating a delicious piece of homemade apple pie.
9. You're looking at interesting pictures of your friend's trip.
10. You just saw a very sad movie.

5.19 Oral Drill: *Sentence Types*

DIRECTIONS: Use a variety of sentence types to **ask questions, give commands, make comments**, and **express surprise** about the situations below.

Example   Your friend is extremely thin. ("Are you sick?" "How thin you are!")

1. You sit down for your lunch break at work, and your office partner pulls out potato chips and a candy bar.
2. During a party, a friend of yours who never smokes is chain smoking.
3. You are walking up the stairs with a friend, and your friend is experiencing shortness of breath.
4. You just heard that a new discovery was made for treating obesity.
5. Your mother is putting six teaspoons of sugar into her coffee.
6. Your father, who experienced a heart attack a year ago, just ran two miles.
7. You are working out with your friend, and she just lifted two 100-pound weights.
8. A friend of yours whom you haven't seen in six months looks extremely tired.
9. You just heard that the government has initiated a campaign to outlaw cigarette smoking.
10. Your sister has just started a diet on which she can't have any sugar, caffeine, or alcohol.

5.20 Written Activity: *Choose two of the situations above and for each one, write all the possible sentence types to respond to the situation.*

5.21 Written Activity: *What's Funny?*

DIRECTIONS: Read the following cartoon and discuss why it's funny. On the lines below, write the man's statement as a **question** and then as an **exclamatory sentence** with a different structure from the original.

QUESTION: _____

EXCLAMATORY: _____

5.22 Paired Activity: *Your Diet*

DIRECTIONS: After recording your diet for three days in the chart, show your partner and discuss how healthy your diet is. As you discuss your diet with your partner, respond to the instructions below the chart on the next page.

MY DIET			
Day 1 Breakfast	Lunch	Dinner	Snacks
Day 2 Breakfast	Lunch	Dinner	Snacks
Day 3 Breakfast	Lunch	Dinner	Snacks

1. Show surprise at two of the things your partner ate.

    a. _____

    b. _____

2. Make two observations or conclusions about your partner's diet.

    a. _____

    b. _____

3. Ask your partner two questions about the diet.

    a. _____

    b. _____

4. Tell your partner to make two important changes in his/her diet.

    a. _____

    b. _____

5.23 Written Activity: *Weight Watchers*

DIRECTIONS: Weight Watchers is a well-known organization that is devoted to helping people reduce their weight. They have a strict diet that their members follow, regular meetings that their members attend, and their own food available in supermarkets. Think of at least five questions that you would like answered to better understand how the Weight Watchers program works. Write your questions in a letter to the organization.

B. Sentence Types According to Structure

The chart below demonstrates different types of English sentences according to their structure.

TYPE	EXAMPLE
Simple Sentence A simple sentence has one independent clause.	• Scientists have developed artificial fat.
Compound A compound sentence has two independent clauses joined by a coordinating conjunction.	• You can eat all the fatty foods you want, **and** your body won't absorb the fat.
Complex A complex sentence contains one independent clause and one dependent clause joined by a subordinating conjunction.	• **Although** you will be ingesting fatty foods, your body won't absorb the fat.
Compound-Complex A compound-complex sentence contains at least one dependent clause, one independent clause, plus one additional clause.* *(Or: Two independent clauses and at least one subordinate clause.)	• Although you will be able to enjoy a variety of your favorite desserts *(dependent clause)* and you will be ingesting all that fat *(independent clause)*, your body won't absorb the fat *(independent clause)*.

5.24 Written Activity: *Sentence Types*

DIRECTIONS: For each of the health disorders below, write a short paragraph with four sentences—**one of each type** from the above chart—describing the disorder. If you have no experience or knowledge of the disorder, do some research in the library. Label each sentence as is shown in the example.

1. Multiple Sclerosis

_____

_____

_____

_____

2. AIDS

_____

_____

_____

_____

3. Leukemia

_____

_____

_____

_____

Focus on Writing

A. Sentence Fragments

A **sentence fragment** is an incomplete sentence that is written as if it were a sentence. A sentence fragment is missing one or more sentence parts such as a subject, a verb, or an object. Read the following passage and notice the sentence fragments that are underlined. Discuss what component of the sentence is missing.

A vegetarian is a person who doesn't eat meat. For several reasons. Some vegetarians are opposed to the killing of animals. And being a vegetarian is a form of protest. These vegetarians don't eat any red meat or poultry. Or use any animal products such as leather or fur. Other vegetarians don't eat red meat for health reasons. Because red meat contains a lot of fat.

There are a few ways to correct sentence fragments. Notice the examples from the above paragraph corrected in the table below:

CORRECTION	EXAMPLE
• Add the components that are missing, e.g. subject, verb.	**1. This is** because red meat contains a lot of fat.
• Connect the fragment to a previous sentence.	**2.** Some vegetarians are opposed to the killing of **animals, and** being a vegetarian is a form of protest.

5.25 Editing Activity: *Sentence Fragments*

DIRECTIONS: In the passage below about the macrobiotic diet, underline the **sentence fragments**. Then, on the lines below the passage, rewrite the passage so that there are no fragments. You may have to add some words.

A macrobiotic diet is based on the concept of yin and yang in Eastern philosophy and the natural balance of nature. An example. There is no meat in a macrobiotic diet. The small number of teeth in our mouth used for chewing meat compared to the other kind of teeth. Macrobiotics believe that we are not designed to have meat in our diet. Sugar also. Brown rice, which requires a lot of chewing, is the primary food in the macrobiotic diet. When we chew the rice, natural sugar is produced in the mouth. So we don't need any sugar from other sources. Of course, vegetables along with brown rice. Because they are such a rich source of vitamins and other essential nutrients.

B. Run-On Sentences

There are two types of run-on sentences as shown in the chart below.

Type	Run-On Sentences	Correct Sentences
• Two or more clauses are incorrectly joined In (1) there are two complete sentences, but the writer did not punctuate the sentence correctly. A period is needed after *habits* as in sentence (2).	1. I used to be a very healthy person, but recently my lifestyle has changed and I have developed some bad **habits they** include smoking cigarettes, drinking coffee, staying up late, and eating junk food.	2. I used to be a very healthy person, but recently my lifestyle has changed and I have developed some bad **habits. They** include smoking cigarettes, drinking coffee, staying up late, and eating junk food.
• Too many clauses in one sentence In (3) the writer includes a series of clauses with no break. A new sentence should begin after *habits* as in (4).	3. I used to be a very healthy person, but recently my lifestyle has changed, and I have developed some bad habits, and they include smoking cigarettes, drinking coffee, and I stay up late and I eat too much junk food because I really can't resist it.	4. I used to be a very healthy person, but recently my lifestyle has changed, and I have developed some bad **habits. These habits** include smoking cigarettes **and** drinking coffee; **I also** stay up late and eat too much junk food because I really can't resist it.
• Comma splice - two independent clauses joined by a comma A connector with the proper punctuation needs to be added as in (6).	5. Recently I've improved my diet, I feel much better.	6. Recently I've improved my diet; as a result, I feel much better.

5.26 Editing Activity: *Run-on Recognition*

DIRECTIONS: Determine whether each sentence below is a run-on sentence and justify your answer. Then, if necessary, make corrections so that it is not a run-on sentence.

1. Because Grace is a vegetarian, she must pay special attention to the amount of protein in the food she eats, so she eats a lot of beans, she also eats eggs.

2. When Grace first became a vegetarian, she missed eating meat since she had always liked the food she eats, so she eats a lot of beans, she also eats eggs.

3. When Grace first became a vegetarian, she missed eating meat since she had always liked the taste of it, but now she can't imagine eating meat because she has grown to appreciate the pure taste of meatless cuisine, and meat tastes very strange to her, and so she is happy to be a vegetarian.

4. Sometimes it's very difficult to eat out in restaurants due to the limited meatless choices on menus although that is changing now with the increase in vegetarian restaurants.

5. Grace is opposed to the killing of animals, so not only is she a vegetarian but she is also very disturbed by the use of animal fur for clothing.

6. She feels better now that she doesn't eat meat anymore, she feels more humane and she feels healthier.

7. Being a vegetarian and feeling that she is doing her share to protect animals, Grace becomes irritated when people question her motives for being a vegetarian although she tries to be patient with such people, and she tries to make them understand the value of saving animals, but often people just don't understand.

V. Special Problems

Pay careful attention to those special problems with sentences.

PROBLEM	EXPLANATION
Inserting An Object After An Intransitive Verb 1. INCORRECT: I get up **the morning.** 2. CORRECT: I get up **in the morning.**	• If the verb is intransitive, there is no direct object as in (2).
Double Subject 3. INCORRECT: My sister **she** is healthy. 4. CORRECT: My **sister** is healthy. OR 5. My **sister and brother** are happy.	• A sentence can have a compound subject connected by *and* as in (5) but not a double subject as in (3).
Sentence Fragment 6. INCORRECT: Taking care of your health. 7. CORRECT: Taking care of your health is very important.	• A sentence fragment is missing key components as in (6). • A sentence must have a subject, a verb, and usually a direct object or complement as in (7).

Continued on next page.

Continued from previous page.

PROBLEM	EXPLANATION
Run-On Sentence 8. INCORRECT: The mind affects the body in many ways for example we can become ill as a result of stress. 9. CORRECT: The mind affects the body in many ways; for example, we can become ill as a result of stress. 10. INCORRECT: One way that the mind affects the body can be seen when depression or stress results in illness, which proves that the mental state is causing the illness and doctors are now treating these illnesses by treating the psychological problem. 11. CORRECT: One way that the mind affects the body can be seen when depression or stress results in illness, which proves that the mental state is causing the illness. Doctors are now treating these illnesses by treating the psychological problem.	• One sentence cannot contain two independent clauses as in (8) unless joined by the proper punctuation and/or sentence connector as in (9). • Do not include too many clauses in one sentence as in (10).

5.27 Editing Activity

DIRECTIONS: Correct the errors in the sentences below. Do not change anything that is already correct.

1. To play soccer, baseball, and hockey.
2. Because this is such an important meeting, I'm wearing nice.
3. The professor told about the experiments in cardiovascular improvement.
4. This new method of losing weight seems.
5. How many times you ran around the track?
6. How that concert was enjoyable!
7. After the game, the crowd left the parking lot in a very orderly fashion there were no problems.
8. Doctors they make me nervous.
9. Although many people haven't read this book.
10. After the lecture was over, where you went?

Composition Topics

1. Describe your diet and physical activities, and explain how they help you to stay healthy and fit.
2. Write a persuasive essay about the advantages and disadvantages of certain diets.
3. Describe a recent breakthrough or discovery in medicine and discuss its implications.

[xpanding Horizons

• Noun Clauses, Direct and Indirect Speech

DISCUSSION QUESTIONS

1. How do you gain knowledge? Through reading? direct experience? observation? introspection? from teachers? Is one way of knowing better than another? Is one method valued more in your culture than another?

2. Some people look to teachers, masters, or gurus to guide them through their lives. Have you ever done that? Describe such a person.

3. What are some of the events or experiences in a person's life that may mark the transition from childhood to adulthood? What are some other important transitions in a person's life?

OBJECTIVES

In this chapter you will learn:

1. To identify the function of noun clauses

2. To use proper punctuation and capitalization for direct speech

3. To report statements, questions, and imperatives using indirect speech

4. To use a variety of introductory noun clause verbs

5. To use the subjunctive form in noun clauses

Preview

DIRECTIONS: The following is an excerpt from the first lecture in an Introduction to Statistics class. The professor is discussing the process of investigation with the students.

How Do You Know What You Know?

I'd like you to take a minute and think about how you know what you know. As children, we are very curious and we want to know why and how things happen. When our parents or other adults give us an answer, we accept it. That is called hierarchical learning. What a trusted authority tells us is the truth.

As we get older, however, we need more proof. Then we may believe what scientists tell us. Scientists base their knowledge on something called the "scientific method." Most Western research is carried out in this way: scientists form a hypothesis, which they test in a controlled experiment, and which other scientists replicate. Scientists rarely talk about "truth" in absolute terms. Instead they use terms like "support for this" or "research indicates this."

In the past few decades, however, some people have criticized the scientific method. They say, "This method assumes that there is a single objective reality that we can know about." They point to the discovery in quantum physics that on an atomic scale, the observer is actually part of what he or she sees and helps to create what he or she observes. Therefore, atomic particles do not have properties which are independent of the observer.

Several scholars have suggested that people have different "ways of knowing." A female colleague told me that she found this to be true in her class last semester. She said that her female students were more interested in subjective truths and how people interact and that her male students were more interested in objective truths.

So as we learn more about the scientific method in this class, I would like you to think about its value and its limitations. Keep in mind that there may indeed be other ways of knowing.

FOCUS ON GRAMMAR

The following questions are based on the preview text and are designed to help you find out what you already know about the structures in this chapter. Some of the questions may be hard and some of them may be easy. Answer as many of the questions as you can. Work with a partner if your teacher tells you to do so.

1. Find the example of an exact record of what someone has said (that is, **direct speech**) in the lecture. Write that here. Note the punctuation.

2. The professor recounts something he heard from a female colleague. He uses **indirect speech.** Find that statement and rewrite it in direct speech, using quotation marks, paying careful attention to the punctuation.

_____

3. What is the direct object in this sentence from paragraph 2: "Then we may believe what the scientists tell us"?

_____

4. What is the subject of the following sentence from paragraph 1: "What a trusted authority tells us is the truth"?

_____

Grammatical Patterns Part One

I. Forms of Noun Clauses

A noun clause can replace a noun phrase or a pronoun in a sentence, as in the following examples (the nouns and noun clauses are in bold):

a. **Your paper** was excellent.
   noun phrase

b. **What you wrote** was excellent.
   noun clause

c. I read **it.**
   pronoun

d. I read **what you wrote.**
   noun clause

In (a) **your paper** is a noun phrase and the subject of the sentence; this is replaced by the noun clause **what you wrote** in (b). In (c) the pronoun **it** is the object of the sentence and it is replaced by the noun clause **what you wrote** in (d).

A noun clause consists of a connecting word (**CW**), a subject (**S**), and a verb (**V**) as follows:

- I read **what you wrote.**
       (CW) (S)   (V)

- **What you wrote** was excellent.
  (CW) (S)   (V)

Connecting Words
There are two types of connecting words.

Connecting Words	Example
1. that-connectors If **that** introduces the object of the verb, as in sentence (1), then it can be deleted.	1. Critics believe **(that) there isn't one objective truth.**
2. wh-connectors You cannot delete wh- connecting words. **what** . . . . **how/how much** . . . . **when** . . . . **whether/if** . . . . **where** . . . . **why**	2. Then we may believe **what the scientists tell us.** 3. Her students were interested in **how people interact.** 4. I don't know **when the universe began.** 5. I'm not sure **whether I'll be a black belt in karate.** 6. I don't know **where I should begin.** 7. I can't understand **why he didn't leave.**

II. Functions of Noun Clauses

A noun clause can have five grammatical functions in a sentence.

Function Of The Clause	Examples
1. As subject of the sentence A noun clause can replace the subject of a sentence, as in sentences (1)–(4). (The noun clause is in bold.)	1. **What a trusted authority tells us** is the truth. 2. **That he became a black belt** surprised his parents. 3. **Whether or not he'll pass his classes** is another question. 4. **Whoever misses the test** will fail.
2. As the complement of a sentence A complement comes after the verb **be** and other linking verbs (**seem, look, appear,** etc.).	5. It is exactly **how I pictured it.** 6. It seems **that he likes his school.**
3. As the object of the verb As the object of the verb, the noun clause (in bold) comes after the main verb in the sentence as in (7) and (8).	7. Scholars have suggested **that there are several ways of knowing.** 8. You can imagine **how difficult statistics is.**

Continued on next page.

Continued from previous page.

FUNCTION OF THE CLAUSE	EXAMPLES
4. As the object of a preposition Note how the noun clause comes after the preposition **about** in sentence (9).	9. Think about **what you know.**
5. As an appositive A noun clause completes the noun, **the fact,** and is introduced by the connecting word, **that.** Such appositives occur after abstract nouns like **fact, belief, idea, doubt,** etc.	10. The fact **that I preregistered** made all the difference. 11. The idea **that I would graduate soon** frightened me. 12. The belief **that the universe began with a "big bang"** is quite popular.

6.1 Recognition Drill: *Breaking Away*

DIRECTIONS: Read the following statements made by parents and children about the difficulty of breaking away. Underline the noun clauses and indicate their function in the sentence: S (subject), C (complement), OV (object of the verb), OP (object of a preposition), or A (appositive).

Example   CUE: I told my mother that I was moving out.
              ANSWER: I told my mother <u>that I was moving out</u>.

            FUNCTION: _____OV_____

1. The most difficult thing about living away from my parents is that I have to do my own cooking and cleaning! (Kathy)

   Function: _____

2. What I like the best is the freedom I have to make my own decisions. (Sara)

   Function: _____

3. My mother told me that I would miss her, and she was absolutely right! (Jeremy)

   Function: _____

4. The age at which children leave home depends on how mature they are. (Arnold)

   Function: _____

5. The fact that my children want to live with me during their college years doesn't mean that they are weak or immature. (a mother)

   Function: _____

   Function: _____

6. I want whatever is best for my kids. If they are ready to leave, then they should have the freedom to do so. (a father)

   Function: _____

6.2 Recognition Drill: *Identifying Noun Clauses*

DIRECTIONS: Read the following letter that Jack wrote to his friend, Roberto, after his first week at a community college. Underline the noun clauses and indicate their function in the sentence: **S** (subject), **C** (complement), **OV** (object of the verb), **OP** (object of a preposition), or **A** (appositive). The first one has been done for you.

Dear Roberto,

1 The first week of college is over and I can tell you <u>it really wasn't easy</u>. I never thought that it would be so difficult to work and go to school. I miss our high school days so much. What I miss the most are the basketball games—our families cheering and our friends screaming. You can imagine how competitive sports are here.

object of the verb

2 The **campus** is modern. The professors are exactly how I **pictured** them—middle-aged, with beards and glasses! The people in my classes are **pretty friendly.** There was a party for new students this weekend and my classmate introduced me to many of his friends. "Jack was the star player on his basketball team in high school," he said to all the women he knew. I told him later that he had embarrassed me.

3 I got into all the classes I wanted. The fact that I had **preregistered** last spring made all the difference. Some of the other first-year students didn't do that and now they're **stuck with dud** classes.

4 Well, I'd better do some studying now. I hope that I can go to **homecoming weekend** at Wilson High. It all depends on how much work I have. I hope you will come to town. I miss you a lot! I'm sure the second week will be better. Don't worry!!

See ya,

Jack

Jack

Vocabulary

campus: the land and buildings of a school
to picture: to imagine how something looks
pretty friendly: very friendly (informal)
to preregister: to sign up ahead of time
to be stuck with something: to end up with something that is less than desirable and hard or impossible to change
dud: not exciting (informal)
homecoming weekend: a high school or college weekend for former students who come back for the occasion

6.3 Paired Activity: *Leaving Home*

DIRECTIONS: Do you think that young adults (ages 18–22) should be encouraged to leave home and live on their own? Do you think that they will grow up faster and be stronger individuals if they do? If they choose to stay with their parents, should they pay for room and board or should everything be given to them? At what age should a parent suggest his or her child break away and live independently?

Discuss these questions in pairs or small groups. Then write several sentences based on your discussion, using the five types of clauses listed on pages 118–119. Underline the clauses and identify their functions in the sentence.

III. Direct Speech

When repeating a person's words exactly, use **direct** (or quoted) **speech**. Note the punctuation, capitalization, and use of quotation marks (" ") in the following examples of direct speech, which reflect some people's ideas about breaking away.

TYPE OF QUOTATION	EXAMPLE
Statements • The period (.) comes at the end of the entire sentence, not the quote as in (1). • If the end of the sentence and the end of the quote are the same, then the period appears inside the quotation marks as in (2).	1. "What I like the best is having the freedom to make my own decisions," Sara said. 2. Sara said, "What I like the best is having the freedom to make my own decisions."
Questions/Exclamations • The (?) and (!) come at the end of the quote, not the sentence as in (3) and (4). Put a period at the end of the sentence. • The (?) comes at the end of the sentence and inside the quotation marks when the end of the quote is also the end of the sentence as in (5).	3. "My mother told me I would miss her, and she was absolutely right!" Jeremy exclaimed. 4. "Didn't you think you would miss your family?" her sister asked. 5. His sister asked, "Didn't you think you would miss your family?"
One sentence, separated • Insert commas before and after *Kathy said* and do not capitalize the second part of the sentence.	6 "The most difficult thing about living away from my parents," Kathy said, "is that I have to do my own cooking and cleaning."
Two sentences, separated • Place the period after *one father said.* Capitalize the first word of the second sentence.	7. "I want to do whatever is best for my kids," one father said. "If they are ready to leave, then they should have the freedom to do so."

6.4 Written Activity: *Punctuating Quotations*

DIRECTIONS: Read the following well-known quotations and rewrite them using proper punctuation, capitalization, and quotation marks.

1. To be or not to be Hamlet stated that is the question.

_____

_____

_____

2. Those who lack belief Lao Tzu said will not in turn be believed.

_____

_____

_____

3. I think therefore I am wrote Descartes.

_____

_____

_____

4. The great question that has never been answered Sigmund Freud is noted as saying and which I have not yet been able to answer despite my thirty years of research into the feminine soul is: what does a woman want?

_____

_____

_____

5. Mankind must put an end to war John F Kennedy once said or war will put an end to mankind.

_____

_____

_____

6. Mark Twain is noted for saying put all your eggs in one basket and then he added and watch that basket!

_____

_____

_____

7. We are here on earth to do good to others W.H. Auden stated what the others are here for, I don't know he added humorously

---

8. A Japanese proverb goes like this Fall seven times Stand up eight

---

9. Advice Erica Jong wrote is what we ask for when we already know the answer but wish we didn't

---

10. There is more to life than increasing its speed Gandhi once said

---

6.5 Written Activity: *A Memorable Conversation*

DIRECTIONS: Reconstruct a memorable conversation from your past with a person who gave you guidance or advice. Record the conversation in writing using direct speech and the appropriate punctuation. Indent the first line of each new speaker as follows:

"What should I do about the job offer?" Steve asked Patricia.

"Why don't you think about it for a day," she answered. "That will give you some time to sort things out."

"You're right. I don't have to make the decision today," John said.

IV. Reporting Speech

To report speech after a certain time has passed, use **indirect speech** and follow these guidelines:

1. Do not use quotation marks.
2. Change the verb to a past tense, if possible.
3. Change the pronouns and adverbs to show that it is reported, not quoted, speech.
4. Use an appropriate introductory clause verb (say, tell, answer, ask, etc.).

A. Reporting Statements

DIRECT SPEECH	INDIRECT SPEECH
Change the verb to a past form when reporting direct speech. Past perfect verbs (e.g., sentences 6 and 8 below) do not change. Begin the sentence by naming the speaker.	
1. "I **want** to attend a U.S. university," John said.	1. John said that he **wanted** to attend a U.S. university.
2. "I **am looking** for a program in computer science," John said.	2. John said that he **was looking** for a program in computer science.
3. "I **sent** away for the program description," John said.	3. John said that he **had sent** away for the program description.
4. "I was **thinking** about starting this September," John said.	4. John said that he **had been thinking** about starting that September.
5. "I **haven't filled out** the application form yet," John said.	5. John said that he **hadn't filled out** the application form by that time.
6. "I **had written** the statement of purpose before," John said.	6. John said that he **had written** the statement of purpose before.
7. "I **will apply** for my visa tomorrow," John said.	7. John said that he **would apply** for his visa the following day.
8. "I **had been writing** for two hours when the electricity went out," John said.	8. John said that he **had been writing** for two hours when the electricity went out.
Note how **modals** change their form when reporting direct speech.*	
9. "My academic counselor **can help** me with the paperwork," John said.	9. John said that the academic counselor **could help** him with the paperwork.
10. "The Consul **may be** available now," the receptionist said. (possibility)	10. The receptionist said that the consul **might be** available then. (possibility)
11. "You **may go** in now," the receptionist said. (permission)	11. The receptionist said that he **could go** in at that time. (permission) .
12. "You **must bring** 3 photographs," the receptionist said.	12. The receptionist said that he **had to bring** 3 photographs.
The following modals **do not change their form.**	
13. "I **couldn't come** yesterday because of my work schedule," John said.	13. John said he **hadn't been able to come** the day before because of his work schedule.
14. "I **should ask** my bank for the financial statement," John said.	14. John said that he **should ask** his bank for the financial statement.
15. "The bank **couldn't have sent** the documents yet," John said.	15. John said that the bank **couldn't have sent** the documents by that time.
16. "I **shouldn't have waited** so long," John said.	16. John said that he **shouldn't have waited** so long.

*See Chapter 12 for more details on modals.

6.6 Written Activity: *Reporting Statements*

DIRECTIONS: The generation born between 1948 and 1964, called the baby boomers, has been labeled the "Me Generation" because of their excessive concern with themselves and their own happiness. When Joanne, a baby boomer, began feeling that her life was empty, she went on a quest for meaning and spoke to many people to help her. She got a lot of advice. Below is the direct speech of the advice people gave her. Change that into reported speech using the sequence of tenses outlined in the chart above.

Here is the advice Joanne received:

1. Guru Atmananda: "You have squandered your life on the acquisition of material things. You need to let go of your attachments and find inner peace."

   _____

   _____

2. Her mother: "Joanne, honey, you will be a lot happier if you settle down and have a family."

   _____

   _____

3. Her advisor at school: "I had a similar experience when I was your age. I was looking for the perfect life. When I realized that I would never find it, I applied to graduate school to get my Ph.D. You should do the same thing."

   _____

   _____

4. Her psychiatrist: "You may just be depressed and have a serotonin deficiency. You can take antidepressant medication and you will probably feel much better."

   _____

   _____

5. Her best friend: "You've been working too hard. You shouldn't have taken on that new position at work. You could take a vacation."

   _____

   _____

6. Her boyfriend: "You had been feeling this way when I met you. I think it must be your personality. You need to accept yourself."

   _____

   _____

SPECIAL NOTE

ADVERB AND PRONOUN CHANGES IN REPORTING SPEECH

Pronouns and adverbs of time and place must also be changed when you report direct speech. Here are some of the most common changes.

DIRECT SPEECH	INDIRECT SPEECH
Changes in adverbs:	
yet	by that time
today	that day
tomorrow	the next day/the following day/a day later
yesterday	the day before/the previous day
last week/month, etc.	the previous week/the week before
this week/month, etc.	that week
next week/month, etc.	the following week/the next week/a week later
now	then/at that time
this	that
these	those

Changes in pronouns:

"I will write to **my** mother," John said.	John said that **he** would write to his mother.
"**You** can always call **me** collect," Sarah told John.	Sarah told John that he could always call **her** collect.
"**We** will miss **you**!" John's sisters told him.	John's sisters told him that **they** would miss **him**.

6.7 Oral Drill: *Reporting Statements*

DIRECTIONS: A group of students in an English class were talking about the difficulties of learning a second language. Report their statements using the sequence of tenses just listed.

Example   CUE: "I feel like a baby every time I come into my English class," Lise said.
           ANSWER: Lise said that she felt like a baby every time she went into her English class.

1. "I've been studying English for six years and I still can't get the tenses right!" Paolo said.

2. "When I'm writing, I can get the grammar right. But when I'm speaking, it's impossible," said Mariko.

3. "Yesterday, I was talking to the airlines on the phone and I understood nothing!" said Pietro.

4. "Even though the classes in this school are terrific, we really need contact with Americans," said Fattaneh.

5. "Tomorrow I'll take the TOEFL exam. I wonder if I will get the score I need," Ali said.

6. "Pronunciation is the problem for me. I tried to order lunch today at the restaurant and the waiter couldn't understand me. I was really embarrassed," said Than.

7. "I love learning English grammar. It's so logical!" said Heidi.

8. "All I know is that I must study harder," said Takashi.

9. "Last week I had trouble with verb tenses. This week I'm having trouble with pronouns!" said Francoise.

10. "I just can't spell in English. I should take a course in spelling," said Ibrahim.

11. What are your problems in learning English? Share them with a partner and then report your partner's problems to the class.

■ B. Reporting Questions

Follow these guidelines when reporting questions:

1. Use statement, not question, word order in the indirect speech.
2. For *yes/no* questions, use **if** or **whether** as the connecting word.
3. For *wh*-questions, retain the appropriate *wh*-word (what, where, etc.).
4. Use an appropriate introductory clause verb (ask, inquire, etc.).

NOTES	DIRECT SPEECH	INDIRECT SPEECH
Reporting **Yes/No** questions: • Use **if** or **whether** as connecting words. • Use statement word order in indirect speech. • Use a past form of the verb in indirect speech.	"**Do** you **have** your passport with you?" the receptionist asked John. "**Have** you **been** to this office before?" the receptionist asked John.	The receptionist asked John **if** he **had** his passport with him. The receptionist asked John **whether** he **had** been to that office before.
Reporting **Wh**-questions: • Keep the **wh**-connecting word in the indirect speech. • Use statement word order.	"**Where should I pay** for my visa?" John asked the receptionist. "**Where is** the cashier's desk?" John asked the receptionist. "**How can I apply?**" John asked. "**When did** you **send** us the form?" the receptionist asked John.	John asked the receptionist **where** he **should pay** for his visa. John asked the receptionist **where the cashier's desk was.** John asked **how he could apply.** The receptionist asked John **when he sent them the form.**

6.8 Oral Activity: *Reporting Questions*

DIRECTIONS: Making decisions about professional life can be difficult, so some people go to career counselors for help. Here are some questions people ask career counselors. Imagine that you are the career counselor, and report the following questions using indirect speech and the sequence of tenses outlined above. Then offer an answer to the question.

Example   CUE: "Do I need a college education to get a good job?" (Gloria)
ANSWER: Gloria asked me if she needed a college education to get a good job, and I told her that it wasn't necessary but it was recommended.

1. "Where can I find jobs in my field?" (Bob)
2. "Can I have a successful career and a family too?" (Sally)
3. "Where are the best jobs?" (Jennifer)
4. "How can I write a good resumé?" (George)
5. "What will be the fastest growing jobs in the future?" (Linda)
6. "How should I ask my boss for a raise?" (Gary)
7. "How can I find out what my skills are?" (Kim)
8. "Do I need a degree in business to start my own business?" (Fred)
9. "Did I make a mistake by leaving my first job after one year?" (Louise)
10. "Is it possible to work in the same office as my spouse?" (Teresa)

■ C. Indirect Questions

Note how a question can be embedded in a sentence by using a noun clause. In this case, you are not reporting speech, just including the question in a statement. Therefore, use statement word order and do not change the verb tense.

QUESTION	INDIRECT QUESTION (NOUN CLAUSE)

1. What *is* the *population* of China? . . . .
   (verb)   (subject)
	1. I don't know what the *population* of China *is*.
	   (subject) (verb)

2. What does **vendetta mean?**	2. I'm not sure **what vendetta means.**
3. Whose **book is** this?	3. I can't say **whose book this is.**

6.9 Paired Activity: *How Much Do You Know?*

DIRECTIONS: Work in pairs. Take turns formulating questions about the following information. Begin your question with the **wh-word** in parentheses. Use *I don't know* or a similar phrase if you can't answer your partner's question. Do not shift to a past tense.

Example   CUE: the fifth president of the United States (who)
STUDENT A: Who was the fifth president of the United States?
STUDENT B: I don't know who the fifth president of the United States was.

STUDENT A:

1. the author of *The Old Man and the Sea* (who)
2. The president of Thailand (who)

3. [the meaning of] *leap year* (what does)

4. Universal Studios (where)

5. [the meaning of] *gangrene* (what does)

6. the capital city of the state of Nebraska (what)

STUDENT B:

1. the winner of the Nobel Peace Prize in 1989 (who)

2. the population of the world (what)

3. [the meaning of] *get off my back* (what does)

4. Flagstaff (where)

5. the next president of your country (who)

6. the distance between Vancouver, B.C. and Miami, Florida (what)

D. Reporting Imperatives

You can report imperative statements in two ways.

IMPERATIVE DIRECT SPEECH	INDIRECT SPEECH/ INFINITIVE	INDIRECT SPEECH/ NOUN CLAUSE + MODAL
1. "Complete this assignment for homework," the teacher told the students.	1. The teacher told the students **to complete** the assignment for homework.	1. The teacher told the students **that they should complete the assignment for homework.** (Use the modals **should, had to, ought to, had better**.)
Negative Imperatives: 2. "Don't do exercise 12," she added.	2. The teacher told the students **not to do** exercise 12.	2. The teacher told the students **that they shouldn't do exercise 12.**

6.10 Oral Drill: *Reporting Imperatives*

DIRECTIONS: Report the following imperative statements in the two ways just outlined. Use **told** when you report and imagine who might have given that imperative.

Example   CUE: "Be quiet!"
           ANSWER: (infinitive): The librarian told the students to be quiet.
                   (modal): The librarian told the students that they should be quiet.

1. "Clean up your room!"

2. "Type up this report!"

3. "Don't come late anymore!"

4. "Stand up straight!"

5. "Don't forget my birthday!"

6. "Take out your passport!"

7. "Stop smoking!"

8. "Get me the newspaper!"

9. "Get in line!"

10. "Don't turn away when I'm talking to you!"

11. Practice giving and reporting commands with your classmates.

SPECIAL NOTE

SAY AND TELL

Note how **SAY** and **TELL** are used differently.

I. Say is followed by a noun clause. (To + indirect object can follow **say**, but it is not common):

- She said (to me) <u>that she was leaving.</u>
  noun-clause

2. Tell is always followed by an indirect object (IO) and a **noun** clause.

- She told **me** <u>(that) she was leaving.</u>
  IO   noun-clause

3. Tell is usually used with imperatives and is followed by an indirect object (IO) + infinitive.

- She told **me** <u>to go.</u>
  IO   infinitive

6.11 Paired Activity: *Reporting Imperatives*

DIRECTIONS: Choose one of the following situations to discuss with your partner. Write down the solutions to the problem presented that you and your partner decide upon. Write them in two ways: (a) using a modal and (b) using an infinitive. (See the chart on page 129 for assistance.)

Example   Jack told me that he hated American food and I told him **to learn** to cook. (infinitive)
Jack told me that he hated American food and I told him he **should learn** to cook. (modal)

SITUATION A: You and your partner are living in a new city. You are having difficulty adjusting to this new place and are not at all happy. Take turns with your partner stating your problems and offering solutions. Be ready to write down or report your conversation orally using both an infinitive and modal form, as shown in the examples above.

SITUATION B: Sotha is a Cambodian immigrant who is very confused about her future. She wants to go to school and work at a job before she gets married and has a family. Her mother agrees with her, but her boyfriend is eager to get married now. Sotha loves her boyfriend, but she is worried that she will not finish college if she gets married now. With your partner, decide on five things Sotha can do to make her decision easier. Then be ready to report your advice using both an infinitive and modal form.

6.12 Error Analysis: *Indirect Speech*

DIRECTIONS: Read the following sentences written by students and find any errors in direct and indirect speech. Correct the errors clearly.

1. When I first came to the United States, the customs man said me since I was a tourist that I didn't need a visa. Two weeks later, immigration stopped me and asked me where was my visa? I told him that immigration tells me I don't need one. Then he asked me whether if I knew that I can't be in this country without a visa and that did I want to go back to my own country.

2. The most memorable conversation I have ever had was with my father before he passed away. Two days before he died, he said me that he loved me very much, and that would I take care of my younger sister. I assured him that I would do that, and then he asked me whether was I happy today. I replied that I was very happy to be his son, but I was very sad to see him sick.

3. My most memorable conversation was with my boyfriend, who is now my husband. I remember when he asked me would I marry him. I told him yes I would. When he asked me when did I want to get married, I told him I think we should do it right away! And we did.

V. Reporting Connected Discourse

A. Reporting Phrases and Exclamations

Note how the following phrases and exclamations are reported in indirect speech.

DIRECT SPEECH	INDIRECT SPEECH
"Hello!"	She greeted him.
"What a nice day!	She exclaimed that it was a nice day.
"No."	She refused./She disagreed.
"Yes."	She accepted. She agreed.
"Sure."	She agreed (enthusiastically, hesitantly, etc.)
"I'd love to go with you!"	She accepted the invitation.
"Thank you."	She thanked him.

B. Reporting Several Statements by One Speaker

When you are telling a story or reporting extended discourse, it is important to link the many ideas or statements logically and concisely. Note how this has been done below.

DIRECT SPEECH	INDIRECT SPEECH
1. "We would love to send Martha away for college. We just can't afford it," Mrs. White said.	Mrs. White said that they would love to send Martha away for college **but that** they just couldn't afford it.
2. "Is it possible for Martha to get a scholarship for the tuition? Then we could afford the room and board," Mrs. White told the college counselor.	She asked if it was possible for Martha to get a scholarship for the tuition **because in that case** they could afford the room and board.
3. "Yes, it is possible to get a scholarship. There are many possible sources of funding," the college counselor said.	The college counselor told Mrs. White that it was possible to get a scholarship **and that** there were many possible sources of funding.

6.13 Written Activity: *A Memorable Conversation*

DIRECTIONS: Report the memorable conversation that you wrote in direct speech on page 112 earlier in the chapter. Use indirect speech and a variety of introductory clause verbs.

6.14 Paired Oral Activity: *Roleplay*

DIRECTIONS: Create a short dialogue based on one of the following situations. Then present it to the class. Have your classmates reconstruct the dialogue using connected discourse.

1. A teacher catches her student cheating on a final exam.
2. Your friend asks you about living and studying in the United States.
3. You're at the Canada–U.S. border, trying to come back into the United States. Your realize that you have forgotten your passport. Create a dialogue between you and the Immigration Officer.
4. Create your own situation.

6.15 Oral Activity: *Reporting Connected Discourse*

DIRECTIONS: Work in groups of three. While two of the students are discussing one of the following topics, the other student will take notes of the conversation. After 5–10 minutes, switch roles and discuss another question. After each student has had a turn to take notes, report the discussion in writing or orally, as instructed by your teacher.

1. Should young children (ages 3–6) be enrolled in a school and be taught skills to prepare them for elementary school, or should they simply be allowed to play without structure? Why?
2. Should adolescents (ages 12–16) be allowed to choose their school and leisure activities (for example, music, sports, etc.), or should they follow their parents' desires? Why?
3. Should high school students who are planning on studying science at a university be required to study language and literature? Should language and literature students be required to study science? Why?
4. Should international students be required to have a 550 TOEFL score in order to be admitted to a U.S. university, or should each school have its own entrance exam? Why?

Grammatical Patterns Part Two

Preview

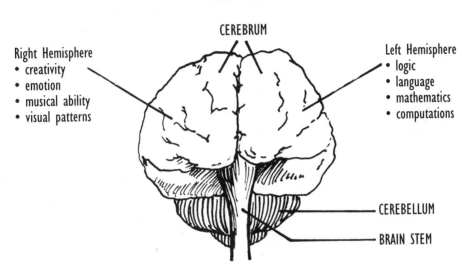

CEREBRUM

Right Hemisphere
• creativity
• emotion
• musical ability
• visual patterns

Left Hemisphere
• logic
• language
• mathematics
• computations

CEREBELLUM

BRAIN STEM

DIRECTIONS: Do you know the difference between the right and left brain? Read the following lecture on this distinction, given in a university psychology class. Then answer the questions that follow.

1 "In our last meeting, I told you that two facts regarding the brain have recently become apparent. **2** First, the brain has two parts, called *hemispheres,* which function independently. **3** Second, each hemisphere interprets the world through distinctly different processes. **4** Today we will look at how each hemisphere functions.

5 "That the left brain processes information in a linear and logical way is one of the most basic differences. **6** The left brain draws on rules. **7** Thus, yesterday when I prepared my lecture, I made an outline of the talk. **8** I used my left brain to organize the information in a clear and logical way.

9 "The right brain, on the other hand, is the creative hemisphere. **10** It processes information simultaneously and is able to relate that information. **11** My daughter used her right brain last week when she painted a picture of our house.

12 "Tomorrow we'll see how the two hemispheres talk to each other.

13 Why don't you review chapter 6 in the textbook before class? **14** There'll probably be some difficult terminology. **15** It's essential that you be very familiar with the technical terminology. OK. See you next week. Have a good weekend!"

FOCUS ON GRAMMAR

The following questions are based on the preview text and are designed to help you find out what you already know about the structures in this chapter. Some of the questions may be hard and some of them may be easy. Answer as many of the questions as you can. Work with a partner if your teacher tells you to do so.

1. What is the subject of sentence 5? _____
   Rewrite sentence 5, beginning your sentence with "One of the most basic . . ."

   One of the most basic differences _____

   _____

   Which of the two sentences would you most hear in an informal conversation?

   _____

2. What is unusual about one of the verbs in sentence 15?

   _____

   Can you explain why a special form of the verb is used in this sentence?

   _____

3. Imagine that one of your classmates was sick and asked you to report what the professor said.

   a. For sentence 9, which verb tense would you use in indirect speech? _____

      Why? _____

   b. In sentence 13, what is the meaning of "Why don't you . . .?"

      _____

      How would you report that statement?

      _____

I. Special Considerations in Indirect Speech

Native speakers do not always follow the sequence of tenses listed in the chart on page 124. There are many factors to consider that influence this choice, which are discussed below. In some cases, a change in the tense of the verb is optional in indirect speech. At other times, a specific change is **not possible.**

A. Optional Cases

It is not necessary to change the verb tense in the following cases. However, it is always grammatically correct to do so.

FACTORS TO CONSIDER	**EXAMPLE**
1. Immediate Reporting It is not necessary to change the verb when the speech is reported **immediately.**	**A:** I hate this professor's voice. **B:** What did you say? **A:** I said that I **hate (hated)** this professor's voice.
2. Factual or Accepted Information If the information is **factual** or **generally accepted,** you may use the present tense in the reported speech.	• The professor said that water **freezes (froze)** at 32 degrees F.
3. Habitual Activity, Still True If the information is related to **habitual action,** and is still true at the moment of reporting, you may use the present tense in the reported speech.	• She said she **writes (wrote)** to her boyfriend daily.
4. Informal Speech, Past Tense • In **informal** conversation, speakers often do not change the past to a past perfect form. • In **formal** English, it is best to change a past verb to a past perfect form.	• "I had a great time at the party," Corinne said. Corinne said she **had (had had)** a great time at the party. • The lecturer stated that there **had been** many causes of the economic recession.

6.16 Oral Activity: *Optional Cases*

DIRECTIONS: Match the quote with the probable speaker. Then report the speech. Indicate when it is necessary to change the verb tense.

1. "Intelligence is 70% genetically determined and 30% environmentally determined."

2. "I can't come to the phone right now because I'm in the shower."

3. "Did you have a hard day at work?"

4. "You must learn how to control your eating habits."

5. "I've been working out at the gym about once a week."

6. "We've been to Tokyo three times."

7. "The 1980s was a decade of unprecedented buying."

a. Maria told her roommate to tell her friend on the phone

b. The newscaster claimed

c. The doctor told the patient

d. The husband asked his wife

e. The neighbor boasted

f. The patient told the doctor

g. The psychology teacher stated

B. Other Cases

Note that the following cases do not follow the sequence of tenses for reported speech that appears in the chart on page 135.

FACTORS TO CONSIDER	EXAMPLE
1. Requests and Suggestions If the direct speech is a **request, suggestion,** or **order,** the reported speech must express that.[a] • In (a), for example, you do not report the "why don't you" as "why didn't you" because the intention of the author is to make a suggestion. • In (b), it would not be accurate to report the direct speech as "The judge said he wanted . . ." since the judge is really issuing an order, not simply saying what he wants.	**a.** "Why don't you take me to a nice restaurant?" the woman asked the man. *(request)* • The woman asked the man if he would take her to a nice restaurant. • The woman suggested that the man take her to a nice restaurant. **b.** "I want order in this courtroom!" the judge said. *(order)* • The judge **insisted that there be order** in the courtroom.[b]
2. Future Time If a simple present or present progressive verb form is used to express future time, report the speech using *would* (and not a past form of the verb.)	**c.** "The train leaves at 6:00 P.M. tomorrow," the man said. • The man said that the train **would leave** at 6:00 P.M. the next day.
3. Introductory Verb in Present If the verb introducing the noun clause is in the present tense (e.g., **says** in d), do not change the verb tense in reported speech. A present tense is often used to report statements which a person makes regularly, as in (e).	**d.** The president **says** he will increase funds for education. **e.** Gloria **says** she **loves** her husband.

[a]See Section II on page 137 on **The Subjunctive Form After Expressions of Urgency** for more explanation.
[b]See the detailed list of these verbs on page 137.

6.17 Paired Activity: *Optional and Other Cases*

DIRECTIONS: Work in pairs. Cover your partner's side of the page. Student B asks Student A the questions and Student A finds the appropriate quote and reports the speech. Then switch roles. Change to a past form **only when necessary.**

STUDENT A

1. "You need to buy some new clothes."
2. "Why don't you make dinner tonight, dear."
3. "I'll be 40 years old in two more months!"
4. "I want everyone to be on time for class tomorrow!"
5. "I'm never getting married."

STUDENT B

a. What did the angry teacher say to her students?
b. What did Jack say to his best friend?
c. What did Bob say to his mother?
d. What does Sandra's mother say to her every time she sees her?
e. What did the wife suggest to her husband?

Now switch roles

6. What did George's mother relate to her neighbor?

7. What do presidents always say before getting elected?

8. What did Jackie's Japanese roommate say?

9. What did the doctor suggest to his patient?

10. What did the student ask her teacher?

a. "When does the TOEFL exam start?"

b. "George got a 4.0 grade point average after his first semester."

c. "I promise to reduce taxes this year."

d. "I always take my shoes off before going into someone's home."

e. "How about losing 20 pounds?"

II. The Subjunctive Form After Expressions of Urgency

In the Preview text to Grammatical Patterns Part Two (page 133), the professor states:

> **"It's essential that you be very familiar with the technical terminology."**

The professor wants to stress the importance of knowing the technical terms, so he uses **an expression of urgency** at the beginning of the sentence. When you do this, the verb form after that expression is in the **simple form.** As you will remember, the simple form of the verb is the infinitive without **to.** This is called the subjunctive form of the verb. Normally, you would say "you are," but in this case you would say "you be" because it follows the expression of urgency.

NOTES	VERBS OF URGENCY
• Use the simple form of a verb (the infinitive form without **to**) after the expressions of urgency listed in the opposite column. • Pay careful attention to the form of the third person singular (he, she, it)—**no third person singular -s.**	It is **essential that** she **take** science classes. Other expressions that follow a similar pattern: **important that** **urgent that** **crucial that** **vital that** **desirable that** **best that** **imperative that** **recommended that** **necessary that**
• When forming a negative with these expressions, place **not** before the simple form of the verb.	• It is **essential** that she **not** fail any courses. • It is **vital** that she **not** miss any sessions.

6.18 Oral Drill: *Expressions of Urgency*

DIRECTIONS: Choose three of the following questions to answer using an expression of urgency and a noun clause. Choose the expression of urgency that seems most appropriate. (Refer to the list in the chart above.) Be ready to answer when your teacher calls on you.

Example   CUE: Your sister wants to get into a good university. What must she do?
ANSWER: It is essential that she have a good academic record.

1. Jane is having problems adjusting to life in a big city. What should she do?
2. Robert is worried because he can't seem to make friends in his office. What can he do?
3. Terry just found out that one of his colleagues has been stealing from the shop. What would you tell him?
4. If you want to have a successful party, what must you do?
5. If you want to have a successful job interview, what should you not do?
6. What should you do (or not do) to be healthy?
7. Bob is 40 years old and still single. He'd like to get married. Give him some advice.
8. What should be done to save the environment?

■ III. The Subjunctive Form After Verbs of Request

Use the following verbs to make a strong request. Note the use of the simple form of the verb (the subjunctive form) after these verbs of request.

FORM	VERBS OF REQUEST

The Subjunctive Form
• Use the simple form of a verb (the infinitive without **to**) after verbs of request [e.g., **set** in (1)].
• Pay special attention to the form of the third person singular (he, she, it)
• When forming the negative with these verbs, place not before the simple form of the verb as in (2).
	1. The psychologist **suggested** that **she set** some specific goals for her son.
	2. The psychologist **recommended** that she **not** spank her son.
	Other verbs of request which follow the same pattern (arranged from weak to strong):
	
	    suggested **desired**
	    advised **urged**
	    proposed **insisted**
	    asked **demanded**
	    requested **commanded**

Reporting Verbs of Urgency and Request • When reporting a verb of urgency or request in indirect speech, keep the subjunctive form; that is, do not change the verb to a past form. Note that in (3) and (4) the verb **(have)** is the same. • Note the position of **not** in the indirect speech in sentence (6).	3. "It is best that my wife have her own career." (direct) 4. The husband said it was best that his wife **have** her own career. (indirect) 5. "It is important that she not give up her career." (direct) 6. He said that it was important that she **not give up** her own career. (indirect)

6.19 Written Activity: *The Subjunctive Form*

DIRECTIONS: Choose one of the following situations and write a letter outlining the problem and making recommendations. Use sentences with verbs of request and expressions of urgency.

1. You are the manager of a small store. Recently, one of your employees has been quite negligent in her work and even rude to the customers. You would like to terminate her, but she is a friend of the store owner. Write a letter to the boss, explaining your situation and making some recommendations.

2. You are a junior high school teacher. One of your students, Mark, has been acting up in class and exhibiting quite disruptive behavior. You know that Mark is a very smart student and capable of doing excellent work. You think he is under the influence of some irresponsible students at school. You suspect that his home life is not a happy one. Write a letter to the guidance counselor of the school, describing the problem and making some recommendations.

IV. Reduction of Noun Clauses

Compare the following sentences, which have the same meaning but different forms.

a. It is important that she take science classes. (*more formal, written—for example, a written evaluation by the daughter's teacher intended for the parents*)

b. It is important for her to take science classes. (*informal, conversational—for example, parents talking to each other about their daughter*)

Note that sentence (b) is a **reduction** of sentence (a). The clause **that she take science classes** becomes a phrase **for her to take science classes.**

Other noun clauses can also be reduced to phrases, and the chart below summarizes this. (See Chapter 14 for more details on this topic.)

CLAUSE REDUCTION	EXPLANATION
1. It is best { **that she change her job.** / for her **to change her job.** } 2. The psychologist suggested { **that she quit.** / **to her to quit.** }	• Noun clauses after verbs of request and urgency (e.g., (1) and (2) opposite) can be reduced to infinitive phrases.
3. I don't understand { **what I have to do.** / **what to do.** } 4. I don't know { **when I should go.** / **when to go.** }	• In (3) and (4), the noun clause is the object of the verb in the sentence. In this case, you can reduce the clause to an infinitive phrase but keep the **wh-** word. You will not keep the modal (e.g., have to, should).
5. He told me { **what I should not do.** / **what not to do.** }	• In (5) note the position of **not** in the reduced clause.

6.20 Oral Activity: *Reduction of Noun Clauses*

DIRECTIONS: Read the following situations and make a statement about them by using a reduced noun clause.

Example   CUE: John is in the middle of a busy intersection in a foreign city. He is looking at all the street names. He has a confused look on his face.
ANSWER: He's lost and he doesn't know **where to go.**

1. Suzanne is in her room looking at all her clothes strewn on her bed. Her date is arriving in ten minutes but she still hasn't gotten dressed.
2. Joe has gained a lot of weight. He went to the doctor to get some advice.
3. Kyoko has six brochures on her desk about English-speaking schools in the United States. She must make a decision, but she is not sure which school is the best.
4. Kim and Blake want to adopt a child. They don't know a lot about the procedure, so they went to a lawyer.
5. Benny is failing his economics class. He went to talk to the professor.
6. Emory forgot the time of his dental appointment.
7. Jane is new in town. She's not sure about the stores. She needs to buy a new dress.
8. My dog has fleas. Help!
9. I can't stop smoking. Please give me some advice.
10. Turn to your partner and share a problem you have. Then offer advice to each other.

V. Noun Clauses in Subject Position

Note the following uses of noun clauses in subject position.

USE OF NOUN CLAUSE	EXAMPLE
Stalling for Time • If you wish to gain a little time before answering a difficult question, rephrase it as a noun clause and place it at the beginning of the answer. • Use **whether** for **yes/no** questions as in (2).	1. Mother: What did you do while I was gone? Son: **What I did while you were gone** is a long story! 2. Did you pay a lot of money for your house? **Whether I paid a lot of money for my house** is not important.
Academic/Formal English Placing the noun clause at the beginning of the sentence creates a more formal, academic sentence.	*Informal:* It is obvious that mental well-being is linked to physical health. *Formal:* **That mental well-being is linked to physical health** is obvious.

6.21 Rapid Drill: *Avoiding Personal Questions*

DIRECTIONS: The following questions are very personal and would probably cause embarrassment to any American. To avoid answering such nosy questions, transform each question into a noun clause and place it in subject position. Use the following expressions to help you avoid answering the questions.

How old I am is . . . $\begin{cases} \text{none of your business.} \\ \text{not important.} \\ \text{confidential.} \\ \text{not an issue.} \\ \text{not your problem.} \\ \text{etc.} \end{cases}$

Example   QUESTION: How old are you?
POSSIBLE RESPONSE: **How old I am** is quite frankly none of your concern.

1. How much money does your father make?
2. How much do you weigh?
3. Are your parents divorced?
4. What's your I.Q.?
5. How many friends do you have?
6. When was your first kiss?
7. What did you get on the last grammar test?
8. Are you religious?
9. Are you planning on getting married?
10. Did you take a shower this morning?

Now *you* ask your teacher some personal questions.

11. _____

12. _____

6.22 Written Activity: *Noun Clause in Subject Position*

DIRECTIONS: Read the following text on the human potential movement in the United States to find out what a mind gym is. Then answer the questions that follow.

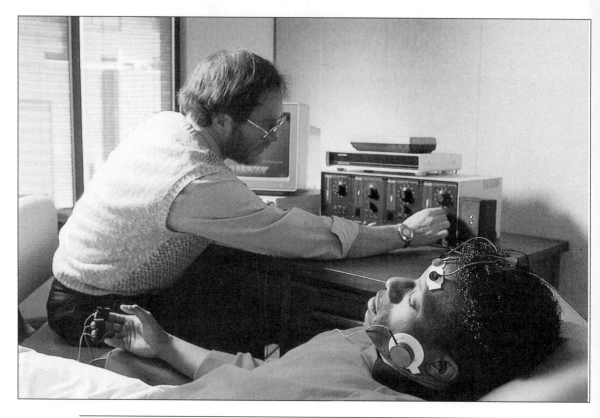

The Human Potential Movement

The human potential movement was an important trend in the United States that started over a quarter of a century ago and still plays an important role in the lives of many Americans today. This movement focused on the spiritual and creative development of the individual. Groups formed to help people explore their inner feelings communally. New approaches to treating the emotional and psychological problems of individuals emerged. Americans were caught up in a desire to achieve complete happiness and fulfillment. Encounter groups, T-sessions, Gestalt therapy, Past Life therapy—these are only a few of the types of activities that flourished during this time.

Today, we see vestiges of the movement in such innovations as a mind gym. A mind gym is exactly what it sounds like: a place to go to relax and exercise your mind using the latest equipment in biofeedback and flotation tanks. Yoga and meditation are increasing in popularity. If you go to a bookstore, you are sure to see recent bestsellers about achieving peace through meditation. It is not surprising that people are turning to these practices as our lives become hectic and stressful. What a curious thought: in the future we won't be taking exotic vacations to Hawaii to get away from it all; we'll be taking out a membership in the nearest mind gym and spending our time in quiet meditation.

Now answer each of the questions based on the text. Begin each of your answers with a noun clause in subject position.

Example   CUE: What is one reason why the Human Potential Movement flourished?
ANSWER: **That Americans were caught up in a desire to achieve complete happiness and fulfillment** provides one explanation.

1. Why did the human potential movement flourish in the United States?
2. What is not surprising to the author?
3. What is a curious thought to the author?
4. In your opinion, what is one explanation for the stress in modern life?
5. What might be one disadvantage of going to a mind gym?

VI. Special Problems with Noun Clauses

Pay careful attention to these special problems.

PROBLEM POINT	EXPLANATION
1. No **to** after **said + subject** (INCORRECT) She said me that she would go. (CORRECT) She told me that she would go.	Don't confuse these constructions: • She **said to me** that . . . • She **told me** that . . .
2. Usng **that** to report a **Yes/No** question (INCORRECT) He asked me that I had any sisters. (CORRECT) He asked me if I had any sisters.	Use **if** or **whether** to report **yes/no** questions.
3. Using incorrect word order to report a **wh-**question (INCORRECT) I don't know what time is it. (CORRECT) I don't know what time it is.	Use **statement** word order to report a **Wh-**question.
4. Using the auxiliary **don't** in reporting imperatives (INCORRECT) She told us to don't go. (CORRECT) She told us not to go.	Use **not** in front of the infinitive.
5. Using incorrect pronouns or adverbs in indirect speech (INCORRECT) She told me that I didn't want to go here. (CORRECT) She told me that she didn't want to go there.	Change the pronouns and adverbs to indicate that it is indirect and not direct speech.
6. Using an incorrect form of the verb after verbs of urgency and request. (INCORRECT) He insisted that she sees a doctor. (CORRECT) He insisted that she see a doctor.	Use the simple form of the verb (the infinitive without *to*) in these cases.

■ **6.23 Error Analysis:** *Noun Clauses*

DIRECTIONS: Find any errors in noun clause construction and tense. Correct the errors clearly above the sentence.

1. A few students asked the teacher why was there going to be a final exam.

2. The teacher told to the students that it is crucial that they learn to take tests.

3. According to the students, however, it was more important that they were given more class time.

4. The president told to the United States to don't worry about the recent stock market problems because the economy was strong and healthy.

5. What is my father's annual income is none of your business.

6. This is exactly that I noticed at my age.

7. What are we in such a situation is only an example for our children.

8. That at what age a parent should suggest her child break away and live independently is that a parent should consider.

focus on Writing

Introductory Clause Verbs

The following is a list of common verbs used to introduce noun clauses that report speech or express ideas. These verbs have been grouped according to their function. Note that this list is not complete. (Anything enclosed within parentheses is optional.) Add your own verbs to this list as you come across them.

FUNCTION	NOTES	VERBS
To Report Almost Any Statements	• Use these verbs to report objective information. They do not convey the speaker's feelings.	He **said (to me)** that he would go. He **reported (to me)** that . . . She **stated (to me)** that . . . He **mentioned (to me)** that . . . He **indicated** that . . . *(An indirect object must follow* **told.***)*

Continued on next page.

Continued from previous page.

FUNCTION	NOTES	VERBS
To Give Additional Information	• Use these verbs to report several bits of information given by the same speaker.	He **further stated (to me)** that he would stay an hour. He **continued to say (to me)** that . . . He **later mentioned (to me)** that . . .
To Present Factual Information	• Use these verbs to report a brief announcement. • You **must** use a pronoun after each.	She **informed us** that the class was cancelled. He **notified us** that . . . She **advised us** that . . .
To Present A Strong Argument Or Opinion	• Use these verbs to report an opinion or argument. • They are arranged from weak to strong.	He **believed** that the death penalty was wrong. She **maintained** that . . . She **claimed** that . . . He **asserted** that . . . She **argued** that . . . He **declared** that . . .
To Respond	• Use these verbs to report a response to a statement or question.	He **replied** that it was a social issue. She **responded (to me)** that . . . He **answered (me)** that . . . She **agreed (with me)** that . . . She **concurred (with him)** that . . . He **disputed (the fact)** that . . . He **disagreed (with him)** that . . .
To Conclude		She **concluded** that her boss was right. He **realized** that . . .

6.24 Written Activity: *Introductory Clause Verbs*

DIRECTIONS: Read the following conversation between Christine and John about male and female intelligence. Then report the conversation in a paragraph, using the introductory verbs listed in the chart above. Avoid using said in your report of their conversation. Add appropriate transition words.

CHRISTINE: Women are more intelligent than men because they are more open-minded.

JOHN: I disagree, Christine. I believe that men and women do not have any inborn differences in their intelligence.

CHRISTINE: So you think that we are born with our intelligence?

JOHN: Pretty much. You can't really increase your intelligence after birth, but you can make good use of it.

CHRISTINE: I disagree with that. I believe that intelligence is both inborn and developed through experience.

JOHN: Well, it appears that we have different points of view on this. Do you think there are different kinds of intelligence?

CHRISTINE: Absolutely! Some people are especially bright in mathematics, and others are brilliant in music.

JOHN: I agree with you on that point. And I don't believe that the I.Q. test can measure all of that.

6.25 Written Activity: *Nature vs. Nurture*

DIRECTIONS: Think about the following questions which ask you to think about intelligence and where it comes from. Then discuss them with a partner or in small groups. Make a note of your classmates' ideas below. There are no right answers to these questions, so feel free to disagree with your partner. Then write a summary of your conversation using a variety of introductory clause verbs from the chart above on pages 144–145. Avoid using **said** in your essay.

1. Define intelligence

_____

_____

_____

2. Are you born with intelligence or is it something that you acquire? Explain your answer.

_____

_____

_____

3. An I.Q. test is often used to measure a person's intelligence. What do you think about these tests? Does a high I.Q. ensure academic or professional success?

_____

_____

_____

4. Is there any difference between men and women in the type or amount of intelligence? If so, what is it? How do you know?

_____

_____

_____

5. What happens to your mental functioning as you age?

_____

_____

_____

Composition Topics

In this chapter, you have had the chance to read about and discuss the question of human experience and learning. Choose one of the following topics and write a composition in which you clearly formulate your own ideas.

1. "Men and women can never have the same type or amount of intelligence." Agree or disagree with this statement and give strong reasons to support your position.

2. A turning point is an event in your life that seriously changed the direction of your life. Graduating from high school, leaving home, the beginning of your career, a marriage, a baby, a divorce, a death—these are events that often change one's life dramatically. Write a composition in which you describe such an event that you have experienced. Explain why it was so meaningful and important to you.

3. Describe a teacher or guide who taught you something important in your life. What did they do to help you learn? What did you learn?

Making a Difference

• Adjective Clauses

To Make A Difference: To have an influence or impact on the people around you or your environment.

DISCUSSION QUESTIONS

1. What is the difference between a celebrity and a hero? Name a living person who is a hero for you and explain why. Name a celebrity you enjoy.
2. How are you presently making or how do you hope to make a difference in the future?
3. How would you like to be remembered after you die?

OBJECTIVES

In this chapter you will learn:

1. To combine sentences using adjective clauses
2. To distinguish and punctuate restrictive and nonrestrictive adjective clauses
3. To reduce adjective clauses

Preview

DIRECTIONS: Read the following text on the Live-Aid Concert to find out more about Bob Geldof. Then answer the questions that follow.

1 Rock concerts and benefits to raise money for good causes were quite common in the United States during the last two decades of the 20th century. One of the first well-known benefit concerts was the Live-Aid Concert in 1985.

2 On July 13, 1985, more than a billion people from all over the world were witness to a rock concert *which hosted over sixty rock acts on two continents simultaneously.* The person *who was responsible for the Live-Aid Concert,* as it was called, was Bob Geldof, an **abrasive** rock singer with the Boomtown Rats. Geldof had one objective in **pulling off** the largest rock concert ever—he wanted to raise money for the **famine** relief effort. Geldof gave tirelessly to a project *for which he did not receive even a penny.*

3 It all began on a quiet evening when Bob and his girlfriend decided to **stay in** and catch a **documentary** on Ethiopia on T.V. It was a program *that Geldof is not likely ever to forget.* He watched as a **relief worker** had to choose 300 starving people out of 10,000 to receive a small ration of butter oil. Greatly moved by that experience, Geldof decided to do something for the hungry of the world. He wrote and recorded **the single** "Do They Know It's Christmas," *which raised $11 million.* The U.S. equivalent, "We are the World," quickly followed, *which raised even more money.* Soon **donations** started pouring into the Live-Aid Foundation set up by Geldof from people *whose conscience had been rattled by this rock singer's dedication and commitment.*

4 However, the single act which *Geldof will always be remembered for* was, of course, the Live-Aid concert. Such well-known groups and musicians as Bob Dylan, Mick Jagger, Phil Collins, U-2, Tina Turner, and Madonna performed in the JFK Stadium in Philadelphia and Wembly Stadium in London. The concert brought in over $60 million for famine relief. It also brought the reality of starvation into the homes of viewers in 90 countries.

5 Even now, well over a decade later, Geldof often wonders what would have happened if he hadn't stayed home that night.

VOCABULARY

abrasive: unrefined, irritating in manner
to pull off: to achieve, to organize successfully
famine: a severe shortage of food
to stay in: to spend the time at home, to not go out
documentary: a film or T.V. program based on factual information

relief worker: a person working for a social project
single: a 45 r.p.m. record
donation: a gift of money or objects given to an organization

CULTURAL NOTE/DISCUSSION

The Live-Aid Concert of 1985 started a trend in which rock stars in the United States began to host benefit concerts to raise money for various social concerns, such as the situation of the farmer in the Midwest of the United States, the spread of AIDS, and human rights. Have you ever attended such a concert? What do you think of rock stars hosting such concerts?

FOCUS ON GRAMMAR

The following questions are based on the preview text and are designed to help you find out what you already know about the structures in this chapter. Some of the questions may be hard and some of them may be easy. Answer as many of the questions as you can. Work with a partner if your teacher tells you to do so.

1. The clauses in italics in the preview are all adjective clauses; that is, they modify nouns. Circle the noun being modified by each clause.

2. Compare the following clauses from paragraph 2.

    a. ". . . a rock concert **which** hosted over 60 rock acts . . ." and

    b. "The person **who** was responsible for the Live-Aid Concert . . ."

    Why is *which* used to introduce clause (a) and *who* used to introduce clause (b)?

    _____

    _____

3. Now look at the following clause from paragraph 3: ". . . a program **that** Geldof is not likely ever to forget."

    Does **that** refer to a person or a thing? Could **that** also refer to a person? For example, could you replace **who** in clause (b) in question 2 with **that**? Now, make a rule for the use of **which, who,** and **that.**

    _____

    _____

4. Compare the following clauses:

    a. ". . . a project **for which** he did not receive even a penny." (paragraph 2)

    b. ". . . the single act **which** Geldof will always be remembered for . . ." (paragraph 4)

    Note the position of the preposition **for** in both clauses. Could **for** be moved to the end of the clause in (a)? Could it be placed before **which** in (b)?

    _____

    _____

Grammatical Patterns Part One

I. Adjective Clause: Form

An adjective clause is a group of words (relative word, subject, and verb) that comes after a noun and modifies and/or restricts that noun, which is called the **antecedent noun.** The adjective clause gets **embedded** in the main clause of the sentence; it becomes a subordinate clause within the main clause.

Note how the second sentences in (1) and (3) below are turned into an adjective clause and embedded in the sentence. (**A** = antecedent noun; **RW** = relative word, **S** = subject, and **V** = verb)

1. The person was Bob Geldof. He was responsible for the concert.

2. The *person* <ins>**who was responsible for the concert**</ins> was Bob Geldof.

          (A)   (RW/S) (V)

                    adjective clause

3. It was a program. Geldof is not likely to forget the program.

4. It was a *program* <ins>**that Geldof is not likely to forget**</ins>.

          (A)   (RW)   (S)   (V)

                    adjective clause

II. Types of Adjective Clauses

There are two types of adjective clauses.

Restrictive:	The single act **which Geldof will be remembered for** was the Live-Aid Concert.	A restrictive adjective clause limits the antecedent noun. It makes it more specific.
Nonrestrictive:	He recorded "Do They Know It's Christmas," **which eventually raised $11 million.**	A nonrestrictive adjective clause gives additional information, not necessary to identify the noun being modified.

Grammatical Patterns One will examine restrictive adjective clauses. Grammatical Patterns Two will look at nonrestrictive adjective clauses.

III. Restrictive Clauses: Relative Words

A relative word connects the adjective clause to its antecedent noun. Relative words can have many functions in the adjective clause, as outlined in the chart below. The relative word is in **bold** and the clause is *in italics*.

FUNCTION OF RELATIVE WORD	EXAMPLE	NOTES
Subject of the adjective clause	1. The person **who/that** was (subject) (verb) responsible for the concert was Geldof. 2. More than a billion people witnessed a concert **that/which** (subject) hosted over 60 rock acts. (verb)	• Use **who** (or **that**) for people as in (1). • Use **that** (or **which**) for things, as in (2).
Object of the adjective clause	3. It was a program **that** Geldof (object) (subject) is not likely to forget. 4. Some of the performers saw musicians **who(m)** they hadn't seen in years. 5. Some of the performers saw musicians ~~whom~~ they hadn't seen in years.	• In (3), **that** is the object of the clause (Geldof is not likely to forget **that**). **Geldof** is the subject of the clause. • Use **who** or **whom** for people in object position. **Whom** is more formal. • When the relative word is an object, it can be deleted as in (5). This does not change the meaning of the sentence.
Object of a preposition	6. Geldof gave tirelessly to a project **for which** he did not receive a penny. 7. Geldof gave tirelessly to a project **that** he did not receive a penny **for**. 8. Geldof gave tirelessly to a project ~~that~~ he did not receive a penny **for**.	• An adjective clause can follow most prepositions. In (6) **for** is the preposition and **which** is the object of the clause. • The preposition can be placed at the end of the clause as in (7). This is informal. • The relative word can be deleted if the preposition is at the end of the adjective clause, as it is in (8).
Possessive	9. Donations poured in from people **whose** consciences were rattled by Geldof's commitment and dedication. (It was the people's consciences that were rattled.) 10. Geldof wanted to do something for the hungry in Ethiopia, **about whose situation** he was very disturbed.	• **Whose** shows possession and usually refers to persons as in (9). • **Whose** can also follow a preposition when it modifies the object of that preposition as in (10).

7.1 Written Drill: *Amnesty International*

DIRECTIONS: What do you know about the organization, Amnesty International? Read the following sentences to find out more. Fill in the blanks with any appropriate relative words **(that, which, who, whom,** or **whose).** Show all possibilities.

Amnesty International is a human rights organization _____ was founded in London. Its
1

work centers on the rights of "prisoners of conscience," men and women _____ governments
2

have imprisoned them for their beliefs, ethnic origin, language, or religion. A program _____
3

Amnesty International has been well known for is its adoption program. This involves a group of

concerned citizens _____ select a prisoner of conscience and write to the government
4

_____ has imprisoned him or her, asking for the prisoner's release.
5

Amnesty International has done a great deal to defend human rights, for _____ it was
6

awarded the Nobel Peace Prize in 1977.

7.2 Written Activity: *Adjective Clauses*

DIRECTIONS: Imagine that you work for a very progressive company which allows workers to take six months off of their work every five years to participate in some activity that will benefit their country. Think about the kind of activity that you would get involved in to make your country a better place to live. Then answer the following questions using an adjective clause. You can use the noun in parentheses as the antecedent for the clause if you wish.

Example   CUE: What type of work will you do? (a cause)
            ANSWER: I would like to work for a cause <u>that will help the homeless</u>.
            (adjective clause)

1. What type of work will you do? (a cause)

   _____

2. Who will benefit from your work? (the people)

   _____

3. What skills do you have to contribute? (the skills)

   _____

4. What problem will you solve? (the problem)

   _____

5. Whom will you go to for money? (the people)

   _____

6. How will you carry out your idea? (the plan)

■ A. Whose

An adjective clause can also show possession. In this case, the relative word (**whose**) replaces the possessive pronoun, as it does in the two sentences below.

I have a friend. His father works for Amnesty International.
I have a friend **whose** father works for Amnesty International.

7.3 Oral Drill: *Whose*

DIRECTIONS: You are the director of a relief organization that sends workers to developing countries. Decide if you would or would not hire the following people to go to Africa to develop their food supply and explain why. Use **whose** in your response.

Example   CUE: His health is poor.
ANSWER: I wouldn't hire a man whose health is poor, because he needs to be strong in order to do his job effectively.

CUE: Her degree is in anthropology.
ANSWER: I would hire a person whose degree is in anthropology because she would be familiar with foreign cultures.

1. His father is dying.
2. Her mother is a famous movie star.
3. His cross-cultural experience is limited.
4. Her husband can't accompany her.
5. His university major was philosophy.
6. Her work experience is on a farm.
7. His age is 50.
8. Her appearance is sloppy.
9. His application was illegible and late.
10. Her skin is sensitive to the sun.

7.4 Paired Drill: *Whose*

DIRECTIONS: Discuss the following questions with a partner, using *whose* in your response. Be honest! Be prepared to share (and defend if necessary) one or two of your answers with the class.

1. What kind of person do you dislike?
2. What kind of man or woman will you (or did you) marry?
3. What kind of people do you like?
4. What do you look for in a friend?
5. What type of person would you never do business with?
6. Say something about the kind of mother you have.
7. Say something about the kind of father you have.

8. What kind of boss do you prefer?

9. What kind of friend do you need?

10. What type of government do you think is the best?

B. Object of Prepositions

Note how these two sentences can be combined in four different ways using an adjective clause. In both cases, the sentences are arranged from **informal** to **formal use.**

1. Amnesty International is the organization.
   I told you **about it.**

   Amnesty International is the organization_∧ **I told you about.**
   Amnesty International is the organization **that** I told you **about.**
   Amnesty International is the organization **which** I told you **about.**
   Amnesty International is the organization **about which** I told you.

2. The prisoner was released.
   Amnesty International wrote to the prisoner.

   The prisoner_∧ Amnesty International wrote **to** was released.
   The prisoner **who(m)** Amnesty International wrote **to** was released.
   The prisoner **that** Amnesty International wrote **to** was released.
   The prisoner **to whom** Amnesty International wrote was released.

7.5 Oral Drill: *Objects of Prepositions*

DIRECTIONS: Combine these sentences in as many ways as possible. **Use the second sentence as an adjective clause.**

Example   CUE: Money is a commodity. We can't live without it.
           ANSWER: Money is a commodity **that/which** we can't live without.
                                       ∧we can't live without.
                                       without which we can't live.

1. I went to an island in the Pacific for vacation. My travel agent had told me about it.

2. My brother has a pen pal. He has been writing to him for 20 years.

3. The student wrote an outstanding paper. She was awarded a prize for it.

4. The bus boycott was in Montgomery, Alabama. Martin Luther King was jailed for it.

5. King believed in Christian principles. He combined nonviolent passive resistance with them.

6. The speech was given in 1963 to 250,000 people. Martin Luther King was famous for it.

7. My sister volunteered to work for a homeless shelter. Ray Kroc of McDonald's paid for the shelter.

8. The local AIDS organization started a food service. Many sick people benefit from it.

9. Many blacks helped slaves escape in the south in the 19th century. We know very little about them.

10. The donor gave over a million dollars to save the symphony orchestra from bankruptcy. The donor remains anonymous.

C. Relative Words of Place and Time

Adjective clauses can modify places and time in the following ways. Note that although the various constructions have the same meaning, they are not equal in degree of formality. **The sentences are arranged from informal to formal.**

1. Place
   The prisons are filthy.
   Many prisoners of conscience were sent **to the prisons.**

   a. The prisons ∧many prisoners of conscience were sent to are filthy.
   b. The prisons **where** many prisoners of conscience were sent are filthy. ·
   c. The prisons **that** many prisoners of conscience were sent to are filthy.
   d. The prisons **which** many prisoners of conscience were sent to are filthy.
   e. The prisons **to which** many prisoners of conscience were sent are filthy.

2. Time
   1980 is the year.
   Amnesty International won the Nobel Peace Prize then.

   a. 1980 is the year∧ Amnesty International won the Nobel Peace Prize.
   b. 1980 is the year **that** Amnesty International won the Nobel Peace Prize.
   c. 1980 is the year **when** Amnesty International won the Nobel Peace Prize.
   d. 1980 is the year **in which** Amnesty International won the Nobel Peace Prize.
   e. 1980 is the year **during which** Amnesty International won the Nobel Peace Prize.

SPECIAL NOTE

RELATIVE WORDS OF TIME
Use these prepositions with the following units of time:
YEAR: during which, in which
DAY: on which
MONTH: during which, in which

7.6 Paired Activity: *Place and Time*

DIRECTIONS: Test your knowledge of dates and places. See if you can identify more than your partner. Take turns identifying these times and places by using an appropriate **preposition** and **relative word. Do not use <u>when</u> or <u>where</u>.**

Example   December 25
           December 25 <u>is the day on which Christians celebrate Christmas</u>.

STUDENT A

1. February 14

2. July 4

3. The ninth month of the Muslim calendar

4. 1776

5. A nursing home

6. 10 Downing Street

7. Epcot Center

8. Mecca

STUDENT B

1. Halloween

2. April 15

3. 1492

4. The fourth Thursday in November

5. The Forbidden City

6. A kennel

7. The Alamo

8. Angkor Wat

7.7 Written Activity: *Using All Types of Adjective Clauses*

DIRECTIONS: Combine the following sentences using the second sentence as an adjective clause. Write the sentences as a unified paragraph.

Mother Theresa

1. Mother Theresa was born into a family in Albania. Her family was very wealthy.

2. Her mother often took her daughter to visit the poor. Their miserable living conditions left a lasting impression on Mother Theresa.

3. She left the convent and started her own congregation. She had to obtain approval from the Vatican for it.

4. In 1954, Mother Theresa set up a home for the dying with 26 volunteers. The volunteers' life was austere: no possessions and a 16-hour work day.

5. In 1979, she received the Nobel Peace Prize. She was criticized by some people for this. These people believed she had helped the poor but had not contributed to world peace. The Nobel Prize was intended for world peace.

6. She has also received criticism in the United States. There, some feminists disagree with her anti-abortion stance.

Harriet Tubman

1. Harriet Tubman was a slave. She escaped from her slave owner and then helped others to escape.

2. Harriet was born in Maryland in 1820. Slavery was legal then.

3. The plantation mistress was cruel. Harriet was owned by this mistress.

4. One night, Harriet escaped the plantation and went to Pennsylvania. Slavery was not legal there.

5. As a free woman, Harriet worked for the Underground Railroad to set the other slaves free. She could not forget those slaves.

6. She became the leader of the Underground Railroad and organized the workers. The workers referred to her as "General Tubman" because she was so strict.

D. Special Uses of Restrictive Adjective Clauses

1. To Define

Restrictive adjective clauses are often used to define or describe as in the following examples. Note the use of the expressions:
   one who or **a person who** (for persons)
   a (time) in which (for periods of time or events)

   • A philanthropist is **one who gives large amounts of money to charitable causes.**

   • The 1950s was a decade **in which conformity was very important.**

   • Capitalism is an economic system which **endorses free enterprise.**

7.8 Paired Activity: *Defining*

DIRECTIONS: Work with a partner to develop clear definitions or descriptions of the following terms and events. Use a dictionary for any difficult terms. Write a definition for each one, using an adjective clause. Then compare and discuss these with another pair of students.

Define these terms:

1. an altruist

2. a misogynist

3. democracy

4. culture shock

5. charity

6. a volunteer

7. a donation

8. a benefactor

9. schizophrenia

Characterize these times:

1. the 1990s

2. middle age

3. motherhood

4. adolescence

5. The Renaissance

6. The 1960s

7. The Middle Ages

2. TO EMPHASIZE

The following construction (called a cleft sentence) is used when speakers or writers want to emphasize a certain point. Compare the following two sentences and note how (b) underscores the writer's point:

a. Karl Benz first developed the automobile, but Henry Ford is remembered for making it affordable to the public.

b. Karl Benz first developed the automobile, but **it is really Henry Ford who is remembered for making it affordable to the public.**

7.9 Oral Activity: *Emphasizing*

DIRECTIONS: Your teacher will identify the following famous people or organizations by what they have done or invented. Some of the statements will be true and others will be false. See if you can identify the errors and correct them. Use the following constructions in your responses:

"**Are you sure? I believe it was really** _____ **who/when/where/that, etc.**"
OR
"**Oh, I think it was** _____**.**"

Example   CUE: Thomas Edison
TEACHER: Thomas Edison invented the telephone.
STUDENT: <u>No, I believe it was really Alexander Graham Bell who invented the telephone.</u>

- Marie Curie
- Charles Darwin
- Florence Nightingale
- Babe Ruth

- Pelé
- Albert Einstein
- Neil Armstrong
- Mao Tse Tung

Grammatical Patterns Part Two

Preview

DIRECTIONS: How would you feel today if you had been somewhat responsible for the development of the atomic bomb? Read the following text on J. Robert Oppenheimer and answer the questions that follow.

The Father of the Atomic Bomb

1 J. Robert Oppenheimer, who was perhaps the most brilliant nuclear physicist of our century, is often referred to as "the father of the atomic bomb." After receiving a bachelor's and master's degree at Harvard University in only three years, Oppenheimer went abroad for his doctorate in the "new" nuclear physics in Cambridge, England, and at the University of Gottingen, where he met other brilliant scientists. These scientists, who would later **figure** prominently in his life, included Edward Teller and Leo Szilard. After that, he taught in Holland, where he was affectionately given the name "Oppie," which **stuck** for life.

2 In 1942, he was made director of the Manhattan District, a project for the development of the atomic bomb, which had not yet been produced by any country. Oppie gathered a **coterie** of brilliant scientists around him who eagerly and willingly worked at finding a way to build this bomb. Oppie had a powerful effect on the people who worked for him. They were amazed at his diverse interests and talents—physics, poetry, gourmet foods, and spiritual matters.

3 It is almost hard to believe that it was this brilliant lover of poetry and fine wine who inspired capable scientists to create the most destructive weapon on earth. In fact, after the bomb had been dropped on Hiroshima and Nagasaki, Japan in August of 1945, Oppie himself was disturbed by the power of his own creation. He then tried to establish a formal agreement between the United States and the Soviet Union which would forbid the production of such weapons. The United States and the Soviet Union, which by that time had begun making its own bombs, were unable **to strike** any such cooperative agreement. Thus, the arms race had begun.

VOCABULARY

to figure: to appear, to have a place
stuck: stayed
a coterie: a group of people
to strike: to make

FOCUS ON GRAMMAR

The following questions are based on the preview text. Answer as many of the questions as you can. Work with a partner if your teacher tells you to do so.

1. Underline all the adjective clauses in the text. (There are eleven.) Circle the noun that each clause modifies.

2. Compare the punctuation of the two clauses in sentences (a) and (b) below:

   a. J. Robert Oppenheimer, **who was perhaps the most brilliant nuclear physicist of our century,** is often referred to as "the father of the atomic bomb." (paragraph 1)

   b. Oppie had a powerful effect on the people **who worked for him.** (paragraph 2)

   Can you explain why the punctuation is different? Could you delete the adjective clause in sentence (a) and still have a meaningful sentence? Could you do that for sentence (b) and keep the same meaning?

3. Rewrite the following sentence, changing the phrase in bold to an adjective clause.

   In 1942, he was made director of the Manhattan District, **a project for the development of the atomic bomb.**

   _____

   _____

■ I. Nonrestrictive Adjective Clauses

Nonrestrictive adjective clauses provide additional information that is not necessary to identify the noun being modified. These clauses, unlike restrictive clauses, are set off by commas in writing and pauses in speech.

MEANING	EXAMPLE	NOTES
Nonrestrictive Adjective Clauses The adjective clauses in (1) and (2) provide added information about the antecedent noun, but it is **not essential** information.	1. My maternal grandmother, **who lived until she was 95,** was active in the civil rights movement. 2. Birmingham, **which is a city in the state of Alabama,** was the site of many civil rights demonstrations. 3. My grandmother met Martin Luther King, **whom** she would never forget.	• Use **who(m)** for people and **which** for things in nonrestrictive adjective clauses. • Always set off the nonrestrictive clauses by commas. • The relative word can *never* be deleted in a nonrestrictive clause, even if it is the object of the clause or of the preposition as it is in (3).
Restrictive Adjective Clauses The adjective clauses in (4) and (5) provide **essential** information. The clause cannot be omitted from the sentence without changing the meaning of the sentence.	4. I have two sisters. My sister **who/that lives in Virginia** is married. 5. The sister **whom I am going to visit** is single.	• The relative word **that** can always replace **who** or **which** in a restrictive clause. • Do not use commas with restrictive clauses. • The relative word **can** be deleted if it is the object of the clause or a preposition.

7.10 Rapid Drill: *Pronunciation of Clauses*

DIRECTIONS: Your teacher will read a series of sentences. If there is a pause before and after the adjective clause, you will know that it is a nonrestrictive clause. If there is no pause, then it is restrictive. Circle the sentence in each pair you hear your teacher say. Note the different pronunciation patterns below. Then answer the comprehension questions that follow.

The book, which I lent you, is on the table.

The book which I lent you is on the table.

1. **a.** My friends, who are from Canada, will be at the party.
   b. My friends who are from Canada will be at the party.
   In which sentence are **all** his friends from Canada?

2. **a.** The students, who were attentive in class, passed the test.
   b. The students who were attentive in class passed the test.
   Which sentence states that only **some** of the students were attentive?

3. **a.** The tennis players, who were women, won the tournament.
   b. The tennis players who were women won the tournament.
   Which sentence states that **all** of the players were women?

4. **a.** My boyfriend, who is from France, is sitting over there.
   b. My boyfriend who is from France is sitting over there.
   Which sentence implies that she has more than one boyfriend?

5. In pairs, practice your own pronunciation. See if your partner can distinguish between the two types of intonation patterns.

A. Test for Restrictive and Nonrestrictive Clauses.

Here is a quick way to find out whether a clause is restrictive or nonrestrictive.

1. First identify the adjective clause.
   - Martin Luther King <u>who was a civil rights leader</u> was assassinated in 1968.
   - People <u>who knew him</u> were devastated.

2. Then take out the adjective clause and ask yourself: Does this sentence make sense without the clause?
   - Martin Luther King was assassinated in 1968. (*This sentence is OK without the clause; the sentence makes sense.*)
   - People were devastated. (*This sentence is not OK without the clause. We don't know which people were devastated. All of them? Some of them? We need the clause for the sentence to be clear and complete.*)

3. If the sentence is OK without the clause, then it is nonrestrictive. In this case you need to put commas before and after the clause.
   - Martin Luther King, who was a civil rights leader, was assassinated in 1968.
   If the sentence is not OK without the clause, then it is restrictive and you don't use commas.
   - People who knew him were devastated.

7.11 Recognition Drill: *Restrictive or Nonrestrictive?*

DIRECTIONS: Read the following sentences and identify the underlined clause as R (restrictive) or NR (nonrestrictive). Insert commas where necessary.

Example   NR   Hillary Clinton, <u>who was the First Lady in 1995</u>, attended a women's conference in Beijing.

1. Susan B. Anthony <u>who was born in N.Y.</u> is famous for her work in getting women the right to vote.
2. She was a schoolteacher <u>who supported a woman's right to vote</u>.
3. Elizabeth Cady Stanton was the other founder of the National Woman Suffrage Association <u>which was instrumental in changing the laws about women's suffrage</u>.
4. Elizabeth Blackwell was the first woman <u>who graduated from a medical school in the United States</u>.
5. She was not accepted by her teachers and later she was rebuffed by her friends <u>who also ostracized her</u>.
6. Eventually, she finished her coursework; she was the student <u>who got the highest grades in her class</u>.
7. She opened a hospital in New York. The hospital <u>which was run by women</u> later expanded to become a medical school.
8. When Shannon Faulkner applied in 1993 for acceptance to The Citadel <u>which is a state-supported military school in Charleston, South Carolina</u> she did not indicate that she was female.
9. The school <u>which was all-male until 1995</u> did not ask if an applicant was male or female at the time because only men were allowed in the school.
10. When the school realized she was female, it withdrew its offer and Faulkner sued. She engaged in a legal battle <u>that lasted several years</u> but she finally won in 1995. The Citadel is no longer an all-male school.

■ II. When to Use Nonrestrictive Adjective Clauses

Use nonrestrictive clauses in the following cases.

CASE	EXAMPLE
1. When the antecedent noun has been previously identified. In (1) the scientists have been identified in the previous sentence.	1. Oppie met some brilliant scientists in Germany and England. **These scientists, who would later figure prominently in his life,** included Edward Teller and Leo Szilard.
2. When the antecedent noun is a proper noun In (2) the antecedent, **J. Robert Oppenheimer,** is a proper noun.	2. **J. Robert Oppenheimer, who was perhaps the most brilliant nuclear physicist of our century,** is often referred to as the father of the atomic bomb.

Continued on next page.

Continued from previous page.

CASE	EXAMPLE
3. When the antecedent is a one-of-a-kind noun. In (3) the antecedent, **the atomic bomb,** is unique. There is only one atomic bomb.	3. The goal of the project was to develop **the atomic bomb, which had not yet been done by any country.**
4. When the antecedent noun is all of a kind.	4. **The scientists, who adored Oppie,** stayed until the end of the project. (All of them adored Oppie.)

7.12 Recognition Drill: *Restrictive vs. Nonrestrictive Clauses*

DIRECTIONS: Read the following sentences and underline all adjective clauses. Label the clauses as restrictive **(R)** or nonrestrictive **(NR)** and be ready to explain why. Insert commas before and after the nonrestrictive clauses.

Example   <u>NR</u>   Sophon and Srey, <u>who were from Cambodia</u>, arrived at the Burlington Airport on a wintry day in Vermont in 1982.

_____ 1. A large group of people some of whom included members of Sophon's family as well as Americans were anxiously waiting for these refugees to arrive.

_____ 2. The American volunteers who had organized this reunion included English teachers, retired physicians, politicians, and homemakers.

_____ 3. As Srey and Sophon walked through the gate, Channel 3 which was the local T.V. station quickly moved in to film and interview them.

_____ 4. Afterwards, everyone went to the apartment which had been rented for them. The apartment which was located in the middle of town was very small.

_____ 5. Sophon and his family were only one of many Indochinese refugee families who were resettled in Vermont.

_____ 6. Their children who are all in high school today barely remember that day.

7.13 Chapter Review

DIRECTIONS: Change each of the following sentences in parentheses into a **relative clause** and write it in the space provided. Insert commas where necessary.

1. Clara, <u>who works at the university</u>, and David _____ went on a drive to
(Clara works at the university.)   (David is her husband.)

the desert _____. The road _____ went up into the
(They had never been to the desert before.)   (They travelled on the road.)

mountains _____ and then down the mountains into a flat area
(The mountains had snow.)

_____. The wind was blowing very hard and David _____
(The area was very dry.)   (His car is small.)

was a little worried about keeping his car on the road.

2. Sigmund Freud _____ was born in 1856 in Austria _____.
(He is known as the Father of psychoanalysis.)   (He studied medicine in Austria until 1881.)

After graduating as a neurologist, Freud studied under Charcot _____.
(Charcot's hypnosis techniques were popular at the time.)

Charcot's interests in "hysteria" convinced Freud to study psychiatry. Freud developed

techniques _____. Freud helped a lot of people _____
(The techniques were designed to uncover a person's unconscious.)   (The people suffered from psychosomatic problems.)

with his methods and laid the groundwork for much of the psychological work going on today.

III. Adjective Clauses That Modify Sentences

Compare the following sentences and note how an adjective clause can modify an entire sentence
and not just a noun.

COMPARE:

1. I don't like our *uniform,* **which the principal picked out this year.**

2. *This year students are required to wear uniforms,* **which I completely agree with.**

PUNCTUATION

- In sentence (1), the nonrestrictive adjective clause modifies the **noun,** *uniform.*

- In (2) the nonrestrictive clause comments on the entire **previous statement,** "students are required to wear uniforms."

- A comma always precedes a sentence clause, just as in any nonrestrictive clause.

7.14 Oral Drill: *Sentence Clauses*

DIRECTIONS: Respond to the following statements with an **adjective clause** that comments on the
statement and expresses your thoughts and feelings.

Example   CUE: Many workers in the United States don't have health insurance, . . .
                ANSWER: . . . which has become a serious problem.

1. The Berlin Wall was torn down quickly, . . .
2. Nelson Mandela, a political prisoner in South Africa, was freed in 1990, . . .
3. The environment has become a very serious political issue, . . .
4. Computers have made information more accessible, . . .
5. The United States allows the death penalty, . . .
6. Most U.S. universities require a score of 550 on the TOEFL, . . .
7. The greenhouse effect is making summers warmer in the Midwest of the United States, . . .
8. Teachers earn low salaries in many states, . . .
9. There are many more fax machines in the world, . . .
10. Practically everyone in the United States has a T.V. now, . . .

11. The rain forests in South America are rapidly being deforested, . . .
12. Most urban areas have more and more homeless, . . .
13. There is no known cure for AIDS, . . .
14. United States citizens can own and carry handguns, . . .
15. Stricter pollution laws have decreased smog in many cities, . . .

IV. Nonrestrictive Clauses After Expressions of Quantity

Note how a nonrestrictive adjective clause can follow an expression of quantity such as **both, many, much, some**, and so on. In this case, the clause modifies all or a portion of the antecedent noun.

Two Sentences	One Sentence + Adjective Clause	Notes
I have many friends. All of **them** can speak a foreign language.	1. I have many friends, **all of whom can speak a foreign language.**	• Replace the pronoun with **whom** for people. In (1) **whom** replaces **them**.
I couldn't decide between two universities. Both of **them** were reputable.	2. I couldn't decide between two universities, **both of which were reputable.**	• Since these clauses are nonrestrictive, use **which**—not **that**—for objects as in (2).
I have many friends. Many of their spouses work at home.	3. I have many friends, **many of whose spouses** work at home.	• Use **whose** for possession as in (3). • Always insert commas before and after the clause.

7.15 Oral Drill: *Clauses After Expressions of Quantity*

DIRECTIONS: Read the following sentences about motivations and explanations for human behavior. Combine the sentences using an **expression of quantity.**

Example   CUE: There are many theories about why people do what they do. The majority of them have some validity.

             ANSWER: There are many theories about why people do what they do, **the majority of which** have some validity.

1. Sigmund Freud believed that people were driven by very basic drives of the pleasure principle and the death wish. Both of these drives originate in the unconscious.

2. B. F. Skinner maintained that the environment shapes our behavior. Any aspect of our behavior can be both learned and unlearned.

3. Carl Rogers firmly held the belief that humans are innately good. All people are motivated by a self-actualizing principle.

_____

4. Abraham Maslow described several stages of human development. The highest stage is self-actualization.

_____

5. There are many other psychologists. Many of their theories about motivation, however, are not well known.

_____

7.16 Written Activity: _Adjective Clauses After Expressions of Quantity_

DIRECTIONS: Complete the following sentences using the **expression of quantity** given and an **adjective clause.**

Example   I have many interests, <u>most of which are not intellectual</u>.

1. In my room there are many objects, the most expensive _____.

2. There are many restaurants in this city, the majority _____.

3. In this class there are many students, few _____.

4. I have known many admirable people, the most _____.

5. I have accomplished a number of things in my life, _____.

6. My father has given me a lot of advice, some of _____.

7. The government has instituted many changes, _____.

8. We have had a lot of tests in this class, many _____.

9. My best friend has many good qualities, all _____.

10. I have made a lot of decisions in my life, many _____.

7.17 Written Activity: _Combining Sentences_

DIRECTIONS: Write a short paragraph about the organization International Physicians for the Prevention of Nuclear War (IPPONW). Use the information listed below, and feel free to include some of your own thoughts about the existence of nuclear weapons in our world. In your paragraph **use at least five different types of adjective clauses,** including both restrictive and nonrestrictive, and underline them. Refer to the chart on page 152 at the beginning of the chapter for a comprehensive list of all types of clauses.

International Physicians for the Prevention of Nuclear War (IPPONW)
- a worldwide federation of medical doctors and health professionals
- founded in 1980 by two U.S. citizens and two Soviet citizens

- the objective of the organization is to consolidate medical opinion against the danger of nuclear arms
- has organized programs to warn the public of these dangers
- supports the following efforts:
  - stopping nuclear testing
  - putting a freeze on the development of atomic weapons
  - not taking funding away from social programs to develop nuclear arms
- won the Nobel Peace Prize in 1985

V. Adjective Clause Reduction of Restrictive Clauses

Note how restrictive adjective clauses can be reduced (shortened).

Full Restrictive Clause	Reduced Restrictive Clause	Pattern/Notes
1a. The relief workers **who were tired** went home.	**1b.** The **tired** relief workers went home.	**Be + Adjective** • Delete the subject relative word and the **Be** verb; move the adjective in front of the noun as in (1b).
2a. The person **who was responsible for the concert** was Bob Geldof.	**2b.** The person **responsible for the concert** was Bob Geldof.	• If a phrase follows **Be**, as it does in (2a), delete the relative word and be, but keep the phrase after the noun as in (2b).
3a. Amnesty International is an organization **which was founded in London.**	**3b.** Amnesty International is an organization **founded in London.**	**Passive Verb** • Delete the relative word + **Be** verb and keep the past participle (e.g., **founded** in 3b).
4a. Oppenheimer had the best scientists who were **working with him.**	**4b.** Oppenheimer had the best scientists **working with him.**	**Progressive Verb** • Delete the relative word + the auxiliary **Be** and keep the verb-ing.
5a. More than a billion people witnessed a concert **which hosted over 60 acts.**	**5b.** More than a billion people witnessed a concert **hosting over 60 acts.**	**Verbs Other than Be** • When the main verb is not **Be**, or the verb is not in a passive or progressive form, change the verb to an -ing form as in (5b)—hosting.

7.18 Oral Drill: *Restrictive Clause Reduction*

DIRECTIONS: Reduce the adjectives clauses in the following questions; then answer the question with a **reduced adjective clause.**

Example   CUE: Do you believe that people <u>who are honest</u> can make a lot of money?
ANSWER: Do you believe that *honest people* can make a lot of money? Of course, honest people can make money.

1. Do you think that corporations that make a lot of money should sponsor charitable programs to benefit the poor?
2. Do you think a child who is forced to do chores in the home develops more responsibility?
3. Do you think that animals which are endangered should be protected?
4. Do you think that foods that are harmful to the body should be regulated?
5. Do you think that teenagers who are under 18 should be allowed to drive?
6. Do you think spouses who physically abuse their husband or wife should be put in jail?
7. Do you believe that students who skip class but who pass the tests should pass the course?

VI. Adjective Clause Reduction of Nonrestrictive Clauses

FULL CLAUSE	REDUCED CLAUSE	PATTERN/NOTES
1. J. Robert Oppenheimer, **who was perhaps the most brilliant physicist of our time,** is often called the father of the atomic bomb.	2. J. Robert Oppenheimer, **perhaps the most brilliant physicist of our time,** is often called the father of the atomic bomb.	• The same rules as in the table on page 169 apply to nonrestrictive clauses. • Be sure to keep the commas in the resulting reduced clause.

7.19 Oral Drill: *Important American Women*

DIRECTIONS: **Reduce the adjective clauses** in the following sentences to **phrases.**

1. Betty Friedan, who was the founder of the National Organization for Women, was one of the first women to recognize the need for a women's organization.
2. Gloria Steinem, who had been a key player in the women's movement, has a number of talents, which consist of brains, comic perception, and extremely good looks.
3. The woman who was given the first license to fly in the United States was Amelia Earhart.
4. Geraldine Ferraro, who is now living in New York City with her family, was the first female to run for vice-president of the United States.
5. At 19 months Helen Keller had a disease that was never diagnosed, and that left her unable to speak, hear, or see until she was helped by her teacher.

VII. Special Problems With Adjective Clause Use

PROBLEM	EXPLANATION
1. Repetition of the Pronoun in the Clause [INCORRECT: I really enjoyed the Vietnamese food that I had it yesterday.] CORRECT: I really enjoyed the Vietnamese food that I had yesterday.	• The relative word replaces the noun in the adjective clause.
2. Agreement [INCORRECT: I met some people who was from my country.] CORRECT: I met some people who were from my country.	• Make sure the antecedent noun agrees with the verb in the clause.
3. Location of the Clause [INCORRECT: We went to a Hawaiian island for our fiftieth wedding anniversary that was deserted and romantic.] CORRECT: For our fiftieth wedding anniversary we went to a Hawaiian island *that was deserted and romantic.*	• Place the clause as close as possible to the antecedent noun.
4. No Preposition or Particle [INCORRECT: The restaurant that she went was crowded and noisy.] CORRECT: The restaurant that she went **to** was noisy and crowded.	• Be sure to place the preposition or particle at the end of the clause.
5. Using **That for Nonrestrictive Clauses** [INCORRECT: I like martial arts, that teach balance and strength.] CORRECT: I like martial arts, **which** teach balance and strength.	• If the clause is nonrestrictive, you **must** use **which** and not **that** for things.

■ 7.20 Error Analysis

DIRECTIONS: Each of the following sentences has an error in adjective clause use. Find the errors and correct them. Refer to the above chart, but note that some errors may not be among the types listed there.

1. You wouldn't believe the test that we had it in our structure class last week!

2. John went to see a friend that his father is the president of his college.

3. My husband adores lumpia that is an Indonesian-style egg roll.

4. There is an old bridge crosses the river in my town.

5. The class schedule that I got it yesterday has many errors on it, which I am going to complain to the administration.

6. My economics professor will let me take my final exam after vacation for that I am very grateful.

7. In my house I have all kinds of paintings, most of them are from the twentieth century.

8. This is the kind of plant that you usually have to fertilize it regularly.

9. I used to have this doctor that I'd never go back to her.

10. 96.5 F.M. is one radio station that I listen a lot.

11. I love Georgia O'Keeffe's paintings that are all on exhibit in Los Angeles now.

12. She left her textbook on the table in the kitchen that she needs for class tomorrow.

13. I had an interesting talk with two students, both of them are from Turkey.

14. For my birthday I got a beautiful piece of crystal, which I love crystal.

15. Montpelier that is the capital city of Vermont has six months of winter.

16. I would never marry a man that his religion is different from mine.

17. The movie that Loretta and Jack went yesterday was *Rain Man*, which they loved.

18. The IPPONW, which was founded in 1980 by two Soviet and two United States citizens.

19. Their objective is to consolidate medical opinion against the danger of nuclear arms which have bad effects on people whose mental and physical are destroyed.

Focus on Writing

Sentence Combining

Learning to use a combination of full and reduced adjective clauses can assist you in becoming a better writer. For example, paragraph (1) below presents information in a loosely connected way, but paragraph (2) uses adjective clauses to combine ideas and tighten the sentence structure.

---

1 Marilyn Monroe was born in Los Angeles in 1926. Her face is perhaps the most famous face of a movie star. She attained stardom quickly. She could not deal with the stardom easily. In 1962, she committed suicide at home. She had just bought her home to begin a new life.

2 Marilyn Monroe, whose face is perhaps the most famous of all movie stars, was born in Los Angeles in 1926. Unfortunately, she could not deal with the stardom that she attained quickly. In 1962 she committed suicide in her home, which she had just bought to begin a new life.

7.21 Written Activity

DIRECTIONS: Read the following paragraphs written by a student about Marilyn Monroe. Although the paragraph is grammatically correct, it requires some editing to combine sentences with adjective clauses. Edit the paragraph to make the sentences tighter.

Marilyn Monroe was born in Los Angeles. Los Angeles is the home to many stars. Marilyn was well-loved by her movie fans. These fans did not know how unhappy Marilyn's personal life was, however.

Marilyn's early life was far from perfect. Marilyn did not live with her family. Her family's psychiatric problems were quite severe. She lived with a cold and rigid foster family. The foster family did not accept her as a full member of their family. This scarred Marilyn a great deal.

At six, Marilyn returned to live with her mother. Her mother had a mental breakdown after nine months. After that, Marilyn lived in a number of foster homes. None of the homes were nurturing.

It's not surprising that Marilyn's personal life was hard. She wanted to be loved and accepted. At 16, she married her first husband. He was a neighbor. Their marriage only lasted three years. That marriage was the first of many. Marilyn was on her way to becoming a star.

Composition Topics

1. Imagine that you were organizing a rock concert to benefit a good "cause," similar to Live Aid described in the Preview section of this chapter. Write a letter to a musical group that you would like to invite to play at your concert. In the letter, explain why you are hosting this concert and try to persuade the musician(s) to play at little or no cost.

2. Each year *Time* magazine chooses the Man of the Year, a man or woman who has contributed a great deal to the world during that year. If you were on the staff of *Time* magazine and were asked to submit a recommendation for the year that has just passed, who would you recommend? In a short essay, explain why you think that individual deserves to be called the Man of the Year. Describe the person's accomplishments and why you think he or she has made a difference.

3. Describe a person or an event that has made a difference in your life. Be specific in explaining how that person or event changed you.

Making Choices

• Adverb Clauses

DISCUSSION QUESTIONS

Read the poem on the next page. Then answer the following questions:

1. Do you believe in fate (destiny)? Do you believe you have the freedom to shape your life?

2. When you have an important decision to make, to whom do you talk?

3. If a close friend came to you for help in making a difficult decision (for example, a marriage or career choice), would you just listen or would you give him or her specific advice? Is there any danger in giving people advice?

4. In the Robert Frost poem, "The Road Not Taken," what does it mean when he says, "Yet knowing how way leads on to way,/I doubted if I should ever come back"?

OBJECTIVES

In this chapter, you will learn:

1. To form and use adverb clauses of time, place, reason, result, direct contrast, opposition, purpose, and manner

2. To punctuate these clauses

3. To reduce adverb clauses

Preview

The Road Not Taken

Two roads diverged in a yellow wood,
And sorry I could not travel both
And be one traveler, long I stood
And looked down one as far as I could
To where it bent in the undergrowth;
Then took the other, as just as fair,
And having perhaps the better claim,
Because it was grassy and wanted wear;
Though as for that the passing there
Had worn them really about the same,
And both that morning equally lay
In leaves no step had trodden black,
Oh, I kept the first for another day!
Yet knowing how way leads on to way,
I doubted if I should ever come back.
I shall be telling this with a sigh
Somewhere ages and ages hence;
Two roads diverged in a wood, and I—
I took the one less traveled by,
And that has made all the difference.

—Robert Frost

DIRECTIONS: Read the following letter that Joanne wrote to her friend Carole. Then answer the questions that follow.

Dear Carole,

1 At last I've got a moment to write to you! I really wish that we lived closer to each other *so that* we could have lunch together once in a while. *Although* we've only seen each other twice in the past five years, you're still my very best friend.

2 The baby **is due** in two months. Jack and I are truly excited! But, Carole, I'm so undecided about what to do *after* the baby arrives. *Whenever* I try to decide between staying home and continuing my job, I just get more confused. The **dilemma** has really come to a head now that my boss is **putting on the pressure** for a definite answer. Maybe you can help me, *since* you were always better than me at making decisions. **3** I think I know what you would advise me to do: make a list of the advantages and disadvantages and write them down. That's what I did and here's what I came up with. *While* my **heart** tells me to stay home, my **head** tells me to go back to work. One side of me says, "How can you leave your beautiful baby at home *while* you **trudge off** to work all day?" The other side says, "Joanne, *if* you leave your job now, you won't get another one that pays so well." It's true; I like working, and we could sure use the income. I also think I would like being with my baby. You know that it would be nearly impossible to survive on Jeff's salary alone. However, we could probably manage it *unless* he **gets laid off**.

4 Please write and let me know what you think I should do. And Carole, I hope you're planning a visit soon!

Love,

Joanne

Joanne

VOCABULARY

to be due: will be born
a dilemma: a problem with two equally likely resolutions
to come to a head: to reach a critical point
to put on the pressure: to demand immediately
my heart: my feelings
my head: my rational thinking
to trudge off: to go somewhere slowly and unwillingly
to get laid off: to lose one's job

CULTURAL NOTE/DISCUSSION

Many mothers in the United States must choose between staying home with their baby and struggling financially or going back to work and putting the baby in daycare. Some mothers must work for financial reasons, but more fortunate ones can live on their spouse's salary. What are the advantages and disadvantages of each alternative? What would you advise Joanne to do?

FOCUS ON GRAMMAR

The following questions are based on the preview text and are designed to help you find out what you already know about the structures in this chapter. Some of the questions may be hard and some of them may be easy. Answer as many of the questions as you can. Work with a partner if your teacher tells you to do so.

1. The words in italics in the preview letter introduce adverb clauses. Which of those words have approximately the same meaning as the words below? Write them in the space provided.

   a. at the same time as _____

   b. each time _____

   c. if not _____

2. What type of relationships do the following words show between the ideas in the sentence (e.g., purpose, time, contrast/opposition, condition)?

   a. although (paragraph 1) _____

   b. so that (paragraph 1) _____

   c. after (paragraph 2) _____

3. Locate and underline the two sentences in the letter that use the word <u>while</u>. Does <u>while</u> have the same meaning in each sentence? If not, what is the difference?

   _____

4. Compare the punctuation of these two sentences. How do they differ? Can you explain why there is a difference?

   a. "Although we've seen each other only twice in the past five years, you're still my very best friend."

   b. "Maybe you can help me since you were always better at making decisions."

   _____

Grammatical Patterns Part One

I. Adverb Clauses: Position and Punctuation

Adverb clauses are **dependent clauses.** As you will remember from Chapter 5, dependent clauses cannot stand alone. They require a **main clause** to complete them in a sentence. The words that introduce the adverb (dependent) clauses are called **subordinating conjunctions.**

Sub.Conj
While my *heart tells* me to stay home, my *head says* otherwise.
    Subject + Verb,   Subject + Verb

    (Adverb) Dependent Clause   Main Clause

In the example above, the adverb (dependent) clause (while my heart tells me to stay home) appears at the beginning of the sentence, introduced by the subordinating conjunction, **while.** The main clause (my head says otherwise) comes after the adverb clause in this sentence. This is not always the case, however. Adverb clauses can come after the main clause.

Note the position and punctuation of the adverb clauses below (in bold).

EXAMPLE	NOTE
1. **Although we've only seen each other twice in the past five years,** you are still my very best friend. *(initial position in sentence)*	**Position of adverb clause** • The adverb clause can occur in initial position as in (1) or after the main clause as in (2).
2. You are still my very best friend **although we've only seen each other twice in the past five years.** *(position after the main clause)*	**Punctuation of adverb clause** • Place a comma after an adverb clause in initial position as in (1). No comma is necessary in (2) because the main clause comes first in the sentence.

■ II. Summary Chart of Adverb Clause Use

Adverb clauses modify the verb or main clause in a sentence. These clauses express a relationship of **time, place, reason, contrast, opposition, condition, purpose,** and **manner.** They answer questions such as *when, where, how,* or *why.* Below is a list of these clauses and the subordinating conjunctions for each type. Since many of these may not be new to you, test yourself by covering the far left column and trying to identify the type of clause by looking at the example.

TYPE OF CLAUSE	SUBORDINATING CONJUNCTIONS	EXAMPLE
1. Time	• after • before • when • while • as • whenever • since, until/till • as soon as • once • as long as	a. I'm undecided about what to do *after the baby arrives.* b. *As soon as the baby is born,* I will have to make a decision. c. I will work *as long as* I am able to.
2. Place	• where • wherever • everywhere • anywhere	d. *Everywhere I look,* I see mothers with their newborn babies!

Continued on next page.

Continued from previous page.

Type Of Clause	Subordinating Conjunctions	Example
3. Reason/Result	• because/since/as • now that • inasmuch as • as long as • so that/such that	e. Maybe you can help me, *since* *you were always better at* *making decisions.*
4. Direct Contrast	• while • whereas	f. *While* **my heart tells me** **to stay home,** my head tells me to go back to work.
5. Opposition	• although • even though • though • despite the fact that • in spite of the fact that	g. *Although* **we've seen** **each other only twice in** **the past five years,** you are still my very best friend.
6. Condition	• if • unless • provided that • only if • whether or not • in case • even if	h. *Unless* Jeff gets laid off, we could probably manage it. (See Chapter 13 for a more complete explanation of adverb clauses of condition.)
7. Purpose	• so that • in order that	i. I wish we lived closer *so that* **we could have lunch** **together once in a while.**
8. Manner	• as • as if • as though	j. You look *as though* **you are** **ready to have the baby** **soon!**

8.1 Recognition Drill: *The Pros and Cons of Staying Home*

DIRECTIONS: Below is the list that Joanne made of the advantages and disadvantages of staying home with her baby.

1. Underline the **adverb clauses** in each sentence.

2. Circle the **subordinating conjunctions** and identify them by type (for example, time). Refer to the above chart for a complete list.

3. Put a check (√) next to those sentences that require a comma and then insert one where necessary.

Example ___√___ (After) her baby is born, **a mother's life changes dramatically.**

time

The advantages of staying home:

1. _____ The mother can give her baby a great deal of attention as she will not be gone during the day.

2. _____ Whenever the child is hungry the mother will be able to feed him or her.

3. _____ The mother will be the primary caregiver so that the child will feel secure.

4. _____ Although the mother won't have the social contact she is used to at work she won't be completely exhausted at the end of the day by trying to juggle what are in fact two full-time jobs.

The disadvantages of staying home:

1. _____ Despite the fact that she must leave her child at day care the mother will be able to retain her position and salary at work.

2. _____ The mother will lose her job unless she returns to work after the maximum six-week maternity leave.

3. _____ Wherever you live there are many competent and caring day care workers who need the income.

4. _____ While the baby is at day care he or she will have social contact with other babies and adults.

III. Time Clauses

The following chart summarizes adverb clauses of time.

SUBORDINATING CONJUNCTION	EXAMPLE	NOTES
after	1. **After** I *finish* college, I will work in my father's company.	• In (1) the speaker is talking about the future, but note that a future tense is **not** used in the adverb clause. Always use the simple present tense in adverb clauses of time that talk about the future.
before	2. **Before** I started this job, I (had) worked for a travel agent.	• The use of the past perfect in sentences with **before** and **after** clauses is optional, as in (2).

Continued on next page.

Continued from previous page.

SUBORDINATING CONJUNCTION	EXAMPLE	NOTES
when	3. Joe was in college **when** he met Jill. 4. They *had known* each other two years **when** they got married.	• In (3) **when** means *during* or *at that time*. • In (4), **when** means before; the past perfect is necessary in the main clause.
while/as	5. The children are in day care **while** Lou Anne *is working*. 6. **As** Lou Anne was taking her children to day care, she saw a bus hit a tractor trailer.	• A **progressive** tense is usually used in **while** and **as** clauses, as it is in (5) and (6). • **While** and **as** have the same meaning *(at the same time.)*
by the time	7. **By the time** the baby is born, Jack and Linda will have been married for four years.	• See the Special Note on page 183 for a detailed explanation of **by the time**.
since	8. *Sue has been working* **since** Johnny was born.	• Use an appropriate perfect tense in the independent clause of a sentence with a **since** clause. In (8), the present perfect progressive is used.
whenever	9. **Whenever** George thinks about getting married, he gets butterflies in his stomach.	• **Whenever** = each time that. • Use a simple present or past tense in a **whenever** clause; (9) uses a simple present to express his habitual activity.
once	10. **Once** Carole graduates from high school, she will move to New York.	• **Once** = after Note that (10) is a sentence about the future; use the future tense in the main clause, but the simple present tense in the adverb clause.
as soon as	11. **As soon as** she moves there, she will rent an apartment.	• **As soon as** = immediately after As in (10), don't use a future tense in the adverb clause.
until/till	12. Alex won't get married **until** he can afford a house.	• **Until** = up to that moment
as long as/ so long as	13. Joan will never leave her hometown **as long as** her mother is alive.	• **as/so long as** = during the entire time that

SPECIAL NOTE

INTENSIFIERS WITH SUBORDINATORS

Intensifiers can be used with the following subordinating conjunctions of time. These intensifiers show emphasis.

- **just as/just when** . . . . The plane took off **just as (when)** we
  (at precisely that time)   arrived at the airport.
- **shortly before/after** . . . . He changed his will **shortly**
- **immediately before/after**   **(immediately) before** he died.
- **long before/after** . . . . She had divorced him **long before** he died.
- **ever since** . . . . She has been afraid to fly **ever since** she was
                                         a child.

8.2 Rapid Drill: *Adverb Clauses of Time*

DIRECTIONS: State what types of decisions you will make or have made before, during, or after these events. Use the subordinating conjunction in parentheses. Use the intensifiers listed above when appropriate.

Example   CUE: leave home (before)
              ANSWER: Before I leave home, I must decide where to live.

1. have a baby (as soon as)
2. buy a house (long before)
3. look for a job (while)
4. enter the university (once)
5. change jobs (whenever)
6. retire (once)
7. travel to another city (immediately after)
8. get married (before)
9. get divorced (shortly before)
10. move to another city (whenever)
11. make a will (before)
12. ask my boss for a raise (as soon as)
13. have my parents live with me (by the time)
14. put my parents in a nursing home (as long as)
15. go to graduate school (when)

8.3 Written Drill: *Verb Tenses with Adverb Clauses*

DIRECTIONS: Fill in the blanks using any appropriate verb, paying careful attention to the use of the verb tenses.

Example   Right after Bob *brushes his teeth,* he will go to bed.

1. Long before he was elected president, Ronald Reagan _____ a movie actor.

2. Once I _____ save up enough money, I can make a deposit to rent a nicer apartment.

3. As soon as an earthquake _____, you should run for cover.

4. As long as she _____, Mrs. Rose never missed having Sunday dinner with her children.

5. I _____ when the telephone rang.

6. As Mr. Jones _____ at Sweetwater's restaurant, his wife was sitting at the Waterworks restaurant.

7. She _____ since I have known her.

8. Whenever my teacher _____, I get really frustrated.

9. I will study English until I _____.

10. I will retire from my job after I _____.

11. We _____ ever since class began.

12. Once _____, I will go and get some lunch.

13. When I was in elementary school, I _____.

14. When I finished high school I (already) _____.

15. My English _____ since I came here.

SPECIAL NOTE

BY THE TIME

Note the verb tenses used in the main and adverb clauses with **by the time**.

- By the time she <u>leaves</u>, I <u>will have finished</u> dinner.
  (present)   (future perfect)

- By the time she <u>left</u>, I <u>had already finished</u> the test.
  (past)   (past perfect)

(See Chapter 3 for an explanation of the future perfect tense.)

8.4 Written Activity: *A Life Story*

DIRECTIONS: Write a composition in which you describe the major events in the life of one of your parents or grandparents. Use at least four adverb clauses of time. Underline the subordinating conjunctions.

IV. Place Clauses

SUBORDINATING CONJUNCTION	EXAMPLE	NOTES
where	1. I want to live **where** my children will be safe.	• **where** = a specific place
anywhere/wherever	2. I will not raise my children **anywhere (wherever)** there is crime.	• **anywhere/wherever** = any place
everywhere	3. **Everywhere** he travels, he sees poverty in the big cities.	• **everywhere** = all places

8.5 Rapid Drill: *Place Clauses*

DIRECTIONS: Complete these statements using a place clause.

1. I like to shop anywhere . . .
2. I love restaurants where . . .
3. I don't go anywhere . . .
4. Everywhere I look, . . .
5. Wherever there are rich people, . . .
6. Anywhere there is political repression, . . .
7. I will always go wherever . . .
8. In a movie theater, I always sit where . . .
9. I will buy a house anywhere . . .
10. Everywhere you go in this town, you can find . . .
11. I can find an ATM anywhere . . .
12. I need to find a place where . . .
13. I will settle down anywhere . . .
14. Everywhere I went, I . . .
15. Wherever the movie star went . . .

V. Reason Clauses

SUBORDINATING CONJUNCTION	EXAMPLE	NOTES
because/as/since	**1. Because** her parents divorced when she was small, Marie is reluctant to marry.	• All of these subordinating conjunctions state a cause and have the same meaning as **because.**
as long as/so long as	**2. As long as** you are in the kitchen, could you get me a glass of water?	• **As/so long as** is used more in conversation.
now that	**3. Now that** Maria's father has moved far away, she only sees him once a year.	• **Now that** is used to express time and cause; it means **because now.**
inasmuch as in view of the fact that on account of the fact that as a result of the fact that on the grounds that due to the fact that	**4.** Her parents were granted a divorce **inasmuch as** they had irreconcilable differences. **5. Due to the fact that** you failed to file your income taxes on time, you must pay a penalty.	• These subordinating conjunctions all mean **because.** • They are more formal and are mainly used in **formal writing and speaking.**

8.6 Paired Activity: *Adverb Clauses of Reason*

DIRECTIONS: First answer yes, no, or maybe to the following questions. Then discuss the **reasons** for your answers with a partner. *Use other subordinating conjunctions than* because!

Example   Would you marry someone from a different culture than your own?
"Yes."

"Of course I would marry someone from another culture, since it is not the person's nationality that counts, but their personality."

1. Would you marry someone from a different religion than yours?
2. Would you put your parents in a nursing home when they get old?
3. Would you think of donating some of your money to a good cause?
4. If you couldn't have children of your own, would you adopt one?
5. If a family member needed a kidney transplant, would you donate yours?
6. If you saw someone cheating on an important test, would you report that person?
7. If you saw a friend's child shoplifting at a record store, would you report that child?
8. If you inherited a lot of money, would you donate some of it to your school?
9. Would you work in a foreign country if you were offered a job there?
10. Would you ever live on a farm? On a boat?

8.7 Written Activity: *Adverb Clauses of Reason*

DIRECTIONS: Choose one of the questions in exercise 8.6 and write a short paragraph explaining your decision. Use at least three adverb clauses of reason. Do not use **because** in your paragraph.

■ VI. Result Clauses

Compare how result can be expressed in the two constructions below. A review of count and noncount nouns (Chapter 1) would be helpful at this point.

Note how **so** can be followed by an adjective or adverb only; **such** must be followed by a noun phrase.

EXAMPLE	So + ADJECTIVE/ADVERB + THAT	SUCH + NOUN PHRASE + THAT
The population is small. The mail carrier knows where everybody lives.	1. The population is **so** small **that** the mail carrier knows where everybody lives.	2. This town has **such** a small population **that** the mail carrier knows where everybody lives.

A. Such . . . That Constructions

SUCH . . . THAT CONSTRUCTION	EXAMPLE
With singular count nouns: Use such + a/an + adjective + singular count noun (e.g. population as in (1).	1. This rural town has **such a small population (that)** the mail carrier knows where everybody lives.
With plural nouns: Use such + adjective + plural noun + (that)	2. The town sells **such tasty apple pie (that)** tourists can't resist buying some to take away.
With mass nouns: Use such + adjective + mass noun + (that)	3. The local restaurant serves **such good food (that)** people go there from miles away.
With abstract nouns Use such + abstract noun +(that)	4. At night there is **such quiet (that)** I don't have any trouble sleeping.

B. So . . . That Constructions

So . . . That Construction	Example
So + adjective + that	1. The city is **so polluted that** I often think of moving to the country.
So + adverb + that	2. But my job pays **so well that** I can't afford to give it up.
So much/little + (adjective) + mass noun + that	3. There is **so much (noisy) traffic on my street that** I have to keep the windows closed. 4. There is **so little entertainment in the country that** I would probably be bored.
So many/few + (adjective) + count noun + that	5. I've got **so many friends here that** it would be hard to leave. 6. American cities have **so few parks that** I often long for open green spaces.

Special Note

So/That and Such/That in Initial Position

Occasionally, the such/that or so/that phrase is placed at the beginning of a sentence for emphasis. Note that this is not a common construction; however, when it does appear in this position in the sentence, then you must use **question (inverted) word order** as in the following examples:

• **Such good food** does that restaurant serve that people go there from miles away.
• **So polluted is that city** that many people suffer from respiratory problems.

8.8 Written Drill: *So* or *Such?*

DIRECTIONS: Here are a few reasons people gave for choosing to marry their husbands and wives. Fill in the blanks with **so** or **such**, as appropriate.

1. Mark has _____ beautiful eyes that I fell in love with him at first sight.

2. My wife is _____ intelligent that she runs her own business now.

3. Jill and I had _____ stimulating conversations that I was immediately attracted to her.

4. His family was _____ a welcoming group of people that I immediately felt accepted.

5. _____ witty was my husband that I couldn't stop laughing on our first date!

6. Jack had _____ few financial difficulties that I found him very stable.

7. Rhonda had _____ many friends that I was sure she was a special person.

8. I had _____ an easy feeling around her that I knew I wanted to spend my life with her.

9. He was _____ patient around children that I wanted him to be the father of my children.

10. We had _____ a good time together that I fell in love.

8.9 Written Activity: *Homeschooling*

DIRECTIONS: Read the following paragraph about homeschooling. Then answer the questions using a **so . . . that** or **such . . . that** construction in each answer.

Bill and Laura Gold live in rural Ohio. They have three children. When it was time to send their children to school, Bill and Laura decided that they wanted to teach their children at home, to do "homeschooling." They made this decision because they didn't want their children exposed to some of the negative aspects of public schools such as the poor food in the cafeteria, the possibility of drugs and violence, and the discipline problems in the classroom. In addition, Laura felt that because of the large number of students in each class, the children wouldn't get enough attention. She believed that with more individual attention at home, the children would learn more quickly. She also thought that their children would have more confidence in their ability to learn if they studied at home with her in a nonthreatening atmosphere. In short, Laura felt that their children would get a better education if they were schooled at home. The only possible problem would be a lack of time. If Laura got too busy at home with other activities, she might not devote enough time to teaching.

1. Why did Laura and Bill decide to do homeschooling for their children? _____

_____

2. In particular, how did Laura feel about the class size in the public schools? _____

_____

3. What is the one problem Laura thinks she might have? _____

_____

4. What is your opinion about homeschooling? What are some advantages or disadvantages?

_____

_____

8.10 Error Analysis: *Clauses of Time, Place, Reason, and Result*

DIRECTIONS: Find the errors in the following sentences and correct them clearly. Some sentences may not have any errors.

1. Alaska is such cold state that few people want to live there.

2. Earthquake insurance is such an important in some states that more and more homeowners are buying it.

3. I have so few good friends that I often get lonely.

4. I would really like to go to Egypt. Because I would like to see the pyramids there.

5. As the professor spoke about the causes of the greenhouse effect, he showed many slides.

6. Gloria and Jack will try a six-month separation before they will get divorced.

7. Gerald will move where are clean air and water.

8. Cheryl was talking to her mother during that the earthquake hit.

9. Because an imported car is very expensive, so I will buy a domestic one.

10. By the time I will get there, the plane already left.

8.11 Written Activity: *Adverb Clauses of Time, Place, Reason, and Result*

DIRECTIONS: Choose one of the following situations and write a letter. Use at least four adverb clauses of time, place, reason, and result and underline the subordinating conjunctions.

1. You are studying at a university in the United States. Your family expects you to return home at the end of this semester, but your academic department has asked you to stay for at least two years as a teaching assistant. You are torn between pleasing your family and pleasing yourself. You like the United States, you like the people in your department, and you think that you would learn a lot as a teaching assistant. Make a decision whether to stay or return home. Then write a letter to your family or to the department explaining the situation and your decision.

2. While you were in a distant city attending a training session in your field, you were asked to stay on for one month to help set up a new office there. Your employer in your own city completely agreed and encouraged you to take advantage of the opportunity. After one month, your colleagues liked your work so much, they asked you to take a job there in the new city. You love the challenge of the work and the people you work with, not to mention the increase in salary. However, you know it would be very hard for your elderly parents, who are not well physically, to have you live so far away. Make a decision and write a polite refusal letter either to your employer or the new employer, explaining your situation and your decision.

VII. Direct Contrast and Opposition Clauses

SUBORDINATING CONJUNCTION	EXAMPLE	NOTES
Direct contrast: • While • Whereas	1. **While** private schools are very expensive, public schools are free in the United States. 2. Private schools provide a lot of individual attention **whereas** public schools don't have the means to cater to individual students. 3. Private schools are very expensive **while** public schools are free in the United States.	• Use **while** and **whereas** to show that two things or situations are in direct opposition or contrast. • **While** and **whereas** have the same meaning, but **whereas** is more formal. • Unlike other subordinating conjunctions, **while** and **whereas** may occur before either the main or adverb clause with **no change in meaning.** • A comma is sometimes placed after the main clause, but it is not necessary.
Concession: Although even though though	4. **Although** private schools provide careful supervision, many students still use drugs and alcohol. 5. Private school students often get accepted into good colleges, **though** some choose to go to work instead.	• A concession clause shows contrast by placing limits on the ideas in the main clause. The main clause shows surprising or unexpected results, as in (4). • **Although, even though,** and **though** have basically the same meaning. • A comma is sometimes placed after the main clause as it is in (5), but it is not obligatory.
In spite of the fact that despite the fact that	6. **In spite of the fact that** public schools have bad reputations, there are many qualified and caring teachers who work there.	• These phrases have the same meaning as **although.**

8.12 Rapid Drill: *Contrast Clauses*

DIRECTIONS: Transform the following sentences using an appropriate subordinating conjunction of contrast from the list above.

Example   CUE: It's hot in Texas, but it's bitter cold in Alaska right now.
ANSWER: While it's hot in Texas, it's bitter cold in Alaska right now. (*This is a direct contrast, so use while.*)

1. A high school diploma is very important, but many students drop out before they graduate.

2. Many wealthy families can afford to send their kids to private school, but they put them in public school.

3. Private school academic programs are excellent, but public school athletic programs are first-rate.

4. The long-term effects of homeschooling have not been determined, but many families feel that this is the best way to protect their children from negative influences found in public schools.

5. Some students graduate from high school, but they have difficulty reading and writing.

SPECIAL NOTE

As . . . As

The following constructions may be substituted for **although.**

1. **As + Adjective + As + Subject + Linking Verb**
   - **Although** he is intelligent, he couldn't pass the law exam.
   - **As intelligent as he is,** he couldn't pass the law exam.

2. **As + Adverb + As + Subject + Verb**
   - **Although** he cooks well, his dinner last night was a disaster!
   - **As well as he cooks,** his dinner last night was a disaster!

3. **As + Much + As + Subject + Verb**
   - **Although he studied a lot,** he failed the exam.
   - **As much as he studied,** he failed the exam.

8.13 Rapid Drill: *Contrast Clauses*

DIRECTIONS: Gloria was engaged to Mike for one year. Two weeks before the wedding she decided that he was not the right person for her to marry. Below are some of the things that Gloria said to Mike. Transform them using the **as . . . as construction** from the special note above.

Example   CUE: Although I enjoy your company very much, I don't love you.
            ANSWER: As much as I enjoy your company, I don't love you.

1. Although you are very wealthy, money isn't the only factor.

2. Although you tried very hard to make me love you, I never fell in love.

3. Although you are good looking, I am not attracted to you.

4. Although you have been very kind to me, your parents never accepted me.

5. Although you love me very much, I don't believe this marriage can work.

6. Although you are very ambitious, I don't think I would be happy being moved around by your corporation.

7. Although I admire your drive, I believe that I would be happier with someone who is more relaxed.

8. Although I really wanted this relationship to work, deep down I don't believe we were meant for each other.

9. Although I am openminded about religious differences, I would like to marry someone from my own faith.

10. (Add your own sentence.) _____

■ VIII. Reduction of Contrast and Cause Clauses to Prepositions

Note how the following clauses can be reduced to prepositional phrases.

A. CONTRAST Clauses

To change a clause into a prepositional phrase, reduce the subject verb group in the adverb clause (e.g., **it rained**) to a noun phrase (e.g., **the rain**). Replace the subordinating conjunction with an equivalent proposition (e. g., despite).

> **Clause: Despite the fact that** *it rained*, we went to the game.
> **Phrase: Despite** *the rain*, we went to the game.

> **Clause: In spite of the fact that** *the weather was bad*, we held the picnic outdoors.
> **Phrase: In spite of** *the bad weather*, we held the picnic outdoors.

> **Clause: Although** *he had planned it carefully*, there were still some transportation problems.
> **Phrase: Regardless of** *his careful planning*, there were still some transportation problems.

8.14 Written Drill: *Despite* or *Despite the Fact That?*

DIRECTIONS: Read the following statements made by public school teachers and fill in the blanks with **despite** or **despite the fact that.**

Example   CUE: I enjoy teaching at a public school *despite* the discipline problems.

1. _____ the media often gives bad reports, many of my students are hardworking and honest kids.

2. _____ the great dropout rate, many of our students go on to college and become professionals.

3. _____ the low pay, I would never change my job.

4. _____ they get an eight-week break in the summer, public school teachers get burned out easily.

5. _____ better working conditions, I would never teach at a private school.

6. Now transform the above sentences using the alternative form. That is, change **despite + noun** to **despite the fact that + clause** and vice versa.

Example   CUE: I enjoy working at a public school despite the discipline problems. (**despite + noun**)
   ANSWER: I enjoy working at a public school despite the fact that I face discipline problems every day. (**despite the fact that + clause**)

B. CAUSE Clauses

Clauses of reason/cause can be reduced to prepositional phrases (e.g., **as a result of, due to, in view of,** and **because of**) in the following ways.

> **Clause: Because** *she worked hard*, she got a promotion.
> **Phrase: As a result of** *her hard work*, she got a promotion.

> **Clause: Because** *the economy was strong*, business was good.
> **Phrase: Due to** *the strong economy*, business was good.

Clause: Because *the stock market* was strong, she invested in stocks.
Phrase: **In view of** *the strong stock market,* she invested in stocks.

Clause: Because *she got an important account,* she won an award.
Phrase: **Because of** *her getting an important account,* she won an award.

SPECIAL
NOTE

> **POSSESSIVES BEFORE GERUNDS**
> Note how the following sentence has been reduced using a possessive before the gerund
> *donating.*
> • Because he donated a kidney, she was able to live.
> • **Because of** *his* **donating a kidney,** she was able to live.

8.15 Oral Drill: *Reducing Clauses to Prepositional Phrases*

DIRECTIONS: Below are a number of reasons Jack gave his family explaining why he chose not to go to college. Reduce these clauses to phrases using the prepositions provided.

Example   CUE: Jack doesn't want to go to college because it is too expensive. (because of)
ANSWER: *Jack doesn't want to go to college because of the high cost.*

Jack doesn't want to go to college . . .

1. . . . because he got poor grades in high school. (because of)
2. . . . because he doesn't need a college degree for his work. (due to)
3. . . . because he doesn't like school. (in view of)
4. . . . because his friends told him not to. (as a result of)
5. . . . because he wants to make some money. (because of)
6. Now use prepositional phrases to explain to Jack why it is important for him to go to college.

8.16 Group Activity: *The Death Penalty*

DIRECTIONS: In some countries of the world, the death penalty is legal while in others it is not. In small groups, discuss the laws in your countries and the possible causes for these death penalty policies. Then take a personal stand on this issue. After your group discussion, complete the sentences that follow.

1. I believe the death penalty should _____.

2. Despite _____, I believe _____

_____.

3. It is best that _____ in view of _____

_____.

4. Because of _____, my _____ country

_____.

8.17 Paired Activity: *Using Although to Concede*

DIRECTIONS: When you are presenting an argument either in writing or speaking, it is common to concede, or recognize, another point of view and then to point out the problems or flaws with this point of view. For example, if a teenage son wanted to persuade his parents to buy him a car, he might make the following argument.

"Although a car is very expensive, I will be able to do your errands for you and you will have more free time."

Choose one of the following topics to discuss with your partner. Take opposing sides on the issue. Debate the issue, using **although** to concede to your partner's opposing point of view. Be ready to write your ideas in a paragraph if instructed by your teacher.

1. Children should be required to wear uniforms to school.
   Children should be able to choose what to wear to school.

2. A woman would make a fine president of the United States.
   A woman would not be suitable as president of the United States.

3. Handguns should be available for individuals to buy.
   People should not be able to buy handguns.

4. Men and women should sign financial agreements before getting married.
   Men and women should not sign financial agreements before getting married.

IX. Purpose Clauses

Compare the following sentences.

1. John went on vacation to see his family. He ate more than he usually does, **so** he gained five pounds.	• John did not intend to gain weight. He did not do it on purpose. This is a result.
2. Jack went to the doctor, who told him he was too thin and needed to gain some weight. He ate a lot last week **so that** he could gain some weight.	• Jack **wanted** to gain weight. He did it on purpose.

Paragraph 1 expresses a result. Paragraph 2 expresses **purpose**. It states **why** he ate a lot. When you want to talk about purpose, you can use the **so . . . that** construction. Note how this construction and other expressions of purpose are used in the following examples.

SUBORDINATING CONJUNCTION OF PURPOSE	EXAMPLE	NOTES
so that + modal	1. Jim studied business **so (that)** he could work for his father.	• **So that** is always followed by a modal—will, would, can, could, may, might. In (1) it is followed by **could**. • **That** is sometimes deleted with no change in meaning.

Continued on next page.

Continued from previous page.

SUBORDINATING CONJUNCTION OF PURPOSE	EXAMPLE	NOTES
in order that	2. Ruth studied architecture **in order that** she could design the house of her dreams.	• **In order that** has the same meaning and use as **so that**, but it is not commonly used.
Reduction to preposition, in order to + infinitive	3. Jim studied business **in order to** work for his father. 4. John wore a raincoat **in order not to** get wet.	• The above clauses can be reduced to infinitive phrases, e.g., **in order to work** in (3). • Note the position of **not** in (4).

A. Modal Choice with *So That* Constructions

The type of modal used in the **so that** clause depends on the verb tense used in the main clause. Note the examples below.

TENSE OF MAIN CLAUSE	EXAMPLE	MODAL USED IN SO THAT CLAUSE
Simple Present (Habitual)	1. I **eat** fiber regularly **so that** my cholesterol level **will** not increase. 2. I **take** the kids to the babysitter **so that** I **can** have some free time.	• In (1) **will** means **to be sure that** • In (2) **can** means **to be able to**
Past	3. I **got** a babysitter **so that** I **could** go to the race. 4. I **helped** my brother train **so that** he **would** win the race. 5. I **helped** my brother train **so that** he **might** win the race.	• Use **could** (to be able to) after clauses in the past tense as in (3). • Use **would** (to be sure) after clauses in the past tense as in (4). • **May** and **might** are sometimes used as in (5), but are not common.
Future	6. I **will join** a diet center **so that** I **can** lose 20 pounds. 7. I will only shop when I am not hungry **so that** I **won't** buy any junk food.	• Use **can** after main clauses in the future tense as in (6). • Use **will** after main clauses in the future tense, as in (7).

8.18 Written Drill: *Can/Could or Will/Would?*

DIRECTIONS: Fill in the blanks with **can, could, will,** or **would,** as appropriate.

1. He became a doctor so that he _____ earn money.

2. She became a doctor so that she _____ help people.

3. The government raised taxes so that it _____ pay back its debts.

4. A bird protects its nest so that none of the chicks _____ get hurt.

5. Mark studied hard so that he _____ get an A.

6. The presidential candidate will campaign nonstop so that he _____ win the election.

7. The policeman stopped the drunk driver so that no one _____ get killed on the road.

8.19 Rapid Drill: *You Are What You Eat*

DIRECTIONS: Read the following sentences about food choices. Transform the **in order to + infinitive** phrase to a **so that + modal** construction.

Example   CUE: Jack drinks coffee **in order to** wake up in the morning.
              ANSWER: *Jack drinks coffee so that he can stay awake in the morning.*

1. Early settlers in the United States dried fruits and vegetables in order to have something to eat in the winter.

2. Robert will go on a fruit fast in order to cleanse toxins from his system.

3. Some people give up dairy products in order to avoid winter colds.

4. Claire ate a box of chocolates this morning in order to feel better after her boyfriend left her.

5. David will eliminate sugar from his diet in order to lose some weight.

6. My mother fed us a lot of dairy products in order to strengthen our bones.

7. My husband eats a lot of leafy green vegetables in order to get enough calcium.

8. Many vegetarians don't eat meat in order to spare animals from a brutal death.

X. Manner Clauses

SUBORDINATING CONJUNCTION	EXAMPLE	NOTES
as if/as though	1. This room looks **as if** a tornado hit it. 2. My boss treats me **as though I were** a secretary, which I definitely am not! 3. You look **as if** you **are** very tired.	• **As if** and **as though** are used to answer the question "how?" as in (1) and (2). • When the **as though/as if** clause is untrue, as it is in (2)—the speaker is not a secretary—use **were**, not **was**. • If the statement is possibly true, as in (3)—you could be tired—then the verb **be** takes its usual form.

Continued on next page.

Continued from previous page.

SUBORDINATING CONJUNCTION	EXAMPLE	NOTES
(like)	4. This room looks **like** a tornado hit it.	• **Like** is a preposition, so it is followed by a noun, not a clause. It may be followed by a clause in informal conversation as in (4), but it is not considered standard English.
as	5. It happened just **as** we imagined it would.	

8.20 Oral Drill: *As If/As Though*

DIRECTIONS: Work with a partner and write the answers to the following questions using **as if** or **as though** in your response.

Example   CUE: How does your house look after a party?
ANSWER: It looks as though a hurricane swept through it.

1. How does your teacher look when you don't do your homework?
2. How do you feel after a two-week break from school?
3. How do you look after taking a hard exam?
4. How do you feel after spending two hours in rush hour traffic?
5. How does a person look after falling asleep at the beach in the sun?
6. Jason is giving a presentation to the board of directors of his company. How should he speak to the group?
7. Georgette is singing at her opera debut tonight. How should she sing?
8. Ron is leaving for a year in the army. How should he and his girlfriend spend their last day together?
9. Lydia is going to her first formal dance tonight. How should she dress?
10. Mark is running for mayor of his city and he is going to his first political rally tonight. How should he act there?

8.21 Paired Activity: *All Adverb Clauses*

DIRECTIONS: Roleplay the following situations with a partner. Use the subordinating conjunctions listed. Be ready to present your roleplay to the class if instructed by your teacher.

SITUATION 1: The director of personnel of IBM is interviewing a potential candidate for a job.
SUBORDINATING CONJUNCTIONS: **since, so that, whenever**

SITUATION 2: A boss has given his employee too much work. The employee is trying to complain politely but firmly to the boss.
SUBORDINATING CONJUNCTIONS: **as soon as, before, in spite of the fact that, despite**

SITUATION 3: A police officer has stopped a driver for speeding.
SUBORDINATING CONJUNCTIONS: **while, once, as if**

SITUATION 4: A tenant is complaining to his landlord about a leaky faucet.
SUBORDINATING CONJUNCTIONS: **such that, everywhere, while**

■ 8.22 Section Review

DIRECTIONS: Fill in the blanks with any appropriate answer. **There may be more than one correct answer.**

1. _____ his illness, Jack continued to work.
   - **a.** In spite of
   - **b.** Despite of
   - **c.** Despite the fact that
   - **d.** Inasmuch as

2. _____ David tried, he couldn't remember his first grade teacher's name.
   - **a.** As hard as
   - **b.** Although
   - **c.** Despite the fact that
   - **d.** Due to the fact that

3. Many people decrease their fat intake so that they _____ control their cholesterol.
   - **a.** can
   - **b.** will
   - **c.** could
   - **d.** would

4. Jack is leaving his job because his boss treats him as if he _____ his personal slave.
   - **a.** is
   - **b.** was
   - **c.** were
   - **d.** had been

5. Frank had _____ on his vacation that he didn't want to return.
   - **a.** a so good time
   - **b.** so much good time
   - **c.** such a good time
   - **d.** so much fun

6. By the time the hurricane _____ the coast of Florida, most of the people living there will be gone.
   - **a.** hit
   - **b.** has hit
   - **c.** will hit
   - **d.** hits

7. Although I'd like to travel, _____ .
   - **a.** but I don't have enough money
   - **b.** I plan to leave soon
   - **c.** I don't have enough money
   - **d.** I can't

8. We decided not to get married _____ .
   - **a.** in spite of our love
   - **b.** despite the fact we love each other
   - **c.** despite we love each other
   - **d.** because of we love each other.

9. Carmina stopped studying _____ .
   - **a.** after she went to bed
   - **b.** after she had read 100 pages
   - **c.** after she reading 100 pages.
   - **d.** after she read 100 pages.

10. _____ , she graduated with honors.
   - **a.** Because of her hard work
   - **b.** Because she work hard
   - **c.** Because her hard work
   - **d.** Because she worked hard

Grammatical Patterns Part Two

Adverb Clause Reduction

Preview

DIRECTIONS: Read the following letter written to Edith, an advice columnist. Find out what the writer's problem is. Then answer the questions that follow.

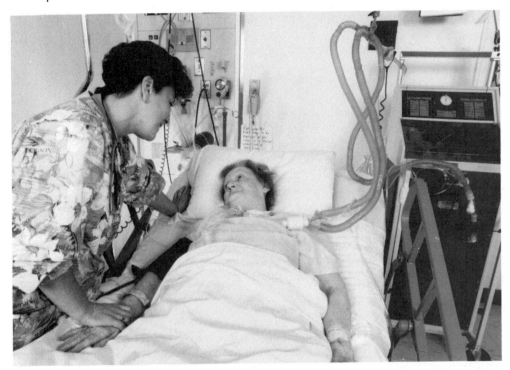

Dear Edith,

   I never thought I would find myself writing a "Dear Edith" letter, but I don't know who else **to turn to.**

   Four years ago my sister found out she had **a degenerative disease** for which there was no cure. *Being optimistic,* she lived her life normally. She believed that scientists would surely find some sort of treatment. Well, they haven't. Last year *while visiting friends in California,* she had a serious attack and she had to be hospitalized. *Upon returning to Des Moines,* she came to me and told me how horrible her hospital visit had been. She said she wouldn't want to endure that again. *Having realized that **her prognosis** was* *not good,* she made me promise that when her condition worsened and she became nonfunctional, that I would have the doctors withdraw all **life-support systems.** *Not really believing that such a situation could ever occur,* I assured her that I wouldn't let her suffer.

Edith, two months ago she relapsed into **a coma.** The doctors have told me that there is no hope for recovery. They also said that soon she will need a life-support system, and that she could go on living with that for quite a while. I don't know what to do. *Having promised my sister not to let her suffer,* I feel that it is my duty to do what she asked. On the other hand, I believe that as long as there is time, there is hope.

I hope that you can help me with this very difficult decision.

Distressed in Des Moines

VOCABULARY

to turn to: to go for advice
a degenerative disease: an illness which gets worse and worse
a prognosis: a prediction about the future state of a disease
life-support systems: devices that perform bodily functions and allow a person to live
a coma: an extended period of unconsciousness caused by injury or disease

CULTURAL NOTE/DISCUSSION

There is an increasing number of patients in the United States who choose to refuse life-saving treatment in order to die naturally when all life-support systems are withheld. A patient who is still relatively healthy can sign a document (called a **living will**) making this request. What is your reaction to the dilemma stated in the letter? Do you agree that ". . . as long as there is time, there is hope?" What would you do in such a situation?

FOCUS ON GRAMMAR

1. All the phrases in italics in the "Dear Edith" letter are adverb clauses of time and reason that have been reduced (that is, shortened by omitting words). Work with a partner to transform these phrases into clauses.

   Example   CUE: Being optimistic, she lived her life normally. (reason)
                ANSWER: *Because she was optimistic,* she lived her life normally.

   a. *Not really believing that such a situation could ever occur,* I assured her that I wouldn't let her suffer. (reason)

   Since I _____, I assured her that I wouldn't let her suffer.

   b. Last year *while visiting friends in California,* she had a serious attack and she had to be hospitalized. (time)

   Last year _____ she had a serious attack and she had to be hospitalized.

2. How did you change sentence (b) above from a phrase to a clause?

3. Compare these two sentences:

   a. While she was visiting friends in California, she had a serious attack.

   b. While she was visiting friends in California, her illness became worse.

   Sentence (a) can be shortened to *While visiting friends in California,* she had a serious attack. Sentence (b) cannot be shortened in this way. Can you guess why?

4. Compare these sentences from the preview:

   a. Having realized that her prognosis wasn't good, she made me promise that when her condition worsened and she became nonfunctional, I would have the doctors withhold all life-support systems.

   b. Having promised my sister not to let her suffer, I feel that it is my duty to do what she asked.

   Which sentence best expresses a time relationship? A cause-effect relationship? Could either sentence express **both** relationships?

I. Adverb Clause Reduction: An Overview

Adverb clauses of **time, reason,** and **opposition** can be reduced to adverb phrases without any change in meaning. Below is a brief overview of adverb clause reduction. (The clauses are in bold and the phrases are in italics in the sentences below.)

Clauses of Time:

   Clause: **While she lived in the nursing home,** she had good care.
   Phrase: *(While) living in the nursing home,* she had good care.

   Notes:
   • The subjects of both clauses must be the same; otherwise reduction is not possible. In the example above, **she** is the subject of both clauses, so reduction is possible.
   • The subject **(she)** is deleted in the reduction.
   • The verb form **(lived)** is changed to a participial "-ing" (living) in the reduced phrase.
   • Keeping the subordinator **(while)** is optional in the reduction.

Clauses of Reason:

   Clause: **Because she was healthy,** she didn't need special care.
   Phrase: *Being healthy,* she didn't need special care.

   Notes:
   • The subject **(she)** and the subordinator **(because)** are deleted.
   • The verb **(was)** is changed to **verb-ing (being).**
   • *Being healthy* = because she was healthy.

Clauses of Opposition:

   Clause: **Although she was happy in the nursing home,** she missed her house.
   Phrase: *Although happy in the nursing home,* she missed her house.

   Notes:
   • The subject **(she)** and **be** are deleted.
   • Keep the subordinator **(although)** and the adjective **(happy).**

All three types of reduction will be discussed in detail beginning on page 202.

8.23 Recognition Drill: *Clause Reduction*

DIRECTIONS: As previously stated, you may reduce a clause **only if the subjects in the two clauses are the same.** Read the following story about Mrs. Rose and underline the subjects in each sentence. Then put a check (✓) next to the sentences that can be reduced.

Example   CUE: _____ Because <u>Mrs. Rose</u> was alone, <u>her children</u> put her in a nursing home.
(The subjects are different—Mrs. Rose and her children—so this can't be reduced.)

CUE: __✓__ Because <u>they</u> lived far away, <u>Mrs. Rose's children</u> were unable to care for their mother themselves.
(Here the subjects are the same and so reduction is possible.)

_____ 1. Before her husband died, Mrs. Rose was happy living in her Victorian house.

_____ 2. Because her house was so big, Mrs. Rose didn't want to stay there alone after her husband's death.

_____ 3. Her children found a very good nursing home for her because they were worried about her being alone in the house.

_____ 4. While she was well, Mrs. Rose was quite comfortable in the home.

_____ 5. After she had a heart attack, the doctors advised her to have a pacemaker implanted.

_____ 6. The pacemaker allowed her to lead a normal life while it was functioning well.

_____ 7. However, after she wore it for two years, she began to have heart problems again.

_____ 8. The doctors advised her to have a new one put in since the old one was not working well.

_____ 9. Mrs. Rose decided not to have a new pacemaker installed because she didn't want to prolong her life.

_____ 10. Her children were outraged because they felt she should try to live as long as possible.

■ II. Reduction of Time Clauses

FULL CLAUSE	REDUCED CLAUSE	NOTES
BEFORE 1. Before she had her heart attack, Mrs. Rose was happy in the nursing home.	1a. Before having her heart attack, Mrs. Rose was happy in the nursing home. OR 1b. Before her heart attack, Mrs. Rose was happy in the nursing home.	With **before, after,** and **since:** • Delete the subject; note how **she** has been deleted in (1a) and (1b).

Continued on next page.

Continued from previous page.

FULL CLAUSE	REDUCED CLAUSE	NOTES
AFTER 2. **After she had worn it for two years,** she began to have problems with the pacemaker.	2a. **After wearing it for two years,** she began to have problems with the pacemaker. OR 2b. **After two years,** she began to have problems with the pacemaker.	• Change the verb to a participial phrase (1a) **verb-ing** form; in (2a) **wearing** is the verb-ing from of **wear,** the main verb in (2).
SINCE 3. Mrs. Rose's children have visited her twice **since they arrived in town.**	3a. Mrs. Rose's children have visited her twice **since arriving in town.**	• Keep the subordinator. • Sometimes the clause can be reduced to a prepositional phrase as in (1b) and (2b).
WHILE 4. Mrs. Rose had a heart attack **while she was visiting with her daughter.**	4a. **While visiting with her daughter,** Mrs. Rose had a heart attack. OR 4b. **Visiting with her daughter,** Mrs. Rose had a heart attack.	With **while:** • Delete the subject; • Change the verb to an **-ing** form; • **While** may be deleted when the meaning is "at the same time." Note how this has been done in (4b).
AS 5. Mrs. Rose had a heart attack **as she was visiting with her daughter.**	5a. **Visiting with her daughter,** Mrs. Rose had a heart attack.	With **as:** • **As** must be deleted; • The phrase must come at the beginning of the sentence.
AS SOON AS 6. **As soon as the children heard about their mother's heart attack,** they rushed to the hospital.	6a. **Upon hearing about their mother's heart attack,** the children rushed to the hospital. OR 6b. **On hearing about their mother's heart attack,** the children rushed to the hospital.	With **as soon as:** • Replace **as soon as** with **upon** as in (6a); • change the verb to an **-ing** form; • **On** can also replace **as soon as** like in (6b).

8.24 Oral Drill: *Reduction of Time Clauses*

DIRECTIONS: Reduce the following clauses whenever possible.

Example   CUE: Mrs. Rose had a heart attack while she was visiting her daughter.
           ANSWER: Mrs. Rose had a heart attack while visiting with her daughter.

1. As soon as Lila discovered that she won the lottery, she called her mother.
2. While she was talking to her mother, a van from the T.V. station pulled up to her house.
3. Once the T.V. crew had set up their equipment, they knocked on Lila's door.
4. Before they had a chance to ask her what she was going to do with the million dollars, Lila shut the door.
5. As soon as she got rid of the TV reporters, the telephone rang.
6. As she was talking to the newspaper reporter on the telephone, she heard the doorbell ring.
7. After Lila talked to 14 reporters that day, she decided she never wanted to win the lottery again.

8.25 Written Drill: *Clause Reduction: Time*

DIRECTIONS: Complete the following sentences using an adverbial clause of time. Then reduce the clause. Use each of the six subordinators listed in the chart on page 202 (i.e., before, after, since, as, while, as soon as).

Example: CUE: _____, he decided to take a trip around the world.
           ANSWER: *After he got fired from his job*, he decided to take a trip around the world.
           After getting fired from his job, he decided to take a trip around the world.

1. She decided to quit school _____.
2. He decided to paint his house _____.
3. They decided to get married _____.
4. The teacher decided to cancel the test _____.
5. The student decided to cut class _____.
6. The athlete decided to quit the team _____.
7. The teenager decided to quit smoking _____.
8. The employer decided to fire his worker _____.
9. The man decided to lose weight _____.
10. The woman decided to learn English _____.
11. The old man decided to write a novel _____.

8.26 Written Drill: *Reduction of Time Clauses*

DIRECTIONS: Turn to Exercise 8.3 on page 182 of this chapter. Decide which clauses in that exercise can be reduced and restate the full clauses with a reduced clause.

III. Clause Reduction: Reason

CLAUSE	REDUCTION	NOTES
Because/Since/As **1. Because (Since/As) she lived all alone, Mrs. Rose was happy to move to a nursing home.**	**1a. Living all alone, Mrs. Rose was happy to move to a nursing home.**	To reduce clauses of reason: • Delete the subject and the subordinator; • Change the verb to an **-ing** form.
Be Verbs **2. Because she was all alone, Mrs. Rose was happy to move to a nursing home.**	**2a. Being all alone, Mrs. Rose was happy to move to a nursing home.**	If the verb is **be** as it is in (2), change it to **being** as in (2a). This expresses reason.
Negative Verbs **3. Because she didn't want to prolong her life any longer, Mrs. Rose refused a new pacemaker.**	**3a. Not wanting to prolong her life any longer, Mrs. Rose refused a new pacemaker.**	If the adverb clause is negative, as in (3), place not in front of the **-ing** verb, as in (3a).
Because Of **4. Because she was lonely, Mrs. Rose was happy to move to a nursing home.**	**4a. Because of her loneliness, Mrs. Rose was happy to move to a nursing home.**	**Because of** is already a reduction of a reason clause. (See Grammatical Patterns One of this chapter for more explanation.)

8.27 Rapid Drill: *Reduction of Reason Clauses*

DIRECTIONS: Below are some for and against statements about the right to refuse life-saving treatments in cases of terminal or severe illness. Reduce these clauses of reason to participial phrases **whenever possible**. (Remember that the subjects in both clauses must be the same to reduce adverb clauses.)

Example   CUE: Many people refuse such treatment because they don't have the money to pay for it.
          ANSWER: Not having the money to pay for it, many people refuse such treatment.

For

1. Since some patients are octogenarians, they feel that they have lived long enough.
2. Many patients don't want to be a burden to their children so they choose not to have further treatment.
3. Other patients choose to die because the pain is intolerable.

Against

5. Many people disagree with a person's right to die because they believe there is always hope for a cure.

6. Some doctors disagree with a person's right to die since it can create serious legal complications for the hospital.

7. Because many people believe that only God can make such decisions, they oppose the right-to-die decision.

8.28 *Reduction of Reason Clauses*

DIRECTIONS: Turn to Exercise 8.27 on page 205. This time, complete the sentences by stating **why** the people made their decision using an adverb clause of reason. Then reduce the clause.

Example   CUE: _____, he decided to take a trip around the world.
ANSWER: *Because he liked to travel*, he decided to take a trip around the world
Liking to travel, he decided to take a trip around the world.

■ IV. Clause Reduction: *Opposition*

CLAUSE	REDUCTION	NOTES
Although/Though/While **1. Although (Though/While) she was lonely,** Mrs. Rose tried to have a positive attitude.	**1a. Although (Though/While) lonely,** Mrs. Rose tried to have a positive attitude.	• Adverb clauses with **although, though,** and **while** (of opposition) can be reduced to phrases in the same way.
2. Although (Though/While) she is an old person, Mrs. Rose still feels young.	**2a. Although (Though/While) an old person,** Mrs. Rose still feels young.	• Note how (1a) reduces to a **subordinator + adjective** in (1a).
3. Although (Though/While) she missed her house, she was glad for the company at the nursing home.	**3a. Although (Though/While) missing her house,** she was glad for the company at the nursing home.	• Note how (2) reduces to a **subordinator + noun** in (2a). • Note how (3) reduces to a **subordinator + verb-ing** in (3a).

8.29 Written Activity: *Reduced Clauses of Opposition*

DIRECTIONS: Read the following statements. Choose five that you do not completely agree with. Write a sentence for each one and present your ideas by using a reduced clause of opposition.

Example   CUE: The only way to learn English is by going to an English-speaking country.
ANSWER: Although extremely beneficial, going to an English-speaking country can be very expensive for students; they can also learn by taking classes in their town.

1. The English make the best cars.

2. Money is the root of all evil.

3. Mothers should stay home with their children.

4. Husbands should share equally in the housework and child care.

5. When people have personal problems, they should go to a psychologist.

6. Teenagers should not be allowed to own their own cars.

7. Capitalism is the best economic system in the world today.

8. The United Nations should have an army.

9. Large corporations should be obliged to donate 1% of their profits to charity.

10. One day the world will solve its conflicts in ways other than war.

8.30 Written Activity: *Reduced Clauses of Time, Reason, and Opposition*

DIRECTIONS: Answer the letter to Edith found on page 199. Use at least four reduced clauses in your answer. Underline them.

■ V. Clause Reduction: Having + Past Participle

Having + past participle can express **time** or **reason**, or both.

CLAUSE	REDUCTION	NOTES
Time **1. After the patient (had) refused the life-saving treatment,** he was released from the hospital.	**1a. After refusing the life-saving treatment,** the patient was released from the hospital. **1b. (After) having refused the life-saving treatment,** the patient was released from the hospital.	• Sentences 1, 1a, and 1b have the same meaning. • Retain **after** in sentence 1a. • You may delete **after** in sentence 1b, but doing so may express a cause-effect relationship. (See below.)
Reason (because/since/as) **2. Because he had lost his close relatives,** the patient didn't want to live any longer.	**2a. Having lost his close relatives,** the patient didn't want to live any longer.	• The patient lost his relatives **before** his decision. A time and reason relationship is expressed in (2). • Use **having + past participle** to express that time-reason relationship. • Delete **because, as,** or **since.**

8.31 Written Activity: *Having + Past Participle*

DIRECTIONS: Complete the following sentences to demonstrate your understanding of clause reduction.

1. After having lost the game, _____.

2. Having lost the game, _____.

3. The Berlin Wall came down _____.

4. The United States and the Soviet Union signed an arms agreement _____.

5. Having realized _____.

■ VI. Clause Reduction: The Passive

Note how passive adverb clauses can be reduced to phrases in the following sentences.

Passive Clause	Reduction	Notes
(Time) **1. Before the patient was released,** he had to sign a hospital form.	Being + Past Participle **1a. Before being released,** the patient had to sign a hospital form.	• If the action in the adverb clause occurs after or at the same time as the action in the main clause, reduce the clause with **being + past participle** of the verb in the adverb clause.
(Reason) **2. Because he had been given his last treatment,** the patient was able to go home.	Having Been + Past Participle **2a. Having been given his last treatment,** the patient was able to go home.	• If the action in the adverb clause occurs before the action in the main clause as it does in (2a), reduce the clause with **having been + past participle** of the verb in the adverb clause.

8.32 Written Activity: *Clause Reduction*

DIRECTIONS: Rewrite the statements in parentheses as reduced adverb clauses if it is possible. If it is not possible, simply write the full clause. Add subordinators when necessary. Pay special attention to punctuation.

I have had this battle with my parents about euthanasia and living wills. _____,
(Because they are Catholic)

it is against their religion to do anything to end a person's life. _____, I do not
(Since I am not a practicing Catholic)

have any religious problems with this behavior; in fact, there are many reasons why I may choose

to sign a living will. For example, _____, my uncle became extremely ill and
(after he had spent 6 months in the hospital)

depressed. In fact, he often talked about wishing he would die, but he said that he wanted to see

me married _____.
(before he died).

_____, I would prefer to have all life-support devices withheld for myself. It can
(Because I have seen my uncle suffer with a terminal illness)

also be a great expense for the family. My uncle was in great debt from his medical bills

_____.
(before he was operated on for the last time)

VII. Special Problems With Adverb Clause Use

PROBLEM	EXPLANATION
1. Sentence Fragment [INCORRECT: He wasn't accepted at the university. Because his grades were low.] CORRECT: He wasn't accepted at the university because his grades were low.	An adverb clause is a dependent clause. Make sure you have two subject-verb groups.
2. Punctuation [INCORRECT: Because his grades were low he wasn't accepted at the university.] CORRECT: Because his grades were low, he wasn't accepted at the university.	If you begin your sentence with the adverb clause, it must be followed by a comma.
3. Dangling Participles [INCORRECT: While painting the house, the telephone rang.] CORRECT: While painting the house, I heard the telephone ring.	You can only reduce the adverb clause when the subjects are the same in both clauses. The incorrect sentence indicates that the telephone painted the house. This, of course, is impossible. The correct sentence expresses the speaker's intended meaning.
4. Because of + Noun Clause [INCORRECT: Because of he had low grades, he wasn't accepted at a university.] CORRECT: Because of his low grades, he wasn't accepted at the university.	Don't use a clause after **because of**. Use a noun.
5. Using So Instead of Such [INCORRECT: She has so big feet that she can't find shoes to fit her.] CORRECT: She has such big feet that she can't find shoes to fit her.	**So** is followed by an adjective only. **Such** is followed by an adjective + noun.
6. Using Double Connectors in the Same Sentence [INCORRECT: Although it was raining, but we went swimming anyway.] CORRECT: Although it was raining, we went swimming anyway. [INCORRECT: Because it was cold, so we built a fire.] CORRECT: Because it was cold, we built a fire.	Do not use **but** and **although, because** and **so** in the same sentence.

◼ 8.33 Error Analysis: *Adverb Clauses*

DIRECTIONS: Find any errors in the following sentences and correct them clearly. Do not change anything that is already correct.

1. Because coming from a very conservative family, Carlos was shocked at coeducational dormitories in the United States.

2. While painting the house, the thunder struck.

3. She slipped as walking to school.

4. Having been being an English teacher, Cheryl can explain grammar very well.

5. Before coming to the United States, Ali studied statistics.

6. Although schools on the east coast are prestigious and well-respected, but schools on the west coast are less expensive.

7. I know that I have a good friend when I was lonely.

8. As soon as I will fix my bike, I'll ride over to your house.

9. I will trust a friend as long as that friend will be honest with me.

10. I must tell you that one condition of my scholarship is that once I graduated, I must return to my country.

11. I wish we could live together in the United States so that you should come to this country.

12. While my rational side tells me to go back, on the other hand, my mind tells me to stay here.

13. If I go back, I will have no job at home so I have to live far from you, so that I prefer to live in Toledo than at home.

14. Even though I tried my best, but I didn't pass the final examination.

15. Many people choose to die because of a lack of money or the medicine to cure them has not been found.

ƒocus on Writing

ſentence (ombining

Using adverb clauses in your writing will express the relations among ideas more precisely. In the examples below, note how sentence (2) is clearer than sentence (1):

1. The streets were flooded. Traffic was backed up for miles.

2. Because of the flooded streets, traffic was backed up for miles.

8.34 Chapter Review

DIRECTIONS: Combine the following sentences using a subordinate conjunction from the list below:

so . . . that	so that	while	whereas
inasmuch as	now that	once	despite the fact that

1. I tied a string around my finger. I wanted to be sure to remember to mail my Mother's Day card.

_____

2. There aren't many parking spaces. I had to drive around 15 minutes waiting for one.

_____

3. This quiz is easy. The last one was extremely difficult.

_____

4. I don't have class on Thursday evenings any more. I can watch my favorite T.V. show.

_____

5. Gladys will get 550 on her TOEFL. After that, she will begin her studies.

_____

8.35 Discuss and Write: *A Moral Dilemma—Kohlberg's Theory*

DIRECTIONS PART ONE: Read the following situation and think about the answers to the questions at the end. Discuss your answers in pairs or small groups if instructed by your teacher. This situation was used for a study, the results of which will be explained below.

> A woman was dying of cancer. Only one drug could save her and that drug had just been discovered in the town where she lived. Her husband did not have the money to buy the drug, which cost 10 times as much as it did for the druggist to make. He was able to borrow only half of the money, so he went to the druggist to ask him if he would sell it to him at half price or let him pay for it later. The druggist refused, so the husband broke into the store and stole the drug to save his wife. Should the husband have done that? Why or why not?

Write your thoughts here:

_____

_____

_____

_____

Discuss your answers in small groups if instructed by your teacher.

DIRECTIONS PART TWO: How did you (and your classmates) evaluate the husband's action? What made you approve or disapprove of his action? Read the following paragraphs about one psychologist who used this situation to identify several levels of moral reasoning. Then, rewrite the paragraphs below, combining sentences whenever it is possible and appropriate. Use a variety of adverb clauses and subordinators. You may change words, sentence structures, and sentence order.

1 The psychologist Lawrence Kohlberg studied moral behavior. He wanted to examine the reasoning of a person faced with a moral dilemma. In his experiment, Kohlberg first told his subjects a story with a moral dilemma. Then he asked his subjects to tell him how the person in the story should act and why. Kohlberg analyzed this data. Then he identified three levels of moral behavior. He found that an individual must pass through stage one. Then that individual can move on to stage two.

2 Level One: Preconventional (Early Childhood)
At this stage, the child is influenced by the **outcome** of his behavior. He does not analyze society's standards. A child is punished, so the action is bad. A child is rewarded. The action is good.

3 Level Two: Conventional (Middle Childhood)
The child is influenced by the ideals of the social group (the family, peer group, country). The desire for approval is strong. The child obeys society and authority.

4 Level Three: Postconventional (Adolescence to Adulthood)
The person separates himself from the identity of the group. This is in contrast to what the person does at level two. The individual has his or her own values at this stage but realizes that other values exist. The highest level of moral reasoning is Universal Orientation. The person at this stage has abstract and very broad and complete moral principles.

DIRECTIONS PART THREE: Write a paragraph in which you evaluate your group's decisions in terms of Kohlberg's theory. State what the members of your group thought about the situation in Part One, and identify that according to the levels described above. Give reasons to explain your categorization. Use a variety of adverb clauses in your paragraph.

Composition Topics

1. Respond to the Robert Frost poem on page 175 of this chapter. What does the poem say to you? Have you ever had a similar experience?

2. All people have experienced procrastination at some point in their lives. Why do people procrastinate? What are some techniques for avoiding procrastination?

3. The text that follows is a living will. Read it and decide if you would or could sign such a document. Then write a composition in which you argue for or against such legal documents.

To My Family, My Doctor, My Lawyer, And All Others Concerned

Death is as real as birth, growing up, and getting old. In fact, it is the only certainty we have in this life. If the moment should arise when I am not able to make decisions about my future, let this document be an expression of my desires and directions while I am still of sound mind and body.

If there arises a time when no reasonable expectation of recovery exists for me, either from a physical or mental disability, then I direct that I be allowed to die and not be kept alive by medication or by heroic measures. I do wish that medication be given to me to relieve the intense suffering, even if this should shorten my life.

I have carefully considered everything before signing this document. It is in agreement with my convictions and beliefs. I wish that these instructions be carried out to the extent allowed by the law.

—Rosa Yans

Health and Fitness II

Chapter 9

• The Sentence: Integration

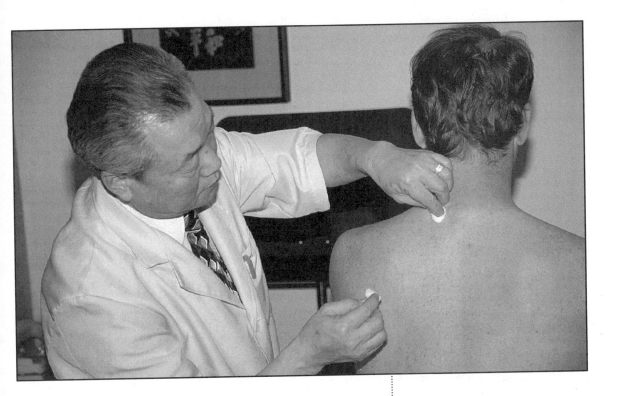

DISCUSSION QUESTIONS

1. Do you know what acupuncture is? Have you ever received an acupuncture treatment? Can you describe how it felt?

2. In your native country, is there a newspaper column where you can write to a doctor?

3. What kind of alternative medical treatments, such as acupuncture, homeopathy, relaxation therapy or biofeedback, are practiced in your native country?

OBJECTIVES

In this chapter you will learn:

1. To use a variety of sentence connectors and sentence types to express relationships between ideas

2. To write more sophisticated sentences through sentence combining

3. To recognize faulty parallelism and to use correct parallel structures in sentences

Preview

DIRECTIONS: Read the following letter from a newspaper column entitled "Doctor Jones" in which a medical doctor answers health-related questions submitted by readers.

Dear Doctor Jones:

1 I have suffered from migraine headaches for years now, and have found no cure for them. The other day a friend suggested that I try acupuncture. However, the thought of those needles really scares me. Since I have found no other **remedy,** I would like to know more about this method. Can it be effective for migraines? How do those needles feel? Would you recommend acupuncture?

Desperate For A Cure

Dear Desperate:

2 At one time, not only was I very **skeptical** about acupuncture but I also wanted to prove that it was merely a **placebo.** Therefore, I conducted a series of experiments using acupuncture needles on animals. I used electrodes to measure the pain responses in individual nerve cells. To my surprise, it worked! The nerves which transmit pain did not respond; as a result, I became convinced that this treatment was more than a placebo.

3 Although many medical doctors are still opposed to such an **unconventional** method of treatment, I now support the treatment of many medical conditions with acupuncture. Furthermore, I see the value of combining conventional methods of treatment with acupuncture at times. For example, acupuncture can be used to prevent **nausea** before administering anesthesia for surgery. Similarly, positive results can be seen with cancer patients using the lifesaving but usually nauseating **chemotherapy** drug cisplatin.

4 Because of the **debilitating** effects of migraines and the lack of effective medication, I would definitely recommend acupuncture as a method of treatment. If you're afraid of the needles, let me assure you that unlike the needles you find in your traditional doctor's office, acupuncture needles are painless. You feel a slight **twinge** when the needle goes in and then a **tingling** or a **buzz,** nothing more. Moreover, due to the release of **endorphins,** you leave an acupuncture treatment feeling something similar to a **runner's high.** Try it and let us know how it goes!

Vocabulary

remedy: cure
skeptical: unwilling to accept something as truth without questioning
placebo: something inert given as medicine; the psychological result of receiving it may have the same effect as the medicine

unconventional: outside the norm, nontraditional
nausea: the sick feeling in the stomach which often precedes vomiting
chemotherapy: a treatment for cancer using a systemic, highly concentrated administration of chemicals or drugs
debilitating: weakening or harming, usually to the point of making it difficult to function
twinge: a very slight sensation, i.e., a "twinge" of pain
tingling/buzz: a slight resonating feeling
endorphins: opiates made in the brain in response to pain
runner's high: a feeling of elation or lightness after vigorous exercise

FOCUS ON GRAMMAR

The following questions are based on the preview text and are designed to help you find out what you already know about the structures in this chapter. Some of the questions may be hard and some of them may be easy. Answer as many of the questions as you can. Work with a partner if your teacher tells you to do so.

1. Read through the Preview and try to find sentences expressing each of the **logical relationships** stated below.

Example   ADDITION: Furthermore, I see the value of combining conventional methods of treatment with acupuncture at times.

ADDITION: _____

_____

CAUSE/EFFECT: _____

_____

CONCESSION: _____

_____

OPPOSITION: _____

_____

COMPARISON: _____

_____

2. Underline the word or phrase that connects the ideas in each of the above sentences and expresses the relationship between the ideas.

Example   ADDITION: <u>Furthermore</u>, I see the value of combining conventional methods of treatment with acupuncture at times.

3. Notice the word order in the following sentence from paragraph 2. What generalization can you make about the word order used with the correlative conjunctions **not only . . . but also?**

   *At one time, not only was I very **skeptical** about acupuncture but I also wanted to prove that it was merely a **placebo**.*

Grammatical Patterns

■ I. Sentence Variety

By using a variety of sentence connectors and sentence types, one idea can be expressed in different ways. The following section shows the variety of possible connectors to express each function.

A. Addition

CONNECTORS	EXAMPLES
Coordinating Conjunction **and**	• Migraine headaches are painful, **and** they cause nausea.
Conjunctive Adverbs **in addition, additionally, furthermore, moreover, also**	• Migraine headaches are painful; **in addition,** they cause nausea.
Correlative Conjunctions **not only . . . but also**	• **Not only** are migraine headaches painful, **but** they **also** cause nausea. (Question order follows **not only,** and the subject of the following clause is usually placed between **but** and **also.**)
Prepositional Phrases **in addition to, along with, as well as**	• **In addition to** being painful, migraine headaches cause nausea.

9.1 Written Activity: *Addition*

DIRECTIONS: Below is a passage about homeopathic medicine. Combine two sentences whenever appropriate, using a connector to introduce the additional idea. *Also* is used as a hint to indicate when an additional idea is being expressed. Use as many different connectors as possible.

Example   Homeopathic medicine can now be found in most health food stores. Also, it is becoming easier to find doctors that prescribe homeopathic formulas.

Not only can homeopathic medicine now be found in most health food stores, but it is also becoming easier to find doctors that prescribe homeopathic formulas.

Homeopathy is an alternative healing method which can be more effective than conventional approaches. It can **also** be safer. In a homeopathic treatment, the patient is given a specific medication. The patient may **also** be given advice on changes in diet and other health-related lifestyle patterns. Homeopathic medicine works on the same principle as all effective vaccines—"treat like with like." The medication is composed of whatever is making the patient sick. The advantage is that rather than treat the symptoms, homeopathic treatment helps the body to build resistance to the bacteria or virus causing the illness. The patient can **also** avoid many side effects brought on by conventional medication, most commonly antibiotics. Many people are turning to homeopathy due to this holistic approach. **Also,** in many cases a homeopathic treatment produces results where conventional methods fail.

SPECIAL NOTE

NOT ONLY . . . BUT ALSO

The correlative conjunction **not only ... but also** can be difficult to use because of the following rules:

1. Question word order follows **not only,** and the subject of the following clause is usually placed between **but** and **also.**

   Not only *do I exercise,* **but** *I also walk* to work every day.

2. Parallel structures must follow the conjunctions:

   Vitamins are **not only** *popular* **but also** *effective.*
   (adjective)   (adjective)

   Acupuncture can **not only** *heal* **but also** *prevent* illness.
   (verb)   (verb)

B. Concession

In a sentence expressing concession, the second idea is surprising or unexpected based on the information in the first idea.

CONNECTORS	EXAMPLES
Coordinating Conjunction **but**	• The relationship between mind and body is obvious, **but** many traditional doctors still reject healing methods based on this relationship.
Subordinating Conjunctions **although, despite the fact that**	• **Although** the relationship between mind and body is obvious, many traditional doctors still reject healing methods based on this relationship.
Conjunctive Adverbs **however, nevertheless**	• The relationship between mind and body is clear; **however,** many traditional doctors still reject healing methods based on this relationship.
Prepositional Phrases **despite, in spite of**	• **Despite** the obvious relationship between mind and body, many traditional doctors still reject healing methods based on this relationship.

9.2 Written Drill: *Concession*

DIRECTIONS: Complete the sentences to express **concession**.

1. Despite _____, Robin gets sick often.

2. _____; nevertheless, Jim is a vegetarian.

3. Stephen buys organic fruits and vegetables despite the fact that _____.

4. Carla has a very healthy diet; however, _____
_____.

5. In spite of a daily workout at the gym, _____
_____.

6. _____ although home-coooked meals are time-consuming.

7. Despite the effectiveness of acupuncture, _____
_____.

8. _____, but he smokes anyway.

9. In spite of the medication Juan takes for his headaches, _____
_____.

10. The city I live in has few recreational facilities; nevertheless, _____
_____.

C. Opposition

The following connectors help to express opposition or difference between two things or ideas.

CONNECTORS	EXAMPLES
Coordinating Conjunctions **but, yet**	• A migraine is one continuous headache, **but** cluster headaches repeatedly start and stop over a period of time.
Subordinating Conjunctions **whereas, while**	• **Whereas** a migraine is one continuous headache, cluster headaches repeatedly start and stop over a period of time.
Conjunctive Adverbs **in contrast, on the other hand**	• A migraine is one continuous headache; **in contrast,** cluster headaches repeatedly start and stop over a period of time.
Prepositions **unlike**	• **Unlike** a migraine, which is one continuous headache, cluster headaches repeatedly start and stop over a period of time.

9.3 Written Activity: *Opposition*

DIRECTIONS: Use the connectors from the chart to write a sentence expressing **opposition** between each of the two ideas presented below.

Example   running/swimming
         While running is very good aerobic exercise, swimming is considered to be better for you.

1. antibiotics/herbal medication

   _____

2. taking a walk/taking a nap

   _____

3. hiking up a mountain/running around the track

   _____

4. fast food/home-cooked meals

   _____

5. good nutrition/regular exercise

   _____

6. tennis/ping pong

   _____

7. going to the doctor/going to the dentist

   _____

8. junk food/fruits and vegetables

   _____

9. body building/aerobics

   _____

10. taking vitamins/eating well

    _____

SPECIAL
NOTE

CONCESSION VS. OPPOSITION

Note the difference between **concession** and **opposition**:

Concession
Although she smokes, she supports the anti-smoking campaign.
(The ideas in the second clause express the opposite of what we expect.)

Opposition
Whereas some people support the campaign, some people think it's unconstitutional.
(The ideas in the second clause express a difference from the ideas in the first clause.)

9.4 Written Activity: *Concession/Contrast*

DIRECTIONS: The sentences below are about proposed legislation to prohibit advertising tha encourages smoking. In each pair of sentences determine whether the relationship is **concessior** or **contrast**. Then combine the sentences using an appropriate connector. Use a variety o connectors.

1. Some people believe the government has no right to prohibit advertising of a product that is legal but dangerous. This administration is fighting to institute such a law.

    Relationship: _____

    New Sentence: _____

    _____

2. Adults may be immune to cigarette advertising. Children are very impressionable.

    Relationship: _____

    New Sentence: _____

    _____

3. There is free speech protection in the First Amendment to the Constitution. The government must protect citizens from misleading claims by advertisers.

    Relationship: _____

    New Sentence: _____

    _____

4. Some lawyers are defending the proposed restrictions on cigarette ads. Others are fighting to uphold the First Amendment.

    Relationship: _____

    New Sentence: _____

    _____

5. In 1971, cigarette ads were banned from radio and television by the Federal Communications Commission. Advertising in magazines and on T-shirts is not so easy to regulate.

    Relationship: _____

    New Sentence: _____

    _____

6. Three thousand children a day begin smoking and nearly a thousand will go on to die. Many people support unlimited advertising by the tobacco industry.

    Relationship: _____

    New Sentence: _____

    _____

7. The tobacco industry claims their advertising is intended to draw smokers to their brand of cigarettes, not to persuade nonsmokers to take up the habit. Two administration officials proposed several restrictions on tobacco-related advertising.

Relationship: _____

New Sentence: _____

_____

D. Cause/Effect

CONNECTORS	EXAMPLES
Coordinating Conjunctions **for** (cause) **so** (effect)	• A high stress level can contribute to many illnesses, **for** stress weakens the immune system. • Stress weakens the immune system, **so** a high stress level can contribute to many illnesses.
Subordinating Conjunctions **because, since**	• **Because** stress weakens the immune system, a high stress level can contribute to many illnesses.
Conjunctive Adverbs **therefore, as a result, consequently**	• Stress weakens the immune system; **therefore,** a high stress level can contribute to many illnesses.
Prepositions **because of, due to, as a result of**	• **Because of** the potential of stress to weaken the immune system, a high stress level can contribute to many illnesses.

9.5 Written Activity: *Cause/Effect*

DIRECTIONS: Go back to the Preview and answer the questions below using a variety of **sentence connectors** from the above chart to express **cause/effect**. Use complete sentences to answer the questions.

Example   Why do people write to Dr. Jones?
(Many people have medical questions that they would like answered without having to visit a doctor; therefore, they write to this column for advice.)

1. Why did "Desperate" write to Dr. Jones?

2. Why do you think Dr. Jones was skeptical about acupuncture in the beginning?

3. What convinced him that acupuncture was more than a placebo?

4. How can acupuncture be used for surgery?

5. How could cancer patients benefit from acupuncture?

6. Why do patients feel so good immediately after an acupuncture treatment?

7. Do you think "Desperate" will try acupuncture?

9.6 Oral Activity: *Interview*

DIRECTIONS: Interview at least two English-speaking people and find out about their knowledge of and experience with acupuncture. Use the questions below for the interview. Then report to the class using a variety of sentence connectors to express cause/effect.

QUESTIONS

1. Have you ever tried acupuncture? Why/why not?

2. Do you think acupuncture can be an effective healing method? Why/why not?

3. Do you think alternative healing methods such as acupuncture should be covered by health insurance? Why/why not?

E. Comparison

CONNECTORS	EXAMPLES
Coordinating Conjunction **and . . . too**	• Holistic medicine views the patient as a whole person, **and** acupuncture takes this approach **too**.
Subordinating Conjunction **just as**	• **Just as** many holistic treatments view the patient as a whole person, acupuncture treats the body as an interdependent system.
Conjunctive Adverbs **similarly, in comparison**	• Holistic medicine views the patient as a whole person; **similarly,** acupuncture treats the body as an interdependent system.
Prepositions **like, similar to**	• **Like** other holistic treatments, acupuncture is based on viewing the patient as a whole person.

9.7 Written Activity: *Cause/Effect and Comparison*

DIRECTIONS: The percentage of overweight Americans is twice as high today as it was in 1900, because of the change in the environment in which Americans live. The box below lists some of those changes. For each change write one sentence expressing **comparison** between the past and the present and another sentence expressing the **effect** of that change on a person's diet, health and lifestyle.

Example   1900s: People walked or rode bicycles as their primary mode of transportation.
PRESENT: Many people drive instead of walking to get places.
COMPARISON: Whereas in the past, people walked or rode bicycles as their primary mode of transportation, today people drive instead of walk to get places.
CAUSE/EFFECT: Because many people drive instead of walk to get places, they don't burn as many calories during the day.

1. 1900s: Much time was spent preparing fresh meals.

   PRESENT: Microwave ovens make it possible to prepare fast food meals very quickly.

   COMPARISON: _____

   CAUSE/EFFECT: _____

2. 1900s: People ate fresh fruits and vegetables for snacks.

   PRESENT: There are over 1000 new commercially produced snack foods every year.

   COMPARISON: _____

   CAUSE/EFFECT: _____

3. 1900s: Families spent time together talking or in other activities, with little focus on food outside of mealtimes.

   PRESENT: People sit and watch T.V., where they see advertising that encourages them to go to the kitchen for a snack.

   COMPARISON: _____

   CAUSE/EFFECT: _____

4. 1900s: People rarely went out to restaurants, and when they did it was a special occasion.

   PRESENT: It is common to go to restaurants that feature "all you can eat" for a low price.

   COMPARISON: _____

   CAUSE/EFFECT: _____

5. 1900s: People were physically active throughout the day attending to their survival needs.

   PRESENT: Convenience stores, moving sidewalks at airports, drive-through banking and fast food restaurants encourage laziness and lack of movement.

   COMPARISON: _____

   CAUSE/EFFECT: _____

9.8 Written Activity: *Sentence Combining*

DIRECTIONS: For each of the following pairs of sentences, identify the relationship between the two sentences. Then, combine each pair of sentences into one sentence, using one of the **connectors** from the preceding charts. Write the new sentence on the line.

Example   Most fitness centers provide a variety of exercise equipment for their members. A running track, a sauna, and a pool are available too.

RELATIONSHIP: *Addition*
In addition to a running track, a sauna, and a pool, most fitness centers provide a variety of exercise equipment for their members.

1. Some members come to the fitness center to work out daily. Other members can only fit it into their schedule once or twice a week.

   RELATIONSHIP: _____

   NEW SENTENCE: _____

2. The membership is supposed to be limited. My fitness center is often too crowded.

   RELATIONSHIP: _____

   NEW SENTENCE: _____

3. Sometimes my fitness center is full of people. Sometimes I can't even use the equipment.

   RELATIONSHIP: _____

   NEW SENTENCE: _____

4. At my fitness center there are qualified, professional instructors. There is state-of-the-art equipment.

   RELATIONSHIP: _____

   NEW SENTENCE: _____

5. I never buy any snacks at the juice bar. The prices are very high.

   RELATIONSHIP: _____

   NEW SENTENCE: _____

6. Most fitness centers have a membership fee that members must pay on an annual basis. My fitness center does too.

   RELATIONSHIP: _____

   NEW SENTENCE: _____

7. I've been a member of this fitness center for one year. I've never attended an aerobics class.

   RELATIONSHIP: _____

   NEW SENTENCE: _____

8. I like to work out on equipment that is straightforward and fun. I stay away from the more technically difficult machines.

   RELATIONSHIP: _____

   NEW SENTENCE: _____

9.9 Written Activity: *Sentence Variety*

DIRECTIONS: Read the paragraph below about Jennifer's decision to improve her health. For each function given below the paragraph, write three sentences using different connectors to express the same idea from the paragraph. As the example shows, identify the connector and circle the connector in the sentence.

One year ago, Jennifer decided that she was going to change her lifestyle and start taking better care of her health. She was overweight from a diet high in fat and sugar. She was out of shape from a lack of exercise. She also felt tired most of the time, with hardly enough energy to climb the stairs to her apartment at the end of the day. She smoked a pack of cigarettes a day and frequently drank beer. When she decided to change her ways, she started by changing her diet so that grains, legumes, vegetables, and fruits took the place of the fat and sugar. She quit smoking, signed up for an aerobics class, and started cycling on weekends. Since then, she has lost 25 pounds, and is now in excellent shape. Only one problem remains. She still gets tired climbing the stairs to her tenth-floor apartment.

Example   FUNCTION: Cause/Effect

COORDINATING CONJUNCTION: *Her diet was very high in fat and sugar, (so) she was overweight.*
SUBORDINATING CONJUNCTION: *(Because) her diet was very high in fat and sugar, she was overweight.*
CONJUNCTIVE ADVERB: *Her diet was very high in fat and sugar; (therefore,) she was overweight.*

1. FUNCTION: Addition

_____

_____

_____

2. FUNCTION: Contrast

_____

_____

_____

3. FUNCTION: Opposition

_____

_____

_____

4. FUNCTION: Cause/Effect

_____

_____

_____

II. Special Problems with Sentences

PROBLEM	EXPLANATION
Double Connector INCORRECT: (1) **Because** people have become so health conscious, **so** the life span of the average American has increased. CORRECT: (2) **Because** people have become so health conscious, the life span of the average American has increased.	• Two clauses can be joined as in (1) by **one** connector that expresses the logical relationship between the ideas in the two clauses.
Illogical Placement of Connector INCORRECT: (3) I smoke cigarettes **although** my lungs are healthy. CORRECT: (4) **Although** I smoke cigarettes, my lungs are healthy.	• Be careful of illogical sentences as in (3). Be sure that the sentence connector **logically** relates one idea to another as in (4).
Faulty Parallelism INCORRECT: (5) My doctor told me **that I should take an iron supplement** and **I should eat more iron-rich foods.** CORRECT: (6) My doctor told me **that I should take an iron supplement** and **that I should eat more iron-rich foods.**	• Be careful not to omit necessary components of the parallel structure as in (5). Include all the necessary components as in (6).

■ **9.10 Editing Activity**

DIRECTIONS: Find and correct the error in each of the following sentences. Some of the sentences may be correct as they are.

1. Because a very good diet, Sandra is always healthy.

2. The common cold can make you feel very miserable; therefore, staying at home in bed.

3. Although I've been maintaining a very healthy diet, but I've been sick.

4. She is in very good shape; consequently, she exercises regularly.

5. With excellent nutrition, a generous supply of vitamins, a lot of rest, and plenty of exercise.

6. Not only is medicine important when you're sick, but take care of yourself too.

7. But the relationship between body and mind is very interesting.

8. Many doctors charge very expensive rates for example my doctor.

9. The magazine that I read, it is about how to increase longevity through better health.

10. The sun shines my window, so I have my plants in the window box.

11. I heard about an acupuncture clinic it also has a specialist on herbal medicine.

focus on Writing

Parallelism

■ In English, any time two similar structures are joined, they must be parallel. Notice how the first sentence below contains two parallel structures. Compare this with the second sentence, which is incorrect because the structures are not parallel.

a. In addition to **playing tennis** and **hiking in the mountains**, I also enjoy surfing.

b. In addition to **playing tennis** and **I hike** in the mountains, I also enjoy surfing.

The following chart demonstrates the variety of parallel structures that are possible.

PARALLEL STRUCTURES	EXAMPLES
Single Words Nouns Verbs Adjectives Adverbs	1. John writes **poetry** and **novels**. 2. Coleen **runs** and **works out**. 3. This diet is not only **difficult** but also **effective**. 4. Bill started his new diet **reluctantly** yet **aggressively**.
Phrases Noun Phrases Verb Phrases Adverbial Phrases Gerund Phrases Infinitive Phrases Participial Phrases	5. **A balanced diet** is as important as **a regular program of exercise**. 6. When Jack gets a cold, he **takes a lot of vitamins** and **drinks a lot of fluids**. 7. Linda and Dan walk a mile **in the morning** and **at night**. 8. Jim's doctor recommended **cooking healthier meals** and **getting more rest**. 9. Ruth wanted to lose ten pounds, so she tried to **eat less** and **exercise more**. 10. **Hoping to reduce the stress in her life** and **not having to worry about money**, Joyce quit her job.
Clauses Noun Clauses Adjective Clauses Adverb Clauses	11. Gary realized **that he was losing weight** but not **that he was becoming anemic**. 12. This is the diet **that promises instant results** and at the same time **that can cause malnutrition**. 13. **Because she couldn't swallow** and **since she had good medical insurance**, she decided to have her tonsils out.
Correlative Conjunctions	14. I enjoy not only **camping** but also **mountain climbing**. 15. Acupuncture is **neither** painful **nor** harmful.

■ **9.11 Editing Activity:** *Faulty Parallelism*

DIRECTIONS: Find the **faulty parallelism** in each of the following sentences and correct it.

1. What great shape she's in, and she looks healthy!

2. The doctor wanted to find out why Linda was underweight and about her blood sugar level.

3. Following a regular program of exercise is more beneficial for me than to be on a fad diet.

4. What I like best about my fitness center are the modern Lifecycle™ machines and they have such a beautiful Olympic size swimming pool.

5. Not only is Jim healthy, but how athletic he is.

6. Due to his son's persistence and because he wanted to lose 10 pounds, Frank decided to join a fitness center.

7. When Richard realized that his eating habits were the cause of his illness, he began to plan his meals more conscientiously and in a careful way.

8. Julian decided to try a homeopathic treatment as well as he changed his diet.

9. Shari really enjoys ocean kayaking and to go hiking in the desert.

10. This is a combination of vitamins that build up the immune system and they prevent infection from spreading.

9.12 Written Activity: *Parallel Structures*

DIRECTIONS: To each sentence below, add a structure that is **parallel** to the one that is underlined. Use the information provided in parentheses for the additional structure.

Example   CUE: *Kathy knows that she has too much stress in her life.* (As a result, Kathy's health is not very good.)
NEW SENTENCE: *Kathy knows that she has too much stress in her life and that she is unhealthy as a result.*

1. *Because she has two jobs,* Kathy leads a very stressful life. (She is a single mother.)

   _____

2. In order to reduce the level of stress in her lie, Kathy has *quit one of her jobs.* (She now has a live-in housekeeper.) _____

3. Kathy is not happy *with her present physician's attitude about stress.* (She doesn't like the way he treats the problem.) _____

4. *Despite the fact that she gets a lot of exercise, which supposedly reduces stress,* she still feels stressed out. (She's taking special vitamins designed to lower stress.)

   _____

5. *Joining a stress-management program* has helped her. (She learned how to meditate.)

   _____

6. The program has taught her *how to prioritize her responsibilities.* (She is also finding out what she can do in stressful situations.) _____

7. *Taking positive action to change her routine,* Kathy has begun to experience less stress. (She is also seeking help from outside sources.) _____

9.13 Written Activity: *Research Report*

DIRECTIONS: Choose one of the healing methods below and write a report about it using what you have learned in this chapter. Find information about the method by doing research in the library and through oral interviews. In your report you should describe the method, explain what kind of conditions it is most effective in treating, and discuss response to the method by people who have experienced the treatment.

Biofeedback
Homeopathy
Aromatherapy
Herbal Medicine
Diet—e.g., Yeast-Free, Pritikin™

Analysis of an Authenic Text

DIRECTIONS: Read the following text about fast food, referring to the vocabulary below.

Fast Food Fare and Nutrition
by Connie Roberts, M.S., R.D.

1 Every second, an estimated 200 people in the United States order one or more hamburgers. The U.S. National Restaurant Association estimates that on a typical day 45.8 million people—a fifth of the American population—are served at fast-food restaurants. The fast-food industry boasts phenomenal growth. From 1970 to 1980, the number of fast-food outlets increased from 30,000 to 140,000, and fast-food sales increased 300%. Fast-food chains have expanded to college campuses, military bases, and other countries. The menus have become more varied, and hours of operation have expanded to include breakfasts.

2 The trend toward increased consumption of fast foods by Americans has been attributed to the growing employment of women outside the home, the increasing number of people

living alone, smaller families, the **prevalence** of less formal lifestyles, the increase in **disposable income,** and consumers' desire and demand for convenience. These trends suggest a growing reliance on fast food for more than one meal a day, beginning at a young age. Because such foods serve a need in a fast-paced society, they are probably a permanent part of the lifestyle of many Americans. We must, therefore, be concerned about the effect of fast foods on our health and nutritional status.

3 . . . Fast-food dining has been so well accepted that recommendations to reduce or eliminate it are likely to meet with little or no success. The more **efficacious** approach is to improve the nutritional quality of fast foods and the eating practices of its consumers.

4 Fast-food chains should be regarded as one of many possible food sources, with advantages and limitations that must be considered within the context of one's total diet. For such considerations, consumers need to be educated about how to choose foods, especially when eating out. Health professionals should be able to provide some advice, but much more could be done by the fast-food establishments themselves. First, in addition to **disclosing** the protein and vitamin contents of their foods, fast-food restaurants should provide information on the number of calories and the levels of important minerals and fats (quantity and type), so that consumers can make informed choices. Second, they should provide printed menus for consumers wishing to restrict their intake of sodium, calories, or fats, indicating the best choices for such a meal. Third, they should expand their efforts to identify the nutrient content of foods—for example, at salad bars. Fourth, they should make readily available such items as skim or low-fat milk, margarine, low-fat salad dressings, and 100% whole-grain buns, so that **consumers** will find it easier to make healthful choices. Finally, for the health of all of us, these important **purveyors** of food should work with experts to provide optimal nutrition for the public.

VOCABULARY

prevalence: frequency or noticeability
disposable income: the part of a salary that can be spent after all fixed expenses are paid
efficacious: having a result
disclosing: giving information
consumers: those who eat or use a commodity
purveyors: suppliers

DISCUSSION

1. What kind of fast food is available in your country? How would you rate this food in terms of nutritional value?
2. Do you think it is possible to produce fast food that is healthy?
3. What cultural differences or similarities exist between your country and the United States as reflected by the prevalence or scarcity of fast-food chains?

WRITTEN EXERCISE

1. The following is a revised version of the beginning of the first sentence in paragraph 2. Complete the sentence by making the other necessary changes. Then discuss which sentence is better.

   Americans are eating more fast foods because _____

   _____

2. Paragraph 3 is composed of two sentences. Combine them into one sentence.

   _____

   _____

3. In the following sentence, replace **in addition to** with **not only**, and make any other necessary changes.

   First, in addition to disclosing the protein and vitamin content of their foods, fast-food restaurants should provide information on the number of calories and the levels of important minerals and fats.

   _____

   _____

   _____

Composition Topics

1. Write a composition describing the general health and fitness of people in your country. Include information about diet, exercise, illness, and attitudes about health.

2. Write a composition about the ideal lifestyle a person should have for optimal health.

3. Describe the medical system in your country, emphasizing its strong and weak points.

American Culture II

Chapter 10

- Article Use
- Subject-Verb Agreement

Discussion Questions

1. When you meet someone for the first time, what do you say? How do you greet your friends? Your teacher or boss? What do you say or do when you leave? Are these customs different from conventional means of greeting people in the United States?

2. If a close friend were coming to the United States for the first time, what single piece of advice would you give him or her?

Objectives

In this chapter, you will learn:

1. To use the definite and indefinite articles correctly

2. To understand when **not** to use an article

3. To use articles with proper nouns

4. To use articles in making generalizations

5. To use correct subject-verb agreement

6. To understand collective nouns

Preview

DIRECTIONS: The following selection includes the first three paragraphs from an essay on adjusting to life in the United States. The essay was written by Rupa Joshi, a Fulbright scholar from Nepal who studied in the United States. Read the excerpt and then answer the questions that follow. The essay will be continued later in the chapter.

A Crash Course in Americana
by Rupa Joshi

When I came to the United States last year, I was given **a crash course** on how to get by. I was flooded with tips **to tide me over** any cultural shock. Before I had time to recover from jet lag, I had learned about the Boston Tea Party, seen a Native American museum, eaten barbecue, listened to Dr. Martin Luther King's "I Have a Dream" speech and watched a rodeo.

I was told not to be offended if most Americans didn't look me in the eye while replying to my questions. I was advised to feel comfortable calling elders, including professors, by their first names or nicknames. "It's OK to eat chicken with your fingers," they said, "provided it's not a formal dinner." They told me not to be alarmed if just-introduced males kissed or embraced me . . . .

My orientation advisers taught me the important things, all right. But after living here for nearly a year and a half as a graduate student, I still find myself trying to **fine-tune** myself to the new lifestyle. These are small things, nuances that probably seem insignificant to those who have lived here longer. But to me they are constant irritants, sand in my shoes.

(To be continued)

VOCABULARY

a crash course: a rapid introduction to
to tide me over: to get me through
to fine-tune: to adjust more precisely

CULTURAL NOTE/DISCUSSION

The rest of the essay by Rupa Joshi describes the irritants, or the "sand in my shoes" the author describes. If you were going to finish this essay, what "irritants" would you talk about? Discuss your ideas with the class or with a partner.

FOCUS ON GRAMMAR

The following questions are based on the preview text and are designed to help you find out what you already know about the structures in this chapter. Some of the questions may be hard and some of them may be easy. Answer as many of the questions as you can. Work with a partner if your teacher tells you to do so.

1. Consider the following sentence from the preview text:

   "I had learned about **the** Boston Tea Party, seen **a** Native American museum, eaten barbecue, listened to Dr. Martin Luther King's "I Have a Dream" speech and watched **a** rodeo."

   Can you explain why *the* appears before the noun phrase "Boston Tea Party" and *a* appears before the other two nouns?

   _____

   _____

2. Consider the following phrase:

   "I still find myself trying to fine-tune myself to **the** new lifestyle."

   Using *the* before **new lifestyle** indicates that the lifestyle the author is describing has been previously mentioned in the text. What is this new lifestyle?

   _____

   _____

3. Consider the following sentence:

   "But to me they are constant irritants, sand in my shoes."

   Why is no article used before the noun, **sand?**

   _____

   Why is no article used before the noun, **irritants?**

   _____

Grammatical Patterns Part One

I. Article Use: An Overview

Nouns in English can be preceded by the articles **a/an** or **the**, or by no article, depending on their use. Note the examples below. This section will examine all three possibilities in detail.

a/an	I bought **a** book yesterday.
the	**The** book I bought was very interesting.
Ø (no article)	It was about **culture shock.**

A. Using A/An (indefinite articles)

A and **an** are indefinite articles. They are used only with count nouns that have not been specified. Note their uses on the next page.

	RULE	EXAMPLE
Count Nouns	• Use **a** or **an** before an unspecified noun, i.e., one that has not previously been identified. In (1), the sentence does not specify a particular car.	1. Most families own **a car**.
Noncount Nouns	• Do not use a and an before a noncount noun. In (2), **ice cream** is a noncount, mass noun. (See Chapter One for an explanation of count and noncount nouns.)	2. Most children love **ice cream**.

SPECIAL NOTE

DO I USE *A* OR *AN*?

Use **a** before:

1. Nouns or adjectives beginning with a consonant sound:
   - **a** fire
   - **a** book
2. Nouns or adjectives beginning with the vowel **U**, when it sounds like "**you**":
   (long vowel)
   - **a** united front
   - **a** university
3. Nouns or adjectives beginning with the consonant **H** when it is aspirated:
   - **a** helper
   - **a** hostage

Use **an** before:

1. Nouns or adjectives beginning with a vowel:
   - **an** American
   - **an** edge
2. Nouns or adjectives beginning with the vowel **U** when it **doesn't** sound like "**you**": (short vowel)
   - **an** uptight businessman
   - **an** underfed child
3. Nouns or adjectives beginning with the consonant **H** when it is silent:
   - **an** hour
   - **an** honest politician

10.1 Written Drill: *Greetings*

DIRECTIONS: Read the following paragraph on advice for foreign visitors about greetings in the United States. All indefinite articles (a/an) have been omitted. Insert **a** or **an** wherever it is necessary.

What should you do when you meet American for the first time? Some people suggest that you smile and say "Hi!" in informal situation or "How do you do?" in formal situation. Others recommend firm handshake. Everyone ᵥ agree that kiss is not appropriate, even on the cheek. It is common to make **small talk** when you first meet person. You can talk

about the weather, recent sporting event, or better yet, ask the person question about his or her life. In any case, don't remain silent when you meet people for the first time because if you do, the person might think you are snob!

Special Note

IMPORTANT GRAMMATICAL TERMS

Review these terms before continuing with this chapter.

- **prepositional phrase**
- **restrictive adjective clause***
- **nonrestrictive adjective clause***

- **superlative adjective**

- The book is **on the table**.
- The book **that I read** was excellent.
- *Moby Dick*, **which was written by Herman Melville**, is an American classic.
- *Moby Dick* was **the best book** I have ever read.

*See Chapter 7 for more details.

B. Using The (definite article)

The definite article, **the**, can be used with both count and noncount nouns. Its use indicates that the speaker (or writer) and the listener (or reader) share a definite knowledge about the noun referred to. Note the ways in which this definite reference can be made.

USES OF *THE*	EXAMPLE
Noncount Nouns **A.** Before a noun that has been qualified or limited by a prepositional phrase.[a] In (1) **in the bottle** limits the milk.	**1. The** milk *in the bottle* has soured.
B. Before a noun that has been qualified by an adjective clause.[a] In (2) **wine** has been limited by the clause **that I bought.**	**2. The** wine *that I bought* is on the table.
Count Nouns **C.** Before a noun that has been qualified by a prepositional phrase, such as **in the lot** in (3) or an adjective clause, such as **that I picked out** in (3).[a]	**3. The** car *in the lot* is not **the** car *that I picked out.*
D. Before a noun that has been previously specified. In (4), the first sentence indicates that the car belongs to Mr. Jones.	**4.** Mr. Jones bought a car yesterday. **The** car is a 1989 Toyota.
E. Before a noun that refers to the class or the thing in general. In (5), the sentence is describing the class of cars, Cadillacs.	**5. The** Cadillac symbolized prestige in the 1950s.
F. In a superlative adjective + noun construction as **the most expensive** in (6).	**6. The most expensive** car I ever bought was a 1960 Corvette.
G. Before a noun that is one of a kind. In (7), there is only one Earth.	**7. The Earth** is round.

[a]*There are a few exceptions to this rule. See section E,* **Some Exceptions to the Article Rules.**

10.2 Recognition Activity: *Education in the United States*

DIRECTIONS: Read the following sentences about the state of education in the United States. Then indicate why a definite article **(the)** precedes the italicized nouns. Refer to the chart on page 240 for a list of cases requiring definite article use.

Example   The *personal computer* now plays an important role in secondary education in the United States. *The* precedes **personal computer** because it's a count noun and it refers to the computer in general.

1. The *high school diploma* used to be a valuable degree for getting a job in the United States at the beginning of the century. The *job* one got depended on a number of factors.

_____

_____

2. In today's world, the *job seeker* has a better chance of finding a good job after earning a college degree.

_____

_____

3. The *attitude* that our grandparents had towards school was quite different from the *attitude* our children now have.

_____

_____

4. It is very sad to many Americans that a country such as the United States—one of the *richest countries* in the world—does not place a high priority on the *education* of its young people.

_____

_____

5. Many parents are fighting against the *problems* of public schools—overcrowding, gang violence, apathy—and they are demanding that their children be given the *best possible education.*

_____

_____

10.3 Written Drill: *Definite and Indefinite Articles*

DIRECTIONS: The following paragraphs are a continuation of the essay from the Preview selection of this chapter. Fill in the blanks with **the, a** or **an** as appropriate. Be ready to explain your choices.

Coming from Nepal, _____ country where people drive on _____ left side of the road, I received ample warnings to be careful while crossing the street. But people failed to tell me that in this country even pedestrian traffic flows _____ wrong way. Walking in malls or down school corridors, I constantly seem to get in _____ way of people going the opposite direction. _____ situation gets more tricky when the footpath—sorry, pavement—is used by people on roller blades and skateboards.

2 I still have not been able to fathom some of _____ mysteries of bathrooms, or restrooms. (I haven't even figured out when _____ bathroom becomes _____ restroom.) It's taken me _____ long time to get used to these plush-carpeted, heavily scented and color-coordinated rooms that put to shame many living rooms back home.

C. No Article

There are some cases in which **no article** is used before a count or noncount noun. Study the following chart for a list of these cases.

USE NO ARTICLE	EXAMPLE
Noncount Nouns **A.** Before unspecified noncount nouns. In (1) **success** is a noncount noun which has not been limited in any way.	**1. Success** is often determined by wealth.
B. Before gerunds **(verb-ing)**. In (2), **making** is a gerund.	**2. Making money** is important to many parents in their 30s.
C. Before nouns which identify social institutions. In (3) **marriage** refers to the social institution of marriage. Other nouns like this include **divorce** and **retirement**.	**3. Marriage** is increasing in the United States and so is **divorce**.
D. Before references to academic subjects of study, e.g., **history** in (4).	**4.** My sister is studying **history**.
Count Nouns **E.** Before plural count nouns that refer to the class or thing in general, as **Cadillacs** and **symbols** in (5).	**5. Cadillacs** are **symbols** of status. (See section D, Generalizations.)

Continued on next page.

Continued from previous page.

Use No Article	Example
F. Before locations that imply a specific activity. In (6), **work** is both a place and an activity. Other nouns like this include **school** and **church**.	**6.** She drove to **work**. (See the special note below.)
G. Before titles, e.g., **president** in (7), or appointments, e.g., **chairperson** in (8).	**7.** Clinton was elected **president**. **8.** She was appointed **chairperson**.

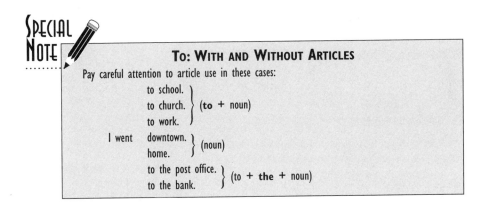

Special Note

To: With and Without Articles

Pay careful attention to article use in these cases:

$$\left.\begin{array}{l}\text{to school.}\\ \text{to church.}\\ \text{to work.}\end{array}\right\} \text{(to + noun)}$$

$$\text{I went}\left.\begin{array}{l}\text{downtown.}\\ \text{home.}\end{array}\right\} \text{(noun)}$$

$$\left.\begin{array}{l}\text{to the post office.}\\ \text{to the bank.}\end{array}\right\} \text{(to + the + noun)}$$

10.4 Written Drill: *Article Use*

DIRECTIONS: Fill in the blanks with **a/an, the,** or **Ø** (for no article), as appropriate. Be ready to explain your choices. Work with a partner if your instructor tells you do to so.

Dear Chris,

I arrived at _____ airport in Charlottesville on time! _____ director of my school was
  1   2

waiting for me with _____ sign. _____ sign said, "Welcome to Virginia, Jean-Pierre!"
  3   4

I was _____ little embarrassed, but it was such _____ nice welcome.
  5   6

After we got _____ suitcases, he drove me to _____ apartment that had been rented
  7   8

for me. I can't believe how big _____ apartments in this city are. I have two bedrooms,
  9

_____ kitchen, _____ bath, and _____ living room all to myself.
  10   11   12

I wish I had _____ car, because _____ public transportation here is not very good. It
            13   14

takes me about one hour to go to _____ school by bus. If I had _____ car, I could get
                                  15   16

there in about 20 minutes. Charlottesville is _____ small city, so _____ traffic isn't
                                              17   18

heavy. And _____ roads here are nice and wide.
            19

_____ classes which I am taking are all excellent. I've gotten to know _____ other
  20   21

foreign students who are also studying _____ business. Most of them are from Asian
                                        22

countries, but there are _____ few from Europe.
                          23

Well, I had better "hit _____ books" as you Americans say. Please write me soon. I miss
                         24

_____ French food!
  25

Bye, Bye

Jean Pierre

Jean Pierre

10.5 Written Activity: *A Letter Home*

DIRECTIONS: Write a letter to a friend or family member and tell him or her about your first week
in a foreign country. If you have never lived in a foreign country, then write about a week that you
spent in a different city. Pay careful attention to the use of articles.

■ D. Making Generalizations

You will want to pay special attention to article use when you use nouns in a **generic** way. Generic
means "in general." Note how the article use is different in the following sentences:

   a. The computer has changed life in many ways.

   b. I bought **a** computer in order to do payroll taxes.

Sentence (a) refers to **the computer** as a generic noun. It makes a **generalization** about the effects
of the computer on our lives. Sentence (b) speaks about a specific computer that the speaker
bought, one item in the general class of computers. Note that it would be incorrect to use **the** in
(b), just as you cannot use **a** in place of **the** in sentence (a).

Below are four ways to make general statements about people or things in English. Note the
difference in article and number use in each generalization and also the degree of formality.

COUNT NOUNS		
Form	**Use**	**Example**

A. the + singular noun	• Use **the** when speaking generally about nouns in the following categories:
	  • plants
	  • animals
	  • technical inventions
	  • with certain adjectives used as nouns (e.g., **the rich**)
		1. **The computer** has changed everyday life in the United States. *(technical inventions)*
		2. **The sloth** is a three-clawed animal found in Costa Rica. *(animals)*
		3. The **rich** get richer and the **poor** get poorer. *(adjectives used as nouns)*
		4. The **crocus** is the first flower to bloom in spring. *(plants)*

B. the + plural noun	• Use **the** when speaking generally about nouns in the following categories:
	  • classes of people (ethnic groups, professional groups)
	  • plural proper nouns
		5. In business, **the Americans** are often direct in their refusals. **The Japanese** often find their bluntness disconcerting. *(ethnic groups)*
		6. The **medical doctors** have a strong lobby. *(professional group)*
		7. The native **American Indians** lost their land. *(proper plural noun)*

C. a/an + singular noun	• For nouns that do not belong in any of the categories described in (A) or (B) above, use **a/an** when making generalizations about those nouns.	8. **A car** is a necessity in the city. 9. **A house** on oceanfront property can be expensive.
D. plural noun with no article (0)	• The nouns in (C) above can also be made plural and used without an article to make a generalization. This is less formal than the other constructions. Note: It is not possible to use **the** with these plural nouns for generalizations. Sentences (12) and (13) are incorrect.	10. **Cars** are necessary in this city. 11. **Houses** can be expensive in Washington, D.C. 12. **Incorrect:** The cars are necessary in this city. 13. **Incorrect:** The houses can be expensive in Washington, D.C.

NONCOUNT NOUNS		
Form	**Use**	**Example**
E. noncount noun only (no article)	• **Never** use an article with **noncount** nouns when using these nouns generically.	14. **Love** is a many-splendored thing. 15. **Gold** is a precious metal. 16. **Death** and taxes are inevitable.

10.6 Recognition Activity: *Specific or Generic?*

DIRECTIONS: Read the following sentences and identify the noun in bold as **specific** or **generic**. **Generic** means that it refers to the entire class of things or people in that category. **Specific** means it refers to a specific instance or portion of that category.

Example   a. **A modem** sends information across telephone lines. _____*Generic*_____

            b. I will need **a modem** to be able to work at home. _____*Specific*_____

In sentence (a), the writer is describing how **all** modems work, so this is a generic noun. Sentence (b) refers to one modem that the writer is going to buy, so it is a specific noun.

1. There are many surprises for **a foreign student** visiting the United States. _____

2. They might be surprised at the informality between a student and **a professor.** _____

3. A **student** from Japan was surprised when the professor told her to call him by his first name. _____

4. Another student was shocked when **an American student** began arguing in a loud voice with his professor. _____

5. The foreign student believed that such behavior was a sign of **disrespect.** _____

6. Foreigners are also likely to be surprised at the distances between places in **the country.** _____

7. It is not uncommon for people to drive one hour to **work.** _____

8. **Public transportation** is often poor in U.S. cities. _____

9. Foreign students don't always realize they will need **a car.** _____

10. Finally, many foreign students are surprised at how well Americans treat **dogs.** Some people say they treat dogs better than their own children. _____

10.7 Paired Activity: *Generalizations*

DIRECTIONS: Work in pairs. Discuss whether any of the sentences in Exercise 10.6 can be restated using a different noun phrase construction. Put a check next to those sentences. Then compare your answers with those of the entire class.

Example   **A modem** sends information across telephone lines. _____*Generic*_____

> *Modems send information across telephone lines.*
> *The modem sends information across telephone lines.*

10.8 Oral Activity: *Proverbs in English*

DIRECTIONS: Each of the following sentences is a well-known proverb in English. With a partner, read each one and supply an appropriate article in the space provided (**the, a/an, Ø**). Be ready to explain why you made the choice that you did. Then choose two proverbs from the list and discuss the meaning of each one. Be ready to tell the class what you and your partner discussed.

1. _____ variety is _____ spice of _____ life.

2. You can't teach _____ old dog _____ new tricks.

3. _____ beauty is only skin deep.

4. _____ bird in _____ hand is worth two in _____ bush.

5. Every cloud has _____ silver lining.

6. _____ grass is always greener on _____ other side.

7. _____ practice makes perfect.

8. _____ Rome wasn't built in _____ day.

9. _____ money is _____ root of all _____ evil.

10. _____ money makes _____ world go round.

11. Write two proverbs that you know from your culture, or ones your family used, and be ready to talk about their meaning.

    _____

    _____

E. Some Exceptions to the Article Rules

Although you learned that count and noncount nouns qualified by an adjective clause or prepositional phrase are preceded by **the**, there are some exceptions to this rule. These are explained below.

COUNT NOUNS	
Compare: **a.** I want to buy **a** suitcase *from Italy.* **b.** Where is **the** suitcase *that you bought in Italy?*	• The meaning in (a) is "**any** suitcase from Italy," not a specific one, so **a** is used. • In (b), both the speaker and listener **know** which suitcase is being referred to, so **the** is necessary.
Compare: **c. A** car, *which can be quite expensive,* is indispensable to a foreign student in the United States. **d. The** car *that my brother bought* doesn't have any air-conditioning.	• In (c), **car** is generic; it refers to all cars. It is followed by an adjective clause that does not specify which car. Use **a.** • In (d), **car** has been limited by an adjective clause, so you must use **the.**

NONCOUNT NOUNS	
Compare: **e.** I love **cheese** *from Wisconsin.* **f.** Where is **the cheese** *that you bought yesterday?* **g. Hail,** *which is a combination of ice and snow,* can be quite dangerous. **h. The hail** *that we get in my town* can be as big as golf balls.	• In (e), **cheese** is a generic noun meaning "any cheese from Wisconsin." • In (f), the cheese has been specified. • In (g), the noncount noun is generic followed by a nonrestrictive adjective clause. • In (h), the hail has been limited to a specific type, that is, the hail in a specific town. Use **the** to reflect this specification.

10.9 Written Drill: *Exceptions to Article Rules*

DIRECTIONS: Fill in the blanks with **a/an, the,** or Ø, as appropriate.

1. I know _____ place where we can go for lunch.

2. This is _____ place which I told you about.

3. _____ pet, which can be quite a nuisance at times, can also be a joy to elderly people.

4. Most people don't like _____ steak which has been overcooked.

5. I gave _____ steak which I overcooked to the dog.

10.10 Written Exercise: *Articles*

DIRECTIONS: Fill in the blank with any noun that makes sense. You will have to decide whether to use the, **a/an** or Ø.

Example   CUE: _____ you gave me was beautiful.
              ANSWER: <u>The sweater</u> you gave me was beautiful.

1. _____ which bothers me most about a foreign language is the pronunciation.

2. _____ never makes me scared, but _____ sure does!

3. I really need _____; do you know where I can find it?

4. The area which intrigues me the most in the United States is _____.

5. _____ in my first language is quite different from English, but _____ is quite similar.

Grammatical Patterns Part Two

Subject-Verb Agreement

Preview

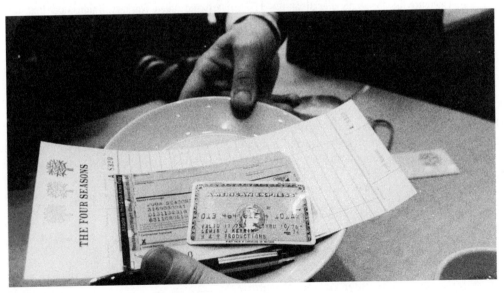

DIRECTIONS: What do you know about tipping in the United States? Should you tip a waiter? How much? Read the following text on tipping customs in the United States to find out. Then answer the questions that follow.

U.S. Visitors Tripping on Our Way of Tipping
By Sehyon Joh

1 A number of tourists visiting the U.S. face more than the language barrier when they visit New York or other large American cities. **The intricacies of tipping** have some of them baffled.

2 France, as well as many other European countries, has a "tip-included" policy which means the service is included in the bill. But if a customer is especially satisfied with the service, he or she might leave an extra franc or two on the table.

3 A tourism official tells the story of a French visitor who felt insulted when an American waiter followed him to the door, handed him the dollar he had left on the table as a tip and told him: "I think you need this dollar more than I do. Take it." The French visitor had assumed, of course, that the tip had already been included in the bill.

4 In many countries in Asia, there is basically no tipping, so **none of the waiters** expects to find a tip on the table after serving customers. In spite of these differences, foreign visitors learn quickly about U.S. tipping customs.

5 Just how much should a person tip? **"Fifteen percent** is acceptable and twenty percent is preferable," says John Turchiano, spokesman for the Hotel and Restaurant Employees Union Local.

6 Lawrence Goldberg, an official at the Taxi Drivers and Allied Workers' Union, said that for taxi drivers, **$25.00 a day** in tips is the average for a large city. This represents about 25–30 percent of his income. When Goldberg was asked who the worst tippers were, he replied, "Those rich old ladies out shopping on Fifth Ave."

FOCUS ON GRAMMAR

The following questions are based on the preview text and are designed to help you find out what you already know about the structures in this chapter. Some of the questions may be hard and some of them may be easy. Answer as many of the questions as you can. Work with a partner if your teacher tells you do so.

1. Locate the following subjects in the preview text, underline them and write the verb which follows them in the space provided.

   a. "A number of tourists" _____ (paragraph 1)

   b. "The intricacies of tipping" _____ (paragraph 1)

   c. "France, as well as other European countries" _____ (paragraph 2)

   d. "None of the waiters" _____ (paragraph 4)

   e. "Fifteen percent" _____ (paragraph 5)

   f. "$25.00 a day" _____ (paragraph 5)

2. Using the examples in (1) above as a guide, fill in the blanks with **is** (singular nouns) or **are** (plural nouns) in the following sentences. Then try to formulate a rule for subject-verb agreement for these cases.

   a. A number of Chinese visitors to the United States _____ surprised by the tipping customs here since tipping is prohibited in their country.

      RULE: _____

   b. $4.35 an hour _____ the average wage of a waiter in the U.S.

      RULE: _____

   c. Ten percent _____ not a sufficient tip for good service at an upscale restaurant.

      RULE: _____

   d. None of the workers in a fast food restaurant _____ given tips for service.

      RULE: _____

   e. A waiter, as well as a taxi driver and a hairstylist, _____ paid wages plus tips.

      RULE: _____

I. Subject-Verb Agreement

A. General Principles

You know that the subject of a sentence or clause must **agree** in number with the main or auxiliary verb of that sentence or clause. Most of the time, deciding if the noun is singular or plural is quite obvious, as in the following examples:

1. <u>The book</u> is missing. (*singular noun; singular verb*)

2. <u>The books</u> were on the table yesterday. (*plural noun; plural verb*)

However, sometimes the subject is longer than one word. Other times, it involves a more complex expression which makes it more difficult to decide whether it is singular or plural.

3. <u>Whatever you want to do</u> is fine with me. (*In this case the subject is a clause and thus requires a singular verb.*)

4. <u>A box</u> of books was delivered to my office. (*The subject here is a box and not books, so the subject is singular.*)

5. <u>Every book</u> is checked out. (*Every + noun requires a singular verb.*)

6. <u>One of the books</u> was missing. (*Only one, so the subject is singular.*)

7. <u>The news</u> is on at 6:00. (*Some nouns which end in -s such as* **economics** *and* **species** *are singular.*)

10.11 Rapid Drill: *Subject-Verb Agreement*

DIRECTIONS: Complete the following phrases using **is** or **are**.

Example   CUE: Most of the houses in the city
                   ANSWER: *Most of the houses in the city* **are** *built of wood.*

1. Most of the cars in this city . . .
2. Many of the women at this school . . .
3. One of the students in this class . . .
4. English classes . . .
5. The homework I have . . .
6. Learning a second language with other students . . .
7. Roses . . .
8. Every grammar class I take . . .
9. A pair of glasses . . .
10. Mathematics . . .

■ B. Some Special Cases

The chart below summarizes some potentially troublesome cases in subject-verb agreement.

QUANTITIES/ADDITIONS	EXAMPLE SENTENCE	RULE/EXPLANATION
a number of vs. **the number of**	1. **A number of** foreign visitors are surprised by tipping customs. 2. **The number of** customers *is 75.*	• **A number of** means "many," so a plural verb is used as in (1). • **The number of** means "the amount," so a singular verb is used with this expression as in (2).
percents/fractions amounts/distances	3. **20%** *is* preferable. 4. **Half** *is* given to the busboy. 5. **$3.35** *is the* minimum wage. 6. **Five miles** *is* an average distance for me to run.	• A singular verb follows **percentages, fractions, amounts,** and **distances** when they are not followed by an "of phrase."
amounts + of phrases	7. **Half of the tables** *are* occupied. 8. **The majority of the customers** *are* happy. 9. **A quarter of the cake** *is* gone! 10. **21% of the population** *is* poor. 11. **21% of the books** *are* paperback.	• When an **-of** phrase follows a **percentage, distance, fraction,** or **amount,** the verb agrees with the noun closest to the verb. Therefore, in (7) the verb agrees with **tables,** a plural noun, and in (9), the verb agrees with **cake,** a singular noun.

Continued on next page.

Continued from previous page.

QUANTITIES/ADDITIONS	EXAMPLE SENTENCE	RULE/EXPLANATION
none	12. **None of the workers** *receives* a tip. 13. **None of the workers** *receive* a tip. *(less formal)*	• Usually, a singular verb follows **none**, even if the noun following it is plural (12). • In conversational English, a plural noun has become acceptable, as in (13).
as well as/ **in addition to/** **together with**	14. **France,** as well as other European countries, *has* a tip-included policy. 15. **Waiters,** in addition to others who work for tips, *are* usually generous tippers.	• With these expressions, the first noun determines if the verb is singular or plural. In (14), **France** is the subject of the sentence and not **other European countries,** so the plural is singular. • Note how these expressions are set off by commas.

10.12 Rapid Drill: *Subject-Verb Agreement*

DIRECTIONS: Complete the following sentences paying careful attention to subject-verb agreement.

1. Half of the English words I learn . . .
2. The majority of students in the class . . .
3. None of the teachers I know . . .
4. A million dollars . . .
5. A number of leaders in the world . . .
6. Doctors, in addition to lawyers, . . .
7. 100% . . .
8. One quarter of my day . . .
9. A number of students in this class . . .
10. Tom Cruise, as well as other movie actors, . . .
11. The number of tests in this class . . .
12. Six miles . . .
13. 55% of the population . . .
14. One-third of my friends . . .
15. Over half . . .

COMPOUND SUBJECTS	EXAMPLE SENTENCES	RULE/EXPLANATION
neither/nor	1. Neither the host nor his guests **were** happy. 2. Neither the guests nor their host **was** happy.	• The noun closest to the verb determines if that verb is singular or plural.
either/or	3. Either John or his brothers **are** going to make dinner.	• In (1), the second noun **guests** determines that the verb is plural.
not only/but also	4. Not only the waiter but also the cook and busboy **work for tips.**	• In (2), **host** is closest to the verb, so a singular verb is required.
both/and	5. Both John and his sister **are** going to be at the party.	• Use a plural noun with subjects using **both/and.**
and	6. Carol and Bob **were** at the party. 7. The administration and interpretation of educational tests **is** an important part of her job.	• Compound subjects connected by **and** are always plural as in (6). • Occasionally, the compound subject describes two parts of a single process as in (7). Use a singular verb in this case.

10.13 Written Drill: *Compound Subjects*

DIRECTIONS: Complete the following sentences.

1. Neither my mother nor my father . . .
2. Not only cigarette smoking, but also drinking and overeating . . .
3. Neither Italy nor other European countries . . .
4. Not only New York, but also other cities, . . .
5. The city of San Francisco . . .
6. I'm not sure who is going; either my friend or my parents . . .
7. Walking and running . . .
8. The collection of water . . .

10.14 Written Activity: *Customs in Your Culture*

DIRECTIONS: Write about four customs from your cultural background that you think your teacher or classmates might not know about. These customs could be related to tipping, sharing food, birthdays, holidays, etc. Use the following expressions and pay careful attention to subject-verb agreement. Be ready to give an oral account of your written work.

1. A number of . . .
2. None of the . . .

3. The majority of . . .

4. . . . , in addition to . . .

10.15 Editing Activity: *Subject-Verb Agreement*

DIRECTIONS: Read the following paragraph, which provides statistics on women around the world. Correct any errors in **subject-verb agreement** clearly.

Facts about Women Around the World

Women's lifespan varies around the world. For example, 64 years are the average age around the globe, but 40 years is the average age in Sierra Leone. A Japanese woman, as well as an American or French woman, has an expected lifespan of around 80.

The majority of women lives in Asia. 13% lives in Africa, while only 5% of the world's women lives in North America. The fewest number of women in the world lives in Oceania.

The average wage of women are substantially less than that earned by men. Forty cents for every dollar are what the average worker in Bangladesh earns. In Sweden it is much better; almost 90% of male wages is paid to women there. The average percentage of all countries is 75.

C. Collective Nouns

A collective noun refers to a group of something. Examples of collective nouns include **audience, class, government, committee, family, flock, herd,** etc. Collective nouns may be followed by either singular or plural verbs. Note the difference in use in the following examples.

EXAMPLE SENTENCE	EXPLANATION
1. The family **arrives** together at 7:00. 2. John just arrived and now the family **are** all here.	• When a **singular verb** is used with a collective noun, it emphasizes the group as a unit. In (1), the family will arrive together as one group. • When a **plural verb** is used with a collective noun, it emphasizes that the group members are acting individually.[a] In (2), group members have arrived separately, so a plural noun is used.
Exceptions: 3. The **police** carry guns in the U.S. 4. The **military** often retire at 45. 5. The **people** don't trust the news.	• These collective nouns are **always** plural.

[a]*Collective nouns are more often plural in British English than American English (for example, "The family are all in London.").*

10.16 Written Drill: *Collective Nouns*

DIRECTIONS: Circle the **appropriate singular** or **plural verb**, depending on the meaning of the sentence. Refer to the chart on page 255 to help you decide.

1. The committee is/are having a heated debate about the question of summer vacations.

2. The Bush family is/are spending the summer in Kennebunkport, Maine.

3. Meanwhile, the Smith family is/are taking separate vacations this year.

4. The government always keep/keeps in close contact with the president while he is on vacation.

5. People in the United States do/does not usually take vacations that are longer than four weeks.

6. The military is/are granted leaves or vacations, upon request.

10.17 Paired Activity: *Collective Nouns*

DIRECTIONS: Complete the following sentences and choose the **appropriate verb**. Then discuss your answers with a partner. See if your impressions are similar or different.

1. The police in the United States is/are _____.

2. I think the military in the United States has/have _____.

3. An audience at a rock concert is/are _____.

4. An American family value/values _____.

5. The government in the United States is/are _____.

6. This class is/are _____.

II. Special Problems with Article Usage and Subject-Verb Agreement

Pay special attention to these very common errors.

PROBLEM/INCORRECT FORM	EXPLANATION
1. Most [incorrect: Most of students here eat fast food.] correct: **Most students** here eat fast food. correct: **Most of the students** here eat fast food.	Plural count nouns after **most** are followed by **of the** or **no article** + the plural noun.
2. Generic Abstract Nouns [incorrect: The money is very important to my host family.] correct: **Money** is very important to my host family.	Don't use **the** before a noncount noun when you are referring to that noun in general.

Continued on next page.

Continued from previous page.

PROBLEM/INCORRECT FORM	EXPLANATION
3. Indefinite Article [incorrect: She is teacher of English.] correct: She is a teacher of English.	Students often forget to put **a/an** before a singular count noun, especially if it refers to a profession.
4. Count/Noncount Nouns [incorrect: She did a lot of **researches**.] correct: She did a lot of **research**. [incorrect: Do you have much ski **equipments**?] correct: Do you have much ski **equipment**?	Be very careful about the use of articles and quantifiers with noncount nouns.

■ **10.18 Written Activity:** *Error Analysis*

DIRECTIONS: Examine the following sentences, which were written by ESL students, for errors in **article usage** and **count and noncount nouns**. If you find an error, circle it and make your correction clearly above the error. Some sentences may not have any errors. If a sentence is already correct, do not change anything.

1. Confucianism influence Korea greatly because it was a dominant ideology of Yi Dynsty.

2. So Korean has the characteristics of courtesy, desire for higher education, and quietness.

3. The swimming in the ocean requires more strength than the swimming in a pool.

4. Rick won a prize of a trip around the world, but he didn't accept the prize because it was sponsored by the weapons company.

5. The happiness that she is looking for can never be found during the life.

6. The traveling can be great experience for people because it provides exposure to other cultures.

7. In 1950s, the average American family consumed much more loaves of bread than they do today.

8. Many Americans think the divorce is increasing because most of families do not share time together.

9. The Earthquake Commission offers the following advices to people in high-risk areas: when an earthquake hits, stand under the door or the table.

10. If you ever visit the Great Lakes, be sure to go to Niagara Falls.

11. Louisa is planning the trip to southern part of France where she hopes to visit Roman ruins.

12. It is difficult for new parents to make decisions regarding the discipline.

13. Japanese has skillfulness.

14. Success in work in Japan is closely related with superior's evaluation.

15. In other words, vertical relationship is more important than horizontal one.

16. Most of Koreans learn some English in high school.

17. When you ask the direction, the Japanese will be very kind and have patience to tell you what to do.

18. None of us likes to pay taxes.

19. The crowd are going wild over the new song by the Rolling Stones.

20. The majority of houses in this state is made of stucco.

Focus on Writing

Definitions

When you define a term, you will probably use generic nouns in your definition. Note how this occurs in the following definition.

The <u>sloth</u> is a <u>three-clawed animal</u> <u>found in Costa Rica.</u>
term being defined   class to which it belongs   distinguishing feature

In the example above, **the** is used before **sloth** as a generic marker and not as a reference to a specific sloth. You may use **the** when defining nouns (both count and noncount) that belong to clearly identified classes of things. For example, these classes include animals, plants, professionals, inventions, and so on.

You would not use **the** in your definition of an object such as a chair, a house, etc. In such a case you would use either **a + noun** or a plural noun, as follows:

   a. **A soup tureen** is a serving bowl which has a top to keep the soup warm.

   b. **Soup tureens** are serving bowls which have tops to keep the soup warm.

Note the adjustments that have been made in subject-verb agreement in sentence (b) above.

10.19 Written Activity: *Defining*

DIRECTIONS: Imagine that you have encountered beings from another planet and these beings do not understand the use or function of many things on this planet. Choose five objects from the following list and write brief (2–3 sentences) **definitions** of the objects which include what they are used for or what they do. Use **the** when it is possible to define your terms.

   1. computers

   2. rollerblades

   3. surfboards

   4. lipstick

5. watches

6. nail polish

7. neckties

8. tattoos

9. toothbrush

10. snakes

11. psychologists

12. English teachers

13. bread

14. vitamins

Composition Topics

1. Foreign visitors and immigrants often experience culture shock when they first go to a foreign country. Using the Preview essay on page 236 as a model, describe what you were prepared for and what you were not prepared for when you first arrived in this country. If you do not remember because you were too young when you came here, interview a family member. If you have spent any time in a foreign country, describe that experience.

2. Write about the tipping customs of another country. Draw from your own experiences or interview a person from another culture.

3. Write about different forms of greetings around the globe. Draw from your own experience and the experiences of others.

The Spirit of America

Chapter 11

• Passives

The Spirit of America
(Life, Liberty and the Pursuit of Happiness)

DISCUSSION QUESTIONS

1. Why do you think so many people from around the world immigrated to America?

2. How would you define "the American dream"?

OBJECTIVES

In this chapter you will learn:

1. To form the passive voice of English verbs in all tenses

2. To form and use the passive voice of modals, infinitives, and gerunds

3. To understand which English verbs have a passive voice

4. To understand when the passive voice should be used

5. To understand when the agent should be included in a passive sentence

6. To use passive verb forms as adjectives

Preview

DIRECTIONS: Martin Luther King, Jr., was an African American civil rights leader who fought for equality through peaceful resistance. Below is a famous speech delivered by Martin Luther King, Jr., in Washington, D.C., on August 28, 1963. Read the speech, referring to the vocabulary list when necessary.

I Have a Dream
by Martin Luther King, Jr.

I say to you today, my friends, so even though we face the difficulties of today and tomorrow, I still have a dream. I have a dream that one day this nation will **rise up** and live out the true meaning of its **creed,** "We hold these truths to be self-evident, that all men are created equal." I have a dream that one day on the red hills of Georgia, sons of former slaves and the sons of former slave owners will be able to sit down together at the table of brotherhood. I have a dream that one day even the state of Mississippi, a state sweltering with the heat of injustice, **sweltering** with the heat of **oppression,** will be **transformed** into an **oasis** of freedom and justice. I have a dream that my four little children will one day live in a nation where they will not be judged by the color of their skin, but by the content of their character.

I have a dream today!

I have a dream, that one day down in Alabama—with its vicious racists, with its Governor having his lips dripping with the words of interposition and nullification—one day right there in Alabama, little black boys and black girls will be able to join hands with little white boys and white girls as sisters and brothers.

I have a dream today!

I have a dream that one day every valley shall be **exalted,** every hill and mountain shall be made low. The rough places will be plain and the crooked places will be made straight, "and the glory of the Lord shall be **revealed,** and all flesh shall see together."

This is our hope.

VOCABULARY

rise up: stand
creed: a statement of the beliefs of a certain group of people
sweltering: giving off intense heat
oppression: the state of being subordinated through unjust power or authority
transformed: changed from one state to another
oasis: figuratively, anything which is a relief from difficulty or hardship
exalted: raised up
revealed: uncovered

CULTURAL NOTE/DISCUSSION

What do you know about Martin Luther King, Jr.? How does he symbolize the American spirit of independence, opportunity, and freedom?

FOCUS ON GRAMMAR

The following questions are based on the preview text and are designed to help you find out what you already know about the structures in this chapter. Some of the questions may be hard and some of them may be easy. Answer as many of the questions as you can. Work with a partner if your teacher tells you to do so.

1. A passive verb in English is formed with a form of **be** and the **past participle** of the verb, for example, **is taught.** The auxiliary **be** verb indicates the tense. For example, "is" is in the present tense, so the verb tense is in the present tense.

    Underline the passive verbs in the speech. See if you can identify the verb tenses of the passive verbs in the preview text. Write the tenses used and an example of each below:

    TENSE   EXAMPLE

    _____   _____

    _____   _____

    _____   _____

    _____   _____

    _____   _____

2. Find an example of a negative passive sentence in the text. Write it here:

    _____

    Based on this example from the text, what is the rule for forming the negative passive?

    _____

3. Below is a sentence from the speech containing a passive verb. Following the sentence is a paraphrase of the same sentence, written with an active verb and the agent of the action. Why do you think the passive form of the sentence was used in the speech?

    "I have a dream that one day my four little children will live in a nation where they will not be judged."

    I have a dream that one day my four little children will live in a nation where the people of that nation will not judge them.

Grammatical Patterns Part One

I. Active to Passive Transformation

An English sentence can either be stated in active voice or passive voice. The diagram below demonstrates how the active to passive transformation is made.

SENTENCE IN ACTIVE VOICE	
The <u>average American</u> <u>seeks</u> <u>independence</u> subject verb object There are three steps to making this active sentence passive:	
1. Make the direct object of the active sentence the subject of the passive sentence.	The <u>average American</u> <u>seeks</u> **independence.** subject verb object **Independence** _____ subject
2. Make the verb passive: **be + past participle**	The <u>average American</u> **<u>seeks</u>** <u>independence.</u> subject verb direct object Independence **is sought** _____ subject passive verb
3. If necessary, add **by** to the subject of the active sentence and make it the agent.	**<u>The average American</u>** <u>seeks</u> <u>independence.</u> subject verb object Independence is sought **by the average American.** subject passive verb agent
SENTENCE IN PASSIVE VOICE	
<u>**Independence**</u> <u>**is sought**</u> <u>**by the average American.**</u> subject passive verb agent	

11.1 Rapid Drill: *Active* to *Passive Transformation*

DIRECTIONS: Change each of the following active sentences to passive.

1. Whites forced blacks to sit in the back of school buses.
2. Martin Luther King, Jr., encouraged peaceful resistance.
3. Whites prevented blacks from eating at the same restaurants.
4. Whites discriminated against blacks in many other ways.
5. The constitution guarantees equality for all.
6. The constitution protects the rights of every American citizen.
7. Through such discrimination, whites were violating the basic human rights of blacks.
8. Americans are still taking steps to prevent discrimination.
9. Hopefully, by the end of the century we will make progress in our ability to uphold human rights.
10. One of the major challenges is to remember the damage that we have caused in the past.

II. Passive Voice in Different Verb Tenses

The chart below shows how the passive voice is formed in the various verb tenses. There is **no passive form** for present perfect progressive, simple future progressive, and past perfect progressive.

Active Verb	Passive Verb Form	Passive Verb
Simple Present The Constitution **guarantees** equality for all.	**is/are + past participle**	Equality for all **is guaranteed** by the Constitution.
Present Progressive Many leaders **are taking** steps to enforce the Constitution.	**is/are + being + past participle**	Steps **are being taken** by many leaders to enforce the Constitution.
Present Perfect We **have violated** the principles of the Constitution in the past.	**has/have + been + past participle**	The principles of the Constitution **have been violated** in the past.
Simple Past School segregation **violated** a constitutional right.	**was/were + past participle**	A constitutional right **was violated** by school segregation.
Past Progressive The Montgomery police **were violating** a constitutional right when they arrested a black woman on a bus.	**was/were + being + past participle**	A constitutional right **was being violated** by the Montgomery police when they arrested a black woman on a bus.
Past Perfect The government **had feared** a violent uprising.	**had + been + past participle**	A violent uprising **had been feared** by the government.
Future We **will feel** the impact of the civil rights movement for years to come.	**will + be + past participle**	The impact of the civil rights movement **will be felt** for years to come.
Future Perfect By the time our children are grown, we **will have taught** them many lessons about civil rights.	**will + have + been + past participle**	By the time our children are grown, they **will have been taught** many lessons about civil rights.

II.2 Rapid Drill: *Passive Voice in Different Verb Tenses*

DIRECTIONS: Change each **active verb** below to **passive**.

Example   CUE: catches
              RESPONSE: is caught

1. teaches
2. have written
3. was showing
4. will see
5. is eating
6. were striking

7. had spoken

8. will have performed

9. bring

10. are selling

11. makes up

12. measured

13. was demonstrating

14. is filling

15. will have found

11.3 Written Drill: *Fill in the Blanks*

DIRECTIONS: In the passage below about Martin Luther King, Jr.'s life, fill in the blanks with the **passive form** of the verb in parentheses. Be sure that the verb is in the correct tense.

Martin Luther King, Jr., who _____ (born) in Atlanta, Georgia, on January 15, 1929, _____ (recognize) today as having been one of America's leading social reformers. His role as leader of the civil rights movement began in 1959 when a black woman in Montgomery, Alabama _____ (arrest) for refusing to give up to a white man her seat in the front of the bus. This incident served as the impetus for a bus boycott throughout Montgomery, which _____ (direct) by King. At the time, blacks _____ (discriminate) against severely all over the country, especially in the South, so they were ready for a fight. King's belief in nonviolent demonstrations, however, which _____ (inspire) by Gandhi, _____ widely _____ (adopt) by the civil rights movement. Although blacks _____ still _____ (discriminate) against to some degree at the present, Martin Luther King, Jr. made significant gains in the struggle for greater equality. He will always _____ (remember) as the leader who peacefully convinced many Americans that the principles of the Constitution _____ (not uphold). In 1964, he _____ (award) the Nobel Peace Prize, the first black to receive this award. In 1968, just as he was preparing to lead a nationwide campaign on behalf of the poor, Martin Luther King, Jr. _____ (assassinate). His life _____ (commemorate) every January on Martin Luther King Day.

11.4 Paired Activity: *Freedom*

DIRECTIONS: Discuss the following topics as they relate to the history of your native country. Use the passive voice in a variety of tenses.

Example   FREEDOM: Freedom has not always been respected in this country. Many people were and still are being persecuted for the color of their skin, their religious background, their political views, and their nationality.

1. Freedom of speech

2. Freedom of religion

3. Political opportunity

4. The right to vote

5. Equal rights for men and women

Now choose one of the topics and write five sentences in the passive voice based on your discussion.

11.5 Written Activity: *Civil Rights*

DIRECTIONS: Write a short paragraph about an important leader in your country who fought for civil rights for a group of people that were being oppressed or discriminated against. Use a variety of verb tenses in the passive voice to describe the events and actions that took place. If you have difficulty thinking of someone, write about a person from another country, such as Bobby Kennedy or Nelson Mandela.

III. Verbs That Can be Passive

Not all English verbs have both an active and passive form. The chart below provides guidelines about which verbs can be passive.

GENERALIZATION	EXAMPLE
1. Most **transitive** verbs can be active or passive: **take, bring, eat, teach, write, read, drive, etc.**	Ships **brought** immigrants across the ocean. (active) Many immigrants **were brought** across the ocean by ship. (passive)
2. **Intransitive** verbs cannot be passive: **be, seem, appear, sleep, rise, arrive, weigh** (when it is intransitive), **happen, occur, die, etc.**	The children **were been** sick by the food. (incorrect use of passive) Many **were arrived** in America with no money. (incorrect use of passive) Sasha **was weighed** only 90 pounds when she arrived. (incorrect use of passive)
3. **Have** cannot be passive.	These immigrants **had** many problems. (active) Many problems **were had** by these immigrants. (incorrect use of passive)
4. The verb **to be born** can only be used in the passive.	Her daughter **was born** in March. (correct use of passive) She **born** her daughter in March. (incorrect use of active)

For more information on transitive and intransitive verbs, see Chapter 5.

11.6 Rapid Drill: *Verbs That Can Be Passive*

DIRECTIONS: If possible, change the active sentence to a **passive sentence**. Discuss the reason why the change may or may not be possible.

1. Alicia lay down on the cot to rest during the trip.
2. The sun rises at 6:00 A.M. every day.
3. In the beginning, immigrants earned their salary through manual labor.
4. This country has a very diverse ethnic makeup.
5. Hispanics make up a large percentage of the immigrant population.
6. As Li was preparing to board, the officer weighed his baggage.
7. When the immigrants saw the Statue of Liberty, they knew they had arrived in America.
8. Something strange happened when Sachi spoke with an American for the first time.
9. Many people died during the trip due to the harsh conditions.
10. The highest wave of immigration occurred during this period.

IV. Modals, Infinitives, and Gerunds in the Passive Voice

The following patterns are used for the passive voice of modals, infinitives, and gerunds.

MODALS   Simple: **Modal + Be + Past Participle**
Immigrants **couldn't be convinced** that their lives would be more difficult in America.
Perfect: **Modal + Have + Been + Past Participle**
Immigrants **must have been told** about the opportunities in America.

INFINITIVES   Simple: **To + Be + Past Participle**
Many immigrants waited **to be processed** at Ellis Island.
Perfect: **To + Have + Been + Past Participle**
Many Immigrants felt lucky **to have been rescued** from their former lives.

GERUNDS   Simple: **Being + Past Participle**
Some people hated **being packed** onto a ship like sardines.
Perfect: **Having Been + Past Participle**
Many were grateful for **having been given** the opportunity to come to America.

11.7 Rapid Drill: *Forming Passive Modals, Infinitives, and Gerunds*

DIRECTIONS: Change each of the active verb forms below to the **passive**.

Example   can't drive   can't be driven

1. shouldn't take _____
2. want to carry _____
3. like teaching _____
4. could have refused _____
5. regret having accepted _____
6. denied promising _____
7. have to tell _____
8. hope to hire _____
9. hated reminding _____
10. must sell _____

11. must have sent _____   13. can't deliver _____

12. attempt to educate _____   14. remember checking _____

11.8 Written Drill: *Using Passive Modals, Infinitives, and Gerunds*

DIRECTIONS: The sentences below contain information about the immigrants to the United States who arrived in New York at Ellis Island in the late 1800s. Paraphrase each of the sentences, using a passive modal, gerund, or infinitive. For some sentences, there will be more than one choice.

Example   It was impossible for the government to accept all the immigrants.
            All the immigrants <u>couldn't be accepted</u> by the government.
            It was impossible for all the immigrants <u>to be accepted</u> by the government.

1. It was necessary to impose limitations on the number of immigrants.

   _____

2. When they arrived at Ellis Island, it was impossible to process them immediately.

   _____

3. They left their countries because they wanted freedom from hunger and poverty.

   _____

4. They really enjoyed it when the boat was taking them far from the problems of their native country.

   _____

5. Many of them didn't want to go through the examination and questioning at the port of entry because they feared rejection.

   _____

11.9 Paired Activity: *A New Constitution*

DIRECTIONS: What is freedom? How much freedom should people have? Discuss these questions with your partner and decide on five principles that you would include in a constitution if you were writing it for your country. Write the five principles on the lines below. Each statement should include a passive modal.

Example   People shouldn't be refused the right to choose and practice their religion.

_____

_____

_____

_____

_____

Grammatical Patterns Part Two

Preview

DIRECTIONS: Read the following editorial that appeared in a local newspaper on July 5, the day after Independence Day in America.

Happy Fourth of July

1 Yesterday, on the Fourth of July, American independence once again was celebrated across the nation. Fireworks were **set off,** picnics were held in parks and on beaches, and parades were attended by young and old alike.

2 This is a holiday that has been celebrated by Americans every year for the last 200 years. We all **get caught up in** plans and activities so that we can **get the most out of** a day off from work, and if the holiday falls on a Friday or a Monday, the three-day weekend is an opportunity to take off from the city to a favorite **getaway.**

3 However, as with many holidays, the purpose and origin of the holiday itself are often lost in the excitement and **preoccupation** of the celebration. In the heat of the summer, the American memory should be taken back to the heat of a battle that was won by the spirit of independence, equality, and freedom. The American way of life should be characterized by that spirit, and that spirit should provide the **impetus** and inspiration to continue the fight to uphold these principles. As the hamburgers are **barbecued** and the baseball games won, each American should reflect on the independence that was gained by our country many years ago, and which is still being sought by many. This is the independence that many in our country and all over the world are still struggling to achieve—independence from poverty and hunger, independence from **repression** and hatred, independence from the limitations that prevent human beings from living to their full potential.

VOCABULARY

set off: ignited and as a result exploded
get caught up in: get involved in
get the most out of: receive as much benefit as possible from something
getaway: a place to escape to
preoccupation: something that occupies all your time, energy, or thoughts
impetus: stimulus, incentive, impulse
barbecued: cooked outdoors over hot coals
repression: control that prevents natural development or expression

CULTURAL NOTE/DISCUSSION

Parades and picnics are the two most characteristic activities for the Fourth of July in America. Are these activities common for any holidays in your native country? What is a typical parade in your native country like? Describe a typical picnic.

FOCUS ON GRAMMAR

The following questions are based on the preview text and are designed to help you find out what you already know about the structures in this chapter. Work with a partner if your teacher tells you to do so.

1. Why are the first two sentences in the preview written in the passive voice?

2. The first sentence in paragraph 3 has no agent. Who is the agent? Why is the agent omitted?

3. Underline the agent in the second sentence in paragraph 3. Is it possible to omit this agent? Why or why not?

I. When To Use the Passive

The passive voice in English is actually used much more infrequently than the active voice. It is used most commonly in formal written English. The chart below explains when it is appropriate to use the passive voice.

GENERALIZATION	EXAMPLE
To emphasize the receiver or the result of the action.	1. **Americans are taught** independence and self-sufficiency at an early age. (The emphasis is on Americans being taught, not on someone teaching them.)
If the writer wants to *purposely* omit the agent because the agent is unnecessary.	2. Coffee **is drunk** in America. (Obviously it is drunk by Americans.)
To achieve objectivity by concealing the source of information.	3. **It is often thought** that American families are not close because the children want to live independently. (We don't know who is thinking this.)

Continued on next page.

Continued from previous page.

GENERALIZATION	EXAMPLE
To provide information about the topic after the topic has already been stated.	4. **Baseball** is a very popular American sport. **It is played** all over the country. (We know this second sentence is referring to baseball.)
To avoid clumsiness, bad style, or inappropriateness in writing.	5. Incorrect: American parents instill the value of independence in their children from an early age, which some psychologists **suggest** in this study that this may be why American families are not close. Correct: American parents instill the value of independence in their children from an early age, which may be why American families are not close, as **was suggested** by psychologists in this study.

11.10 Recognition Drill: *Passive vs. Active*

DIRECTIONS: Each pair of sentences below contains an active sentence and a passive sentence. Discuss the distinction between the two sentences and the rationale for using one rather than the other.

Example   a. American parents teach their children independence at an early age.

   b. American children are taught independence at an early age.

In sentence **a**, the active voice is used to make it clear that it is parents who are teaching children independence, as opposed to teachers, society, etc.

   In sentence **b**, the passive voice is used to emphasize the fact that independence is taught regardless of who may be the teacher.

1. a. In 1846, men, women, and children packed up and prepared for the journey west.

   b. In 1846 men, women, and children were packed up and prepared for the journey west.

2. a. "Every day was like a picnic," a girl remembered of her earliest weeks on the trail.

   b. It was said that for the young children every day was like a picnic during the earliest weeks on the trail.

3. a. Circumstances often left children with responsibilities. They were asked to drive ox teams, care for herds, and join in family decisions.

   b. Circumstances often left children with responsibilities. Their parents or other group members asked them to drive ox teams, care for herds, and join in family decisions.

4. a. These children faced hardships and responsibilities that others never face until adulthood, which is why some psychologists suggest that they never really had a childhood.

   b. These children faced hardships and responsibilities that others never faced until adulthood, which is why, as suggested by some psychologists, they never really had a childhood.

5. a. Disease and exhaustion were common during the journey. They were fought with the desire to stay alive.

   b. Disease and exhaustion were common during the journey. The children and their parents fought disease and exhaustion with the desire to stay alive.

6. a. This journey taught these children many lessons that children today will never have the opportunity to experience.

   b. Children were taught many lessons that children today will never have the opportunity to experience.

11.11 Written Activity: *Cowboys*

DIRECTIONS: The passage below about cowboys is written in the active voice. Decide which verbs should be written in the passive and make the changes in the text. Discuss your reason for making the changes.

Being a cowboy was not a romantic life as legend made it out to be. Cowboys had many problems as they traveled across the country rounding up cattle so that they could sell the animals in a different location. For example, in 1866 herders drove approximately 200,000 longhorns north across Indian territory toward Missouri. First, the Indians demanded payment for the grass the cattle ate along the way. Then, a group of angry Missouri farmers stood in the path of the herd demanding that they turn back because disease-carrying ticks had infested the cattle. Sometimes the cowboys sent the cattle to a distant town by railroad, in which case the cowboys had to prod the cattle up ramps with poles, a job that resulted in a lasting nickname—"cowpokes."

11.12 Paired Activity: *National Holidays*

DIRECTIONS: Interview your partner about a national holiday he or she knows about such as Independence Day. Get as much information as possible about the history and traditions associated with the holiday. Write a short report on the holiday, using the passive whenever appropriate. Be prepared to present the information to the rest of the class if your teacher asks you to do so.

II. When To Use the Agent

As well as knowing when the passive voice is necessary, it is important to know when the agent should be used. The chart below provides guidelines on when to use the agent in a passive sentence.

Do Not Use the Agent	Example
When the agent was previously mentioned.	1. **The president** gave a speech last night. Many questions about immigration reform were answered.
When the agent is unknown.	2. An anonymous letter was written to protest this action.
When the agent is obvious.	3. The operation was performed at 3:00. (A surgeon performed the operation.)
When the speaker or writer wants to conceal the agent.	4. A mistake was made when war was declared.
Use the Agent	Example
To identify by proper name a person responsible for a certain work.	1. "This Land is Your Land" was written **by Woody Guthrie.**
To provide new information by providing an indefinite noun phrase.	2. The shopping cart was invented **by a young entrepreneur.**
To emphasize the fact that the agent is inanimate, since omitted agents are usually animate.	3. America was founded **in a spirit of independence and freedom.**

11.13 Rapid Drill: *Using the Agent*

DIRECTIONS: Each passive sentence below contains an agent. Discuss whether the **agent** is necessary, and if possible, omit the agent in the sentence.

Example   Because "The Star Spangled Banner" is the national anthem of the United States, it is sung by Americans before major sporting events. (The agent is unnecessary because it is obvious.)

1. Many pioneers were killed by the cruel weather and harsh living conditions.
2. A gross error was made by the president when he declared war.
3. "Paul Revere's Ride" was written by Henry Wadsworth Longfellow.
4. The Navaho are a tribe of Native Americans. They are known by people for their turquoise and silver jewelry.
5. Ranchers kept their cattle in pens until they were sold and shipped out by the ranchers.
6. Many of the Texas rangers were Mexican. Their feelings about the difficult cattle drives were expressed by them in trail songs.

7. Life on the trail was described by one young, dedicated cowboy as an exciting but harrowing experience.

8. After the president was inaugurated by the people, he gave a speech.

9. The many experiences of life on the trail were recorded by writers to preserve the memory of such a rich experience.

10. Many current problems can be overcome by the same spirit of cooperation and commitment that helped to move the country foward in the early days of its history.

11.14 Written Activity: *O.K.*

DIRECTIONS: Below is a short passage about the origin and use of the word *O.K.* Above the box is a list of agents that can be used for the passive sentences in the passage. For each passive sentence, choose an appropriate agent. Then decide whether the agent should be added, and if so, where it should be added. Be prepared to justify your decision.

a. by the public

b. by reporters

c. by an amazing fact

d. by the average American

e. by speakers of English

f. by Americans

g. by Allen Walker

h. by travelers

O.K.? O.K.!

1 Recently, international travelers who pay attention to the languages they encounter have been surprised. Conversations with the word "O.K." can be heard all over the world.

2 The word is used in the United States at least seven times per day. Therefore, the utterance "O.K." is emitted into the American air more than 1.4 billion times every twenty-four hours. The word **O.K.** in English has replaced the expression **all right,** which is still used although far less frequently than it was one hundred years ago.

3 The most significant research into the history of **O.K.** has been done at Columbia University. **O.K.** was first seen in print in the Boston *Morning Post* of March 23, 1839. When the editor, Charles Gordon Green, was interviewed, he said it stood for **all correct,** spelled **oll korrect.**

11.15 Written Activity: *Collecting Data*

DIRECTIONS: Listen carefully to your teacher or other English speakers for the next few days and take notes as you listen for the word **O.K.** Report your findings to your partner or the class as a whole. Use the passive voice in a variety of tenses to describe each situation, and omit the agent when appropriate.

III. Passive Verbs that Function as Adjectives

There are some verbs that can function as adjectives when used in the passive voice. There are a few distinct categories of these verbs.

Type	Active Verb	Passive Verb	Passive Verb as Adjective
Stative Passive (e.g., **open, close, break**)	The teacher **closed** the window.	The window **was closed** by the teacher.	The window is **closed**. (The passive form of the verb describes a state.)
Participial Adjectives of Feeling or Mental State (**surprise, amuse, bore**)	The new music called jazz **surprised** many Americans.	Many Americans **were surprised** by the new music called jazz.	They were **surprised**. Many **surprised** Americans listened to the new music called jazz.
Idiomatic Use of Passive Form (**be + lost, gone, finished, done**)	no active counterpart	no passive counterpart	I am **lost**. New Orleans is **located** in Louisiana. Those times are **gone**.

SPECIAL NOTE

ACTIVE AND PASSIVE PARTICIPIAL ADJECTIVES

There is often confusion about the difference between the participial adjectives that are formed from a passive verb and those that are formed from an active verb, for example, **surprised-surprising**. Here are some ways to remember the distinction.

PASSIVE PARTICIPIAL ADJECTIVE
- The new music **surprised** many Americans. *(Active verb)*
- Many Americans **were surprised** by the new music. *(Passive verb)*
- The **surprised** Americans listened to the new music. *(Passive adjective)*

The passive participial adjective:
1. has an **-ed** ending: surpris**ed**
2. can be used in a passive sentence: The Americans **were surprised**.
3. usually describes an animate noun: **Americans**

ACTIVE PARTICIPIAL ADJECTIVE
- The new music **surprised** many Americans. *(Active verb)*
- The new music was **surprising**. *(Active adjective)*

The active participial adjective:
1. has an **-ing** ending: surpris**ing**
2. can be used in a passive sentence
3. usually describes an inanimate noun: **the new music**

11.16 Rapid Drill: *Active vs. Passive Participial Adjectives*

DIRECTIONS: Below are some sentences about the origins of jazz. For each active sentence, make one sentence with a passive participal adjective and one sentence with an active participial adjective.

Example   The music *amazed* the public.
   a. The public was amazed.
   b. The music was amazing.

1. The drumbeat in Congo Square *excited* the people who gathered there to dance.
2. Ragtime music *astonished* the Creole musicians who first heard it.
3. The use of improvisation *baffled* other musicians.
4. The new rhythms of jazz *confused* traditional musicians.
5. The intensity of the music *frustrated* listeners.
6. This music sometimes *bored* people who couldn't understand it.
7. The new music *surprised* the public as it spread.
8. The opportunities this new music represented *interested* young musicians.
9. The response of the public *amused* the first jazz musicians.
10. The freedom of this music *annoyed* conservative segments of the population.

11.17 Paired Activity: *First Impressions*

DIRECTIONS: Discuss with your partner your first impression of the United States or another country that you have visited. If you've never been abroad, discuss your first impressions of a city you've traveled to in your country. You will make a statement using either the active or passive participal form of one of the following verbs. Your partner will ask a question for more information, using the other form of the same verb. Choose from these verbs: **surprise, shock, amaze, interest, amuse, frustrate.**

Example   STUDENT 1: When I visited France, I was very **surprised** at how friendly the French people were.
   STUDENT 2: Oh, really? Why was that friendliness so **surprising** to you?
   STUDENT 1: Because I had been told that the French were not friendly to Americans.

11.18 Oral Activity: *American Specialties*

DIRECTIONS: Your teacher will assign you one of the following typical American foods. Interview an American to get the information listed at the top of page 277. If you are unable to interview an American, look for the information in the library.

FOODS

peanut butter	corn on the cob
watermelon	pancakes
coffee	banana split
hamburgers	french toast
pumpkin	corn on the cob

ORIGIN OF FOOD:
HOW IT IS PREPARED
HOW/WHEN/WHERE IT IS EATEN OR DRUNK
ANY ADDITIONAL CUSTOMES RELATED TO THIS FOOD

11.19 Written Activity

DIRECTIONS: Use the information you collected to write a paragraph that you will use as the basis for an oral presentation about the food you were assigned. Use the passive voice whenever possible and appropriate.

11.20 Written Drill: *Review*

DIRECTIONS: Use what you have learned about the passive voice to fill in the blanks below. Use the passive voice in the appropriate tense of the verbs in parentheses.

PHILIP: Hey, Gina, I hear you're going to America soon.

GINA: Yes, I _____ (invite) to visit my relatives in Florida.

PHILIP: Oh really? _____ (tell) much about your family?

GINA: Well, I know that my grandfather's cousin _____ (send) to America before the outbreak of war. He _____ (promise) a job in the butcher shop that another cousin owned at the time.

PHILIP: Boy, that must have been hard. _____ (prepare) for what was waiting for him? Did he know any English?

GINA: I don't think so, but apparently he _____ (teach) by his cousin's wife once he got to America. She was an English teacher.

PHILIP: That was fortunate. I guess immigrants _____ (give) the kind of public assistance with English back then that they have now.

GINA: That's right. They _____ (expect) to learn on their own.

PHILIP: Well. I have a lot of respect for people like your uncle. They _____ (confront) with a lot of obstacles.

GINA: Yes, but he _____ (bring up) in poverty, so he could only look forward to a better life.

IV. Special Problems with the Passive

PROBLEM	EXPLANATION
1. Incorrect form of past participle (INCORRECT: Immigrants were **brung** across the ocean on ships.) CORRECT: Immigrants were **brought** across the ocean on ships.	The past participle form of irregular verbs must be memorized.
2. Omission of one component in the passive construction (INCORRECT: If there is inequality, the Constitution **not being upheld.**) CORRECT: If there is inequality, the Constitution **is not being upheld.**	For certain tenses the verb **be** is used twice in a **passive** construction.
3. Use of the active voice when the passive voice is more appropriate (INCORRECT: American folk songs reflect the spirit of the people. **The writers wrote these songs** about every aspect of American life.) CORRECT: American folk songs reflect the spirit of the people. **These songs were written** about every aspect of American life.	In some situations, the passive voice is more appropriate than the active voice.
4. Incorrect omission or inclusion of the agent (INCORRECT: The Constitution was written.) CORRECT: The Constitution was written **by the fifty-five delegates** to the Constitutional Convention. (INCORRECT: In May, 1787, fifty-five delegates arrived in Philadelphia to write the Constitution. By the end of the summer, the Constitution was written **by these delegates.**) CORRECT: In May, 1787, fifty-five delegates arrived in Philadelphia to write the Constitution. By the end of the summer, the Constitution was written.	It is important to know when the agent should be included or omitted.

Continued on next page.

Continued from previous page.

PROBLEM	EXPLANATION
5. Using the passive in verb tenses for which it should not be used (INCORRECT: I have been being taught English for many years.) CORRECT: I have been learning English for many years.	Do not use the passive voice in present or past perfect progressive, simple future progressive, or future perfect progressive.

■ **11.21 Editing Activity**

DIRECTIONS: Some of the sentences below contain errors in the use of the passive voice. If there is an error, correct it clearly above the sentence. Some of the sentences may be correct.

1. America was establish on the principles of liberty, equality, and justice for all.

2. These principles are of utmost importance to Americans, so countless battles have been fought by Americans when equal rights have been abused.

3. The Constitution was written as a declaration of every American's commitment to these principles.

4. It is sometimes said that these are idealistic notions.

5. Visitors to America are sometimes surprising by the variety of ethnic groups that make up the population.

6. Many minority groups have helped by persistence of civil rights leaders.

7. "The Star Spangled Banner," the national anthem of the United States, was wrote by Francis Scott Key.

8. Halloween is an American holiday that children particularly enjoy. Americans celebrate Halloween on October 31.

9. Any tourist who crosses the border has to checked for proper immigration documents.

10. Jazz was born in America and is now played all over the world.

Focus on Writing

Differences Between the *Be* Passive and the *Get* Passive

Sometimes **get** can be used in place of **be** in passive constructions. The difference in meaning is demonstrated in the chart below.

DIFFERENCE	EXAMPLE
Be expresses a state **Get** expresses a process of becoming	Many women **were convinced** that their lives could be better. Many women **got convinced** that their lives could be better.
Be is formal **Get** is informal	Many women **were told** that their place was in the home. A lot of women **got told** that they had to stay home.
Be requires no involvement from the subject **Get** = subject has some influence over the result	Most women **were hired** as secretaries. (They didn't have much choice in the matter.) Most women **got hired** as secretaries. (This was **their** accomplishment.)
Be often takes an agent **Get** rarely takes an agent	Many women **were told by men** that their place was in the home. Many women **got told** that they had to stay home.

11.22 Written Drill: *Fill in the Blanks*

DIRECTIONS: In each pair of sentences, fill in the blank of one sentence with the correct form of **be** and the blank of the other sentence with the correct form of **get**. Be prepared to justify your choice.

Example a. Before the women's liberation movement, women *were* paid less than men.

b. After the women's liberation movement, women still *got* paid less than men for some jobs.

1. a. Some women _____ swept into the movement.

   b. Some women _____ opposed to becoming involved with the movement.

2. a. *The Feminine Mystique* _____ written by Betty Friedan, a feminist.

   b. Betty Friedan's book, *The Feminine Mystique,* _____ published as a result of changing attitudes towards women.

3. a. Many women _____ promoted from office work because of the victories they had won.

   b. Many women _____ promoted to higher-paying positions.

4. a. The effects of the women's liberation movement _____ felt by men all over the country.

   b. The message of the women's liberation movement _____ carried across the country.

11.23 Paired Activity: *Family Life*

DIRECTIONS: Read the following short passage about the American family. Write a short essay about the characteristics of American family life and compare them with family traditions in your country. Use **be** and **get** with the passive whenever appropriate.

American family traditions are very different from family traditions in other countries around the world. American children are taught independence at an early age, so it is not uncommon for American teenagers to get hired at their first jobs when they're 16 years old. This strong independence can also be seen when young people reach the age of 18. At this age, they usually move out of their parents' house if they get accepted at a university or if they are offered a job. At a later age, it is not uncommon for families to be separated by long distances, although this doesn't necessarily mean that a close relationship is not maintained.

SPECIAL NOTE

BE VS. GET

Notice the strong distinction in meaning between the passive formed by **be + past participle** to describe a **state** and the use of **get + past participle** to describe a **process.**

is married/get married	**is broken/get broken**
is hurt, get hurt	**is dressed/get dressed**

11.24 Rapid Drill: *Oral Paraphrase*

DIRECTIONS: In each pair of sentences below, if the sentence describes a state, paraphrase it with **be + past participle** of the given verb. If the sentence describes a process, paraphrase it with **get + past participle** of the given verb.

Example   MARRY

    a. Susan and Bill took their vows yesterday. <u>They **got married.**</u>

    b. Susan and Bill live together. <u>They **are married.**</u>

1. DRESS

    a. Sharon has clothes on. _____

    b. Sharon has put her clothes on. _____

2. HURT

    a. Marc smashed his finger in the door. _____

    b. Marc has a bandage on his finger. _____

3. LOSE

    a. They can't find the street they are looking for. _____

    b. They took a wrong turn. _____

4. BURN

    a. The toast is black. _____

    b. Somebody forgot to watch the toast. _____

Composition Topics

Use what you have learned in this chapter to write a well-developed essay about one of the following topics. Use the passive voice whenever appropriate.

1. Define the American dream giving examples of how that dream has been realized.

2. Describe the spirit of your native country, drawing on examples from the history, culture, and character of the people.

3. In your opinion, what human rights should be respected in any country? Give specific examples of how these rights can be upheld and how they are being disregarded.

- Modals

The Dating Scene (If You're Single, It's a Must)

DISCUSSION QUESTIONS

1. Are you single? If so, do you want to get married someday?
How is it possible to meet your future husband or wife? If
you're already married, how did you meet your husband or
wife?

2. What are the dating customs in your native country?

OBJECTIVES

In this chapter, you will learn:

1. To use a variety of modals and
their functions by reviewing them

2. To use several new functions for
the modals that you already know

3. To use the past forms of modals
for a variety of functions

4. To use passive and progressive
forms after modals

5. To understand question formation
for modal constructions

Preview

DIRECTIONS: Read the following telephone conversation between Jill, 28 years old, and Patty, 30 years old. Jill and Patty work together in a computer company and are very good friends.

1 Jill: Hi, Patty, this is Jill.

2 Patty: Hi, Jill. How was the party?

3 Jill: Oh, it was just great. You should've come.

4 Patty: I know, but I had to help my sister move. Did you meet anyone?

5 Jill: Yeah, I met a couple of really nice guys. One of them **asked me out**. And listen to this! His friend wants to make it a **double date**. You should get a call from him tonight.

6 Patty: Oh come on, Jill, I haven't been on a **blind date** since high school. You must be kidding!

7 Jill: You can't really call this a blind date. After all, I've seen him, and you know what good judgement I have **in this department**. You should see his eyes. They're your favorite color.

8 Patty: They aren't green! You can't be serious!

9 Jill: And he likes to play tennis. I'd say it's a **match made in heaven**. You have to come. It's a must!

10 Patty: I don't know. I've been so turned off by the whole dating scene since Gary **stood me up** last time.

11 Jill: Oh, Patty, **that's history**. Besides, this guy puts Gary to shame. You should really give him a chance. I can promise you won't regret it.

12 Patty: O.K. I guess I'll **go for it**.

13 Jill: Great! Call me as soon as you hear from him.

14 Patty: O.K. Bye.

15 Jill: Talk to you later.

VOCABULARY

to ask someone out: to ask someone to go on a date
to double date: two couples go out on a date together
a blind date: a date with someone you've never met, usually arranged by a friend
in this department: in this matter (that we're discussing)
a match made in heaven: a couple who are perfectly suited to each other
to stand someone up: to fail to show up for a date
that's history: that is finished, over
to go for it: to attempt something that involves some risk or difficulty

CULTURAL NOTE/DISCUSSION

In the United States it is not unusual for men and women to wait until they are in their late 20s or early 30s to get married. This is often because people, especially women, are concerned about becoming established in their careers before they get married and have children. Therefore, there are many men and women in this age bracket who are single, have careers, and go out frequently on dates. They are part of the dating scene. Is there such a dating scene in your native country? At what age do men and women get married in your country?

FOCUS ON GRAMMAR

The following questions are based on the preview text and are designed to help you find out what you already know about the structures in this chapter. Some of the questions may be hard and some of them may be easy. Answer as many of the questions as you can. Work with a partner if your teacher tells you to do so.

1. Find an example in the dialogue of the following generalizations. Write the example in the space provided.

   a. Jill uses *should* to tell Patty about something she expects to happen.

   _____

   b. Patty uses a form of *have to* to tell Jill about a commitment she made in the past.

   _____

   c. Patty uses *can't* to express disbelief.

   _____

   d. Jill uses *should* to describe something.

   _____

2. Now, find the following sentences in the dialogue and come to an agreement with your partner about the function of each of the underlined modals. Make a generalization and write it in the space provided.

   Example   You *should* really give him a chance. (line 11)
              FUNCTION: *Should is used to give a suggestion.*

   a. I *can* promise you won't regret it. (line 11)

      FUNCTION: _____

   b. You *have to* come. (line 9)

      FUNCTION: _____

   c. You *must* be kidding! (line 6)

      FUNCTION: _____

Grammatical Patterns Part One

I. Modal Forms

The following chart shows the possible modal forms and their time reference.

FORM	EXAMPLE	TIME
Modal + Simple Verb	• I **can promise** you won't regret it. • You **should get** a call from him tonight. • I **had to help** my sister move.	Present Future Past
Modal + Progressive Verb	• You **must be kidding.** • She **had to be kidding.**	Present Past
Modal + Present Perfect Verbs	• You **should have come.**	Past
Modal + Present Perfect Progressive Verb	• They **could have been dating.**	Past

The context of the sentence will determine the time reference of the modal. Usually, time expressions are used to clarify the time reference. For example:

Carol has a big date tonight. She should wear something special.

Since the date is tonight, it can also be assumed it is tonight that Carol will wear something special.

II. The Functions of Modals

A. Expectation and Conclusion: *Should/Ought to/Must*

These two functions are similar because we have expectations or make conclusions based on previous information. However, notice the distinction in meaning, as pointed out in the chart on the next page.

FUNCTION	MODAL	EXAMPLE	GENERALIZATION
Expectation	**should** **ought to**	You **should** get a call from him tonight about the upcoming stag party. The divorce rate **ought** to go down with the increased popularity of marriage counseling.	• **Should** and **ought to** express what **is expected to happen** in the future. • Usually used to express something positive about the future.
Conclusion (Probability)	**must**	These statistics **must** mean that most women prefer to establish a career first.	• Expresses what **is true** at the present.

12.1 Written Activity: *Single Mother*

DIRECTIONS: Below are some sentences about a single working mother, Marj. After each sentence, there is one statement expressing *expectation* and one statement expressing *conclusion*. Decide whether each statement expresses expectation or conclusion and fill in one blank with **must** and the other with **should**.

Example   CUE: Marj has been divorced with primary custody of her four-year old son, Nicholas, for two years.
RESPONSE: She *must* be very busy. She *shouldn't* be so busy once her child starts school.

1. Marj works full-time at an advertising agency to support herself and her son.

   She _____ be getting a raise in the next six months, which will make life easier.

   She _____ be tired when she gets home at the end of the day.

2. She receives some child support from her ex-husband, Joe.

   She _____ appreciate having that extra support for Nicholas.

   She _____ be able to afford music lessons for Nicholas next year.

3. Nicholas goes to stay with his father every other weekend.

   Nicholas _____ look forward to those visits since he is very close to his father.

   By next summer, Nicholas _____ be old enough to learn how to fish with his father.

4. Both Marj and Joe contribute to an educational savings account for Nicholas.

   They _____ have $3,000 in the account by next summer.

   They _____ be very concerned about being able to pay for Nicholas' education.

5. Marj and Joe communicate often about Nicholas.

   They _____ understand the importance of continuity and stability in a child's development.

   With this kind of communication, Nicholas _____ have a better chance of growing up in a stable environment.

Sᴘᴇᴄɪᴀʟ Nᴏᴛᴇ

PROBLEMS WITH *MUST* VS. *SHOULD*

Don't use *must* to predict the future.

(Iɴᴄᴏʀʀᴇᴄᴛ: Lori and George have been dating
for two years. They **must** get married.   Obligation, not conclusion
They **must be going** to get married.)   Impossible form
Cᴏʀʀᴇᴄᴛ: They **must** love each other.   Conclusion

***Should* can be used for *expectation* or *suggestion* with no difference in form.**
They **should** get married soon.   Expectation (This is what we expect to happen.)
                                          Suggestion (This is what we think would be best.)

12.2 Paired Activity: *Expectation* and *Conclusion*

DIRECTIONS: Work with a partner to ask and answer the following questions. Use **should, ought to,** or **must** depending on whether the question is asking you to make a conclusion or express an expectation.

Example   QUESTION: Why do some people stay single?
              ANSWER: They must not want to give up their independence.

1. What will the next six months of your life be like?
2. Why is divorce so common now?
3. Why are so many people starting relationships through e-mail?
4. What will your city be like in ten years?
5. How can some people stay married to the same person for so many years?
6. How do you think it feels to give up a baby for adoption?
7. How will your English ability change by the end of this course?
8. Do you think there will be more women in the work force in the future?

B. Suggestion/Recommendation/Advice

The chart below demonstrates how the modals used to give suggestions differ in strength.

Weak	might[a]	You **might** make pizza.	Perhaps it's a good idea.
	could[a]	You **could** make bread.	I believe it's a good idea.
	should	You **should** make soup.	I believe it's the best idea.
	have to/must (conversational)	You **must** make pizza.	I very strongly believe it's the best idea.
Strong	had better	You'**d better** make steak.	I am convinced that if you don't make steak, you'll be sorry.

[a]*Pronunciation Hint: In order to express the above examples as suggestions, the following intonation pattern should be used:*

You might make pizza. ↘   NOT   I might make pizza.
You could make bread. ↘   NOT   I could make bread.

12.3 Written Activity: *Marriage Counseling*

DIRECTIONS: In the dialogue below, a husband and wife are talking to their marriage counselor. For each suggestion given, fill in the blanks with the most **appropriate modal** from the chart beginning on page 288. There may be more than one correct answer.

WIFE: Rick just isn't willing to contribute at home. He thinks that because I'm the woman, I should do all the housework.

HUSBAND: Well, I'm at work all day. How can I do housework with a full-time job?

COUNSELOR: Yes, but Rick, don't forget that Cindy has a full-time job too. I don't know how you feel about this, but you _____ share equally in the housework. Perhaps each of you _____ have specific chores that you're responsible for.

HUSBAND: I don't know if that will work because even if I do some of the housework, I can't seem to do it right.

COUNSELOR: Cindy, if you want Rick to contribute more, you _____ trust him to do a good job.

WIFE: I realize that, but it's very difficult for me because he never does the kind of job that I would do.

COUNSELOR: That's because he's not you. You _____ start accepting him for what he is, or he'll never trust you. You _____ appreciate the effort he makes and overlook the kind of job he's done.

12.4 Paired Activity: *Making Suggestions*

DIRECTIONS: Work in pairs. You and your partner have a brother, Rick, who is 32 years old and still single. You are very concerned about him because you know he really wants to get married. Use the above modals to make a variety of **suggestions** about how he can meet someone.

Example   He might try joining a club.

12.5 Paired Activity: *Should* vs. *Must*

DIRECTIONS: Comment on the following situations using **should** for expectation or suggestion, and **must** for conclusion.

Example   SITUATION: Ted just got hired as a consultant to a large computer company after a six-month job search. This is a position he has dreamed about for a long time.
CONCLUSION: Ted must be happy he finally found a job.
SUGGESTION: He should be satisfied with the position.
EXPECTATION: He should receive a good salary for this position.

1. Coleen and Joe have four children. Joe has been unemployed for one year, and Coleen has been working as a nurse to support the family. Coleen and Joe just found out that they won $50,000 in the lottery.

2. Sharon is a university student who has done very poorly this semester. She still has a chance of passing if she does well on her final exams, so for the past week, she has been studying very hard.

3. Mohammed just arrived in the United States for a six-month intensive course of English language study. His wife and children were not able to come with him. He's hoping to improve his English and learn about American culture while he's in the U.S., but right now, he is very homesick.

4. Tina and Joe went out on their first date and had a wonderful time. Joe has been very busy, but he hopes to call Tina next week. Tina is surprised that she hasn't heard from Joe.

5. Leo just returned to his country after spending six months in America. His English became very fluent while he was in America, and he made many American friends. He feels out of place back in his own country and is surprised to find that his friends don't understand him when he talks about his experiences.

C. Description: Should

This is a function that is most common in conversational English.

FUNCTION	MODAL	EXAMPLE
Description	should + verb of perception (see, hear, taste, smell)	You **should see** his eyes! They're your favorite color.

12.6 Oral Drill: *Using "Should" for Description*

DIRECTIONS: When your teacher or partner gives a cue below, use **should** to describe it.

Example   CUE: You just returned from a trip to the Grand Canyon.
               RESPONSE: You should see the Grand Canyon! It's amazing.

1. You just bought a brand new sports car.
2. You have been to a wonderful exhibit at the art gallery.
3. You really like the new CD that your favorite band or singer just released.
4. You're cooking soup and you think it's really good.
5. A friend of yours started wearing a new perfume that you think is very nice.
6. You've discovered a great dating service on the Internet.

SPECIAL NOTE

> **FUNCTIONS OF SHOULD**
>
> Be careful not to confuse the use of **should** for suggestion, expectation, and description. Compare the following:
> - From what I've heard about the price they paid, their wedding rings **should** be exquisite. (expectation)
> - You **should** reconsider before you choose such an expensive wedding ring. (suggestion)
> - You **should** see their wedding rings. They're beautiful! (description)

12.7 Paired Activity: *Functions of "Should"*

DIRECTIONS: Read the short passage below about divorce in the United States and ask your teacher any questions you may have about it. After you have read and understood the passage, discuss with your partner or the class as a group the issue of children in divorce and joint custody. As you discuss, use **should** to express expectation, suggestion, and description.

> In a recently published report on divorce in the United States, statistics show that in the last ten years the divorce rate in the United States has increased significantly. Because of the increase in divorce, more attention is being paid to how divorce is affecting children and what arrangements are being made for custody of children when their parents get divorced. In the past, custody of the child in a divorce case was awarded to the mother. However, today many couples are trying joint custody, which means the child spends an equal amount of time with each parent. It is best if a couple can agree on a custody arrangement, but sometimes if the child is old enough, a parent will have the child testify in court in order to win the custody case.

D. Present and Past Habitual Activity: Used To/Would

The chart below shows the modals that are used to express present and past habits.

TIME	FORM	EXAMPLE
Present Habitual Activity	be + ing used to + verb + -ing	Sharon **is used to taking** the bus.
Past Habitual Activity	**used to** **would**	Women **used to** stay at home with their children instead of having careers. They **would** sacrifice a career for their children. *Notice that "Used to" introduces the past habitual activity and "would" is used to show continuation.

12.8 Oral Drill: *Used to/Would*

DIRECTIONS: For each of the statements below about American marriage in the present, make a contrasting statement about what the **past habit or custom** was. Begin your statement with one of the following phrases: "In the past," or "Years ago."

Example   CUE: Today many women don't get married until their late 20s or early 30s.
            RESPONSE: In the past, women would get married in their early 20s.

1. Many couples choose to devote their lives to their careers and a variety of outside interests in place of having children.
2. If a married couple has children, they usually have only one or two.
3. Many women continue in their career after they have a child.
4. Some fathers stay home with a young child while the mother is working.
5. When both the husband and wife are working, the child is taken to a day care center, or a babysitter comes to take care of the child.
6. Very often the extended family does not live in the same city, and the parents of a child can't depend on the child's grandparents or aunts and uncles for support.
7. If a couple gets divorced, they often share custody of the child.

12.9 Written Activity: *American Dating Customs*

DIRECTIONS: The box below shows the difference in some American dating customs before and after the women's liberation movement. Write a paragraph contrasting the dating practices of yesterday and today. Use **would, used to,** and **be used to** whenever possible.

WHAT MEN DID BEFORE	WHAT WOMEN CAN DO NOW
• asked the woman out on a date	• call the man for a date
• opened car doors for women	• open their own doors
• paid the tab	• pick up the tab or share costs
• lit a woman's cigarette	• light their own cigarettes
• made all the decisions about the date	• take responsibility for the date

E. The Communicative Functions of *Can/Could/Be Able To*

Can, could, and *be able to* are used for requests, offers, permission, ability, and possibility. As shown below, sometimes only the context will determine the distinction in these functions.

EXAMPLE	MEANING	FUNCTION
I **can't** read the letter.	• I am not **allowed** to read it because it's private.	Permission
	• I am **unable** to read it because of your handwriting.	Ability
	• It's **impossible** for me to read it because I don't have time.	Impossibility
Can you help me?	• I am **asking** you to do this for me.	Request
	• Is it **possible?** Do you have the time?	Possibility

SPECIAL NOTE

EXPRESSING ABILITY

Can, could, and **be able to** are used to express ability.
Notice the distinction between the functions of these forms in the following examples:
I **could not** call him last night. (unsuccessful one-time action in the past)
I **was able** to call him last night. (successful one-time action in the past)
I **could** call him whenever I wanted to. (repeated successful action in the past)

12.10 Oral Drill: *State the Function*

DIRECTIONS: For each of the sentences below, paraphrase any meanings that the sentence can have according to function.

Example   We can't get married in my fiancé's church.
The church will not give us permission because I am divorced. (Permission)
The church doesn't have any openings on the day we planned to get married. (Impossibility)

1. I can't walk home from work.

2. Can you type this letter?

3. When I was young, I could swim in the lake whenever I wanted to.

4. I can work for you tomorrow.

5. I was able to call my family from the post office last week.

6. I can't write this letter.

7. I can arrive at the church early.

8. I couldn't pick up my package yesterday.

9. Could you help me fix my computer?

10. I couldn't play sports when I was in school.

The chart below demonstrates how **can, could,** and **be able to** are often used with the same time reference. Note also that one form of the modal can be used for different time references.

TENSE	EXAMPLE	FUNCTION
Present	I **can** play the piano.	Ability
	I **am not able** to give speeches.	Ability
	I **could** be in England right now.	Possibility
	(This is used in present unreal conditional sentences e.g., "I could be on the beach right now if I weren't so busy.")	
	I **can** take you home.	Offer
Future	I **can** pick you up tomorrow at 4:00.	Possibility
	I **could** get married next year.	Possibility
	I **will be able to** attend my sister's wedding.	Possibility
Past	I **could** speak Spanish when I was very young.	Ability
	I **was able to** call him last night.	Possibility

SPECIAL NOTE

CAN VS. COULD

As can be seen from the above examples, **can** and **could** are often interchangeable for the same function and tense. However, there is a slight distinction in meaning between these two modals in those cases. Look at the following examples:

I **can** arrive at the reception early to make additional arrangements.

I **could** arrive at the reception early to make additional arrangements.

Both of these examples express possibility in the future, but in the first example, the use of **can** expresses a slightly more *definite* possibility.

12.11 Rapid Drill: *Can/Could/Be Able To*

DIRECTIONS: For each sentence below, change the tense of the modal to the tense given at the end of the sentence. Then state what the function of the modal is. Sometimes there will be no change in the form of the modal despite the tense change.

Example   I *can* arrive at the meeting early to help out. (past)
            I *was able to* arrive at the meeting early to help out.

1. I *couldn't* make any pie for dessert. (future)

2. I *wasn't able to* take a vacation last year. (present)

3. I *can* drop him off at the party on my way home. (past)

4. I *couldn't* attend the meeting because I had a previous appointment. (future)

5. I *can* sing a variety of international folk songs. (past)

6. I *couldn't* call him last week. (present)

7. I *was able to* leave work early yesterday. (future)

F. Requests, Permission, and Offers

Notice in the chart below that nearly the same modals are used for these three functions. Discuss how the functions can be distinguished.

Polite Request	Can /Could/May/Might Can/Could/Would	• **Could** I get a price list, please? • **Would** you drop off the flowers tomorrow, please?
Permission	**May/Might/Can/Could** (Asking for permission) **May/Can/Can't/Could** (Giving/Refusing permission)	• **May** I ask for your daughter's hand in marriage? • You **can** attend the wedding reception even if you can't make it to the church.
Offers	**Can/Could** (Statement) **May/Can/Could** (Question)	• I **could** help you pick out your trousseau if you're having trouble making decisions. • **May** I drive you home after the party?

12.12 Oral Drill: *Requests, Permission, and Offers*

DIRECTIONS: Using the cue provided, make a **request**, make an **offer**, or give **permission**.

Example   CUE: You want to help send the wedding invitations.
            RESPONSE: "I could help with the invitations."

1. You would like to bring a guest to your friend's wedding.

2. You don't want your daughter to stay out late.

3. You would like to pick your friend up on the way to a party.

4. You want to know if your teacher will let you miss class.

5. You would like to borrow a book about American weddings from your teacher.

6. You would like to help your friend move into a new apartment.

7. You want to know if your teacher will let you make up a test you missed.

SPECIAL NOTE

REQUESTS	
It is important to be able to distinguish who is performing the action of requests.	

May **I close** the door?
Can **I close** the door?
Could **I close** the door?
Would you mind if **I closed** the door?
(Never use **would I** for a request.)

⎫
⎬ The speaker **closes** the door.
⎭

Could **you close** the door?
Can **you close** the door?
Would **you close** the door?
Would **you mind closing** the door?

⎫
⎬ The **listener closes** the door.
⎭

12.13 Oral Drill: *Understanding Requests*

DIRECTIONS: For each request below, state what the result would be.

Example   QUESTION: Would you mind lending me $1.00?
                RESULT: The listener would give the speaker $1.00.

1. Can I borrow your book?
2. Would you mind opening the window?
3. Could you turn the stereo down?
4. Would you light my cigarette?
5. May I see your notes from class?
6. Would you mind if I smoked?
7. Would you mind moving to another seat?
8. Could I have seconds, please?

12.14 Paired Activity: *Making Requests*

DIRECTIONS: For each of the following situations, make two requests, one in which **you** want to perform the action and one in which you want **the listener** to perform the action. In most cases, it will be necessary to use a different verb for each request.

Example   CUE: You want the phone number of the person you just met at a party.
                RESPONSE: **Could I have** your phone number?
                              Would you mind giving me your phone number?

1. Your roommate has a beautiful book that you'd like to see.
2. You are going sightseeing and you'd like to borrow your friend's camera.
3. You would like to hear the end of the story that your teacher started telling at the end of the last class.
4. You'd like to talk on the phone sometime with the person you just met at a business lunch.
5. You need change for a dollar.
6. You need a ride to work or school tomorrow.

G. Disbelief and Inappropriateness or Inaccuracy: *Can't* and *Must*

These expressions are usually used in spoken English.

Disbelief	can't	• You called your wedding off? You **can't** mean that!
		• I **can't believe** I ate the whole thing!
	must	• She's going to be a single mother? You **must be** kidding!
Inappropriateness or Inaccuracy	can't	• You **can't** wear that dress! It's indecent.
		• You **can't** really call this a blind date. After all, I've seen her.

12.15 Paired Activity: *Disbelief, Inappropriateness,* and *Inaccuracy*

DIRECTIONS: You and your partner have a friend who has decided to marry someone from another country and live in their country. Take turns making the statements below about your friend. The other person should use **can't** or **must** to show that something is inappropriate or incorrect or to show disbelief and then give a suggestion related to that particular statement.

Example   STUDENT A: Teresa is going to marry someone from another country.
               STUDENT B: You must be kidding! She should think this over before she makes any rash decisions.

1. She's going to live in his country!

2. She's going to change her religion!

3. She's going to give up her career.

4. She'll only come back home to visit once a year!

5. She's going to be living in a very small village.

6. She'll have to bring up her kids speaking a different language.

12.16 Paired Activity: *Cartoon Modals*

DIRECTIONS: Read the following cartoon and underline the modals. Discuss the function of each modal by paraphrasing the sentence in which it is used.

FOX TROT   by Bill Amend

H. Frustration or Annoyance

This function is used primarily in conversational English.

FRUSTRATION OR ANNOYANCE	
has to/had to[a]	• Of course, since we're having the reception outside, it **has** to rain! • They **had to** lower the tax deduction for married couples, didn't they?
must (question)	• **Must** the media print every detail about the lives of the rich and famous?
would	• You **would** show up at this party!
would have to	• The teacher **would have to** announce my engagement to the class.

[a]*If the proper intonation isn't used for this, the meaning can be interpreted as necessity. The falling intonation for tag questions is used and there is strong stress on the modal expression:*

NECESSITY: They had to lower the tax deduction for married couples, didn't they?

ANNOYANCE: They had to lower the tax deduction for married couples, didn't they?

The teacher would have to announce my engagement to the class.

12.17 Oral Drill: *Expressing Frustration or Annoyance*

DIRECTIONS: When you studied progressive verbs, you learned that the progressive tense is used to express frustration or annoyance, for example, "You're always leaving the pots and pans in the sink." Below are a number of statements that a girlfriend used to express frustration to her boyfriend. Your partner or teacher will read the cue sentence, which will express frustration by using the progressive. Restate the sentence using **have to, must, would** or **would have to**.

Example   CUE: You're forever standing me up.
           RESPONSE: You have to stand me up, don't you?

1. You're always taking me to cheap restaurants.

2. You're forever talking about other women/men.

3. You're constantly reminding me about my weight.

4. You're continually talking about your accomplishments, but you show no interest in mine.

5. You're always asking me to make all the arrangements for our dates.

6. You're always asking me to drive.

7. You're forever showing up late for our dates.

12.18 Oral Drill: *Frustrating Situations*

DIRECTIONS: Express frustration or annoyance after your teacher or partner reads each of the situations below.

Example   SITUATION: You receive a telephone call from a friend who says he is getting married. When he tells you the date of the wedding, you realize that you'll be out of the country. FRUSTRATION: You had to schedule your wedding on a day I'm not going to be here, didn't you!

1. You just made arrangements to take your mother to a movie. Your boyfriend/girlfriend calls you up and asks if you want to go out.

2. You are at a family wedding. You see your cousin walking toward you in the same outfit you are wearing.

3. You are sitting at the breakfast table with your family. You're looking in the newspaper for the announcement of your brother's wedding, which took place yesterday. You find it and discover that the newspaper has seriously misspelled your brother's name in the wedding announcement.

4. You're on the way to a wedding and you're 15 minutes late. You run out of gas.

5. You planned a big family reunion to be held at the park. You wake up the day of the party, and it's raining.

6. You're talking to a good friend on the telephone about something important and you hear him/her typing on the computer.

12.19 Written Activity: *Situational Review*

DIRECTIONS: Read each situation and fill in the blanks in the statements that follow the situation with an appropriate modal.

Example   Robin is waiting in the airport for Paul, her husband's brother, whom she has never met. She has only seen pictures of him. Suddenly she sees a man walking towards her.

    a. This man looks different from the pictures, so she thinks, "That <u>can't</u> be Paul!"

    b. The man is waving to her, so she thinks, "That <u>must</u> be Paul."

1. Randy and Maria are engaged to be married, and it is a week before their wedding. Randy has cold feet and wants to call off the wedding. Maria is talking to her best friend, Liz, about this.

    a. Maria is pleading with Liz for assistance and says, "You _____ help me!"

    b. Liz is shocked to hear the news and says, "He _____ be kidding!"

    c. Maria is so frustrated with the situation that she says, "He _____ get cold feet, didn't he?"

2. Sally and Dave are out on a date and have just had dinner. They are discussing their plans.

   a. Dave is really full and knows it is unhealthy to sit after eating so much. He says, "We _____ go sit in a movie after such a big meal!"

   b. Dave doesn't want to get up and leave yet, so he says, "_____ I buy you an after-dinner drink?"

   c. Sally feels very strongly that she needs to get some fresh air, so she says, "We _____ take a walk now."

3. Roxanne and Greg have made plans to go to Hawaii for their honeymoon. Greg's brothers are discussing the plans.

   a. The brothers think that the honeymoon will be great, so one of them says, "They _____ have a wonderful honeymoon in Hawaii."

   b. One of the brothers thinks that the best recreation in Hawaii is water sports, so he says, "They _____ rent a boat."

   c. One of the brothers thinks that it would be impolite for them to leave the reception early, so he says, "They _____ leave for the honeymoon until the reception is over."

4. Lynn has been communicating with Gary through e-mail for one year and is in love with him. In two weeks they are going to meet. She is talking about the situation with her friend, Caroline.

   a. Lynn is expressing her optimism about the meeting and says, "We _____ get along pretty well since we have such a solid relationship already. You _____ see how romantic his messages are!"

   b. Caroline is a bit cynical about e-mail relationships, so she expresses her doubt by saying, "You _____ expect him to be the same in person as he is in cyberspace! There _____ be something that he hasn't told you."

   c. Caroline tries to warn Lynn and says, "You _____ get your hopes up. You _____ be prepared for a surprise."

12.20 Oral Interview

DIRECTIONS: Interview two or three English-speaking people between the ages of 20–35. Explain that you are a foreign student and that you are writing a report about dating and marriage customs.

1. How can a single person meet men/women in this culture?

2. What are some rules about a first date in your native country? (for example, dress, topics of conversation, behavior)

3. How are dating and marriage customs different today than they were in the past?

12.21 Written Feedback

DIRECTIONS: Use modal constructions to report on your interview.

1. Write at least two sentences reporting the information you received about meeting men/women.
2. Write three sentences explaining rules about a first date.
3. Write one sentence explaining how dating and marriage customs are different today than they were in the past.

Grammatical Patterns Part Two

Preview

DIRECTIONS: Read the following letter that a young man wrote to the "Dear Priscilla" advice column in the newspaper.

Dear Priscilla,

1 I am 24 years old and single. For the past six months I've been dating Coleen, a girl that I met at work. I care very deeply for her and have even had thoughts of marriage, but now I'm sure there's no hope for that.

2 On our first date, Coleen told me that she's a very religious person. She also said that she's looking for a man who has the same religious convictions that she has. I know I should've told her the truth right then and there, but I could've lost the opportunity to get to know her better. You see, I'm an **atheist,** but I told her that I am very deeply religious. All these months I've pretended to share her feelings about religion, and she must've believed me because we've become very close.

3 Last night we were at a movie and I made a sarcastic remark about the religious discussion two people were having. Coleen became furious. You should've heard her screaming at me! In my opinion, for such a religious person, she shouldn't have been so hysterical. She might've tried to be more **levelheaded** about the whole issue. Anyway, I became furious too and told her the truth. I apologized and admitted I shouldn't have been pretending to be something I wasn't.

4 On one hand, I feel a bit relieved because I couldn't have pretended much longer. On the other hand, I really love Coleen and she should've called by now to make plans for tonight. Please help . . . .

Afraid That It's Over

VOCABULARY

atheist: a person who has no God or religion
levelheaded: rational and logical rather than irrational and impulsive

DISCUSSION

Is it important that two people who plan to marry share the same religious convictions? Can a relationship work if the man and the woman have extremely different religious beliefs?

FOCUS ON GRAMMAR

DIRECTIONS: Find four examples in the preceding letter of sentences containing modals and write them on the lines provided below. For each one, write what *really happened* and how the writer *feels about it.*

Example   I know I should've told her the truth right then and there, but I could've lost the opportunity to get to know her better.
REALITY: He didn't tell her the truth, and he got to know her better.
FEELING: He regrets not telling the truth, but he's happy that he had the opportunity to know her better.

SENTENCE 1: _____

REALITY: _____

FEELING: _____

SENTENCE 2: _____

REALITY: _____

FEELING: _____

SENTENCE 3: _____

REALITY: _____

FEELING: _____

SENTENCE 4: _____

REALITY: _____

FEELING: _____

What generalization can you make about the meaning of these modal constructions?

I. Perfect Modals

A. Perfect Modal Forms

Perfect modals are formed in the following way:

Simple Perfect **Modal + have + past participle**	I **should have told** her the truth.
Perfect Progressive **Modal + have + been + verb -ing**	I **shouldn't have been pretending** to be something I wasn't.

12.22 Recognition Drill: *Perfect Modal Forms*

DIRECTIONS: Underline all the perfect modals in the "Dear Priscilla" letter.

B. The Functions of Perfect Modals

In general, perfect modals are used to express **unfulfilled** or **unrealized** actions or events. They serve some of the same functions that have already been covered in this chapter, as demonstrated in the chart below.

MODAL	FUNCTION	EXAMPLE
Could have	possibility impossibility disbelief	• I **could've lost** the opportunity to get to know her better. • I **couldn't have** married her anyway because neither of us wanted to move to another country. • You **couldn't have** thought that I would accept such a foolish excuse! • How **could** you **have thought** that I would accept such a foolish excuse?
May/Might have	possibility (may or might) suggestion	• Your advisor **may have been able** to help you with that application. • She **might have tried** to be more levelheaded about the whole issue.
Should have/Ought to have	expectation regret or judgment about past action	• She **ought to have** called by now since it's 8:15 and she said she'd call by 8:00. • I know I **should have told** her the truth right then and there. (But I didn't and I regret it.) • I **shouldn't have been pretending** to be something I wasn't. (I **did** pretend and I regret it.)
Must have	conclusion	• She **must have believed** me because we've become very close.

12.23 Oral Drill: *Judgement* with *Should Have* and *Shouldn't Have*

DIRECTIONS: Below are some problems and some solutions to the problems. Decide on a better solution for each problem and state it using **should have**.

1. John was very shy, so he never asked Maria out.

2. Jack didn't have enough money to pay for the dinner, so he left without paying.

3. Marge didn't know which date to accept for the dance, so she didn't go.

4. Bob didn't want to go out with Jill anymore, so he stood her up yesterday.

5. At the last minute, Annette decided that John wasn't the right person for her to marry, but it was the day of the wedding and everyone was in the church, so she married him anyway.

6. Kathy and Jim have been married for ten years and have a four-year-old son. They haven't been getting along for the past year and don't love each other anymore, so they decided to get divorced.

7. Even though Bill wanted to open the door for Kelly, she insisted on opening it herself.

12.24 Written Activity: *The Rules*

DIRECTIONS: Read the following summary of a book that lists the rules of dating and marriage. Then read each situation which follows, and write two sentences using perfect modals (*should have, shouldn't have, could/couldn't have, must have, might have*) to comment on the situation. For each situation, write the number of the rule that applies. An example is provided for you.

"The Rules: Time Tested Secrets for Capturing the Heart of Mr. Right," by Ellen Fein and Sherrie Schneider, is written for women who want to avoid mistakes in choosing a mate. The premise is that men want a challenge and women can become challenging. Also, if the woman chooses the man, it can lead to a lot of problems, such as not being able to keep his interest. This may sound hokey, but it probably works. It's practical, not anti-feminist.

There are 35 rules. Here are a few:

The Rules At A Glance:

1 Be a "Creature Unlike Any Other" (You're beautiful inside and out.)

2 Don't talk to a man first (and don't ask him to dance).

3 Don't stare at men or talk too much.

4 Don't meet him halfway or go dutch on a date.

5 Don't call him and rarely return his calls.

6 Always end phone calls first.

7 Don't accept a Saturday Night Date after Wednesday.

8 Don't see him more than once or twice a week.

9 No more than casual kissing on the first date.

10 Don't tell him what to do.

11 Let him take the lead.

12 Don't expect a man to change or try to change him.

13 Don't open up too fast.

14 Be honest but mysterious.

Example SITUATION: Michelle was at a party and she really wanted to meet Richard, but Richard saw her biting her nails and twirling her hair out of nervousness and decided not to talk to her.

SENTENCES: *Michelle shouldn't have acted so nervously.*

OR *She couldn't have thought that Richard would be attracted to her when he saw her biting her nails!*

OR *Richard must have thought she had no self-confidence.*

Rule: #1—Be a creature unlike any other.

1. SITUATION: Stephanie and Nick went out on their first date. Stephanie tried to convince Nick to quit smoking. Nick never called Stephanie again.

SENTENCES:

a. _____

b. _____

RULE: _____

2. SITUATION: Mary was at a party and wanted to meet Bruce, who was talking to his friends. She looked at him very intently for a long time to let him know that she was interested in him. He never came over to meet her.

SENTENCES:

a. _____

b. _____

RULE: _____

3. SITUATION: Mark and Cindy were on their first date. They were just finishing a wonderful meal at a restaurant. The bill came, and Cindy insisted on splitting the bill.

SENTENCES:

a. _____

b. _____

RULE: _____

4. SITUATION: Nathan and Julie were on their first date. Julie felt very comfortable with Nathan, so she told him all about her past relationships.

SENTENCES:

a. _____

b. _____

RULE: _____

5. SITUATION: Gina went out with Peter once, and she really liked him. She was hoping to go out with him again, but he didn't call her. She thought maybe he had lost her phone number, so she called him.

   SENTENCES:

   a. _____

   b. _____

   RULE: _____

6. SITUATION: David called Linda on Thursday to ask her out on a date. When he said that he wanted to take her out on Saturday, she said, "Oh, that's wonderful. We can go to the opening at the Art Gallery!"

   SENTENCES:

   a. _____

   b. _____

   RULE: _____

12.25 Written Activity: *Surrogate Mother*

DIRECTIONS: Read the following passage about a surrogate mother. Then, in pairs discuss the questions that follow the passage, using **must have** to make conclusions.

Susan Lee signed a $10,000 contract with Maria and Michael Cole to be a surrogate mother for them because they were unable to have their own child. This meant that she would be artificially inseminated, carry their baby for nine months, deliver the baby, and give it up to them. After she delivered the baby, however, Susan had second thoughts and didn't want to give her to the Coles. She escaped with the baby, but she was found, and the case later went to a court as a custody battle. The Coles won custody of the baby, and Susan was given minimal visitation rights.

Example   QUESTION: How do you think the Coles felt when they found out they couldn't have a child of their own?

They must have been very disappointed and they must have felt desperate to look for a surrogate mother.

1. Why do you think Susan Lee agreed to be a surrogate mother to begin with?

_____

2. How do you think Susan felt after she delivered the baby?

_____

3. What arguments do you think were used on both sides of the court case?

_____

4. How do you think the Coles felt when they won custody of the baby?

_____

5. How do you think Susan Lee felt when the Coles won custody of the baby?

_____

6. What are your opinions about this case? Use **should have/shouldn't have**.

_____

12.26 Written Activity: _Problem-Solving_

DIRECTIONS: The following passage describes some problems that Diane and Tim had after they had their first child. Work with a partner to complete the chart that follows the passage. First, state each problem of this situation in your own words. Then make a conclusion about each particular problem using **must have**. Finally, state how the problems **should have** been solved. Be ready to share your ideas orally with the class. There is an example at the beginning of each column.

Diane had a full-time job as chief editor of a woman's magazine. She and Tim had discussed what her work schedule would be after she had the baby, but they couldn't come to an agreement. She had decided that she couldn't give up her career and she went back to work full time when the baby was six weeks old. Tim didn't agree with this; he thought it was important for the baby to be with his mother for the first year. He was willing to work long hours to provide the extra income for this. Diane was afraid that if she didn't go back to work right away, she would lose her position. John was worried that if Diane went back to work, the baby wouldn't get proper care.

Problems (Real Facts)	Conclusions	Critical Judgments
1. Diane didn't want to give up her job.	1. She must have really enjoyed working at her job.	1. She should have returned to work when the baby was three months old.
2. _____	2. _____	2. _____
3. _____	3. _____	3. _____
4. _____	4. _____	4. _____

5. _____   5. _____   5. _____
_____   _____   _____
_____ .   _____ .   _____ .

6. _____   6. _____   6. _____
_____   _____   _____
_____ .   _____ .   _____ .

12.27 Paired Activity: *Your Past*

DIRECTIONS: Use perfect modals to talk about your past with your partner. Express unrealized possibilities, regrets, disbelief, and untapped abilities. Try to use the following verbs along with any other verbs that you need: **work, do, spend, think, tell, buy, feel, teach.**

Example   I should have worked at a part time job when I was in college, so that I wouldn't still be paying off student loans.

12.28 Written Activity: *Arranged Marriages*

DIRECTIONS: For each situation below about the practice of arranged marriages, write sentences expressing the given functions. Use perfect modals. The first one is done for you as an example.

1. In some countries, there was no dating because arranged marriages were the custom.

   JUDGMENT: Parents should have allowed dating if that's what the children preferred.

   DISBELIEF: _____

   CONCLUSION: _____

2. In the past, a woman was expected to marry the man her family chose for her and devote her life to him.

   CONCLUSION: _____

   DESCRIPTION: _____

   IMPOSSIBILITY: _____

3. Since divorce was uncommon in those days, if either the husband or wife discovered that they were mismatched, they were forced to accept the situation.

   JUDGMENT: _____

   INABILITY: _____

12.29 Written Activity: *Answering the Letter*

DIRECTIONS: Write an answer to the letter on pages 279–280. Use perfect modals in your answer.

II. Special Problems with Modals

PROBLEM	EXPLANATION
Using the Wrong Verb Form After A Modal INCORRECT: • We **must to do** our homework on time • They **can getting** the food for the party. • I **could took** her out on a date. • We **should does** our homework on time. CORRECT: • We **must do** our homework on time. • They **can get** the food for the party. • I **could take** her out on a date. • We **should do** our homework on time.	The present simple form of the verb follows a modal.
Using An Ending On A Modal INCORRECT: • Bill **coulds earn** a higher salary as an accountant. CORRECT: • Bill **could earn** a higher salary as an accountant.	Tense and person markers are never added to modals.
Mixing Two Modals Together INCORRECT: • I **might can attend** the meeting. CORRECT: • I **might attend** the meeting. Or • I **might be able to attend** the meeting.	Only one modal should be used at a time, except when a modal is used before **be able to.**
Making Modals Negative With Don't INCORRECT: • We **don't can solve** this problem easily. CORRECT: • We **can't solve** this problem easily.	Make a modal negative by adding **not** to the modal.
Incorrect Participial Form For Perfect Modals INCORRECT: • I **could have went** out with him, but I didn't want to. CORRECT: • I **could have gone** out with him, but I didn't want to.	The past participle is used for perfect modals.

■ **12.30 Editing Activity**

DIRECTIONS: Find the error in each of the following sentences and correct it.

1. Sarah thought that a computer dating service must to be a more reliable way of meeting eligible men.

2. When she first heard about the service, she didn't was able to decide if she wanted to sign up.

3. After she signed up, she had to deciding which man she wanted to contact.

4. She could have went out with ten different men.

5. She must is going to meet someone she likes eventually.

6. She cans refuse a date with any of these men if she wants to.

7. She had to gave a lot of information about herself when she filled out the application.

8. She should have wrote only the truth about herself, but she lied about her height.

9. She couldn't have meeting any men if she hadn't signed up for this service.

10. Caroline should might meet someone that she really like through the computer dating service.

ƒocus on Writing

Passive and Progressive After Modals

Modals can be followed by passive or progressive verb constructions with present or past time reference. These forms are especially useful in writing.

Modal + Progressive

1. Mothers **should be staying** home with their children! (Present)

2. The immigration office **should have been keeping** you informed about your visa. (Past)

Modal + Passive

3. Because of his outstanding achievement, he **should be awarded** the scholarship. (Present)

4. Contrary to the media reports, her life **couldn't have been saved.** (Past)

12.30 Fill in the Blanks: *Progressive and Passive After Modals*

DIRECTIONS: Below are some sentences about teenage pregnancy. Fill in the blanks with a modal and the passive or progressive form of the verb in parentheses.

Example   Teenage pregnancy is an issue that <u>should be discussed</u> (discuss) by teenagers, their parents, and their teachers.

1. Teenagers _____ (inform) about the dangers of promiscuity.

2. Such a high teenage pregnancy rate _____ (avoid) through better education.

3. After some parents find out that their teenage daughters are pregnant, they realize that they

_____ (educate) their daughters more carefully.

4. Some parents are surprised that this has happened to their daughters and they conclude that

their daughters _____ (pressure) by their peers.

5. There is a lot of controversy about whether contraceptives _____

(distribute) to high school students at school clinics.

6. Some people are convinced that if a teenage girl becomes pregnant, she _____

(neglect) by her parents.

7. Teenagers _____ (learn) to think about the consequences of their actions.

8. This problem _____ (ignore), or it will become more serious.

12.31 Written Activity: *Paraphrasing*

DIRECTIONS: The sentences below are about Stan and Jill, who are getting divorced. Paraphrase each sentence, using a passive or progressive modal. The beginning of the paraphrase is provided.

Example   It's impossible that Stan and Jill were communicating very well.

Stan and Jill *couldn't have been communicating very well.* .

1. I'm not sure if they were going steady when I met them, but it's possible.

They _____.

2. Stan and Jill didn't tell their parents they were getting married, and I think that's wrong.

Their parents _____.

3. They told everyone that were happy, but now we can only conclude that they were lying.

They _____.

4. It was impossible to save their marriage.

Their marriage _____.

5. I can only conclude that they told their children about the divorce.

Their children _____.

6. It's unfortunate that they weren't seeing a marriage counselor.

They _____.

7. I'm sure Jill hired a lawyer to negotiate the settlement.

A lawyer _____.

8. It's possible that Stan was trying to get custody of one child.

Stan _____.

9. I expect that they will resolve the case in court.

The case _____.

10. I can't believe they were expecting to settle this in one month!

They _____.

Analysis of an Authenic Text

PRE-READING DISCUSSION QUESTIONS

Are astrological signs important to you? Do you want to make sure you marry someone with a compatible astrological sign? Is it important to get to know the family of your future husband/wife?

DIRECTIONS: Read the following excerpt from *Linda Goodman's Star Signs*. This description of the Cancer man (June 22–July 23) is addressed to the girlfriends of men born under this sign.

The Cancer Man

1 Let's hope you find his mother **congenial**. If fact, let's pray you do. It's fairly certain she'll pop up in his conversation frequently, in remarks like, "You use frozen pies and instant potatoes? My mother used to bake her own bread when I was a youngster." This **paragon** of virtue is quite likely to pop up just as often in person, when you least expect it. "Darling, I have to cancel our date for the theater tonight. I'm driving mother out to the country for a few days." To put it mildly, the Cancer man may be **reluctant** to **dethrone** Mama and crown you as his new queen.

2 There are certain **traits,** however, that can even up the score in your relationship. For one, he'll be a pretty good chef himself. He may surprise you with his ability to whip up a gourmet meal.

VOCABULARY

Look up the following words in your dictionary if you're not sure of their meanings.
congenial
paragon
reluctant
dethrone
traits

COMPREHENSION QUESTIONS

1. How does the Cancer man feel about his mother?

2. How will a girlfriend of a Cancer man feel about his mother?

GRAMMATICAL ANALYSIS

DIRECTIONS: Decide which modals given in parentheses after each sentence can replace the underlined modal in the sentence without changing the meaning. Discuss how the meaning would change if the other modals were used.

1. My mother <u>used to</u> bake her own bread when she was a youngster. (would, had to, could)

2. Darling, I <u>have to</u> cancel our date for the theater tonight. (had to, must, should, might)

3. To put it mildly, the Cancer man <u>may</u> be reluctant to dethrone Mama. (must, can, should, had better)

4. There are certain traits, however, that <u>can</u> even up the score in your relationship. (may, could, should)

Composition Topics

In this chapter you have had the opportunity to find out about and discuss dating, marriage, and divorce. Now formulate your ideas in a well-organized and well-written composition. Choose a topic from those listed below.

1. Describe your vision of a match made in heaven. What personality traits should this person possess? What requirements does the person have to meet?

2. Discuss your opinion about "The Rules" as listed in Exercise 12.24.

3. Describe a relationship (romantic, social, or business) you had once that was not as successful as you would have liked. State what you could have or should have done differently.

Urban Living

• Conditional Sentences

Chapter 13

Urban Living (Life in the big city)

DISCUSSION QUESTIONS

1. What American cities do you know about? If you could live in any American city, which one would you choose and why?

2. Do you know about any of the problems that exist in American cities? Are these problems similar to those in the cities of other countries?

3. What is being done to solve these problems? If you had power and influence, how would you solve some of the urban problems that you know about?

OBJECTIVES

In this chapter you will learn:

1. To use conditional sentences to express future, present unreal, and past unreal situations

2. To use conditional sentences to describe present and past habitual activity

3. To use mixed time reference in conditional sentences

4. To make inferences with conditional sentences

5. To use **wish** to express conditional meaning and to distinguish between **wish** and **hope**

6. To use several expressions that can replace *if* in conditional sentences

Preview

DIRECTIONS: Read the following letter to the editor written by a resident of Los Angeles who is concerned about the problems that exist in that city.

It's A Nice Place to Visit But I Wouldn't Want to Live Here

Dear Editor:

1 I moved to Los Angeles 40 years ago from the East Coast because it was being **lauded** as the closest thing to **paradise** in this country. For years, Los Angeles lived up to that description, but unfortunately that is no longer true. If someone had asked me 40 years ago, I never would have predicted that this city would change so much in such a short time. It seems that the leaders here should be doing more to put an end to the homelessness, gang violence, drug abuse, and severe smog that are plaguing our city. If there weren't such serious problems here in Los Angeles it would still be a desirable place to live, as it was in the past.

2 Some of our leaders have the habit of claiming that homeless people have the problems they do because they're comfortable in that lifestyle. This is obviously just a **feeble excuse** for supporting what they feel are more worthwhile causes. Well, if they had paid more attention to this problem from the beginning, the number of "comfortable" homeless people on the streets wouldn't have risen so rapidly.

3 Drug abuse and the gang violence that results from it are making our streets unsafe and our schools a threat to our children's lives. If these problems were solved, we could send our children to school without worrying about whether they would make it home. Not long ago, if a child was caught smoking a cigarette on **school grounds,** severe punishment was enforced. Nowadays, children are caught selling or using drugs, and some of them carry weapons to arm themselves in wars against their **peers.**

4 Finally, we all know that the smog level in this city has reached dangerous proportions. If stricter **emission control** laws aren't enforced soon, the air that we breathe to keep us alive will eventually kill us.

5 I certainly hope that my concerns are shared by other people who came here for a higher standard of living and a more comfortable life but are finding their lives at risk instead.

A Concerned Resident

VOCABULARY

lauded: praised
paradise: heaven, a perfect place
feeble excuse: a weak, unconvincing excuse
school grounds: the school building and immediate surrounding area designated as belonging to the school
peers: the people who share one's rank, age, ability, or other general characteristics
emission control: a limit on the amount of dangerous substance that can be let out into the air by cars, factories, and other agents

CULTURAL NOTE/DISCUSSION

Gang violence in American cities is becoming a serious problem. A gang is a group of youth usually of high school age and from one particular ethnic group. Gangs are often involved in dealing drugs and, as a result, there is a high level of competition among different gangs. This very often leads to serious violence. Are there gangs in your country? What kinds of problems do these gangs cause?

FOCUS ON GRAMMAR

The following questions are based on the preview text and are designed to help you find out what you already know about the structures in this chapter. Some of the questions may be hard and some of them may be easy. Answer as many of the questions as you can. Work with a partner if your teacher tells you to do so.

1. The following sentence from the preview describes a situation that is untrue or unreal in the present. In the space provided, write what the truth or reality of the situation is.

   If there weren't such serious problems in our city, it would still be a desirable place to live.

   REALITY: _____

2. Each of the following conditional sentences describes a situation that is untrue or unreal in the past. On the lines after each of the sentences, write what the truth or reality is.

   a. If they had paid more attention to this problem from the beginning, the number of "comfortable" homeless people on the streets wouldn't have risen so rapidly.

   REALITY: _____

   b. If someone had asked me 40 years ago, I never would have predicted that this city would change so much in such a short time.

   REALITY: _____

3. In the *if-* clauses of the following two sentences, notice that the present tense is used in sentence a, and the past tense is used in sentence b. Does sentence **a** describe a **present** situation? Does sentence **b** describe a **past** situation?

   a. If stricter emission control laws *aren't enforced* soon, the air that we breathe to keep us alive will eventually kill us.

   b. If these problems *were solved*, we could send our children to school without worrying about whether they would make it home.

   What conclusion can you make based on these sentences?

Grammatical Patterns Part One

I. The Structure of the Conditional Sentence

Most conditional sentences have a subordinate clause beginning with **if** and a main clause, which in most cases contains a modal and a main verb. As in other complex sentences, the order of the clauses is optional. Look at the following examples and notice the structure and punctuation of both sentences.

If I lived downtown, I could walk to work.
I could walk to work if I lived downtown.

If- (Subordinate) Clause   **Main Clause**
If I lived downtown,   I could walk to work.

II. The Function of Conditional Sentences

The following chart summarizes the main types of conditional sentences and the function each of them serves.

TYPE	EXPLANATION	EXAMPLE
Future	Depending upon the condition, something may happen in the future.	• If we clean up our city, it will be a nicer place to live.
Present Unreal	Describes a situation that is not true or not real at the present time.	• I wouldn't have to deal with these problems if I lived in the country.
Past Unreal	Describes a situation that was not true or real in the past.	• If L.A. hadn't been so desirable years ago, I wouldn't have moved here.
Present or Past Habitual Activity	Depending upon the condition, an activity was done habitually in the present or past.	• If people moved here, it was for the beautiful weather and the wide open spaces.

A. Future Conditional

The following conditional patterns are used to express possibility or probability in the future. Notice that *will* is **not** used in the *if*-clause although the time reference is future.

VERB TENSE/MODALS IN IF-CLAUSE	VERB TENSE/MODALS IN MAIN CLAUSE	EXAMPLE
simple present tense	future tense	• If stricter laws **aren't enforced,** the air we breathe **will kill** us.
	modals: may, might, can, could, should, ought to	• If I **move** to Seattle, I **should be prepared** for a lot of rain. • If the downtown development **continues,** we **could have** a really nice city.

13.1 Rapid Drill: *Future Conditional*

DIRECTIONS: With a partner use the following cues to make statements about the future in the city where you are living now.

1. If the population increases, . . .
2. If the cultural life improves, . . .
3. If more highways are built, . . .
4. If the crime rate goes up, . . .
5. If the immigrant population increases, . . .
6. If the public transportation system improves, . . .
7. If the police force changes, . . .
8. If housing prices go down, . . .
9. If the smog gets worse . . .
10. If traffic problems worsen, . . .

B. Low Probability in the Future Conditional

There are a few additional ways to express future possibility with the conditional. The following expressions added to the simple form of the verb in the *if-* clause emphasize lower probability in the future. Notice that this pattern is similar in structure to the future conditional pattern.

IF- CLAUSE	MAIN CLAUSE	EXAMPLE
should (+verb) happen to (+verb) should happen to (+verb)	future tense/modals: may, might, can, could, should, ought to	If you **should** visit, you **will** see the new mall. If I **happen to** move, I **might** sell my car. If I **should happen to** get that new job, I will move to another city.

13.2 Paired Activity: *Low Probability in the Future Conditional*

DIRECTIONS: A major charity organization is planning a benefit rock concert in a large American city to raise funds for the homeless community. The concert will be held outdoors in the streets of a downtown neighborhood on a Saturday afternoon. The planning committee is having a meeting to discuss the arrangements for the concert, and some of the committee members are asking questions about possible situations. Take turns with your partner asking and answering the questions. Use future conditional sentences and emphasize low probability.

Example   QUESTION: What if it rains?
             ANSWER: If it should happen to rain, the concert will be postponed.

1. What if the city council objects to the idea?
2. What if some businesses don't agree to closing down that day?

3. What if we have a problem selling tickets?

4. What if some of the bands back out at the last minute?

5. What if we run out of food?

6. What if we need first aid?

7. What if the crowd gets out of control?

8. What if people in the neighboring community object to the noise?

13.3 Written Drill: *Fill in the Blanks*

DIRECTIONS: Below are some sentences about **possible future** situations. Fill in the blanks with a correct form of the verb given. Use any of the future conditional forms you have practiced.

1. If I _____ win the lottery next week, I _____ take a trip around the world.

2. I _____ inform my bank if I _____ change my name.

3. If you _____ shave your head, many people _____ look at you strangely.

4. You _____ have a lot of diapers to change if you _____ decide to have a baby.

5. If an earthquake _____ strike tonight, you _____ stand under a doorway.

6. If you _____ lose your car keys and you don't have an extra set, you _____ have to call a locksmith.

7. You _____ take the GRE if you _____ decide to apply for graduate school.

8. If you _____ become famous, you _____ lose your privacy.

The following two patterns also express lower probability in the future. The pattern of these sentences is similar to the present unreal conditional pattern, which will be presented in the next section.

IF- CLAUSE	MAIN CLAUSE	EXAMPLE
were to + verb past tense	would, might, could	If I **were to sell** my car, I **would** have some extra money. If I **got** a new job, I **could** move to another city.

Note: None of these patterns can be used in the negative except for the last one.

13.4 Oral Drill: *What if?*

DIRECTIONS: Use the cue to ask your partner a question. Your partner should answer using the two patterns above for expressing lower probability.

Example   CUE: win a trip around the world
QUESTION: What would you do if you were to win a trip around the world?
RESPONSE: If I were to win a trip around the world, I would quit my job and go.

1. inherit a lot of money
2. find a mouse in your kitchen
3. gain a lot of weight
4. fail a class
5. figure out the meaning of life
6. lose your most valuable possession
7. get a speeding ticket
8. overcome your deepest fear

13.5 Written Activity: *The Pollution Problem*

DIRECTIONS: Los Angeles is suffering serious environmental consequences from being a highly populated metropolitan area and the largest manufacturing center in the United States. In order to improve the situation, certain conditions must be met. For each problem stated below, write a future conditional sentence that expresses the possibility for solving the problem in the future. The first solution is provided for you.

1. PROBLEM: Many polluting ingredients are released into the air by drying paint and solvents on houses, cars, aircraft, and other products.

   SOLUTION: <u>If the polluting ingredients were to be taken out of the paint and solvents, there would be less harm to the environment.</u>

2. PROBLEM: Millions of people commute to work in cars that emit pollutants into the environment.
   SOLUTION: _____

   _____

3. PROBLEM: Many polluting ingredients are being released by factories into the ocean, killing marine life and ultimately upsetting the balance of nature.
   SOLUTION: _____

   _____

4. PROBLEM: With the growing population in Los Angeles, there is an increasing amount of garbage that needs to be dumped.
   SOLUTION: _____

   _____

5. PROBLEM: The beautiful beaches are being littered with trash by inconsiderate sunbathers.
   SOLUTION: _____

   _____

C. Present Unreal Conditional

This conditional structure is probably the most difficult to master. It tends to be confusing because the time reference is present, but the past tense of the verb is used in the *if-* clause. A good way to check your understanding of the unreal conditional is to state what is **real**. The chart below demonstrates how the reality can be stated, based on the unreal situation in the conditional sentence. Notice the following:

If	**Then**
Unreal conditional is negative.	→ Reality is positive.
Unreal conditional is positive.	→ Reality is negative.

IF- CLAUSE	MAIN CLAUSE	EXAMPLE
simple past		If I **lived** in the country, I **would** be happier.
simple past continuous	would / might / could	If I **were working** in the city, I **would** drive.
could + verb		If I **could move**, I would live in the country.

SPECIAL NOTE

If the verb **be** is used, **were** is the proper form regardless of the subject. However, in informal spoken American English, this form is becoming less common, and Americans often use **was**.

13.6 Written Activity: *Gangs*

DIRECTIONS: The existence of gangs and gang violence is on the rise in the United States. Gang members usually come from the same ethnic group and are of high school age. Violence and drug dealing are common among gangs. For each of the following sentences about the existence of gangs and gang violence in U.S. cities, write a conditional sentence stating a present unreality based on the information given.

Example   Some high school kids belong to gangs because it gives them a sense of identity.
<u>If these kids had a stronger sense of identity, they wouldn't belong to gangs.</u>

1. The boys haven't developed a sense of identity because they often have a weak family structure and poor male role models.

_____

2. Some gangs are formed because ethnic groups want to protect their territory.

_____

3. Gang members wear certain colors so that their fellow gang members can identify them.

_____

4. Because many of the gangs are dealing drugs, life is very dangerous for them.

_____

5. Since these kids can acquire dangerous weapons easily, gang warfare is very common.

_____

6. Because these kids don't value human life, they are killing each other foolishly.

_____

7. Leaving the gang can be very dangerous, so many kids stay simply because they're afraid.

_____

13.7 Oral Drill: *If I Lived in Paris*

DIRECTIONS: One student will begin by completing the statement, "If I lived in Paris . . ." The next student will begin a sentence with the new information the previous student provided and will complete that statement. Continue in this manner so that each student can add some information. For the next round, choose a new city.

Example   STUDENT A: "If I lived in Paris, I would buy a lot of expensive perfume."
STUDENT B: "If I bought a lot of expensive perfume, I wouldn't have enough money to eat."

13.8 Paired Activity: *Your City*

DIRECTIONS: For each topic below, write a statement describing either a positive or negative characteristic of your city. Then, discuss each topic with your partner using at least one present **unreal conditional** sentence to qualify or clarify the statement you wrote.

Example   TOPIC: Pollution
WRITTEN: The pollution level in my city is very low.
SPOKEN: "One very positive characteristic of my city is that the air is clean. The pollution level is so low because my city is at a high altitude and there is very little industry there. If there were more industry, I'm sure the air wouldn't be so clean."

1. TOPIC: Population

   STATEMENT: _____

2. TOPIC: Housing

   STATEMENT: _____

3. TOPIC: Culture/Entertainment

   STATEMENT: _____

4. TOPIC: Food

   STATEMENT: _____

5. TOPIC: Mass Transit

   STATEMENT: _____

D. Past Unreal Conditional

The forms in the following chart are used to describe unreal situations in the past. As with the present unreal conditional, it is easier to understand the past unreal if the **reality** is clear.

IF- CLAUSE	MAIN CLAUSE	EXAMPLE
past perfect past perfect progressive	perfect modals (would, could, should, may, might) + have + past participle	If someone **had asked** me thirty years ago, I would never **have predicted** that this city would change so much. If social work agencies **had been receiving** more government assistance, they **could have been doing** much more to help the homeless.

Pronunciation Hint: In spoken English, **would have** is very often contracted in the following way:

I **would have** gone downtown this afternoon if I hadn't finished work so late.
I **would've gone** downtown this afternoon if I hadn't finished work so late.
I'**d have** gone downtown this afternoon if I hadn't finished work so late.
I'**da** gone downtown this afternoon if I hadn't finished work so late. (Not used with the negative.)

13.9 Oral Drill: *Past Unreal Situations*

DIRECTIONS: For each situation given below, make a statement expressing a **past unreality**.

Example   CUE: Evelia's class was at 7:00, so she had to get up very early.
        RESPONSE: If Evelia's class hadn't been at 7:00, she wouldn't have had to get up so early.

1. She stayed up very late the previous night studying for a test.

2. She overslept and missed her bus.

3. There was a bus 15 minutes later, so she had a chance of making it to class on time.

4. She felt nervous about her test, so she studied on the bus.

5. She missed her stop because she wasn't paying attention.

6. The bus driver announced the next stop, so she was able to get off before it was too late.

7. She ran across campus and arrived just in time for the test.

8. She got an A on the test.

13.10 Paired Activity: *Stranger in a Strange Land*

DIRECTIONS: Tell your partner about an interesting, funny, unusual, etc. experience you had in a foreign city (any city other than your own). Your partner will then ask you questions about your story using **past unreal conditional.** You should answer the questions with the past unreal conditional.

Example   STORY: When I was in Aswan, Egypt, many years ago, it was very hot, and since my jeans had not finished drying, I put on a pair of shorts. I knew that it was not appropriate for a woman to wear shorts in public, but I just wanted to go from my hotel room down to the street to buy some fruit. I went out into the street in my shorts, and every person in the marketplace immediately turned to stare in horror at my legs. The people were hissing, whispering, and pointing, which made me feel very ashamed. I quickly ran back up to my hotel room to put my wet jeans on.

QUESTION: What would have happened if you hadn't left the marketplace?
ANSWER: Perhaps, if I hadn't left, someone would have told me to leave.
QUESTION: What would you have done if the people had only stared, but not hissed, whispered, or pointed?
ANSWER: Maybe I would've bought my fruit quickly before running up to my room.

13.11 Written Activity: *Living in a Commune*

DIRECTIONS: Read the following passage about communes. Then write a paragraph about what life would have been like for you if you had lived in a commune. Use **conditional** sentences to express **unreality in the past.**

1. In the 1960s, when idealistic young people grew tired of the problems of city living, many of them abandoned the city to create a utopian way of life in a commune. These were communities of people who escaped to areas far from cities or suburbs and started their lives from scratch. They built their own houses, made their own clothes, grew their own food, and did their own baking.

2. They tried to live as a self-sufficient society. They shared all the tasks of daily life and held their property in common. Communes were based on a variety of popular beliefs such as neo-Buddhism, vegetarianism, and free love.

Example   If I had lived in a commune in the 1960s, I would've baked my own bread.

E. Habits and Facts

The chart below demonstrates how conditional sentences are used to describe habitual activity and make statements of facts. Notice that in these sentences the verb tense in the *if-* clause corresponds to the verb tense in the main clause.

IF- CLAUSE	MAIN CLAUSE	EXAMPLE
Habitual Activity simple present simple past	simple present simple past	(If) (when) people **decide** to move here, it **is** usually because of the weather. If (when) a child **was caught** smoking, severe punishment **was** enforced.
Fact simple present	simple present	If (when) too much exhaust **is emitted,** the smog level **rises.**

*Note: In these two types of conditional sentences, **when** or **whenever** can replace **if,** e.g. **When** people decide to move to this city, it is usually because of the weather.*

13.12 Written Activity: *Habitual Patterns*

DIRECTIONS: Choose from the given cues below to write **conditional** sentences describing the **habits** of people in your city.

Example   CUE: rent an apartment in the city
                   If a person rents an apartment in my city, they must pay very high prices.

1. have an appointment

_____

2. ride the subway

_____

3. go out for lunch

_____

4. want to get some exercise

_____

5. get out of the city

_____

6. see a ballet/hear jazz /go to the theater

_____

7. have a picnic

_____

B. Now, write three sentences describing three more habits of people in your city. For each sentence describing a **present habit**, write one sentence describing a contrasting habit of 50 years ago. Use **if, when,** or **whenever.**

Example   a. If people in Long Island drive to work in New York City, they take the freeway.

              b. Fifty years ago, if people drove into the city they took country roads.

1. a. _____

   b. _____

2. a. _____

   b. _____

3. a. _____

   b. _____

13.13 Paired Activity: *Scientific Facts*

DIRECTIONS: The most common context for conditional statements of fact is in the field of science. Student A should cover the Student B column; Student B should cover the Student A column. Student A will begin a conditional sentence using the information in the A column, Student B should find the information in the B column that completes the sentence.

Example   A: oil is mixed with water   B: sits on the surface
              STUDENT A: If oil is mixed with water,   STUDENT B: it sits on the surface

A	B
1. temperature drops below 0°C	a. it goes out
2. you throw something up	b. it turns to steam
3. you have two opposing forces	c. the result is water
4. water boils	d. they attract
5. a fire has no oxygen	e. it comes down
6. you combine two atoms of hydrogen with one atom of oxygen	f. water freezes

Now, think of at least two additional laws of science or nature and state them using the conditional.

1. _____

2. _____

13.14 Written Drill: *Review*

DIRECTIONS: Restate each of the following sentences with a **conditional** sentence.

Example   Because the crime rate in this city is so low, many people want to live here.
              If the crime rate in this city weren't so low, many people wouldn't want to live here.

1. Washington, D. C., is a very exciting city because of its history as the capital city of the U.S.

   _____

2. Many people wanted to live in Los Angeles years ago because Hollywood was so exciting.

   _____

3. Many residents of Boston go to Cape Cod during their holidays because of its convenient location.

   _____

4. The rich musical and cultural tradition draws people to New Orleans.

   _____

5. In the past, many people went to San Francisco to visit and liked the city so much they returned to live there permanently.

   _____

6. Thousands of people move to Seattle every year, which could mean overcrowding and pollution in the years to come.

   _____

7. New York City is a popular city to visit, especially because of the excellent theater.

   _____

8. Philadelphia offers a rich historical past, which makes it an interesting place to visit.

   _____

13.15 Written Activity: *Letter to the Editor*

DIRECTIONS: Write a letter to the editor of the local newspaper in your hometown or in the city where you are presently living. Discuss ways to improve the city, why certain problems exist, and what will happen if existing problems aren't solved. Use as many conditional sentences as possible in your letter, underline them and identify them.

Grammatical Patterns Part Two

Preview

PRE-READING DISCUSSION QUESTIONS

What are the laws on the sale of guns in your country? Is it possible to acquire weapons illegally? Is there much crime as a result of weapons use? What kind of power does the police force in your city have? What is their primary function?

DIRECTIONS: Jack Warren, a radio talk show host, is interviewing Marianne Brown, the mayor of a large city in the United States, about the drug and related crime problems in that city. Read the interview on the next page with a partner.

1   **WARREN:** Mayor Brown, the statistics show that in the past year the number of **homicides** in your city has soared and that almost 50% of them were prompted by gang warfare or illegal drug dealing.

2   **BROWN:** Yes, I know, but had the voters approved the tax increase, we would be able to afford a larger police force. Right now, we're working with 1.68 officers per 1,200 residents. This means that our officers are unable to respond immediately to every call they get because they're so **swamped.**

3   **WARREN:** Are there any other explanations for these statistics, and if so, what are they?

4   **BROWN:** Well, Jack, even if we increase the police force, the killing will continue unless we restrict the sale of **vicious** weapons. Unfortunately, Assemblyman White's bill to control the spread of **assault rifles** wasn't passed last year. The situation will improve only if the bill is passed this year.

5   **WARREN:** Is there a chance of that happening?

6   **BROWN:** If the **polls** are correct, the bill should be passed. I think that people are finally beginning to realize that the constitutional right to bear arms does not include assault rifles. I really wish there had been more support for this idea last year. I'm sure we wouldn't be experiencing the present increase in homicides if we'd had that support.

7   **WARREN:** Well, Mayor Brown, I certainly hope that the bill does get passed so that you can make your city a safer place to live in.

8   **BROWN:** Thank you, Jack. I hope so, too. If I didn't have such an excellent city council, I wouldn't have been able to gain such extensive support for this campaign to begin with, so I'm sure that, as a team, we'll continue **to make headway.**

9   **WARREN:** Thank you for talking with us, Mayor Brown.

10 **BROWN:** Thank you, Jack.

VOCABULARY

homicide: murder or manslaughter
be swamped: very busy
vicious: terrible, dangerous and/or deadly
assault rifles: a weapon designed for quick attack during war
poll: survey of public opinion
to make headway: to make progress in a difficult situation

FOCUS ON GRAMMAR

Read the three examples below taken from the preview. In each sentence, what is the time reference of the *if-* clause? What is the time reference of the result clause? What generalization could you make about the relationship between the *if-* clause and the main clause? How are these conditional sentences different from the types you've studied so far?

Example   If the freeway system had been designed well, we wouldn't have the present traffic problems.

If the freeway system had been designed well
(Time Reference: Past)

we wouldn't have the present traffic problems
(Time Reference: Present)

GENERALIZATION: A situation in the past affects the present.

1. If the voters had approved the tax increase, we would be able to afford a larger police force.

2. I'm sure we wouldn't be experiencing the present increase in homicides if we'd had that support.

3. If we didn't have such an excellent city council, we wouldn't have been able to gain such extensive support for this campaign to begin with.

I. Mixed Time Reference in Conditional Sentences

In addition to the conditional patterns covered in the previous section, there are cases when it is necessary to **mix** time references to express the appropriate meaning. The chart below demonstrates how mixed time reference is used in conditional sentences.

MIXED TIME REFERENCE	NOTES
Real Past Affects Future: **1.** If you **studied**, you **will** pass. *(simple past)* *(future)* **2.** If **you've paid** attention, you **will understand.** *(present perfect)* *(future)* **3.** If **they've been studying**, they'**ll get** good grades. *(present perfect progressive)* *(future)*	If an action or event already happened or has been happening, it may have some effect on what **will** happen in the future.
Unreal Present Affects Past: **4.** If I **wrote** better, I **wouldn't have failed.** *(simple past)* *(would/could + have + PP)* **5.** If I **weren't studying**, I **couldn't have passed.** *(past progressive)* *(would/could + have + PP)*	An unreal situation or general truth in the present can be related to actions or events in the past.
Unreal Past Affects Present **6.** If I **hadn't moved** here, I **would be living** in Rome. *(past perfect)* *(would/could/should + pres. prog.)*	An unreal event or action in the past would affect what happens in the present.

13.16 Written Drill: *Fill in the Blanks*

DIRECTIONS: The sentences on the next page are about a street fair that was organized by the merchants and residents of one area of a city in upstate New York. Fill in the blanks by using the correct forms of the given verbs. Add any necessary modals. If there is more than one possible answer, discuss the difference in time reference.

1. If there (be) (not) _____ so many enthusiastic residents who support the street fair, we (have) (not) _____ such a successful turnout.

2. If it (rain) _____ yesterday, we _____ (have) the street fair today.

3. If you (enjoy) _____ the fair yesterday, you (want) _____ to come back for next year's fair.

4. If I (go) _____ to the fair, I (tell) _____ you about it now.

5. If I (live) _____ closer to the center of town, I (walk) _____ to the fair yesterday.

6. If I (be/not) _____ so broke, I (spend) more money on crafts at the fair.

7. If the fair (be) _____ profitable for the merchants, _____ (participate) in next year's fair.

8. If the newspaper (print) _____ a story about the success of the fair, it _____ (help) attract more people next year.

13.17 Paired Activity: *Hollywood—Yesterday and Today*

DIRECTIONS: Below is a chart describing what Hollywood was like before it became the center of film production, and some of the changes that took place after that happened. Discuss with a partner what Hollywood might be like today if these changes had not taken place.

Example   If film companies hadn't constructed production studios everywhere, Hollywood would still be a small village.

Before
- small village
- wide treelined streets
- two or three restaurants
- small town atmosphere
- one traffic cop
- residential area

Changes
- Film companies constructed production studios everywhere.
- New people swarmed into the village looking for opportunities in the film business.
- Many movie stars built extravagant homes.
- Supermarkets, banks, and parking lots were built.

13.18 Written Activity: *Past and Present in Your City*

DIRECTIONS: Write a paragraph about your city, describing how it used to be and how it has changed. Use mixed time references to create sentences like the ones about Hollywood.

Example   If my city hadn't grown so quickly over the past five years, we wouldn't be seeing so many new housing developments going up.

II. Wish and Hope

Since **wish** is often used to refer to unreal situations, it is related to some of the conditional forms already covered in this chapter. There is often confusion between **wish** and **hope** because they are similar in meaning. **Wish** usually expresses a feeling of regret about an event whose outcome is known or expected. **Hope** usually expresses a feeling about an event whose outcome is unknown. Both **wish** and **hope** can be used for present, past, and future time reference.

The chart below shows present time references.

	EXAMPLE	NOTES
Wish	• I **wish** I **were** in Hawaii. (I am not in Hawaii, and I regret it.) • I **wish** the sun **was shining.** (The sun is not shining, and I regret it.) • I **wish** I had a bicycle. (I don't have a bicycle, and I regret it.) • I wish I **could sing.** (I can't sing.)	• Main verb is simple past, past progressive, or **could.** • As with the present unreal conditional, **was** is acceptable in spoken English.
Hope	• I **hope** Jim **is enjoying** Tokyo. (I don't know whether he is or not.)	• Usually present progressive is used after **hope** to refer to a present situation.

13.19 Paired Activity: *Wish List*

DIRECTIONS: Think about your favorite restaurant. Wouldn't you like to be there right now? Make a wish list about this restaurant using **wish** and **hope**, and share it with your partner or other classmates.

Example   I wish I were at Café Roma in San Francisco right now. I wish I were relaxing at one of their outdoor tables, waiting to order. I wish I were waiting for my plate of pasta to be served to me. I wish I could have a big basket of their warm, fresh Italian bread. I wish I had ordered cappucino for dessert the last time I was there. I hope I can go back there soon. I hope they haven't changed the menu.

The chart below shows the use of **wish** and **hope** for past time reference.

	EXAMPLE	**NOTES**
Wish	• I **wish** there **had been** more support for this bill last year. (There wasn't support, and I regret it.) • I **wish** I **could have attended** the meeting, but I was busy. (I couldn't attend, and I regret it.)	• Past perfect tenses of the verb or **could have + participle** is used for past time reference after **wish**.
Hope	• I **hope** Jack **didn't forget** the mail. (I don't know whether he forgot it.) • I **hope** you **weren't sleeping** when I called. (I don't know whether you were sleeping.)	• Simple past, past progressive, present perfect, or present perfect progressive tenses are used after **hope** for past time reference.

13.20 Oral Drill: *Wish* and *Hope about the past*

DIRECTIONS: For each situation below, make one comment using *wish* and one comment using *hope*.

Example   CUE: Jack didn't study for the chemistry test.
             WISH: He wishes he had studied.
             HOPE: He hopes he didn't fail.

1. Fred lost his wedding ring.
2. José handed his book report in late.
3. Elaine forgot an appointment she had yesterday.
4. Gina forgot to call her mother on her birthday.

5. Ben failed his English grammar test.

6. Chin said something rude to her colleague.

7. Ernesto cooked Thai food for his friends last night.

The chart below shows the use of **wish** and **hope** for future time reference.

	EXAMPLE	NOTES
Wish	• I **wish** the voters **would** realize that assault weapons are different from weapons. (They don't realize this now, but I would like them to realize it in the future.) • I **wish** it **would rain** tonight. (Most likely, it won't rain.)	• Use **would** to express a **wish** about the future. • A wish about the future is very close in meaning to a hope about the future, except that the probability is much lower when it's a wish.
Hope	• I **hope** it **rains** tonight. (There is a good chance that it will rain.) • I **hope** we'll **receive** our salary soon.	• Use simple present or future tense to express **hope** about the future.

13.21 Written Activity: *Wish* and *Hope* about the future

DIRECTIONS: Write five sentences expressing what you wish and hope about changes you would like to see made in your academic institution.

Example   *I wish we had more choices about classes.*

1. _____

2. _____

3. _____

4. _____

5. _____

13.22 Paired Activity: *Switching Lanes*

DIRECTIONS: Read the cartoon below and ask your teacher about any vocabulary you don't understand. With a partner, discuss the situation of the driver in each lane, using conditional statements and statements with **wish** and **hope**.

Example   If I weren't in this lane, I wouldn't be moving so slowly.

13.23 Written Activity: *Foreign Students in U.S. Cities*

DIRECTIONS: Below is some information about the experiences of some foreign students in U.S. cities. For each sentence given, (a) write a corresponding **conditional sentence**; (b) write a sentence using *wish*; (c) write a sentence using *hope*.

Example   Chikako was driving 80 miles per hour on the freeway and got a speeding ticket.
CONDITIONAL: <u>If she hadn't been driving 80 mph on the freeway, she wouldn't have gotten a speeding ticket.</u>
WISH: <u>Chikako wishes she hadn't been driving so fast.</u>
HOPE: <u>She hopes she doesn't get caught speeding again.</u>

1. Serge visited the new downtown shopping mall and spent too much money.

   CONDITIONAL: _____

   WISH: _____

   HOPE: _____

2. Xin was walking in the city, and a homeless person asked her for some money.

   CONDITIONAL: _____

   WISH: _____

   HOPE: _____

3. Because the public transportation system in this city is so poor, Lorenzo has to drive everywhere.

CONDITIONAL: _____

WISH: _____

HOPE: _____

4. Carlos won't be able to see the Empire State Building when he is in New York because he probably won't have time.

CONDITIONAL: _____

WISH: _____

HOPE: _____

5. Maria asked a stranger for directions to the train station. She got lost because the stranger gave her the wrong directions.

CONDITIONAL: _____

WISH: _____

HOPE: _____

III. Making Inferences

Conditional sentences are used to make inferences. An inference is a conclusion based on previous knowledge or information, as shown in the box below. Notice that almost any combination of tenses is possible in this type of conditional sentence, depending on the meaning being expressed. Very often the modals *should, must, have to,* or *ought to* are used in the main clause to emphasize expectation or conclusion based on the previous information.

INFERENCE	PREVIOUS INFORMATION
• If the polls **are correct,** the bill **will be passed.** • If the statistics **are correct,** the number of homeless in this city **has tripled** in the last five years. • If the smog level **was** that high last week, there **must have been** a heat wave.	• The polls show that people are in support of the bill. • The statistics say that the number of homeless has tripled in the last five years. • The smog level is usually that high only when there is a heat wave.

13.24 Recognition Drill: *Previous Information in Inferences*

DIRECTIONS: When you use a conditional sentence to make an inference, there is previous information upon which you are basing the inference. For each inference below, identify the previous information.

Example   If Sarah is in Florida, she must be enjoying the beaches.
MISSING INFORMATION: <u>Florida has nice beaches.</u>

1. If Jim decided to move to Key West, he must like the beach.

MISSING INFORMATION: _____

2. If Carol has been living in New Orleans for the last five years, she should be hearing some good music.

   MISSING INFORMATION: _____

3. If you have a job on Wall Street, you must work well under stress.

   MISSING INFORMATION: _____

4. If David moved from Dallas to L.A., he should be having better success as a musician.

   MISSING INFORMATION: _____

5. If you live in Seattle, you must not mind rain.

   MISSING INFORMATION: _____

13.25 Paired Activity: *Making Inferences*

DIRECTIONS: Work with a partner. Take turns reading each of the situations below, and use a **conditional** sentence to make an **inference** about each one.

Example   SITUATION: You have heard from many sources that Carnival in Rio de Janeiro is very exciting. You're not sure, but you think that a friend of yours, Sam, is going to Rio this year for Carnival.

         INFERENCE: If Sam is going to Rio for Carnival, he's going to have a great time.

1. The streets in your neighborhood always flood when there is a rainstorm. You've been visiting a friend in another city for two days and have heard reports of a serious rainstorm in your city. What is happening to the streets?

   _____

   _____

2. There was a van Gogh exhibit in Chicago last week. You think that your friend Chris, who loves van Gogh, was in Chicago last week. What did Chris do?

   _____

   _____

3. You have devised a model plan for urban development that you believe can improve every major city in the United States. You have effectively implemented this plan in New York. You are, therefore, convinced that it will work in other cities as well. How can you persuade the city council to adopt it?

   _____

   _____

4. You've heard that Chicago is an exciting city to live in. You think that Kevin, a former colleague, is now working there. How do you think he feels about where he lives?

   _____

   _____

5. Ruth was offered a job as director of Housing and Urban Development. However, she wanted an annual salary of $50,000. You just heard that she took the job. What salary do you think was agreed upon?

_____

_____

13.26 Paired Activity: *Cities of the World*

DIRECTIONS: Below is a chart with information about four major cities in the world. Use the information to the activities that follow the chart. Use **conditional** sentences to make **inferences** based on the information given.

	NEW YORK	TOKYO	RIO DE JANEIRO	LONDON
Time	12:00 P.M.	2:00 A.M.	2:00 P.M.	5:00 P.M.
Weather Nov.–Feb. March–May June–August Sept.–October	very cold snow mild, frequent rain hot, humid, cool occasional rain	cold, dry mild, sunny, dry hot, humid cool, frequent rain	very hot mild, occasional rain very cold warm, humid	very cold, rainy mild, frequent rain hot, humid cool, frequent rain
Serious Problem	crime	pollution	overcrowding	litter

1. What time will it be in the second city, based on the time given for the first city?

   a. New York: 6:00 P.M./Tokyo: ?
   b. Tokyo: 7:00 A.M./Rio de Janeiro: ?
   c. Rio de Janeiro: 3:00 P.M./London: ?

2. Discuss what kind of clothes you expect people to be wearing, based on the given month.

   a. New York: December
   b. Tokyo: October
   c. Rio de Janeiro: January

3. Discuss the problem each person must deal with because of the city that person lives in.

Example   Gary lives in Tokyo and has allergies.
   INFERENCE: If Gary lives in Tokyo, he must be having problems with his allergies.

   a. Chantal comes from a small town in the French countryside and now lives in Rio de Janeiro.
   b. Marcia is a fanatic about cleanliness and is now living in London.
   c. Chikako is living alone for the first time in New York.

IV. Shortened Forms

Very often, shortened forms of conditional constructions are used after yes/no questions. Look at the following example of a yes/no question and the shortened forms of the conditional that follow.

Are you going to be riding the bus to work every day?
AFFIRMATIVE: **If so,** you should buy a pass.
If you **are** going to be riding the bus to work every day, you should buy a pass.
NEGATIVE: **If not,** you don't need a pass.
If you **aren't** going to be riding the bus to work every day, you don't need a pass.

■ **13.27 Paired Activity:** *Shortened Forms of Conditionals*

DIRECTIONS: Ask your partner the given question and add a shortened form of the conditional. Use affirmative and negative forms.

Example   Are you a native of this city? If not, where are you from?

1. Do you like big cities?

2. Have you ever been to New York?

3. Do you have a map of this city?

4. Have you ever ridden the buses in this city?

5. Did you live in an apartment when you were growing up?

■ **13.28 Written Drill:** *Fill in the Blanks*

DIRECTIONS: Fill in the blanks with the correct form of the verb.

1. If I _____ about it more carefully, I never would have left my hometown.
   a. thought
   b. had thought
   c. were thinking

2. I would go to Bangkok if I _____ enough money.
   a. would have
   b. have
   c. had

3. If you should happen to visit me in Jakarta, I _____ show you around the city.
   a. will
   b. would
   c. would have

4. I wish I _____ Tbilisi when I was in Georgia.
   a. would have visited
   b. visited
   c. had visited

5. I wouldn't have made as many friends during my stay in America if I _____ a shy person.

    a. were

    b. had been

    c. would be

6. I _____ I can visit Beijing someday.

    a. wish

    b. hope

    c. want

7. If you _____ two sticks together, you can start a fire.

    a. rub

    b. would rub

    c. are rubbing

V. Special Problems with Conditional Sentences

PROBLEM	EXPLANATION
Reversed order of condition and result INCORRECT: If L.A. didn't attract so many prospective movie stars, it wouldn't be the center of film production. CORRECT: If L.A. weren't the center of film production, it wouldn't attract so many film stars.	The **condition** is placed in the **if-** clause, and the result is placed in the main clause.
Omission of *would* **or other modal** INCORRECT: If I **were** in my country right now, I **had** a job. CORRECT: If I **were** in my country right now, I **would have** a job.	A modal is often used in the main clause of a conditional sentence.
Use of *would* **in** *if-* **clause** INCORRECT: If I **would** be living in a different city, I would be happier. CORRECT: If I **were** living in a different city, I would be happier.	**Will** and **would** are not used in the **if-** clause of conditional sentences.
Incorrect Verb Tense INCORRECT: If I **wasn't** sick yesterday, I wouldn't have missed the concert. CORRECT: If I **hadn't been** sick yesterday, I wouldn't have missed the concert.	A certain verb tense is required depending on the time reference.

■   **13.29 Editing Activity**

DIRECTIONS: Find the error in each of the sentences below, and correct it.

1. If I hadn't moved to a city with such a high smog level, I didn't develop such serious sinus problems.

2. If there is better mass transit in Los Angeles, there wouldn't be such terrible smog.

3. If I lived in Tokyo, Japanese would be my native language.

4. The ozone layer deteriorates if too much carbon monoxide would be allowed to enter the atmosphere.

5. If you had a car, you're required to have a smog check done regularly.

6. If I have more money, I could attend more cultural events.

7. If there wouldn't be so many skyscrapers downtown, I would feel better about taking walks down there.

8. If you are putting two opposite forces together, they are attracting.

9. If I will be going to Atlanta on Saturday, I will drive.

10. If I didn't speak English, I wouldn't have been born in the United States.

focus on Writing

Expressing Ideas

When we write it is useful to have a variety of ways to express our ideas, so that our writing isn't repetitive or redundant. The following words and phrases are used to replace *if* in conditional sentences. Practice using these expressions for variety in your writing.

WORD/PHRASE	EXAMPLE	MEANING
only if	• I would move out of the city **only if** I could live close enough to attend cultural events.	ON THE CONDITION THAT . . .
provided that	• **Provided that** I live in a quiet neighborhood, I enjoy city life.	ON THE CONDITION THAT . . .

Continued on next page.

Continued from previous page.

WORD/PHRASE	EXAMPLE	MEANING
even if	• **Even if** I could live close enough to attend cultural events, I wouldn't move out of London.	REGARDLESS (the condition has no importance)
whether . . .or not (in spoken English)	• **Whether** you live downtown **or not,** the air pollution will affect you. or	
whether (in written English)	• **Whether** you live downtown or uptown, the air pollution will affect you.	
unless	• **Unless** I'm lucky enough to find a cheap apartment, New York City will be too expensive for me. • Tokyo life will not suit you **unless** you like crowds.	IF . . . NOT or EXCEPT ON CONDITION THAT . . .
in case	• **In case** your car breaks down, you can take the subway to work.	IF THIS SHOULD/WERE TO HAPPEN (low probability)
suppose/supposing	• **Suppose** your car breaks down, how will you get to work?	

13.30 Written Activity: *Long-Distance Marriage*

DIRECTIONS: Read the following passage and complete the sentences that follow, based on the information in the passage and your own ideas.

Long-Distance Marriage

Bill and Marilyn are married and have no children. Bill is a stockbroker on Wall Street in New York City, and Marilyn is an assistant production manager at a major movie studio in Los Angeles, California. Because of their professions, they have to live in two different cities and are unable to spend much time together. They talk on the telephone several times during the week and take turns flying to see each other on the weekends. They are able to live happily this way because they are very dedicated to their jobs and they never grow tired or bored with each other.

1. This arrangement will continue to work for Bill and Marilyn **unless** _____
_____ .

2. Bill and Marilyn can have a happy marriage **provided that** _____
_____ .

3. They talk to each other on the telephone several times during the week **even though** _____
_____ .

4. Bill would move to Los Angeles **only if** _____
_____ .

5. **In case** _____ , Bill and Marilyn will have to change their present

    situation and live in the same city _____

6. **Whether** this seems like an ideal living situation for a marriage, _____
_____ .

7. **Suppose** _____ , what will Bill and Marilyn do? _____
_____ .

8. **Even if** _____ , Bill and Marilyn will continue to see each

    other on the weekends.

13.31 Written Drill: *The Brighter Side of Los Angeles*

DIRECTIONS: Below is an editorial response to the letter to the editior which you read at the beginning of the chapter. Fill in the blanks in the letter below with words from the above chart to replace if.

Dear Concerned Resident:

I appreciate your concern for the problems facing Los Angeles at the present. However, from your letter it seems that there is no hope for the city you and I love so much. Let's not forget about all that Los Angeles has to offer. _____ I could live in a city free of smog, crime, and homelessness, I wouldn't move from L.A. Los Angeles offers the opportunity to experience the benefits of its rich ethnic diversity _____ you have the sense to appreciate it. In addition, culturally speaking, there is something for everyone _____ you like film, theater, music, or dance. Finally, _____ you get tired of the fast pace of this exciting city, all you have to do is drive to the beach, or the desert or the mountains. They're all within a 2-hour drive.

I agree that there are many problems here, but _____ concerned residents like you and I take action to solve these problems, they will only continue to worsen. You know we can't depend on politicians to take care of the situation, so it's up to us to do whatever we can in our small way. _____ everyone gave up on the city . . . where would we be then?

Another Concerned Resident

13.32 Written Activity: *Replacing If*

DIRECTIONS: Write a paragraph about your plans for the next six months of your life. Use the expressions from the above chart to replace *if* in conditional sentences.

Analysis of an Authenic Text

DIRECTIONS: Read the following article by Ellen Goodman about the differences between urban and rural life.

Country Music
by Ellen Goodman

1 "Is it quiet up there?" My friend asks this question **wistfully.** She has called long distance, from her city to my countryside, from her desk to my cottage.

2 "Yes," I answer her. There is no urban **clatter** here. No jarring cosmopolitan Muzak of subway and construction, rock and rush-hour voices. We are protected. The water that surrounds this island absorbs the **din** of the other world. Yes, it is quiet up here.

3 Slowly, I sift through the hundred sounds that form this rural chorus. A honeybee shopping the rose hips in front of the porch, a **vole** rustling through the bushes, a hawk piping its song above me. If I concentrate, I imagine that I can even make out different voices of the wind moving through **alder, bayberry, or birch.**

4 . . . I do not live my urban life at such a frequency. Like most city people, I have been trained to listen each day only to the squeakiest wheel, the most insistent, hardest-rock level of audio demands.

5 . . . Some of my friends by now have senses so damaged by the urban **cacophony** that they **squirm** when they are left alone with the crickets. They cannot adjust to country music. And yet it seems to me that it is only when we leave behind the alarms and bells and buzzes and sirens, all these external demands, that the quietest sound of all comes into range: our inner voice.

6   George Eliot once wrote, "If we had keen vision and feeling of all ordinary human life, it would be like hearing the grass grow and the squirrel's heart beat and we should die of that **roar** which lies on the other side of silence." How overwhelming to literally hear the life story of everyone we meet. But I think more often of the **roar** that keeps us from silence, the **roar** of daily life that makes it "impossible to hear myself think."

VOCABULARY

cacophony, clatter, din, roar: loud, disorganized noise, such as the "noise" of the city
wistfully: yearning for something that can't be had
vole: small rodent, similar to a mouse
squirm: writhe, especially in discomfort or pain
alder, bayberry, birch: species of trees

COMPREHENSION QUOTES

1. Why does the author's friend ask the first question wistfully?
2. How is "city music" different from "country music"?
3. Why does the author prefer "country music"?

Written Exercise

A. DIRECTIONS: Use conditional sentences to paraphrase (write in your own words) the following sentences from the text.

1. Some of my friends by now have senses so damaged by the urban cacophony that they squirm when they are left alone with the crickets. (Paragraph 5)

   _____

2. And yet it seems to me that it is only when we leave behind the alarms and bells and buzzes and sirens, all these external demands, that the quietest sound of all comes into range: our inner voice. (Paragraph 5)

   _____

3. How overwhelming to literally hear the life story of everyone we meet.

   _____

B. DIRECTIONS: Write three conditional sentences that would express the feelings of the author's friend about living in the city vs. living in the country.

1. _____

2. _____

3. _____

Composition Topics

Use what you have learned in this chapter about conditional sentences to write a composition about one of the following topics.

1. If you could live in any city in the world, which city would you choose? What would your life be like in that city?

2. How would your life have been different if you had been born in another part of the world? Choose another city or country and discuss how your life would have been different if you had grown up there.

3. If you could design an ideal city, what would it be like?

Age Is a State of Mind

• Gerunds and Infinitives

© 1989 M G N
DIST BY SYNDICATION INTERNATIONAL NORTH
AMERICA SYNDICATE INC

I'M HOME —

THERE'S TEA
IN THE
POT, PET

I SHOULD HOPE SO!
FANCY HAVING TO
BE A WORKING WIFE
AT *MY* AGE

I'VE TOLD YOU
BEFORE — AGE
IS ALL
IN THE MIND

NOT IN MY CASE. NOT WHEN
THE BLOKE WHO PUTS HIS
ARM ROUND ME TO HELP
ME ONTO THE BUS
CALLS ME GRANDMA

4-18

Age Is a State of Mind (You're As Young As You Feel)

DISCUSSION QUESTIONS

1. How do you feel about aging? Do you agree with the expression "age is a state of mind"? At what age will you be "old"?

2. How do you imagine yourself at 60 or 70? What kind of life do you hope to be living?

3. What do people in your native culture do to look and feel younger?

OBJECTIVES

In this chapter, you will learn:

1. To use an infinitive or a gerund as subject of a sentence

2. To use an infinitive or a gerund as the direct object of certain verbs

3. To use a gerund as the object of a preposition

4. To use an infinitive or a gerund as complement of the verb **to be**

5. To use an infinitive as the complement of certain adjectives

6. To use the past, passive, and past passive forms of infinitives and gerunds

7. To use infinitive phrases as replacements for adverb, adjective, and noun clauses

Preview

DIRECTIONS: Deepak Chopra is the author of *Ageless Body Timeless Mind*, a book about how to live a long, healthy life. The letter below was written to him by a college student who is studying to be a doctor.

Dear Dr. Chopra:

1 I read your book recently, and I just wanted to thank you for the work you've done on the relationship between belief and biology. As a medical student and future doctor, it really helped me to understand how the mind affects the body. Now I know how some people can become **centenarians.**

2 I'm really proud to have a 100-year-old great-grandmother who hasn't read your book but refuses to let age get in the way of life. She is very **young at heart.** She has such an active, rewarding life that it seems wrong even to call her old. She still has her garden and her birds, and she always knows what's happening in the world. I especially think it's **cool** that she still has parties with her friends to have fun. To have her energy and spirit for life is an example of your philosophy in action.

3 I hope to be an active, fun-loving **senior citizen** like her when I reach her age. Some of my friends say it's difficult to think about old age because it depresses them. They imagine that anyone over the age of 60 must live in a **nursing home,** helpless and lonely. I think they need to read your book and understand that getting old doesn't have to be depressing at all.

4 For many people, aging can be difficult, and they are really afraid of old age. Their mistake is thinking that at a certain age they will be too old to be happy. Like you, my philosophy is that the way we think is what really **counts.** We have the potential to influence our bodies through our minds.

5 I'm following a course of study that will integrate Eastern and Western medicine. That way as a doctor I can help people to understand the influence of their minds on the aging process.

6 Well, Dr. Chopra, I just wanted to let you know that your book has really influenced me in a very positive way. I am very interested in attending one of your workshops and meeting you someday.

Sincerely,

Derek James

Derek James

VOCABULARY

centenarian: a person who has reached the age of 100
young at heart: to have a young attitude regardless of one's age
cool: a slang expression, especially popular among young people, which is used to express approval of something
senior citizen: an elderly person
nursing home: a place where sick or handicapped elderly people, who are incapable of living on their own, are given medical care and supervision
count: to have value, to be important

CULTURAL NOTE/DISCUSSION

It is common in the United States for senior citizens to remain active for many years beyond retirement age. Many decide to continue working either at a paying job or in volunteer work. There are opportunities for seniors to stay physically and socially active as well. For example, many health clubs have special classes for seniors, such as water aerobics. There are also senior citizen centers where people can meet informally or attend special events such as dances or card parties. Some seniors even go back to school at adult education centers to study something they never had time for before retirement. Do senior citizens in your native country have these kinds of opportunities? What is the society's attitude about lifestyle after retirement?

FOCUS ON GRAMMAR

The following questions are based on the preview text and are designed to help you find out what you already know about the structures in this chapter. Some of the questions may be hard and some of them may be easy. Answer as many of the questions as you can. Work with a partner if your teacher tells you to do so.

1. **a.** In this example from the preview, which of the following verbs could take the place of **hope?** (want, appreciate, enjoy, promise, refuse) Write them on the line below the example: _I hope to be an active, fun-loving senior citizen._

    _____

    Did you use a rule to choose the verbs?

    If you replace **hope** with one of the verbs you did **not** write on the line, what other change will you have to make?

    b. Are the **boldfaced** words in the following two examples from the preview the same part of speech?

    I **hope** to be an active, fun-loving senior citizen when I reach her age.

    I'm really **proud** to have a 100-year-old great-grandmother.

    Based on these examples, what part of speech would you conclude can be followed by an infinitive (**to** + verb)?

    Can you think of any words to replace **proud** in the example above?

2. If you wanted to make **it** the subject of the sentence below, what words would **it** replace?

    To have her energy and spirit for life is a gift.

    Could **having** replace **to have** in this sentence?

3. Why is the gerund (*-ing*) form of **attend** used in the following sentence from the passage?

    I am very interested in **attending** one of your workshops . . .

    Could you use an infinitive (**to attend**) in place of the gerund?

Grammatical Patterns Part One

I. Infinitives

An infinitive consists of **to** + **verb** and takes the place of a noun. An infinitive can have a variety of functions in a sentence.

A. Infinitive As Subject of the Sentence

The box below explains how an infinitive can be used as the subject of a sentence.

GRAMMATICAL FUNCTION	NOTES
Subject of the sentence • **To age** gracefully is difficult. • **It** is difficult to **age** gracefully.	• Using **it** as the subject of the sentence is much more common than using an infinitive. • The infinitive subject is more formal.

14.1 Oral Practice: *Infinitive Subjects*

DIRECTIONS: Below are some stereotypical ideas about getting old. State whether you agree or disagree with each statement, and in your response, instead of using an infinitive subject, use it as the subject. Provide a reason for your opinion.

Example   CUE: **To be** old is depressing.

RESPONSE: I disagree that **it** is depressing **to be** old. There are many happy senior citizens who live full, active lives.

1. To live an active life if you're over 75 is impossible.
2. To get old is terrible.
3. To live in a retirement community must be boring.
4. To date when you're over the age of 60 is uncommon.
5. To travel when you're old is dangerous.
6. To learn a new language is impossible if you're over 50.
7. To enjoy life as a senior citizen is difficult.
8. To be physically active at the age of 70 is unwise.

B. Infinitive As Direct Object

There are certain verbs that are followed by infinitives. Some of them are listed in the charts below along with some helpful hints for memorization. See the chapter appendix for a more complete list.

TYPE A VERBS MUST BE FOLLOWED BY AN INFINITIVE:		
VERBS	**EXAMPLES**	**NOTES**
agree, arrange, decide, deserve, hope, intend, need, learn, promise, plan, prepare, refuse, seem, tend, etc.	• She **arranged** to care for her grandmother. (She will care for her in the future.) • I **expect** to receive a letter today. (I don't know whether I will actually receive it.) • Carol **intends** to change her job. (Whether in fact she will change is unknown.) • She **pretended** to be my sister. (In reality, this is impossible.)	The **verb + infinitive** construction *often* refers to **hypothetical, future, unknown, incomplete,** or **impossible** events although this is not always the case.

14.2 Written Exercise: *Sentence Completion*

DIRECTIONS: A seventeenth-century poet, George Herbert, said, "And now in old age, I bud again." Think about how you would like to have a new life in old age and complete the following sentences by adding an infinitive and additional ideas.

Example   CUE: I need _____.
              RESPONSE: I need <u>to stay active as long as I am able.</u>_____

1. I hope _____.

2. I expect _____.

3. I intend _____.

4. I plan _____.

5. I refuse _____.

6. I will arrange _____.

7. I must prepare _____.

8. I refuse _____.

TYPE A VERBS FOLLOWED BY A (PRO)NOUN + INFINITIVE:		
VERBS	**EXAMPLES**	**NOTES**
advise, allow, cause, convince, encourage, force, get, hire, invite, order, permit, warn, etc.	• The teacher **advised** *us* to study verbs. • The doctor **convinced** *me* to eat less. • The policeman **forced** *them* to pay a fine. • I **hired** *an agent* to sell my house. • The court **ordered** *the man* **not** to speak. • Customers **are allowed** to park there. • I **was encouraged** to buy a new house. • The cashier **was hired** to work nights. • The students **were permitted** to leave.	• Notice that these verbs usually indicate a speech act. • If the construction is made negative, **not** is inserted between the pronoun and the infinitive. • If these verbs are used in the passive, the pronoun is omitted.

TYPE A VERBS THAT MAY BE FOLLOWED BY A (PRO)NOUN + INFINITIVE		
VERBS	**EXAMPLES**	**NOTES**
ask, beg, choose, dare, expect, need, promise, want, would like	• We **begged** to see a movie. (Result: **We** see a movie.) • We **begged** them to see a movie. (Result: **They** see a movie.)	• There is a difference in meaning if the pronoun is omitted.

14.3 Oral Practice: *Verbs Followed By a (Pro)noun + Infinitive*

DIRECTIONS: Based on the cue provided, take turns with your partner asking and answering questions. Use the **verb + pronoun + infinitive** construction.

Example   CUE: friend/invite
            QUESTION: Has a friend ever invited you to do something dangerous?
            ANSWER: Yes, one time a friend invited me to go skydiving.

1. parents/advise
2. teacher/ask
3. friend/convince
4. government/encourage
5. policeman/order
6. doctor/warn
7. law/permit
8. salary/allow
9. company/hire
10. children/beg

14.4 Written Practice: *Anti-Aging Advice*

DIRECTIONS: Below is some advice that a doctor gave a group of people at a lecture on anti-aging. On the lines provided below the lecture, use the **verb + (pro)noun + infinitive** construction to restate what he told them. Use a variety of verbs from the box above.

. . . Summing up, in the fight to hold on to your precious youth, there are many steps that you can take to win the battle. First of all, you should take Vitamins A, C, and E so that body tissue is not so quickly damaged. By slowing down that process, you will increase your body's ability to function. Also, live in a quiet environment so that you won't suffer such drastic hearing loss. One of the most heartbreaking effects of old age is losing the ability to communicate. In addition, if you want to slow down the loss of vision, you'd better use brighter and more focused lighting when you read. Very important, don't forget to maintain a calcium-rich diet so that you can prevent osteoporosis. If you are able to keep your bones strong, you will prevent painful breaks and fractures. Please limit your calorie intake, and your life span will increase significantly. It has been found that people who maintain their optimal weight live longer. Don't smoke! You're automatically cutting your time short if you do. You can exercise well into your eighties, and you will be a healthier 80-year-old as a result. Finally, most important, please keep a positive mental attitude, and I guarantee you'll live longer.

Example   "Avoid caffeine and you will lessen the risk of heart problems." *(He warned them to avoid caffeine.)*

1. _____

2. _____

3. _____

4. _____

5. _____

6. _____

7. _____

8. _____

14.5 Recognition Exercise: *Verbs That May Be Followed by a (Pro)noun + Infinitive*

DIRECTIONS: For each of the following sentences, state *who* would be carrying out the action of the infinitive that is underlined.

Example   CUE: Paul wants his wife <u>to learn</u> English.
             RESPONSE: Paul's wife will learn English.

1. Children expect their grandparents <u>to spoil</u> them.

2. My teacher wants <u>to write</u> an autobiography.

3. Sally begged her mother <u>to stop</u> smoking.

4. Jamie asked his grandfather <u>to buy</u> him a bicycle.

5. My boss chose <u>to give</u> a speech at the company banquet.

6. Jimmy promised <u>to stop</u> lying.

7. Stan's mother needs him <u>to help</u> with the project.

8. Jared dared Nathan <u>to jump</u> over the waterfall.

14.6 Written Exercise: *Verb + Infinitive*

DIRECTIONS: Your government is presently considering cutback of funding for programs to support the elderly. Write a letter to a government representative to protest this decision. Explain why it is important to maintain federally funded programs for the elderly. Use at least ten **verb + infinitive** constructions in your letter. Underline the constructions.

■ II. Infinitive as Complement of an Adjective

An infinitive can be used as the complement of an adjective, which means that the infinitive **adds to** or **completes** the idea expressed in the adjective. The chart below lists some of the adjectives that can be followed by an infinitive complement. See the appendix at the end of the chapter for a more complete listing.

BE + ADJECTIVE + INFINITIVE		
ADJECTIVE	**EXAMPLES**	**NOTES**
afraid	I am **afraid** to tell him that I lost my visa.	• When these adjectives are used, the subject of the sentence is living (animate).
content	She would be **content** to sit in front of the T.V.	
disappointed	We were **disappointed** to hear he was sick.	
happy	I'm very **happy** to be here with you.	
eager	The students are **eager** to improve their grammar.	• Notice that these adjectives express feelings.
glad	I'm sure that you're **glad** to be returning home.	
pleased	I'm **pleased** to announce the winner of the car.	
proud	They were **proud** to be selected as ambassadors.	
sad	My father was **sad** to see me leave.	

BE + ADJECTIVE + (FOR + [PRO]NOUN) + INFINITIVE		
ADJECTIVE	**EXAMPLES**	**NOTES**
boring	It is **boring** (for me) to listen to his stories.	• When these adjectives are used, the subject of the sentence must be **it**. A common error is made by using an animate subject with an adjective that ends in **-ing** in this construction. (See the chapter on passives for more explanation.)
disappointing	It **was disappointing** to hear the test results.	
exciting	It was **exciting** to receive a letter from China.	
easy	It was **easy** to find your house.	
safe	When I was young, it was **safe** to walk at night.	
interesting	It was **interesting** to find out more about Jim. [INCORRECT: I am **interesting** to find out more about Jim.]	

14.7 Written Practice: *Adjectives Followed by Infinitives*

In Deepak Chopra's book mentioned in the preview of this chapter, he describes the seven traits of creative people. These traits ultimately influence the potential we have to counteract the negative effects of aging. Read each of the traits listed below. Then use an **adjective + infinitive** construction to write a paraphrase for each sentence. Use your own words rather than copy the words in the original sentence.

1. They are able to contact and enjoy silence.

   They are content _____.

2. They connect with and enjoy nature.

   They are glad _____.

3. They trust their feelings.

   It is safe _____.

4. They can remain centered and function amid confusion and chaos.

   It is easy _____.

5. They are childlike—they enjoy fantasy and play.

   They are pleased _____.

6. They self-refer: They place the highest trust in their own consciousness.

   They are not afraid _____.

7. They are not rigidly attached to any point of view: Although passionately committed to their creativity, they remain open to new possibilities.

   They are eager _____.

14.8 Oral Practice: *Infinitive as Adjective Complement*

DIRECTIONS: Discuss an elderly person, such as a grandparent, whom you have known and liked all your life. Use adjectives from the chart to describe the person.

Example   *I have always been proud to have such a fun-loving, active grandmother.*

BE + ADJECTIVE + ENOUGH + INFINITIVE	
EXAMPLES	**MEANING**
She's **old enough** to drive in the United States.	• She's 16. She is the **minimum age** necessary in order to drive.
He's **not old enough** to drive in the United States.	• He's 14. He has **not yet reached the minimum age** necessary in order to drive.

BE + TOO + ADJECTIVE + INFINITIVE	
EXAMPLES	MEANING
She's **too old to drive.**	• She's 101. She is **over the maximum age** for driving.
She's 65. She's **not too old to drive.**	• She has **not yet reached the maximum age** for driving.

14.9 Rapid Drill: *Too/Enough and Infinitives*

DIRECTIONS: Change the following sentences so that you are using **too** or **enough** and **an infinitive.** For each sentence make a positive and a negative statement.

Example Nathan can't start preschool yet, because he's only two years old.
POSITIVE: Nathan is not old enough to start preschool.
NEGATIVE: Nathan is too young to start preschool.

1. Rafael can't compete in the Olympics because he's 50 years old.
2. Susan can't buy beer in California because she's only 17 years old.
3. Cherie is 78 years old and still gets jobs playing the piano.
4. Richard will be able to vote in the 1992 U.S. presidential election because he'll be 18 years old.
5. If necessary, Dan could be drafted because he's 18 years old.
6. Mary is 38 and she's pregnant.
7. Sangadji can't study English in this intensive program because he's only 12 years old.
8. Cindy is 40 years old, and she would never date a 23-year-old man.
9. Anthony can't stay home alone because he's only 10 years old.
10. Jenna is 13, and you have to be under 12 to get a discount.

III. Gerunds

A gerund consists of **verb + -ing** and also takes the place of a noun. Like infinitives, gerunds can serve a variety of functions in a sentence.

A. Gerund As Subject of the Sentence

Below are examples of how a gerund can be the subject of the sentence.

EXAMPLE	NOTES
Aging can be difficult for some people.	• Gerund subjects are more common than infinitive subjects.

Continued on next page.

Continued from previous page.

EXAMPLE	NOTES
Creative writing is one of my grandmother's talents.	• The gerund can be part of a noun phrase.
His not appreciating her help surprised me. (The fact that he did not appreciate her help surprised me.)	• A possessive (pro)noun before a gerund phrase can take the place of a noun clause.
Listening to her was difficult. It was difficult **listening to her.**	• As with infinitives, it is possible to replace the gerund subject with **it** when it is followed by the verb **be** and an adjective.

14.10 Rapid Drill: *Gerund Subjects*

DIRECTIONS: Derek's grandmother is 78 years old. Like her mother, she is fairly active. In each pair of sentences below, there is a statement about her activity and a statement describing the effect of the activity. Combine the pairs of sentences into one sentence with a gerund subject.

Example   She gardens every day. This makes her feel useful.
          Gardening makes her feel useful.

1. She has parties with her friends. This makes her feel young.
2. She takes long walks. This helps her to stay in shape.
3. She participates in a theater group and plays the piano on weekends. These activities add to her income.
4. She writes letters to friends in other countries. This keeps her in touch with the world.
5. She visits her grandchildren and plays with them. This is exciting for her.
6. She watches the news on television every day. This keeps her up to date with current events.
7. She takes classes at the community center. This helps her to learn new skills.
8. She cooks for her family. This is rewarding to her.

SPECIAL NOTE

A **possessive** noun or pronoun can precede a gerund subject.
EXAMPLE: **Rachel's continuing** to work past retirement age didn't surprise her friends.

14.11 Written Practice: *Possessives in Subject Gerund Phrases*

DIRECTIONS: Answer all of the following questions with a subject containing a **possessive (pro)noun in a gerund phrase.** Use a noun, pronoun, or the name of the person.

Example   QUESTION: What impresses you about one of your grandparents?
          RESPONSE: My grandfather's playing golf at the age of 80 impresses me.

1. What surprises you about a friend that you have?

_____

2. What is something your teacher does that helps you to learn?

_____

3. What is something your boyfriend/girlfriend/husband/wife does that annoys you?

_____

4. What is something a child does that amuses you?

_____

5. What is something your government does that makes you angry?

_____

6. What is something that disappoints you about a school you attended?

_____

14.12 Paired Oral Practice: *Famous Sayings*

DIRECTIONS: Working in pairs, Student A should look only at the section below labeled Student A. Student B should look at the section labeled Student B. Student A has several explanations for famous sayings that contain infinitives or gerunds as the subject of the sentence. Student B has the list of famous sayings. When Student A reads the explanation, Student B should try to find the famous saying that matches the explanation. Once you have made the match, discuss whether you agree with the saying.

Example   EXPLANATION: I would rather suffer from a relationship that is over than not have had that relationship at all.

SAYING: It is better to have loved and lost than never to have loved at all.

STUDENT A: EXPLANATIONS

1. It is perfectly natural to make a mistake, but it requires special effort and understanding to accept an apology for a mistake.
2. The best way to acquire skills or knowledge is through experience.
3. The more I find out about something, the better I will be able to comprehend it.
4. It's difficult to accept a theory without any physical evidence.

STUDENT A: SAYINGS

1. Seeing is believing.
2. To err is human, to forgive—divine.
3. To know is to understand.
4. Learning is doing.

14.13 Written Practice: *Famous Slogans*

DIRECTIONS: Below are some popular American slogans that encourage people to "hang on" to their youth. Rewrite each saying in your own words using a gerund or infinitive subject.

Example   "Think Young!"

Keeping a fresh, optimistic outlook will keep you young.

1. "Act young!"

_____

2. "Look young."

_____

3. "Stay young."

_____

4. "You're just as young as you feel."

_____

5. "Age is a state of mind."

_____

■ B. Gerund As Direct Object

A gerund can also serve as a direct object after certain verbs. The chart below lists some of these verbs and helpful hints for memorization. See the chapter appendix for a more complete list.

| TYPE B VERBS MUST BE FOLLOWED BY A GERUND | | |
VERBS	EXAMPLE	NOTES
admit, advise, anticipate, avoid, appreciate, deny, defend, dislike, enjoy, finish, mind, recall, recommend, recollect, regret, resent, risk, suggest, tolerate, understand	He **admitted** lying about his age. (He lied in the past.) The students **denied** cheating on the test. (The cheating is a completed action.) I've **finished** writing the report. (The writing has been completed.) Bob **recommends my** going to the theater. (The pronoun emphasizes that I will go.) My boss **resents** my arriving late for work. (I arrive late and he doesn't like it.)	• A **verb + gerund** construction often refers to a **real, past, known, complete,** experience or event. • A possessive (pro)noun is sometimes added before the gerund to indicate who is carrying out the action of the gerund.

14.14 Written Paraphrase: _Retirement Communities_

DIRECTIONS: Following is some information about retirement communities. Read the passage. Then in the space provided below the passage, rewrite it using gerunds as direct objects after verbs. The first one is done for you as an example.

_____

Many senior citizens do not feel bad if they have to live in a retirement community. At one retirement community in Ohio, residents feel good about their living situation because they can come and go as they like. They can live on their own in apartments, cottages, or duplexes that are furnished with their personal belongings. About 40 percent of them drive their own cars because they don't want to be dependent on others for transportation. When Charles Dilgard, the community's chief executive, came to the community 20 years ago, he thought the residents didn't have a sense of independence. He remembers that they were being given too much love and care. At the time, Dilgard said that the residents should have more autonomy. Dilgard also said the residents should be provided with more facilities.

Many senior citizens enjoy living in retirement communities.

_____

_____

_____

_____

_____

_____

_____

_____

_____

_____

SPECIAL NOTE

A **possessive** noun or pronoun can precede a gerund direct object.
EXAMPLE: The teacher appreciated the students' completing their reports on time.

14.15 Rapid Drill: *Possessives In Direct Object Gerund Phrases*

DIRECTIONS: Change each sentence so that the direct object is a **verb + possessive + gerund** construction.

Example   John wanted to give his report after the deadline, and the teacher accepted this.
The teacher accepted John's turning in his report after the deadline since he had been sick.

1. My daughter, Carol, anticipated that I would take her to a movie.
2. She appreciated it when I invited her.
3. She suggested that we go to see a murder mystery.
4. I didn't invite her boyfriend, Steve. Her boyfriend resented this.
5. My daughter understood why Steve was upset.
6. Perhaps he couldn't appreciate the fact that a mother would want to spend some time alone with her daughter.

7. He disliked it that I excluded him.

8. I didn't mind it that Steve wanted to spend time with me.

9. I suggested that he join us next time.

10. In the end, he didn't mind that Carol went without him.

14.16 Written Exercise

DIRECTIONS: For each situation described in the cue, write a sentence by using the **verb** provided in parentheses, a **(pro)noun**, and a **gerund**. Use a noun, pronoun, or a person's name. Sometimes you will have to use the negative form of the verb.

Example   You are on your way to the airport to pick up your mother, and you think that she will arrive late.

(anticipate) <u>I anticipate my mother's arriving late.</u>

1. Your officemate never cleans up his desk, and you don't like it.

   (dislike) _____

2. A friend always lies to you, and you are really upset.

   (forgive) _____

3. You've been having a sleeping problem, and your mother said that you should see a doctor.

   (recommend) _____

4. Your father always gives you lectures, and you are angry.

   (appreciate) _____

5. Your grandmother wants to live alone, and you don't think that it's a good idea.

   (advise) _____

6. Your company decided to prohibit smoking in the building, and you are a smoker.

   (resent) _____

14.17 Written Exercise: *Infinitive or Gerund As Direct Object?*

DIRECTIONS: A plastic surgeon in Miami, Florida, has placed the following advertisement in the local newspaper, hoping to attract elderly people to his clinic for plastic surgery. Fill in the blanks with either the **infinitive** or **gerund** form of the verb in parentheses.

How About a Face Lift?

Do you need _____ (get rid of) some of those unwanted wrinkles

on your face? Do you dislike _____ (find) new wrinkles every day?

I bet you would appreciate _____ (say) goodbye to those

unnecessary age lines forever! If you intend _____ (fight) the look

of old age, I recommend _____ (pay) me a visit for a face lift. We

can arrange _____ (make) you look 20 years younger in a few
short hours. I promise _____ (return) your youthful appearance to
you. I strongly suggest _____ (take) advantage of this opportunity
now. I dare you _____ (look) younger than you are! You won't
regret _____ (place) your faith in my proven skills.

Call For An Appointment Today!

C. Gerund As Object of a Preposition

Any time a verb follows a preposition, the verb must be in gerund form. The chart below lists some common idiomatic expressions with prepositions that are always followed by gerunds.

EXPRESSIONS	EXAMPLES	NOTES
To **look forward to** **be used to**[a] **be accustomed to** **feel up to**	I am **looking forward to** getting a raise. My grandmother **is used to** living alone. I'm **not accustomed to** sleeping late. I don't **feel up to** playing basketball today.	• Because these expressions end in **to** they can be confused with **verb + infinitive** constructions.
About **think about** **talk about** **complain about** **worry about** **be surprised about**	I'm **thinking about** moving to London. We're **talking about** going on strike. She **complained about** getting sick. I'm **worried about** paying my bills. Lenny's **surprised about** getting fired.	• If a verb is used in the progressive, the sentence will contain two **-ing** verb forms.
For **thank someone for** **make an excuse for** **make up for**	I **thanked the nurse for** helping me. I **made an excuse for** being sarcastic. My date **made up for** being late by buying me roses.	• Notice that the gerund construction with the idiom **make up for** is followed by the preposition **by + gerund**.

Continued on next page.

Continued from previous page.

EXPRESSIONS	EXAMPLES
In/On be interested in take part in plan on count on	I'm **interested in** improving my French. We **took part in** helping the poor. You should **plan on** leaving at 6:00. You can **count on** my being early.
Of be afraid of be tired of be proud of approve of	Are you **afraid of** getting bored? She's **tired of** explaining the directions. Jan's **proud of** having so many friends. We don't **approve of** cheating.
With be satisfied with be fed up with put up with be preoccupied with	I'll be **satisfied with** getting a raise. They're **fed up with** being broke. I won't **put up with** your misbehaving. She's **preoccupied with** dieting.

*See the modals chapter for more information on **be used to**.

14.18 Written Exercise: *"Who's Who?"*

DIRECTIONS: Read the following information about people who made significant accomplishments at a late age in life. Then for each sentence find a matching sentence from the sentences which follow. Fill in the blanks with the correct preposition and gerund form of the verb given. Write the person's name on the line provided.

Georgia O'Keeffe:	At the age of 77, Georgia O'Keefe was living in New Mexico, doing some of her most beautiful work.
Ludwig van Beethoven:	Although Beethoven was ill in the last years before his death, he would get up at 5:30 A.M., eat breakfast, and go out into the fields shouting and waving his arms.
Eleanor Roosevelt:	By the age of 56, Eleanor Roosevelt had travelled 280,000 miles as a representative for her husband, the president.
Albert Einstein:	In 1955 at the age of 76, Einstein wrote a public declaration which was signed by a small number of scientists warning against the dangers of hydrogen bombs.

a. She was interested _____ (paint) _____ the beauty of the deserts, flowers, and mountains of the surrounding area.

WHO? _____

   b. He insisted _____ (find) _____ peaceful means for the settlement of all

    matters of dispute between governments of the world.

    WHO? _____

   c. In his last years, the neighboring peasants were used _____ (see) _____

    him walk in the fields speaking in a loud voice and using many gestures.

    WHO? _____

   d. She wasn't afraid _____ (travel) _____ great distances to continue her

    involvement in public activities.

    WHO? _____

14.19 Written Exercise: *The Fountain of Youth*

DIRECTIONS: Try to imagine what it would be like if we could drink from a fountain of youth so that we would never age. Using one expression from each group in the chart beginning on page 362, write six consequences of drinking from the fountain of youth.

Example   People wouldn't **be preoccupied with** getting old and losing their youthful appearance.

1. _____

2. _____

3. _____

4. _____

5. _____

6. _____

Grammatical Patterns Part Two

Preview

DIRECTIONS: Read the following report that describes the characteristics of centenarians.

Centenarians: The Secrets of A Long Life

1 There are an estimated 25,000 centenarians in the United States, and their numbers are rapidly increasing. To better understand what promotes **longevity,** the lives of centenarians and their personal characteristics needs to be closely examined. We are very interested in discovering what kind of lifestyle and particularly what kind of personality determines longevity.

2 Although we may anticipate being told that there are **uniform traits** among centenarians, this is not true. It was originally thought that centenarians must be calm, **serene,** Type B personalities, with stress-free lives. However, there are centenarians who thrive on living **fast-paced, high tension** lives. As far as physical characteristics are concerned, very few claim to have been **obese** at any time in their lives. Many admit to having been social drinkers throughout their lives, and many like to drink coffee. Centenarians have a wide range of nutritional habits—some are vegetarians, but most eat meat. Most of them eat just about everything.

3 There are a few shared traits among centenarians, one of them being a **genetic propensity** toward long life; most centenarians have long-living **forebears.** They also share a sense of **altruism.** Most feel fortunate to have been blessed with **prosperity** and good health and have given help to people who aren't as fortunate. Most centenarians also have a basic love of life. They know how to treasure each day and they enjoy the simple pleasures of life. Centenarians can be party-givers, gardeners, or intellectuals. Many appreciate never having been robbed of their appetite for learning, so they are the kind of people who look for people, experiences, and opportunities that will teach them something. Many of them spend a lot of time reading to satisfy this appetite for learning. You won't find many centenarians who are soft or **slack.** They set high standards and make themselves follow through even if it requires a lot of effort.

VOCABULARY

longevity: the quality or characteristic of living a long life
uniform traits: characteristics which constant or the same
serene: calm, peaceful
fast-paced: moving quickly
high-tension: full of tension, stressful
obese: extremely fat
genetic propensity: a tendency which is inherited through genes
forebears: ancestors
altruism: the quality or condition of giving to or caring about other people
prosperity: wealth, abundance
slack: inactive, lazy

FOCUS ON GRAMMAR

The following questions are based on the preview text and are designed to help you find out what you already know about the structures in this chapter. Work with a partner if your teacher tells you to do so.

1. Find two examples of infinitives in the past tense in the preview text. Write them on the line below. How was the past tense of these infinitives formed?

_____

2. In the following sentence from the preview, is it possible to use a gerund after **like**? Why or why not?

   "Many admit to having been social drinkers throughout their lives, and many like to drink coffee."

3. What question is answered by the infinitive phrase in the following sentence from the preview? Write the question on the line that follows the sentence.

   "Many of them spend a lot of time reading to satisfy their appetite for learning."

I. Type C Verbs: Followed By an Infinitive or Gerund

There are some verbs that can take either infinitives or gerunds as direct objects with little or no difference in meaning, as is shown in the chart below.

TYPE C VERBS ARE FOLLOWED BY EITHER AN INFINITIVE OR A GERUND: WITH NO DIFFERENCE IN MEANING		
VERBS	**EXAMPLES**	
attempt	Tomorrow I will **attempt to surf**.	Tomorrow I will **attempt surfing**.
begin	I **began to study** two years ago.	I **began studying** two years ago.
continue	I will **continue to study**.	I will **continue studying**.
hate	I **hate to sleep** late in the morning.	I **hate sleeping** late in the morning.
like/love	He **loves to receive** her letters.	He **loves receiving** her letters.
prefer	She **prefers to take** the bus.	She **prefers taking** the bus.
start	Tomorrow I will **start to work**.	Tomorrow I will **start working**.

OR WITH A DIFFERENCE IN MEANING		
VERBS	**EXAMPLES**	**MEANING**
try + infinitive + gerund	Many elderly people try to stay active. My grandmother has **tried taking** long walks for her heart problems.	• Make an attempt/make an effort • Experiment to find out if a new method works.

Continued on next page.

Continued from previous page.

VERBS	OR WITH A DIFFERENCE IN MEANING EXAMPLES	NOTES
regret + infinitive (usually used with **say, tell, inform, admit**) + gerund	I **regret to admit** that I'm over the hill. I **regret losing** all my old photographs.	• Feel sorry about saying something negative • Feel sorry about something that has already happened
remember + infinitive + gerund	I always **remember to mail** my bills on time. I **remember** always **mailing** my bills late when I was young.	• The remembering occurs before the action. • Describes a memory of something after it takes place.
forget + infinitive + gerund	My son always **forgets to call** on my birthday. **I'll never forget calling** my son when he was in Europe.	• The result of forgetting is that the action doesn't take place. • **I'll never forget + gerund** describes a memory of something after it takes place.
stop + infinitive + gerund	I always **stop to buy** the newspaper on my way home. I **stopped buying** the newspaper when my eyes went bad.	• Stop for the purpose of accomplishing a task. • Interrupt an action in progress.

14.20 Recognition Exercise: *What Happened First?*

DIRECTIONS: For each sentence below, identify which action of the two that are underlined happens first.

Example   I always <u>stop to look</u> in that shop on the way home.
FIRST: **stop**   SECOND: **look**

1. I <u>must remember to write</u> a letter tonight.

FIRST: _____   SECOND: _____

2. Sharon <u>stopped smoking</u> five years ago.

FIRST: _____   SECOND: _____

3. I'll never <u>forget visiting</u> my great aunt in Italy.

FIRST: _____   SECOND: _____

4. Would you <u>stop</u> at the store <u>to pick up</u> some milk on your way home?

FIRST: _____   SECOND: _____

5. Don't you <u>regret dropping</u> out of high school?

FIRST: _____   SECOND: _____

6. I <u>remember hating</u> physical education classes when I was in high school.

   FIRST: _____   SECOND: _____

7. I didn't <u>forget to call</u> my grandparents on their fiftieth wedding anniversary.

   FIRST: _____   SECOND: _____

8. I <u>regret to admit</u> that I've never been out of this country.

   FIRST: _____   SECOND: _____

■ **14.21 Written Exercise:** *Fill in the Blanks*

DIRECTIONS: Fill in the blanks in the passage below with the correct **infinitive or gerund** form of the verb provided.

Although Caroline Towers is 93 years old, her memory is sharp as a tack. She never forgets

_____ (call) her grandchildren on their birthdays, and she always stops

_____ (buy) them presents when she goes to visit them. She likes

_____ (do) this because she remembers _____ (get)

presents from her grandmother when she was a little girl. She tries _____

(remember) their favorite colors and their special interests. Her sons and daughter always

tell her to stop (buy) _____ presents for the grandchildren because

they are afraid the children will become spoiled. However, Caroline doesn't regret

_____ (show) her grandchildren that they are special to her.

14.22 Written Exercise: *Review of Troublesome Verbs*

DIRECTIONS: After each situation given below, there are two sentences. Fill in the blank in one sentence with a **gerund** form of the verb given and the other sentence with the **infinitive** form.

Example   Robert smokes a pack of cigarettes a day.
<u>Robert stops to smoke a cigarette every day on his way home from work.</u>
<u>Robert would like to stop smoking, but he can't.</u>

1. Gail doesn't want any more wrinkles on her face. (try)

   a. She tries _____ (stay) out of the sun during the hot summer months.

   b. She will try _____ (use) Vitamin E on her skin to prevent additional wrinkles.

2. Although Cynthia is 85, she has many friends all over the world whom she still keeps in touch with. (forget)

   a. She'll never forget _____ (hike) in the mountains in Peru with her friend Luz.

   b. She never forgets _____ (send) Luz a Christmas card.

3. Dan is 74 years old and has never been married. (regret)

    a. He regrets _____ (say) that he lost his chance to get married because he couldn't make up his mind.

    b. He regrets _____ (be) so indecisive.

4. My grandfather met my grandmother at a wedding while she was on a break from playing the piano.

    a. He will always remember _____ (see) her beside the piano when he walked in the door.

    b. He always remembers _____ (take) her out on the anniversary of that day.

II. Infinitives and Gerunds as Complements

Infinitives and gerunds can function as complements of the verb **be** and other linking verbs as shown in the chart below.

COMPLEMENT	EXAMPLES	NOTES
Infinitive	My goal **is to live** an active life. He **appears to be** younger than he is. The children **seem to like** the book. My **hope is to retire** when I'm fifty. My **dream** is **to become** a doctor.	• Occurs after **be, seems, appears** • Often used with nouns that express **incomplete, future, impossible** actions or events such as **hope, dream, goal**
Gerund	Because she is bedridden, the **solution** is **finding** a private nurse. The **result** of the successful interview was **getting** the job. The **key** to staying young is **maintaining** an active life. What I'm really **looking forward to** is **reading** all the books I haven't read. What I appreciate about this school is **meeting** people from other countries.	• Occurs only after **be** • Often used with nouns that express **past, complete, known,** or **fulfilled** actions or events such as **result, solution, secret, key.** • Used in combination with verbs normally followed by gerunds when they occur in a noun clause as subject of the sentence • This pattern is less common than using a gerund subject.

14.23 Oral Practice: *The Stages of Life*

DIRECTIONS: Your teacher will assign you a role: child, adolescent, or adult. Complete each of the following statements with an infinitive or gerund complement according to the stage of life you are in.

1. My primary goal in life is _____ .

2. My dream has always been _____ .

3. What I really enjoy about this age is _____.

4. I seem _____, but _____.

5. The key to being happy is _____.

6. What I am anticipating with great excitement is _____.

7. The solution to all my problems would be _____.

8. The worst part about being this age is _____.

14.24 Written Exercise: *Infinitive and Gerund Complements*

DIRECTIONS: Read the following passage by Ann Guidici Fettner and Pamela Weintraub about longevity research—the study of aging and how to avoid it. Then, with an **infinitive or gerund complement**, complete each statement about the research in the space provided. The first one is completed as an example.

> **1** Scientists in the forefront of longevity research are studying chemical changes that occur in the body over time. They are convinced that information about these changes will provide increased comprehension of the problems related to aging, which may result in an aging cure. **2** The thymosins (a family of hormones) play a key role in keeping people healthy, so scientists are investigating how they work. If we can give the elderly enough thymosin to keep the T-cell level high, we should be able to enhance immunity throughout old age. One type of T-cell is the *killer* cell, which attacks foreign organisms and cancer cells directly. Major progress was made when scientists discovered that thymosins prime the levels of brain hormones involved in reproduction, growth, and development. In five to ten years people will take these thymosins daily to maintain a whole complement of characteristics associated with youth. Scientists realized that daily intake of thymosins could push the average person's vigorous years upward of eighty or ninety simply by boosting the immune system. Scientists know that other substances may also prove to be potent antiaging agents, but they must find them.

1. One way to find an aging cure is <u>to understand the problems related to aging.</u>

2. The goal of scientists is _____.

3. The solution to weakened immunity in old age is _____.

4. The job of the *killer* cell is _____.

5. A major breakthrough in the research was _____.

6. Something we can look forward to is _____.

7. A positive result of the research was _____.

8. One difficulty for scientists is _____.

III. Infinitive of Purpose

Notice in the box below how the infinitive form of the verb is used to explain purpose.

Function	Infinitive Form	Example
Why?/For what purpose?	**to** + verb	• Many centenarians spend a lot of time reading **to satisfy their appetite for learning.**
	in order to + verb	• Many centenarians take long walks **in order to stay in shape.**

14.25 Written Exercise: *How to Stay Young*

DIRECTIONS: Below are some ways to slow down your life which helps to promote longevity. Read each suggestion, and rewrite it using an **infinitive of purpose.**

Example   Reduce irritants: If you tend to get worked up when you're stuck in traffic or in line, your heart may be headed for trouble.
Stay calm when you're stuck in traffic to reduce irritants that can cause heart trouble.

1. Have a good cry. Studies suggest that emotional crying may release stress-related chemicals which have a calming effect.

_____

2. Drive ten miles per hour slower. Try a new route or simply notice the old one more. Slowing down is a good way to appreciate the present moment.

_____

3. Fill your life with rich experiences of all kinds as one way of keeping your mind fresh.

_____

4. Take a moment before eating. Sitting quietly reminds us to notice our meal instead of wolfing it down.

_____

5. Wait a few rings before answering the phone. Rushing to pick it up immediately prolongs your hectic mood.

_____

6. Set aside "boundary time." Pick a part of each day and allow nothing to intrude upon it.

_____

_____

14.26 Oral Interview: *Cosmetic Surgery*

DIRECTIONS: Interview two or three Americans or other English speakers about cosmetic surgery. Ask the following questions.

1. Would you ever consider cosmetic surgery such as a face lift, or liposuction? Why or why not?
2. Why do so many famous people, such as movie stars, have cosmetic surgery?
3. Why do ordinary people agree to such surgery?
4. Why do you think people want to hang on to their youthful appearance?

14.27 Written Feedback

DIRECTIONS: Based on the information you collected from your interview, complete the following sentences with an infinitive of purpose.

1. Many famous people, such as movie stars, have cosmetic surgery done _____

_____.

2. Many ordinary people have cosmetic surgery done _____

_____.

3. People want to hang on to their youthful appearance _____

_____.

14.28 Paired Practice: *Oral Report*

DIRECTIONS: Based on the information already discussed in this chapter and what you have read, prepare an oral report with your partner on the techniques people use to prevent aging. Write at least 10 sentences for the report, and when you present it to the class, divide the sentences up so that each of you is giving half the report. Use infinitive phrases whenever possible to replace either an adverb, adjective, or noun clause.

IV. Causative Verbs: Let, Make, Help, Get

These verbs express cause and are followed by the infinitive form of a verb.

Verbs and Rules	Examples	Meanings
MAKE + (Pro)noun + infinitive (omit *to*) + (Pro)noun + adjective	My teacher **makes me write** an essay every week. Taking tests **makes me nervous.** Watching T.V. **makes me sleepy.**	• Require, force • Cause a physical or emotional reaction

Continued on next page.

Continued from previous page.

VERBS AND RULES	EXAMPLES	MEANINGS
HAVE + (Pro)noun + Simple form of verb **or** + Noun/pronoun + participle (passive)	Kathy **has her kids clean** their rooms on Saturdays. Kathy **has her house cleaned** every Saturday.	• Delegate work or responsibility to someone
LET + (Pro)noun + infinitive form of verb	The IRS won't **let me withdraw** money from my retirement account without a penalty.	• Allow, enable
GET + (Pro)noun + to + infinitive **or** + Infinitive	We should **get my grandmother to go out** dancing with us. **I get my suits dry cleaned** every two weeks. I **got to ride** on my grandfather's tractor when I was small.	• Coerce, persuade • Delegate work or responsibility • Have the privilege or opportunity
HELP + (Pro)noun + infinitive form of verb + (Pro)noun + to + infinitive form of verb	Staying busy **helps my father forget** about his age. Writing **helps me to express** myself.	• Provide assistance in making something happen.

14.29 Oral Practice: *Causative Verbs*

DIRECTIONS: Use causative verbs from the preceding chart to answer the following questions your teacher or partner asks you.

1. Are you easily persuaded? Give some examples.
2. If you had a teenage son or daughter, what kinds of rules would you have?
3. In your job or at home, what kind of work do you delegate to other people?
4. What kinds of things does your English teacher require?
5. When you're studying a second language, how can you best remember vocabulary?
6. How do you feel when you drink coffee?
7. What kind of jobs did your parents give you when you were growing up?
8. What are some things that wealthy people have done for them by hired help?
9. What kind of privileges did you have when you were growing up?

14.30 Written Exercise: *Fill in the Blanks*

DIRECTIONS: Fill in the blank with the appropriate **causative verb**, a noun or pronoun if necessary, and the correct form of the verb in parentheses.

1. When the police officer saw me speeding, he _____ (pull over) to the side of the road. I couldn't remember where the car registration was, so my wife _____ (find) it. I wanted to tell the officer why I was driving so fast, but he wouldn't _____ (explain). Finally, I _____ (listen) by saying that my wife was about to give birth. He jumped into action and _____ his assistant _____ (call) an ambulance. When the ambulance arrived they _____ (get) in. The police officer _____ (leave) without paying a fine.

2. The pleasures of age are much different from the pleasures of youth. First of all, you _____ (learn) how everyone turns out. And of course you are witness to your own unfolding drama or comedy. Nobody _____ (you) _____ (do) things that you don't enjoy. You can also _____ others _____ (win) all the arguments without worrying that your opinion is the one that everyone accepts. Best of all you'll start receiving a lot of assistance in your daily life. You can _____ perfect strangers _____ (carry) your bags and drive you to the store. And even your kids will _____ you _____ (manage) the everyday routine when necessary.

V. Special Problems With Gerunds and Infinitives

PROBLEM	EXPLANATION
For + Gerund or **For + Infinitive** to express purpose: [INCORRECT: I would turn around on the street just **for having** a look at him.] CORRECT: I would turn around on the street just **to have** a look at him. [INCORRECT: John studied his notes **for to prepare** for the test.] CORRECT: John studied his notes **to prepare** for his test.	Use the infinitive form to express purpose. Don't use the gerund after **for** unless you're explaining the use of something.

Continued on next page.

Continued from previous page.

PROBLEM	EXPLANATION
INCORRECT form after certain verbs: [INCORRECT: The mechanic **recommended to change** the oil.] CORRECT: The mechanic **recommended changing** the oil.	Certain verbs must be followed by gerunds, and certain verbs must be followed by infinitives.
Enough before the adjective or **much** after **too**: [INCORRECT: He's **enough old** to drive a car.] CORRECT: He's **old enough** to drive a car. [INCORRECT: He's **too much old** to run marathons.] CORRECT: He's **too old** to run marathons.	**Enough** follows the adjective. **Too** is followed directly by the adjective.

■ **14.31 Error Analysis**

DIRECTIONS: Find the errors with the use of gerunds and infinitives in the following sentences and correct them.

1. The teacher suggested to read the newspaper so that I could improve my English.

2. Some elderly people belong to clubs just for having an opportunity for social contact.

3. Martin is enough educated to get a better job in his profession.

4. It is difficult to imagining what my life would be like if I were 100 years old.

5. The doctor convinced to eat more calcium-rich foods for stronger bones.

6. The mother promised taking the children to the country for the weekend.

7. The spectators were exciting to see their team winning the game.

8. Her brother didn't help her move shocked me.

9. After many months of hard labor, the workers finished to build the apartment complex.

10. The ground was too much wet to play golf.

11. The police officer pulled over the driver for giving him a speeding ticket.

12. I'm used to leave work every day at 5:00.

13. The nursing home residents appreciated we sang folk songs for them.

14. The child always stops buying candy on the way home from school.

15. After the movie, we considered having gone to get some ice cream.

16. These library books need being returned in three weeks.

17. The court made the woman to pay a fine for driving without a license.

18. The foreign dignitaries were interested to meet with the president.

19. After a very persuasive speech, the salesperson got him buy the cologne.

20. My hope is living a long, healthy, happy life.

Focus on Writing

Perfect and Passive Infinitives and Gerunds

It is possible to use gerunds and infinitives for the functions already covered in this chapter in the past tense or in the passive voice. These are especially common in writing. The following chart demonstrates these possibilities.

PERFECT/PASSIVE FORMS	EXAMPLES	NOTES
Perfect Gerund **having + past participle**	I **denied having taken** the money.	• With the perfect gerund form, there is an emphasis on the *completion* of the action in the past. • Some verbs *cannot* be followed by a perfect gerund, e.g. **suggest, recommend, consider, risk** [INCORRECT: He **suggested having gone** to that movie.]
Perfect Infinitive **to + have + past participle**	Centenarians feel lucky **to have lived** long lives. (Past) Centenarians feel lucky **to be living** long lives. (Present) I **hope to have finished** by Friday. (Future)	• Notice the distinction between present, past and future time reference.
Present - Passive Gerund **being + past participle**	We anticipate **being told** that there are uniform traits among centenarians.	• The passive forms emphasize the action or event expressed in the second verb.
Present - Passive Infinitive **to + be + past participle**	Centenarians need **to be** closely **studied.**	• An adverb can be placed between be and the past participle.
Perfect - Passive Gerund **having + been + past participle**	They appreciate never **having been robbed** of their appetite for learning.	• In this construction, the auxiliary **have** will be in the gerund form, followed by the passive form of the verb.
Past - Passive Infinitive **to + have + been + past participle**	Most centenarians feel fortunate **to have been blessed** with prosperity and good health.	• The past-passive infinitive emphasizes the completion of the action in the infinitive.

14.32 Recognition Exercise: *Perfect and Passive Infinitives and Gerunds*

DIRECTIONS: For each sentence, determine the time reference of the **verb + gerund** construction in the sentence. If the time is present, change it to the past. If the time reference is past, change it to the present. If it can't be changed, write "no change."

Example   I appreciate finally being given a chance to meet a centenarian. (present)
          <u>I appreciate finally having been given a chance to meet a centenarian.</u>

1. I dislike reaching the age of 40.

2. My teacher seems to have enjoyed her vacation.

3. I would prefer to have been given a retirement plan at work.

4. Susan recommends teaching at that school.

5. My brother is relieved to have finished his thesis.

6. The lecturer will speak about finding a job.

7. Most centenarians admit to helping other people.

8. My grandmother is pleased to have delivered the good news about increased retirement pay.

9. The lawyer was happy to have received the case.

10. I like having been given a fair opportunity to protest.

14.33 Written Exercise: *Perfect and Passive Infinitives and Gerunds*

DIRECTIONS: Below is a passage about a 97 year-old man who has been hawking newspapers (selling in the street) in San Francisco for 40 years. Fill in the blanks with past and passive forms of the verbs given in parentheses.

Yesterday Harold Douglas celebrated his 40th anniversary hawking newspapers in San Francisco.
He claims _____ (start) hawking newspapers on street corners before
there were automatic streetlights, and he is proud _____ (know)
as the oldest hawker in San Francisco. He happily mentions _____

(greet) yesterday by dozens of people who shook his hand as he stood on his street corner. He is happy _____ (raise) as a hard worker, and he has never liked sitting around. He refuses _____ (restrict) to the house all day, staring out the window at nothing, so he appreciates _____ (permit) to sell newspapers every day on the street corner. He regrets _____ (suffer) from a severe case of pneumonia this past winter, which kept him from his job for the first time since he started hawking.

14.34 Written Practice: *Older Is Wiser*

DIRECTIONS: Write about an experience from your past that made you wiser or taught you a lesson. Use a variety of past and passive forms.

Analysis of an Authenic Text

DIRECTIONS: Read the following article about aging, referring to the vocabulary on page 379.

In the Battle Against Aging, We Forsake Grace For a Larger Arsenal of Weapons
by Ellen Goodman

"I don't intend to grow old gracefully. I intend to fight it every step of the way."

What am I to make of this message? The Census Bureau just announced that the average age of Americans is now a **notch** over 32 years old. The first of the 75 million baby-boomers have passed 40. Their midlife is marked by the emergence of all sorts of products to help them fight it every step of the way.

There are more than the usual number of **unguents** and **elixirs** that promise to rub the age out of our skins and preserve our energy. There are more than the usual products to cover gray hair and fill in the face lines. There are more than the usual **admonitions** to leg-lift a path to eternally youthful thighs.

Men who could accept their baldness or risk the **ridicule** of a toupee now have the chance of growing hair again. Women and men who had to accept their **crow's feet** or risk the knife to retrieve their younger, tauter skin can now chemically iron their skin.

In modest ways, aging has begun to look like a personal choice. How far are you willing to go to stay the same?

Clearly the money is in youth products. There is no way to sell self-acceptance. There may be a profit in the natural look but not in nature.

As we are offered this expanding **array** of weapons, we increase our defense budget. And with each item, with each choice, how much harder it becomes to negotiate a peaceful coexistence with our own age.

How much harder it becomes to age gracefully.

Vocabulary

notch: a little bit
unguents: creams, oils
elixirs: preparations designed to have some medicinal action, such as prolong life
admonitions: warnings
ridicule: mocking, laughing
crow's feet: the wrinkles at the outer edge of the eye
array: selection

Discussion Questions

1. Discuss some of the methods used to fight the aging process and their purpose. How effective do you think these methods are?

2. Do you agree that there is no way to sell self-acceptance? Do you think that by looking and feeling younger, self-acceptance improves?

3. What does the author mean by the difference between the natural "look" and nature?

Composition Topics

Use what you have learned in this chapter about gerunds and infinitives to write a well-organized essay on one of the following topics.

1. Describe the attitude in your country toward aging. What aspects of lifestyle, opportunities, and services for the elderly reflect this attitude?

2. Describe the three stages of your life: childhood, adolescence, and adulthood.

3. Would you like to drink from the fountain of youth? Why or why not?

The Future Is In Our Hands

- Comparative Structures

The Future Is In Our Hands (Bigger Is Not Better)

DISCUSSION QUESTIONS

1. How do you think life will change in the first ten years of the twenty-first century?

2. What important technological advances have you seen in your lifetime? Have any of these had a negative impact on society or the environment?

3. What kind of dangers do we face on this planet as we progress into the future? What can you do personally to lessen these dangers?

4. Why is it important for people all over the world to think and act as a "world community"?

OBJECTIVES

In this chapter, you will learn:

1. To understand the rules for the comparative and superlative forms of adjectives and adverbs

2. To understand the sentence patterns used for making comparisons

3. To use superlative constructions

4. To use equal comparative constructions

5. To use conditional comparative constructions

6. To use comparative words or expressions to express a progressive change of state

Preview

DIRECTIONS: The following article discusses the necessity of returning to a simple lifestyle in order to save the earth. Read the article, referring to the vocabulary list below when necessary.

Voluntary Simplicity
by Duane Elgin

1 Quietly and without **fanfare**, people from all **walks of life** in the United States have been experimenting with a lifestyle called voluntary simplicity. This approach, which stresses **frugal** consumption, spiritual growth, and environmental respect, encourages people to pursue lives that are outwardly simple and inwardly rich.

2 Why? Because the earth has **finite** nonrenewable resources, increasing environmental pollution, and an economic system that promotes an uneven distribution of goods. As economist E. F. Schumacher pointed out, "We must live simply that others may simply live." . . . Some strategies for practicing voluntary simplicity on a personal level include using products that are **durable,** energy efficient, and nonpolluting; recycling metal, glass, and paper products; using public transit, **car pools,** and smaller cars; eating lower on the food chain (fewer processed foods, more simple, healthy foods appropriate for sustaining life on a small planet); becoming more self-reliant; and pursuing work that contributes to the well-being of the world.

3 . . . In short, we must change our everyday habits of consumption. The material possessions that we strive for so **arduously** must lose the intensity of their appeal. **Mainstream** culture under the **sway** of voluntary simplicity would encourage people to live in smaller homes that combine functional simplicity and beauty. The person who was previously envied for having an expensive car and the latest in fashion might be criticized for tasteless **ostentation,** totally inappropriate in a world of great human need.

4 This does not mean that people should completely turn away from the material things of life. Rather, it means that people must increasingly sense that the totality of life is not well served by the endless **accumulation** of luxuries and nonessentials.

5 I believe that if we consciously simplify our lives, finding a satisfying balance between the material and spiritual aspects of existence will be much easier. It is a personal decision and a personal responsibility. Each one of us must act to restore the balance. But the cumulative result of our individual actions can transform our nation and the world.

VOCABULARY

fanfare: a usually noisy and showy display
walks of life: professions, age groups, social status, educational background, etc.
frugal: thrifty, economical
finite: something defined by limits or an end
durable: long-lasting despite frequent use
car pools: two or more people sharing transportation to work or school
arduously: with much energy, strenuously
mainstream: belonging to the largest representative group of a culture or society
sway: persuasion, conviction
ostentation: a showy display of wealth
accumulation: collection, gathering, storing up

CULTURAL NOTE/DISCUSSION

Material possessions, especially cars, have traditionally been highly regarded in American culture. People work very hard all their lives to accumulate as many material possessions as possible. Therefore, the practice of voluntary simplicity would be very difficult to undertake for the average American. Does your culture have the same high regard for material possessions? Would the concept of voluntary simplicity be easily accepted in your culture? What are some specific ways it could be practiced in your country?

FOCUS ON GRAMMAR

The following questions are based on the preview text and are designed to help you find out what you already know about the structures in this chapter. Some of the questions may be hard and some of them may be easy. Answer as many of the questions as you can. Work with a partner if your teacher tells you to do so.

1. Find four adjectives in paragraph 2 that are used to express a comparison between most people's lifestyle and that of voluntary simplicity. Write them below. How are these forms different? What rule can you make about the formation of comparative adjectives?

   _____   _____

   _____   _____

2. In the following sentence from paragraph 3, how would you change the first boldfaced phrase to correspond in form to the second one? What rule can you make about these forms?

   *The person who was previously envied for having **an expensive** car and **the latest** in fashion might be criticized for tasteless ostentation, totally inappropriate in a world of great human need.*

3. Below there is a statement from the preview with the adverb underlined, followed by a second statement containing a blank. Write the comparative form of the underlined word in the blank of the sentence that follows.

   "We must live <u>simply</u> so that others may simply live."

   We must live _____ than before.

Grammatical Patterns Part One

I. Review of Comparative Forms

A. Comparative Forms of Adjectives

The chart below states the rules for the comparative and superlative forms of adjectives.

	COMPARATIVE	SUPERLATIVE	NOTES
One-Syllable Adjectives big small	bigger smaller	biggest smallest	• Add **-er** and **-est** to the adjective.
Two-Syllable Adjectives easy simple humble friendly yellow handsome quiet stupid wasteful	easier simple humbler friendlier more friendly yellower more yellow handsomer more handsome quieter more quiet stupider more wasteful	the easiest the simpliest humblest the friendliest the most friendly the yellowest the most yellow the handsomest the most handsome the quietest the most quiet the stupidest the most wasteful	• If a two-syllable adjective ends in **y, -ple,** or **-ble;** use **-er** and **-est**. If the adjective ends in **y,** change the **y** to **i** and add **-er** or **-est**. • Use either **-er** and **-est** or **more** and **most**[a] if the adjective ends in **-ly, -ow, -er,** or **-some**. • Some words without suffixes can use **-er** and **-est** or **more** and **most**. • For other two-syllable adjectives use **more** and **most**.
Adjectives with More than Two Syllables beautiful	more beautiful	the most beautiful	• If the adjective has more than two syllables use **more** and **most**.
Irregular Forms good bad little far	better worse less farther	the best the worst the least the farthest	• There are a few adjectives whose comparative and superlative forms are completely different words.

[a]**Less** and **the least** can be substituted for more and the most.

15.1 Paired Activity: *Comparative Forms of Adjectives*

DIRECTIONS: As you discuss the following issues related to voluntary simplicity, take turns with your partner, using the adjective in parentheses to ask for a comparison of the two items provided. As you respond, explain your reasons for your choice.

Example   CUE: carpooling/taking the bus (energy-efficient)
          STUDENT A: Which is more energy-efficient, carpooling or taking the bus?
          STUDENT B: Carpooling is more energy-efficient.

1. paper/plastic (bad)
2. potato chips/banana (wholesome)
3. air conditioner/fan (extravagant)
4. airport/train station (quiet)
5. cans/bottles (good)
6. shower/bath (wasteful)
7. fast food/a home-cooked meal (nutritious)
8. recycling paper/throwing paper in the garbage (costly to the environment)
9. oil spills/toxic dumping (harmful to the oceans)
10. styrofoam coffee cups/ceramic coffee cups (convenient)

B. Comparative Forms of Adverbs

The chart below states the rules for comparative and superlative forms of adverbs.

ADVERBS	COMPARATIVE	SUPERLATIVE	NOTES
quickly often seldom	more quickly more often more seldom	the most quickly the most often the most seldom	• With two-syllable adverbs, **more** and **most** are used to form the comparative and superlative forms.
fast hard	faster harder	the fastest the hardest	• There are a few one-syllable adverbs whose comparative and superlative are formed by adding **-er** and **-est**.
little well badly far	less better worse farther	the least the best the worst the farthest	• There are a few adverbs whose comparative and superlative forms are completely different words.

15.2 Written Drill: *A Better Future*

DIRECTIONS: For each pair of sentences below, an adjective is provided. Fill in the blank for one of the sentences with the **comparative** form of that **adjective.** Fill in the blank of the other sentence with the **comparative** form of the **adverb** that corresponds to that adjective.

Example   SAFE: **a.** The air will be <u>safer</u> if the present pollution levels drop.

b. We will be living <u>more safely</u> if we reduce the present pollution levels.

1. PEACEFUL

   a. We must work _____ towards solutions of global problems.

   b. The world will be _____ if nations continue to work together.

2. SIMPLE

   a. People should try to live _____ lives.

   b. We must live _____ so that others may simply live.

3. CONVENIENT

   a. Shopping will be _____ with the help of computers.

   b. We will be able to shop _____ with the help of computers.

4. GOOD

   a. With a mass transit system that is designed _____, we will be less dependent on cars.

   b. With _____ mass transit, we will be less dependent on cars.

5. QUIET

   a. Long before all of the many conveniences of the present, life was much _____.

   b. People used to live _____ before all of the many present-day conveniences.

15.3 Paired Activity: *Getting to Know You*

DIRECTIONS: Circle one of the numbers on the scale to rate yourself on each pair of questions. Then compare and discuss your characteristics with those of your partner's. Use the comparative forms of adjectives and adverbs when you discuss your differences. Be prepared to report to the class if your teacher asks you.

Example   QUESTION: **How competent** are you in English? How **well** do you speak the language?

STUDENT A	0	1	2	3	4	5
STUDENT B	0	1	2	3	4	5

COMPARISON: She is **more competent** in English. She speaks the language **better.**

1. How **friendly** are you? Do you make friends **easily?**

   0   1   2   3   4   5

2. How **conscientious** are you about the environment? Do you recycle **carefully?**

   0   1   2   3   4   5

3. How **ambitious** are you? Do you work **hard?**

    0   1   2   3   4   5

4. How **funny** are you? Can you make people laugh **easily?**

    0   1   2   3   4   5

5. How **adventurous** are you? How **far** away from home have you traveled?

    0   1   2   3   4   5

SPECIAL NOTE

LESS VS. FEWER

Notice the difference in use between *less* and *fewer.*

LESS	FEWER

• Less is used with noncount nouns.
  1. Less traffic means **less pollution.**
	• Fewer is used with count nouns.
	  2. Fewer cars means **fewer accidents.**

• If the noun is understood, it can be omitted after *less.*
  3. In order to conserve water, we should use **less** in our daily routine.
	• If the noun is understood it can be omitted after *fewer.*
	  4. If we solve some of these problems now, we'll have **fewer** in the future.

• Less can be used as an adverb. **5.** If we drive **less,** air quality will improve.	• Fewer cannot be used as an adverb.
• Less can modify another adjective or adverb. **6.** We are **less careful** today than we have been in the past.	• Fewer cannot modify an adjective or adverb.

15.4 Written Drill: *Less/Fewer*

DIRECTIONS: Use *less* or *fewer* before the words below. Add *-s* to the word if it is a count noun. Sometimes you can use both. Discuss the difference in meaning in these cases. (See Chapter 1 for more information on Count/Noncount Nouns.)

1. _____ money

2. _____ mistake

3. _____ resourceful

4. _____ innovation

5. _____ issue

6. _____ time

7. _____ interesting

8. _____ people

9. _____ conservation

15.5 Written Drill

DIRECTIONS: Fill in the blanks with *less, fewer, better,* or *more.*

1. It takes _____ time to throw plastic in the garbage but it is ultimately _____ costly.

2. If we want to save the rainforest we should fight for _____ development.

3. I used to take two showers a day, but I've been encouraged to use _____ water.

4. Jim likes electronic devices but he decided to have _____ in his home.

5. Without energy we are _____ productive.

6. Janet joined a political campaign. She's much _____ serious than I am about this issue.

7. If you plan now, you will be _____ prepared for the future.

II. Comparative Patterns

A. The Basic Comparative Pattern

A comparative sentence has the following basic pattern:

<u>People in America</u> <u>live</u> <u>more extravagantly</u> <u>than</u> <u>many other people</u>.
    noun phrase   + verb   + comparative   + than   + noun plural

The comparative pattern that you are most familiar with is formed on the basis of adjectives and adverbs. However, it is also possible to make a comparison on the basis of nouns and verbs, as is shown in the following examples:

BASIS FOR COMPARISON	EXAMPLE
Adjective	My car is **more expensive** than your car.
Adverb	My car runs **more efficiently** than your car.
Nouns	My car uses **more gas** than your car.
Verbs	My car **costs more** than your car.

SPECIAL NOTE

NOUNS IN THE COMPARATIVE PATTERN

The noun in the comparative pattern can be any form that a noun can take: noun phrase, gerund phrase, and noun clause. For example:
  Plastic bags are more harmful than **paper bags.**
  Riding a bicycle is much less damaging to the environment than **driving a car.**

The second noun in the pattern is often a reduced clause as in the following example:
  You are more accepting of technological advances than **I (am).**

In informal spoken English, the subject pronoun I in the sentence above would become the object pronoun **me.**
  You are more accepting of technological advances than **me.**

15.6 Rapid Drill: *Comparative Patterns*

DIRECTIONS: Use the information below to make **comparisons** about Lisa and Maria and their concern about the environment. Use more than one pattern for each comparison.

Example   LISA:
has written over 100 letters to her congresswoman about environmental protection.

MARIA:
has never written a letter about environmental protection

Lisa has written more letters than Maria has.
Lisa **is more concerned** about environmental protection.

MARIA

1. She doesn't care about the environment.
2. She throws newspapers in the garbage.
3. Her car emits a lot of harmful fumes.
4. She takes 20-minute showers.
5. She uses her car air conditioner when it's hot.
6. She drives everywhere.
7. She drinks from styrofoam coffee cups.
8. She allows the water to run when she's washing the dishes.

LISA

1. She has a strong sense of responsibility.
2. She recycles her newspapers diligently.
3. Her car has an efficient smog control system.
4. She is careful about the length of her showers.
5. She never uses her car air conditioner.
6. She tries hard to avoid driving her car.
7. She uses her own ceramic coffee cup.
8. She conserves water carefully.

SPECIAL NOTE

OMITTING THE SECOND HALF OF THE COMPARATIVE

It is not always necessary to state the second half of the comparison if a comparative statement is being made about an understood topic. For example, in a lecture about global warming you could hear the following comparative statement: **We will experience warmer temperatures and higher water levels.** It is understood that the comparison is between the present and the future.

15.7 Written Activity: *A High-Tech World*

DIRECTIONS: The sentences below describe some recent advances in technology that have changed our lives. For each one, write two **comparative** sentences of different types from the chart above. The sentences should state the effect of the technological advances. The second half of the comparative pattern can be omitted since it is understood that the past is being compared with the present.

Example   Portable phones have become common.
ADJECTIVE: We can be more mobile while we talk on the phone.

ADVERB: <u>People can use the phone more frequently since they don't have to interrupt their activity in order to talk.</u>

NOUN: <u>Talking on the telephone is a less time-consuming activity since we can work and talk at the same time.</u>

VERB: <u>Because of the availability of portable phones, people talk on the telephone more.</u>

1. Camcorders are used by families to record special events and the growth of their children.

_____

_____

2. Fax machines have become a popular medium for the quick transmission of information.

_____

_____

3. Personal computers have become a common addition to the household.

_____

_____

4. E-mail allows friends to communicate on-line and provides access to a variety of information sources.

_____

_____

15.8 Written Drill: *Fill in the Blanks*

DIRECTIONS: Fill in the blanks so that the sentence expresses a logical comparison.

1. Cars in the future will be _____ the cars we have today.

2. Solar energy costs _____ electricity.

3. Recycling is _____ dumping.

4. A large house uses _____ than a small one.

5. Whole foods contain _____ processed foods.

6. Living in the fast lane requires _____ practicing voluntary simplicity.

7. A concerned citizen conserves water _____ one who is apathetic.

B. Substitutions, Omissions, and Additions in the Comparative Pattern

In order to avoid unnecessary repetition when making a comparison, the phrase in the second part of the comparative pattern is often substituted or omitted. The chart below shows several substitutions, omissions, and additions that can be made.

SUBSTITUTION/OMISSION	NOTES
1. My van is better than your van. yours.	• Substitute a possessive adjective + noun with a possessive pronoun.

2. This van is faster than that van.
                     that one.
                     the other van.
                     the other one.
                     the other.
	• Substitute **that** + singular noun with **that one**.
	• Substitute **the other** + singular noun with **the other one** or **the other**.

3. These vans are better than those vans.
                     those.
                     the other vans.
                     the other ones.
                     the other two.
                     the others.
	• Omit the plural noun after **these** and **those**.
	• Substitute **the other** + plural noun with **the ther ones; the other two, three, etc.;** or **the others**.

4. These vans are better than. . .
   the vans I saw.
   the ones I saw.
   those I saw.
	• Substitute **the** + plural noun (before an adjective clause) with **the ones**, or **those**.

5. This information is better than. . .
   the information that I have.
   that which I have.
	• Substitute **the** + noncount noun before an adjective clause with **that**.

6. My car has better smog control than yours.	• Add an auxiliary to the end of the sentence as in (7).
7. My car has better smog control than yours **has**.	• Sometimes the auxiliary is necessary to avoid
8. Wayne likes air conditioning more than Jim.	ambiguity. Notice the ambiguous meaning of (8) as
9. Wayne likes air conditioning more than he likes Jim.	expressed in (9).
10. Wayne likes air conditioning more than Jim **does**.	
11. Wayne likes air conditioning more than Jim likes it.	

15.9 Rapid Drill: *Substitutions and Omissions*

DIRECTIONS: In each of the following sentences, make a **substitution or omission** for the idea that is repeated in the second half of the comparative pattern.

Example   CUE: This water filter is better than **the water filter** you have.
            RESPONSE: This water filter is better than **the one** you have.

1. The city council's solution to the landfill problem is more sensible than the solution proposed by private businesses.

2. The contamination from this oil spill was much worse than the contamination that resulted from the previous spill.

3. The problems we've had with water shortage this summer are less severe than the problems that we had last summer.

4. My recycling efforts have been more productive than her recycling efforts.

5. The loss presented by closing unsafe nuclear power plants is far less than the loss that can result from keeping them open.

6. The problems in the new Metro construction are much more severe than the problems we had predicted.

7. The people working on the toxic waste cleanup this year are much more committed than the people who worked on it last year.

15.10 Oral Drill: *Sentence Completion*

DIRECTIONS: Complete the following sentences with a comparative pattern using **substitutions and omissions.**

Example　　CUE: This school . . .
　　　　　　RESPONSE: This school is much bigger than the one I attended before.

1. Verb tenses in English . . .
2. Your watch . . .
3. The problems we face in the future . . .
4. The education you get in a private school . . .
5. The salary that I make . . .
6. This language learning experience . . .
7. The present political system in my country . . .
8. The friends that I have now . . .
9. Technology in the future . . .
10. The teachers at this school . . .

15.11 Paired Activity: *The Cordless Phone*

DIRECTIONS: Take turns with your partner asking and answering questions about the three cordless phones described in the chart below. Use comparative patterns with **substitutions and omissions.**

Example　　QUESTION: How does the Nova compare to the Sonika and the Echo in price?
　　　　　　ANSWER: The Nova is more expensive than the other two.

	Sonika	Exho	Nova
Price	$30.00	$75.00	$150.00
Reception	• always some static • can be used 100 feet from home	• occasional static • can be used 500 feet from home	• never static • can be used 1 mile from home
Recharge	• can stay off for 15 minutes before recharging	• can stay off for an hour before recharging	• can stay off up to 5 hours before recharging
Special Features	• push button	• push button, redial, call waiting	• push button, redial, call waiting, waterproof

FUNCTION OF COMPARISON

So far, you have studied how to compare one characteristic in two different people, places, or things, for example, *John's life is simpler than Mary's life.* There are two other possible types of comparison:

- Compare two characteristics in two different people, places, or things as in 1 and 2:

    1. *A computer is more efficient than a fax machine is economical.*

    2. *A computer records information more quickly than a fax machine sends it.*

- Compare two characteristics in one person, place, or thing as in 3 and 4.

    3. *John is more ambitious than he is aggressive.*

    4. *John thinks more quickly than he talks.*

15.12 Paired Activity: *Socially Responsible Investment*

DIRECTIONS: The chart below contains information about a few companies where you could invest your money. The information in the chart is related to how socially responsible the company is on the basis of different criteria. The rating scale is 1–5, which means that if the company receives a 1, it is very socially responsible about that particular issue and if it receives a 5, it is probably going to be blacklisted. Use the different types of **comparatives** from the preceding chart to compare the degree of social responsibility of the three companies on a variety of issues. At the end of the discussion, decide which company you would invest your money with.

Examples   City Bank does more to protect the environment than Alcon Corporation does.
City Bank cares more about the environment than it does about health care.
RT Systems invests more money in affordable housing than City Bank does in environmental protection.

CRITERIA	ALCON CORP. (DEVELOPS SOFTWARE)	RT SYSTEMS (TELECOMMUNICATIONS)	CITY BANK (LARGE COMMERCIAL BANK)
ENVIRONMENTAL PROTECTION	5 Stopped using all chemicals that harm the ozone and recycles all paper	3 Recycles paper but still uses some harmful chemicals	3 Stopped using all harmful chemicals but doesn't recycle paper
AFFORDABLE HOUSING	4 Made major investments in affordable housing development	1 Has investments only in commercial property development	3 Has made one investment in affordable housing project, but also has commercial development
ANIMAL RIGHTS	4 Makes annual contribution to animal-protection organization	2 Owns major stock in tuna company that kills dolphins	2 Invests in ivory taken from elephants who must die for the ivory

Continued on next page.

Continued from previous page.

CRITERIA	ALCON CORP. (DEVELOPS SOFTWARE)	RT SYSTEMS (TELECOMMUNICATIONS)	CITY BANK (LARGE COMMERCIAL BANK)
FAIR LABOR PRACTIVE	**2** Doesn't offer the same benefits to male and female employees	**1** Expects employees to work extra hours without pay	**4** Offers bonuses for extra work and has the same benefits package for male and female employees

III. Superlative Constructions

In the chart below are some commonly used superlative constructions. Notice that a few of them use comparative structures to express a superlative meaning.

EXAMPLE	NOTES
1. Alcon is the **more responsible of the two** companies.	• In (1) the pattern is (*the* +comparative adjective + *of the two* + noun)
2. RT Systems is the **most responsible of the three companies.**	• In (2) the pattern is (*the* + superlative adjective + *of the three, four, five* + noun) • These two patterns are used to emphasize the superlative degree of a particular person, place, or thing rather than the characteristic itself.
3. Alcon is being **more responsible than** it's **ever** been before.	• In (3) the pattern used is (comparative adjective + *than ever*)
4. Alcon is being the **most responsible** it's **ever** been.	• In (4) the pattern used is (*the* + superlative adjective + *ever*)
5. Alcon is **more responsible than any other** company I've investigated.	• In (5) the pattern used is (comparative adjective + *than any other*)
6. This company is **the most responsible of all.**	• In (6) the pattern used is (*the* + superlative adjective + *of all*)
7. You're **the greatest!**	• In (7) the pattern used is (*the* + superlative adjective)
8. This was **the best** dinner ever! (This was the best dinner I have ever eaten.)	• In (8) the pattern used is (*the* + superlative adjective + *ever*) • These two patterns are used in colloquial spoken English, usually for the purpose of praising someone or something.

15.13 Written Activity

Write a persuasive advertisement trying to convince investors to choose one of the companies from the above chart.

15.14 Paired Activity: *Superlative Constructions*

DIRECTIONS: Using the cue provided, take turns with your partner to ask each other a question. You should answer the question using one of the superlative constructions from the preceding chart.

Example   telephone/telegraph/fax machine (efficient)
              QUESTION: Which machine is the most efficient?
              ANSWER: A fax machine is the most efficient of the three.

1. solar energy/nuclear energy (good)

2. world peace/one world language/world television system (probable)

3. communities on the moon/communities under water (exciting)

4. the air today/the air in the past (polluted)

5. nuclear war/global warming/earthquakes (threat)

6. a cure for cancer/a cure for AIDS/a solution for famine (probable)

7. parental discretion/violence code on T.V. (sensible)

8. voluntary simplicity/government regulation/citizen groups (effective)

9. electric car/gas-powered car (environmentally safe)

10. writing a letter to a congresswoman/voting in national election/joining a political action committee (powerful)

15.15 Paired Activity: *The Best Ever*

DIRECTIONS: Choose from the topics that follow, and then describe your experiences to your partner, using the superlative constructions from the chart on page 393.

1. Describe three or four friends of yours on the basis of the following characteristics: reliable, interesting, smart, lazy, etc.

2. Describe three movies of one type that you've seen.

3. Compare two cars you've driven.

4. Discuss jobs that you've had or schools that you've attended.

5. Describe beautiful sights you've seen, for example, Niagara Falls, The Great Pyramid, The Grand Canyon, etc.

6. Describe three trips you've taken.

7. Describe two gifts you've received.

8. Discuss accidents or illnesses that you've had.

15.16 Written Practice

Write an essay about one of the above topics using comparative and superlative constructions.

Grammatical Patterns Part Two

Preview

DIRECTIONS: Below is a newspaper article written at the end of the millenium, looking back on the past decades—the 80s and 90s—and forecasting what is to come in the next millenium. Read the article, checking below for any unfamiliar vocabulary.

1 As the millenium comes to a close, it is important to stop and reflect for a moment on the changes that the last decades have brought, and, at the same time, to look at the upcoming years to see what is **in store** for us. The more perceptive we are, especially about the technological advances and environmental changes that we have experienced in the past decades, the better prepared we will be to progress into the next millenium.

2 In the 1980s we saw more and more that man cannot continue to **wreak havoc** on the natural world without producing long-lasting, irreversible damage. We discovered that the gases which industry and the automobile have continually **emitted** into the air are ultimately causing the temperature of the planet to rise by blocking the escape of heat into the atmosphere. This **greenhouse effect** is as frightening as the hole scientists found in the ozone layer. Also a result of synthetic chemicals, such a hole deprives us of the necessary protection from the dangerous ultraviolet light of the sun. There were other disasters similar to these two, which will hopefully force us to **take stock of** how handicapped a planet we are leaving our children. There was the deadly gas leak from a **pesticide** plant in Bhopal, India; a devastating oil spill from a ripped tanker in Alaska; and, of course, the radioactive cloud that swept Europe after an accident at the Chernobyl nuclear power plant. Looking into the future, unless we act, our planet will become increasingly threatened, with greenhouse gases raising temperatures, turning temperate places into tropical ones, and drying up the corn belt.

3 Contrary to expectations, as a result of the technological and scientific advances at the end of the millenium, life has often seemed more confusing than simple. It has become possible for women to **conceive babies for childless couples,** but later they find themselves in **custody battles** because they can't bear to give up the child. **Embryos** are frozen for safekeeping, but more custody battles arise when the parents of such embryos decide to divorce. However, life has become simpler and more exciting in many ways as more machines and **gadgets** such as portable phones, camcorders, fax machines, and computers help to cut down on time and energy spent in everyday activities, and make information more **accessible.**

4 Some **futurists** predict that in the year 2000, humans will live on Mars and will learn how to build and **launch planets**. We may also see a world television system, pizza delivery in space, and a natural form of sugar that doesn't have any calories. Cars will be as safe for the environment as they are for passengers since they'll be solar powered to prevent pollution and computer powered to prevent accidents.

VOCABULARY

in store: to be expected in the future
wreak havoc: cause a lot of destruction
emitted: sent out into the air, especially when referring to gas or odors
greenhouse effect: too much carbon dioxide rises and heats up the atmosphere causing global temperatures to rise
take stock of: make an assessment or conclusion about something
pesticide: chemicals usually used on crops of growing fruits and vegetables to prevent insects from eating them
conceive babies for childless couples: (surrogate mothers) Some women have received money to be artificially inseminated, carry, and deliver a baby for a couple who can't have children
custody battles: a fight that parents undertake to have the legal right to a child
embryos: the form of human life up to the third month after conception
gadgets: small machines or devices that have a very specific purpose
accessible: available
futurists: people who predict the changes that will come in the future
launch planets: design a planet here on earth and send it into space

DISCUSSION

What are some of the predictions made in the article? Which do you agree with? What other predictions would you make about the future?

FOCUS ON GRAMMAR

DIRECTIONS: Look at the article in the preview to find examples of the following generalizations. Write the examples on the lines provided.

1. The author compares the greenhouse effect and the hole in the ozone layer. Find that sentence in paragraph 2. What structure is used? What is the relationship between the greenhouse effect and the hole in the ozone layer expressed by this comparative structure? Can you find a similar structure in paragraph 4?

   _____

2. In the first sentence of paragraph 2 what words does the author use to emphasize the step-by-step change? Can you find a word in the last sentence of paragraph 2 that is used for the same emphasis?

   _____

3. The second sentence in paragraph 1 uses a comparative pattern to express a conditional relationship. Rewrite the sentence, beginning with **if**.

   If _____

   _____

4. Underline the words in the following sentence that are used to make a comparison. Can you think of any other words that could replace these words? What is the opposite of these words?

   There were other disasters similar to these two, which will hopefully force us to take stock of

   how handicapped a planet we are leaving our children.

1. Using As . . . As For Equal Comparative Constructions

   When a comparison is based on two equal qualities or characteristics, the following patterns are used.

EQUAL RELATIONSHIP (SAME)	UNEQUAL RELATIONSHIP (NOT THE SAME)	COMPARATIVE STRUCTURE
1. John is **as tall as** Mary.	2. John is **not as tall as** Mary. (Mary is taller than John.)	• In (1) the pattern is (*as* + adjective + *as*) • In (3) the pattern is (*as* + adjective + noun + *as*).
3. John is **as tall a person as** Mary.	4. John is **not as tall a person as** Mary.	• In (2) and (4) *not* is added to make the relationship unequal.
5. John runs **as quickly as** Mary	6. John does **not** run **as fast as** Mary. (Mary runs faster than John.)	• In (5) the pattern is (*as* + adverb + *as*).
7. John makes **as much money as** Mary.	8. John does **not make as much money as** Mary. (Mary makes more money than John.)	• In (7) the pattern is (*as* + *much* + *as*). • Depending on the noun, *many, little,* or *few* is used in place of *much*.
9. John works **as much as** Mary.	10. John does **not** work **as much as** Mary. (Mary works more than John.)	• In (9) the pattern (*as* + *much* + *as*) follows the verb.

15.17 Oral Drill: *As . . . As*

DIRECTIONS: Compare life in the future with life in the present, using **as . . . as** and the cues below. Make either a positive or negative statement.

Example   people/work/hard

   People will work as hard as they do now.

 1. be/international conflict

 2. computers/necessary

 3. cars/damaging to the environment

 4. people/travel

 5. English language/popular

 6. Americans/compete/aggressively

 7. young people/like computer games

 8. pollution/problem

 9. e-mail/use

10. disease/in the world

11. international terrrorism/widespread

12. time-saving devices/on the market

15.18 Written Drill: *The End is Coming*

DIRECTIONS: Read the cartoon below and complete the following.

1. Replace **sooner** with the following words: **fast, quick, slow.**

2. Change the sentence in the cartoon to the negative.

"It's coming sooner than I expected..."

SPECIAL NOTE

So . . . As

Sometimes **so . . . as** is used in this construction when the two items being compared are unequal. For example: This computer is not **so efficient as** the other one.

15.19 Written Activity: *The Earthling and the Extraterrestrial*

DIRECTIONS: It is the year 2030. An extraterrestrial has been saved from a spaceship that landed on earth. Below are some sentences making comparisons about the extraterrestrial and an earthling. Paraphrase each pair of sentences by using the **as . . . as** comparative pattern.

Example   The earthling is six feet tall. The extraterrestrial is seven feet tall.
             The earthling is not as tall as the extraterrestrial.

1. The extraterrestrial's planet has four seasons. Earth has four seasons.

   _____

2. The earthling is a little anxious to help the extraterrestrial return home. The earthling is very eager to learn about the extraterrestrial's planet.

   _____

3. The earthling sleeps about eight hours every night. The extraterrestrial only sleeps four hours.

   _____

4. The extraterrestrial is hungry every three hours. The earthling is hungry every three hours.

   _____

5. The earthling has only one solution for the greenhouse effect on earth. The extraterrestrial has a few solutions for the greenhouse effect on earth.

   _____

6. There is a very advanced recycling system on the extraterrestrial's planet. Earth has a primitive recycling system.

_____

15.20 Paired Activity: *Technological Advances?*

DIRECTIONS: Interview your partner about the state of technology in two countries that s/he knows about. Then write ten statements using the **as . . . as** pattern to express the equality or inequality of the two countries. After you have written the statements, discuss the advantages and disadvantages of the technological innovation. Here are some suggestions for topics.

Phone system   Electronic equipment
Computer use   Transportation
Household appliances   Space exploration
Telecommunications   Medical equipment

Example   Portable phones aren't as popular in my country as they are in my partner's country.

1. _____

2. _____

3. _____

4. _____

5. _____

6. _____

II. Conditional Comparative Constructions

The comparative pattern below is used to express a conditional relationship between the two things being compared. Notice how the meaning of the comparative sentence corresponds to that of the conditional sentence.

Example 1   CONDITIONAL COMPARATIVE
The more relaxed John is, the more productive he is.
The   +comparative   +subj. +verb, +_the_   +comparative   +subj. +verb.
CONDITIONAL SENTENCE
If John is relaxed, he is productive.

Example 2   CONDITIONAL COMPARATIVE
The more carefully I study, the better chance I have of passing.
The   +comparative   +subj. +verb, +_the_   +comparative   +subj.+verb.
CONDITIONAL SENTENCE
If I study for an exam carefully, I have a better chance of passing.

15.21 Written Drill: *Conditional Comparative Constructions*

DIRECTIONS: Read the following conditional sentences and change each to a comparative construction.

1. If we release more chloroflourocarbons into the atmosphere, the hole in the ozone layer will get bigger.

2. If we wait longer to actively recycle waste, our landfill problems will get worse.

3. If we are less careful about industrial waste, our waters will become more polluted.

4. If we make more intelligent decisions about our future, our future will be better.

5. If we think more responsibly, we will act more cautiously.

15.22 Oral Drill

DIRECTIONS: Your teacher will begin the drill by saying the first clause of a conditional comparative sentence, e.g., *The more we drive. . .* One student will complete the sentence, e.g., *the more polluted the air gets.* The next student will begin the new sentence with the last clause of the preceding sentence, e.g., *The more polluted the air gets. . .* The next student will complete the sentence, e.g., *the faster the ozone layer disappears.* When the drill winds down, begin with a new cue.

1. The more toxic waste we dump in the oceans . . .

2. The more crowded our cities get . . .

3. The more natural resources we deplete . . .

4. The more junk food we create . . .

5. The more populated the world becomes . . .

15.23 Paired Activity: *Your Child's Future*

DIRECTIONS: Take turns with your partner choosing from the statements below to discuss what you would like for the future of your children. When one student makes a statement, the partner should ask, "Why?" The student who made the statement should explain with a conditional comparative sentence.

Example   STUDENT A: I want my children to read a lot.
              STUDENT B: Why?
              STUDENT A: Because the more they read, the more knowledgeable they'll be.

1. I hope they (make a lot of friends, earn a lot of money, find a lot of opportunities, have a lot of experiences, speak many languages, see many countries).

2. I want them to (live peacefully, act cautiously, make decisions wisely).

3. I want them to be (ambitious, self-confident, creative, honest, healthy).

4. I don't want them to (get bad grades in school, get into trouble, have bad luck, lie to me).

5. I don't want them to be (lazy, dishonest, unsuccessful, sick).

15.24 Interview Activity: *The Future of Your Country*

DIRECTIONS: Interview two English-speaking people about the future of the country you are presently living in. Ask for three ways the country can be improved in the future. For each statement your respondents make, ask for a reason why that will make the country better. Record your responses below.

Example   STATEMENT: People in my country should be less wasteful.
              REASON: There will be a more even distribution of goods.

RESPONDENT #1

1. STATEMENT: _____

   REASON: _____

2. STATEMENT: _____

   REASON: _____

3. STATEMENT: _____

   REASON: _____

RESPONDENT #2

1. STATEMENT: _____

   REASON: _____

2. STATEMENT: _____

   REASON: _____

3. STATEMENT: _____

   REASON: _____

15.25 Written Activity

DIRECTIONS: Paraphrase each statement and reason you were given with a conditional comparative sentence.

Example   (based on example above)
              The less wasteful people are, the more even the distribution of goods will be.

1. _____

2. _____

3. _____

4. _____

5. _____

6. _____

III. Expressing a Progressive Change of State

The following chart lists some words and expressions that are used to express a progressive change of state, which is very closely related to the comparative.

WORD/EXPRESSION	EXAMPLE
REPETITION OF THE COMPARATIVE **more and more** **bigger and bigger**	**More and more** countries are realizing that we are all part of one world community.
ADVERBS **increasingly** **progressively**	We are becoming **increasingly** aware of the ways we can work together as a world community.
VERBS **increase (become more)** **decrease (become less)** **worsen (become worse)** **improve(become better)** **lessen (become less)**	The need to work together **increases** every day.
ADJECTIVES **-ing** forms of the above verbs	There is an **increasing** need to work together as a world community to prevent destruction of the planet.

See Chapter Four for more information on progressive verb tenses.

15.26 Rapid Drill: *Oral Paraphrase*

DIRECTIONS: Paraphrase each statement below with one of the words or expressions from the preceding chart to express a progressive change of state.

1. The pollution is getting worse.
2. Prices are getting higher every day.
3. Our chances for saving our planet are quickly going down.
4. People are becoming more involved in positive action to save the environment.
5. The acid rain problem is becoming very dangerous.
6. There is a need for greater community involvement in the recycling program.

15.27 Written Drill: *Progressive Change of State*

DIRECTIONS: Below are some suggestions for implementing the concept of voluntary simplicity, the plan for simplifying our lives in the future. Paraphrase each suggestion by using a word or expression from the preceding chart to express a **progressive change of state**.

Example   There must be moderation of the overall level of consumption in developed nations.
There must be a decreasing amount of consumption in developed nations.

1. There should be more extensive use of electronic communication as a substitute for indiscriminate expensive physical travel.

2. We should see a mounting consumer revolution as people boycott companies whose policies are unethical with regard to the environment.

3. There should be massive investments in cleaning up the environment.

4. We should force a decline in agribusiness, with its heavy reliance on petrochemicals, coupled with a rebirth of family farming using organic modes of food production.

5. We should create a redefinition of the good life—an overall lowering of material expectations, with an increase in appreciation of the nonmaterial aspects of life.

6. We should encourage international cooperation to impose limitations on indiscriminate use and abuse of natural resources.

7. People should be educated in responsible investment to encourage support of businesses that demonstrate prudence and a sense of conscience in their practices.

IV. Other Words Used in Comparative Constructions

The following words and expressions are often used to express comparative relationships.

EXAMPLE	WORD/EXPRESSION	NOTES
My T.V. is **similar to** his.	similar to, like, different from, the same as	• These expressions are used with the verb **be**. • The expressions connect two noun phrases.
Mike and Susan have **similar** stereos.	similar, different, the same, alike, like, compared to, unlike	• These words function as adjectives.
Their stereos are **similar**.	similar, different, the same, alike	• These words end a clause or sentence.

Continued on next page.

Continued from previous page.

EXAMPLE	WORD/EXPRESSION	NOTES
Like your computer, mine has an internal hard disk drive.	like, compared to, unlike	• These words are prepositions which are placed before one noun that is being compared to another.
What is **the difference between** these two radios? The **difference between** the two radios is the price.	the difference between	• This expression is often used in a question asking for a comparison. • When used in a statement, this expression is followed by a noun phrase and the verb **be**.
While your computer is compatible with two other computers, mine is compatible with none.	while	• *While* is a subordinating conjunction.
How does this microwave **differ from** that one? How do the two **differ**?	differ from, compare to	• These verbs can be used to compare and contrast.

15.28 Written Drill: *Fill in the Blanks*

DIRECTIONS: The dialogue below takes place in a robot store in the year 2010. Fill in the blanks with an appropriate expression from the chart above.

SALESPERSON: May I help you?

CUSTOMER: Yes, I'm looking for a robot to do my housework, _____ _____ the one my friend has.

SALESPERSON: I see; well, could you give me a little more information? Each robot we carry is _____.

CUSTOMER: The one my friend has looks _____ the one over there holding the broom and dustpan. Oh yes, and it has the same name, Robo-Clean. I'm sure they're _____.

SALESPERSON: Well, I don't know if you've seen any others, but _____ _____ Robo-Clean, this one over here, Mr. Domestic, does windows, and it whistles while it works.

CUSTOMER: Oh, really? How does Mr. Domestic _____ Robo-Clean in thoroughness?

SALESPERSON: That's a very good question! _____ Mr. Domestic will get the dust out of every corner in your house, Robo-Clean will sweep the dust under the rug.

V. Special Problems With the Comparative

PROBLEM	EXPLANATION
Using a double comparative INCORRECT: (1) Computers are **more better** than typewriters. CORRECT: (2) Computers are **better** than typewriters.	• Don't add **more** to an adjective or adverb that is already in its comparative or superlative form as was done in (1).
Replacing than with *from* INCORRECT: (3) The 90s will be better **from** the 80s. CORRECT: (4) The 90s will be better **than** the 80s.	• Use **than** in the basic comparative pattern as in (4).

Continued on next page.

Continued from previous page.

PROBLEM	EXPLANATION
Attaching a regular ending to an irregular form INCORRECT: (5) The pollution here **is badder** than in my city. CORRECT: (6) The pollution here is **worse** than in my city.	• Use the correct irregular forms as in (6) instead of a regular ending as in (5).
Using *more* for an adjective that requires an *-er* or *-est* ending INCORRECT: (7) We will have **more big** problems in the future. CORRECT: (8) We will have **bigger** problems in the future.	• Don't use **more** if you can use the **-er** and **-est** endings as in (8).
Placing *more* after the adjective or adverb INCORRECT: (9) Janet is intelligent **more** than Pete. CORRECT: (10) Janet is **more** intelligent than Pete.	• Place **more** before the adjective or adverb as in (10) rather than after it as in (9).

Focus on Writing

■ **15.29 Error Analysis:** *Comparative Structures*

DIRECTIONS: Find any error in the use of comparative constructions in the following sentences. Correct the errors clearly above the sentences.

1. Pollution control is more better now than it was ten years ago.
2. This machine is alike a machine I saw in a science fiction movie ten years ago.
3. This city has the worstest recycling program I've ever seen.
4. The simpler our lives become the planet will survive longer.
5. In the future, houses will be functional more than they are now.
6. People are becoming involved in saving the environment quicker than we had ever hoped.
7. The cars of the future will not look the same than the ones we drive today.
8. The day when we see smog-free cities is more far in the future than we think.
9. Nuclear energy poses a much bigger threat from solar energy does.
10. Hopefully, the acid rain problem won't get more worse in the future.
11. The technological progress in this country is the same the other countries.
12. If we take action soon, the sooner we will resolve these problems.
13. Overpopulation is becoming an increasing worse problem.
14. Sankiyo is a company more conscientious than Tryon.

15.30 Essay

DIRECTIONS: Imagine what a house of the future will look like and write an essay comparing it to a house of today. Discuss the design of the house, kitchen appliances, entertainment equipment, methods of cleaning, etc. Take into consideration changes in the house that will protect the environment as well as make our lives simpler. Use the comparative expressions from the chart on page 404.

Example   Compared to the house of today, a future house will be designed to be energy efficient with many windows and skylights to let in the light and heat of the sun.

Analysis of an Authenic Text

A Union for Peace and Survival
by Dawna Nolan

1 Earth. One small planet in a seemingly infinite universe. Ever since the first photos of our earth as it looks from space captured the imaginations of people around the world, the reality of living in a global village has seemed much more immediate.

2 And since the time when Canadian educator Marshal McLuhan first **coined the term,** the concept of all of humanity belonging to a *global village* has become more of a technological reality as well. Scientific advances from jet travel to nuclear weaponry to telecommunications have lessened the distances between peoples making us speedily aware of, and affected by, events in the far corners of the earth.

3 . . . There are many organized groups working for peace, human rights, and the environment, who also provide the means for differences to be resolved and similarities shared. An innovative, valuable tool for them is a global computer network called PeaceNet. This computer-based communication system helps groups such as Greenpeace, Global Link, the Christic Institute, and many others to communicate and cooperate more effectively and efficiently.

4 One of these groups, Beyond War, based in Palo Alto, California, is built on **the premise** that war is obsolete in the nuclear age. Its many educational projects are designed to raise public awareness of the value of **conflict resolution.** The annual Beyond War Awards is one such project, and this year's theme is Building Our Common Future.

5 **Grassroots groups** have also been active in promoting global peace and survival. For example, the Boise Peace **Quilt** Project was begun in 1981 by two Idaho women who wished to make a concrete statement in support of world peace. They and 40 other people made a

quilt and sent it to the Soviet Union as a **gesture** of friendship. Since then, the endeavor has involved **scores** of men, women, and children and has produced more than a dozen quilts.

6 One of the quilts, the National Peace Quilt, is a vibrant red, white, and blue, and is made up of one square for each of the 50 states. The intent is to have every United States senator spend one night sleeping under this quilt. Said Senator Spark Matsunaga of Hawaii, "I swear I woke with the biggest smile my face has ever worn. I realized the power of the human spirit, represented by thousands of women and children from the 50 states who have united to create an inspirational symbol for the political leaders of this great nation to direct it towards unseen greatness, if not plain survival."

VOCABULARY

coin(ed) the term: to make a word or expression familiar to people when it was previously unknown or unfamiliar
the premise: the understanding
conflict resolution: a systematic method of solving problems peacefully
grassroots groups: average people who work together to promote change
quilt: a large bed covering made up of small individual squares of material; each square can have a picture or symbol sewn into it
gesture: symbol
scores: a large number of

COMPREHENSION QUESTIONS

1. What do we mean by the concept of *global village?*
2. What is the benefit of the global computer network, PeaceNet?

GRAMMATICAL ANALYSIS

1. Senator Matsunuga said that he woke with the biggest smile his face has ever worn. What did he mean? What is another way he could have described the way he felt when he woke in the morning?
2. Paragraph 1 ends with the words "much more immediate." How could you finish the comparative pattern? (. . . much more immediate than . . .?)
3. Write three sentences using comparative structures to describe the effect that this quilt project must have had on the people involved.

_____

_____

_____

Composition Topics

In this chapter you have mastered the use of a variety of comparative constructions. Use what you have learned to write a composition about one of the following topics.

1. Compare life in your country when you were growing up with life in the present. Focus especially on technological advances and environmental changes.

2. In the preceding text, Dawna Nolan mentions that the work of one group is based on the premise that war is obsolete. What is necessary in order to make war obsolete? How much we change our behavior individually and globally?

3. Write an essay with your own recommendations for what the average person can do to improve the future of our children.

Appendices

Appendix A: Irregular Verbs

The following list provides the base form, past form and past participle form of most irregular verbs. The base form is the infinitive form of a verb without *to*. This form is used, for example, after modals (*I can begin.*) The past form is used for the simple past (*I began school yesterday.*) The past participle is used after the auxiliaries has/have/had (*I have begun.*) and in the passive (*The window was broken.*)

BASE FORM PARTICIPLE	PAST	PAST
arise	arose	arisen
awake	awoke	awoken
be (is/are)	was/were	been
bear	bore	borne; born
become	became	become
begin	began	begun
bend	bent	bent
bind	bound	bound
bite	bit	bit/bitten
bleed	bled	bled
blow	blew	blown
break	broke	broken
bring	brought	brought
broadcast	broadcast	broadcast
build	built	built
burst	burst	burst
cast	cast	cast
catch	caught	caught
choose	chose	chosen
cling	clung	clung
come	came	come
cost	cost	cost

BASE FORM PARTICIPLE	PAST	PAST
creep	crept	crept
cut	cut	cut
deal	dealt	dealt
dig	dug	dug
dive	dived/dove	dived
do	did	done
draw	drew	drawn
drink	drank	drunk
drive	drove	driven
eat	ate	eaten
fall	fell	fallen
feed	fed	fed
feel	felt	felt
fight	fought	fought
find	found	found
flee	fled	fled
fling	flung	flung
fly	flew	flown
forget	forgot	forgotten
forgive	forgave	forgiven
forsake	forsook	forsaken
freeze	froze	frozen
get	got	got/gotten
give	gave	given
go	went	gone
grind	ground	ground
grow	grew	grown
hang	hung	hung
have	had	had
hear	heard	heard
hide	hid	hidden
hit	hit	hit

BASE FORM PARTICIPLE	PAST	PAST
hold	held	held
hurt	hurt	hurt
keep	kept	kept
kneel	knelt	knelt
know	knew	known
lay	laid	laid
lead	led	led
leave	left	left
lend	lent	lent
let	let	let
lie	lay	lain
light	lit/lighted	lit/lighted
lose	lost	lost
make	made	made
mean	meant	meant
meet	met	met
pay	paid	paid
prove	proved	proven/proved
put	put	put
quit	quit	quit
read	read	read
ride	rode	ridden
ring	rang	rung
rise	rose	risen
run	ran	run
say	said	said
see	saw	seen
seek	sought	sought
sell	sold	sold
send	sent	sent
set	set	set
shake	shook	shaken

BASE FORM PARTICIPLE	PAST	PAST
shoot	shot	shot
show	showed	showed/shown
shrink	shrank	shrunk
shut	shut	shut
sing	sang	sung
sink	sank	sunk
sit	sat	sat
sleep	slept	slept
speak	spoke	spoken
spend	spent	spent
spin	spun	spun
split	split	split
spread	spread	spread
spring	sprang	sprung
stand	stood	stood
steal	stole	stolen
stick	stuck	stuck
strike	struck	struck/stricken
swear	swore	sworn
sweep	swept	swept
take	took	taken
teach	taught	taught
tear	tore	torn
tell	told	told
think	thought	thought
throw	threw	thrown
understand	understood	understood
wear	wore	worn
weave	wove	woven
wind	wound	wound
write	wrote	written

Appendix B: Article Use with Proper Nouns

GENERAL RULES:

1. Use **the** before CLASS + OF + NOUN.

2. Use **the** before all **plural** proper nouns.

CATEGORY	NO ARTICLE	USE THE	EXCEPTIONS
LAND MASSES	**Planets** • Uranus, etc.		• the Earth
	Continents • South America, etc.		
	Countries • France, etc.		• the U.S. • the Sudan • the Ivory Coast
	Islands—singular Maui, etc.	**Islands—plural** • the Virgin Islands, etc.	
	Cities • San Diego, etc.		• the Hague
	Streets • Fifth Avenue, etc.		• the Champs Elysées
REGIONS		• the south (of France) • the northwest, etc.	• southern France • New England
BODIES OF WATER	**Lakes—singular** • Victoria Lake, etc.	**Lakes—plural** • the Great Lakes, etc.	
	Bays • San Francisco Bay, etc.	**The Bay of X** • the Bay of Biscayne, etc.	
		Rivers • the Rhine River, etc.	
		Oceans • the Atlantic Ocean, etc.	
MOUNTAINS	• Mt. Everest, etc.	**Canals** • the Erie Canal, etc. • the Matterhorn • the Rocky Mountains	
DESERTS		• The Mojave Desert, etc.	

BUILDINGS/ INSTITUTIONS	Universities (Name + University) • Harvard University, etc.	Universities (The University of X) • The University of Texas, etc.
		Museums • The Prado, etc.
		Libraries • The Library of Congress, etc.
DATES	• July 4, 1776, etc.	• the fourth of July, etc.
		Decades • the 1980s, etc. • the Roaring 20s (era), etc.
HOLIDAYS	• Christmas, etc.	

Appendix C: Article Use and the Names of Illnesses

A/AN + NOUN	THE + (PLURAL) NOUN	0 + PLURAL/NONCOUNT NOUN
an allergy	the flu	**Noncount:**
an earache	the measles	arthritis
a fever	the mumps	asthma
a headache		depression
a heart attack		diarrhea
an infection		cancer
a sore throat		turberculosis
a stomachache (and		pneumonia
other ailments ending		schizophrenia
in -ache).		
an ulcer		**Plural:**
		AIDS
		diabetes
		herpes

Appendix D: Formation of Plural Nouns

1. REGULAR PLURAL NOUNS

SINGULAR NOUN	PLURAL NOUN	RULE OR PATTERN TO FORM PLURAL
1. value	values	1. Add -s
tradition	traditions	
Cadillac	Cadillacs	
2. tomato	tomatoes	2. Add -es to nouns ending in o, s, x, ch, sh. (See exception below—2, Irregular Plural Nouns.)
mass	masses	
box	boxes	
church	churches	
dish	dishes	
3. mystery	mysteries	3. Change (**consonant + y**) to i and add -es.
4. toy	toys	4. Add -s to (**vowel + y**).
5. Nancy	Nancys	5. Add -s to proper names.
Bundy	Bundys	

2. IRREGULAR PLURAL NOUNS

The following list includes some of the most common **exceptions** to plural formation, arranged by category. **Note that this is not a complete list.**

SINGULAR NOUN	PLURAL NOUN	PLURAL FORMATION PATTERN
1. shelf	shelves	1. **Change -f or -fe to -ves.** **Exceptions:**
knife	knives	• proof—proofs
wife	wives	• chief—chiefs
		• belief—beliefs (**believes** is a verb)
		• roof—roofs

SINGULAR NOUN	PLURAL NOUN	PLURAL FORMATION PATTERN
2. zoo video solo Eskimo	zoos videos solos Eskimos	2. Add -s (**not** -es) to: • nouns ending in **vowel + o**; • foreign words ending in **o**; • proper nouns ending in **o**.
3. man goose mouse	men geese mice	3. These are some examples of nouns that form their plural by changing the middle vowel(s).
4. sheep deer species series fish	sheep deer species series fish	4. The singular and plural forms are the same for these nouns.
5. analysis basis hypothesis	analyses bases hypotheses	5. These are some examples of nouns that form their plural by changing **-is** to **-es**.
6. phenomenon criteron	phenomena criteria	6. Change **-on** to **-a** to form the plural.
7. nucleus stimulus syllabus	nuclei stimuli syllabi	7. Change **-us** to **-i** to form the plural. **Syllabuses** is also acceptable as a plural form.
8. curriculum datum	curricula data	8. Change **-um** to **-a** to form the plural.
9. ox child index	oxen children indices/indexes	9. These nouns do not follow a pattern.

3. Nouns that are Always Singular or Plural

These nouns are **always plural.** They do not have a singular form.

eyeglasses; pliers; trousers; slacks; pajamas; clothes; people; scissors

These nouns end in -s, but they are **always singular.**

mathematics; economics; physics; news

4. Plural of Compound Nouns

SINGULAR NOUN	PLURAL NOUN	PLURAL FORMATION PATTERN
1. doormat dateline disk drive	doormats datelines disk drives	1. Make the **last word** of a compound noun plural when the nouns are about the same in importance. (Follow the rules above to form the plurals.)
2. sister-in-law passerby	sisters-in-law passersby	2. If the **first word** of the compound word is the important one, then make that word plural. (**Exceptions:** add-ons; sit-ins; two-year-olds)
3. spoonful handful	spoonfuls handfuls	3. If the compound word ends in **-ful,** add **-s** to form the plural.

ndex